Alva and Gunnar My[illegible]
Sweden and America

Alva and Gunnar Myrdal are the only couple ever awarded Nobel Prizes as individuals: Gunnar won the prize in Economics in 1974, and Alva won the Peace Prize in 1982. This dual biography examines their work as architects of the modern welfare state and probes the connections between the public and private dimensions of their lives. Drawing on their extensive personal correspondence and diaries between their electrifying first meeting in 1919 and their protracted marital crisis in the early 1940s, this book presents the psychologist and the economist as they sought to combine love and work in an equal partnership. Alva and Gunnar simultaneously experimented with a new kind of intimate relationship and designed the social supports necessary for women both to bear and raise children and to contribute their talents and energies to society. Like all genuine revolutionaries, they struggled to free themselves from the burdens of their upbringings; to evaluate their own actions with what they called "unsparing honesty"; and to test their policy recommendations in practice, measuring everything against the values they shared.

Walter Anderson Jackson III (1950–2015) is best known for *Gunnar Myrdal and America's Conscience: Social Engineering and Racial Liberalism, 1938–1973* (1990), which analyzes the making of Myrdal's *An American Dilemma: The Negro Problem and Modern Democracy* (1944) in relation to early twentieth-century Swedish and American social thought. Jackson grew up in the South during the Civil Rights Movement and earned a BA (mcl) from Duke and a PhD from Harvard. His life's work was prompted by questions about racial inequality in the United States and the perspective a European social democratic thinker brought to this fraught issue. Jackson published numerous articles on white racial liberalism, African American sociologists and anthropologists, and theories of interracial relations. Beloved by students and the public for grounding the civil rights struggle in local history and highlighting the voices and viewpoints of participants, he appeared on the 2015 PBS program, "American Denial."

Routledge Studies in Modern History

Eurasian Empires as Blueprints for Ethiopia
From Ethnolinguistic Nation-State to Multiethnic Federation
Asnake Kefale, Tomasz Kamusella and Christophe Van der Beken

Atlantic Crossroads
Webs of Migration, Culture and Politics between Europe, Africa, and the Americas, 1800–2020
José Moya

Food History
A Feast of the Senses in Europe, 1750 to the Present
Edited by Sylvie Vabre, Martin Bruegel and Peter J. Atkins

Chinese Theatre Troupes in Southeast Asia
Touring Diaspora 1900s —1970s
Zhang Beiyu

Labour and Economic Change in Southern Africa c.1900–2000
Zimbabwe, Zambia and Malawi
Rory Pilossof and Andrew Cohen

Engaging with Historical Traumas
Experiential Learning and Pedagogies of Resilience
Edited by Nena Močnik, Ger Duijzings, Hanna Meretoja, and Bonface Njeresa Beti

Sun Yatsen, Robert Wilcox and Their Failed Revolutions, Honolulu and Canton 1895
Dynamite on the Tropic of Cancer
Patrick Anderson

For more information about this series, please visit: https://www.routledge.com/history/series/MODHIST

Alva and Gunnar Myrdal in Sweden and America, 1898–1945

Unsparing Honesty

Walter A. Jackson

Routledge
Taylor & Francis Group
NEW YORK AND LONDON

First published 2021
by Routledge
52 Vanderbilt Avenue, New York, NY 10017

and by Routledge
2 Park Square, Milton Park, Abingdon, Oxon OX14 4RN

Routledge is an imprint of the Taylor & Francis Group, an informa business

British Library Cataloguing-in-Publication Data
A catalogue record for this book is available from the British Library

Library of Congress Cataloging-in-Publication Data
A catalog record has been requested for this book

ISBN: 978-0-367-49707-1 (hbk)
ISBN: 978-0-367-49708-8 (pbk)
ISBN: 978-1-003-04705-6 (ebk)

Typeset in Times New Roman
by codeMantra

Contents

Figures

Author Biography and Bibliography

Walter Anderson Jackson III (1950–2015) is best known for *Gunnar Myrdal and America's Conscience: Social Engineering and Racial Liberalism, 1938–1973* (1990), which analyzes the making of Myrdal's *An American Dilemma: The Negro Problem and Modern Democracy* (1944) in relation to early twentieth-century Swedish and American social thought. Jackson grew up in the South during the Civil Rights Movement and earned a BA (mcl) from Duke and a PhD from Harvard. His life's work was prompted by questions about racial inequality in the United States and the perspective a European social democratic thinker brought to this fraught issue. Jackson published numerous articles on white racial liberalism, African American sociologists and anthropologists, and theories of interracial relations. Beloved by students and the public for grounding the civil rights struggle in local history and highlighting the voices and viewpoints of participants, he appeared on the 2015 PBS program, "American Denial."

Jackson's first book, published by the University of North Carolina Press, won the Anisfield-Wolf Prize in Cultural Diversity and the Gustavus Myers Human Rights Award and was nominated for the Pulitzer Prize, Bancroft Prize, and National Book Award. His other publications include:

Alva Myrdals kritik av amerikansk politik och det amerikanska samhället under New Deal-eran. *Arbetarhistoria* 27, no. 106–107 (2003): 62–73.

Gunnar Myrdal, social engineering, and American racial liberalism. In *Models, Modernity, and the Myrdals*, ed. Pauli T. Kettunen and Hanna Eskola, 13–33. Helsinki: Renvall Institute, 1997.

White liberal intellectuals, civil rights, and gradualism, 1954–1960. In *The Making of Martin Luther King and the Civil Rights Movement*, ed. A.J. Badger and Brian Ward, 96–117. London: MacMillan, 1996.

Between socialism and nationalism: The young E. Franklin Frazier. *Reconstruction* 1, no. 3 (1991): 124–134.

The "American creed" from a Swedish perspective: The wartime context of Gunnar Myrdal's An American Dilemma. In *The Estate of Social*

Knowledge, ed. Jo Anne Brown and David van Keuren, 209–227. Baltimore, MD: Johns Hopkins University Press, 1991.

Melville Herskovits and the search for Afro-American culture. *History of Anthropology* 4 (1986): 73–103.

The making of a social science classic: Gunnar Myrdal's An American Dilemma. *Perspectives in American History*, new series, 2 (1985): 221–267.

Acknowledgments

On behalf of my late husband, Walter Anderson Jackson III, I would like to thank some of the many people who helped him trace and interpret Alva and Gunnar Myrdal's lives and careers in Sweden and the United States.

I owe a special debt to Kaj Fölster and Sissela Bok, Gunnar and Alva's daughters, for encouraging Walter throughout this project. They generously granted him interviews and shared important documents and photographs with him.

Kaj Fölster followed this project from its beginning to its conclusion. She and Walter had stimulating discussions about the Myrdal family and Swedish society. She took him to places in Sweden where the Myrdals and their relatives had lived, and introduced him to friends and family members. I am particularly grateful to Annika Reimer, the late Urban Myrdal, Gunnel Holst, Arne Fetveit, and Ann-Mari Carlman for their help.

The members of the Myrdal family valued Walter's work and his commitment to high standards of scholarship and objectivity, and I owe them more than I can say.

I would like to acknowledge some of the many scholars and friends in Sweden and the United States who were interested in this project and offered crucial assistance at various stages.

Stellan Andersson, the former archivist at the Swedish Labour Movement's Archives and Library who interviewed Gunnar Myrdal, and Örjan Appelqvist, who studied Gunnar Myrdal's economic thought, provided continuous support over many years and commented on portions of the manuscript. Archivist Lars Gogman provided essential guidance to the photographs in the Myrdals' extensive collection.

Faculty members at Uppsala University in Sweden, where Walter spent a year as a Fulbright scholar, were very helpful. I especially thank Erik Åsard, a historian of the labor movement, who was then the director of the Swedish Institute for North American Studies (SINAS). He and Walter collaborated closely, and they often met when Walter returned to Sweden every summer to conduct research.

Swedish scholars whose expertise and collegiality were particularly valuable to Walter include Dag Blanck, the current director of SINAS; Sven Eliaeson, who studied the Myrdals' contributions to social theory; Hedvig Ekerwald, who analyzed the Myrdals' work on family policy; the late Tore Frängsmyr, a historian of science who was deeply knowledgeable about the history and culture of rural Sweden; and Per Wisselgren, who examined Alva Myrdal's contributions to international social science. Charlotte Fellenius also provided valuable assistance during the research process.

Other scholars who commented on portions of the manuscript include Fred W. Anderson, a historian of colonialism, and Richard H. King, a British historian of the United States.

Walter's colleagues at the University of North Carolina at Chapel Hill were supportive of his work and provided helpful feedback. The members of the Global South group, anthropologist James Peacock, and cultural historian William R. Ferris deserve special mention. Walter's colleagues in the History Department at North Carolina State University, especially David Zonderman, Gerald D. Surh, James E. Crisp, and David Gilmartin, were deeply engaged with his work. Zonderman and the library director, Gregory Raschke, have assisted us during the final preparation of the manuscript.

Many academic institutions and fellowship programs provided essential support for this project, including the W.E.B. Du Bois Institute for Afro-American Studies and the Charles Warren Center for American History at Harvard, the Institute for Advanced Studies at Princeton, the Virginia Center for the Humanities, the Mellon Faculty Fellowship at Stanford, North Carolina State University, the University of North Carolina at Chapel Hill, the Swedish National Archives, Uppsala University, Umeå University, the American Scandinavian Foundation, and the Fulbright Scholar Program.

I gratefully acknowledge the invaluable support I have received from our friend and lawyer, Stewart Fisher. His professionalism, enthusiasm, and kindness made this project run very smoothly.

It is a pleasure to thank Grey Osterud for editing the manuscript. Her skill and dedication made the publication of this book possible.

Max Novick, senior editor at Routledge, responded enthusiastically to this project, and the staff at Routledge have efficiently guided the work from acceptance through production.

Finally, I would like to thank our daughter, Sarah Naomi Jackson, for her patience, love, and joyful spirit.

Rachida Chbihi Jackson
Chapel Hill, North Carolina
2020

Editor's Preface

When I took on the task of producing a publishable book manuscript from the drafts that remained unfinished at the time of Walter Jackson's death, I had worked as his editor for six months. As a historian of women and gender, I knew that his dual biography of Alva and Gunnar Myrdal would make a major contribution to scholarship, not simply because of the Myrdals' role as architects of the welfare state but also because of Jackson's insightful analysis of the connections between the public and private dimensions of their lives. The economist and the policy advocate are presented in their full personal and interpersonal contexts as they sought to combine love and work in an equal partnership. Alva and Gunnar simultaneously experimented with a new kind of intimate relationship and designed the social supports necessary for women both to bear and raise children and to contribute their individual talents and energies to society. Like all genuine revolutionaries, they struggled to free themselves from the burdens of their upbringings; to evaluate their own actions with what they called "unsparing honesty"; and to test their policy recommendations in practice, measuring everything against the values they shared.

Jackson's project was possible because the trove of personal letters and autobiographical reflections the Myrdals preserved in their extensive archive was opened to researchers in 2000, and their descendants and relatives made other documents available as well. Jackson pored over every word Alva and Gunnar wrote, interviewed their families and friends, and investigated the many intellectuals and reformers whose ideas and proposals influenced their thinking. He wrestled with the task of interpreting their private writings, often scribbled in longhand with incomplete sentences and many dashes but revealing the vital interplay of thought and feeling with an immediacy that more carefully crafted documents lack. Focusing clearly on central themes, he traced the changing dynamics of their interactions over time.

At the time of his death, Jackson had completed the first third of his planned book, which examines Alva's and Gunnar's family backgrounds and childhood experience and their relationship from their electrifying initial encounter in the summer of 1919 through the next two years.

He had outlined the middle third, which would have explored their personal and intellectual development up to World War II. Fortunately, he left a complete draft of the final third, which probes the crises that occurred in their relationship from 1941 through 1944 while Gunnar was writing *An American Dilemma* and Alva was coming into her own as a feminist. Since Alva found introspection more rewarding than Gunnar, who was frightened by his history of bleak depression, she left much richer first-person material than he did from this time of trial. These chapters take Alva's perspective more than her husband's, probing her dilemmas as a woman who aspired to equality in a partnership that was marked both by intimacy and distance, and based on a shared project of social reconstruction.

In editing the work that Jackson left unfinished, I have not added anything except an occasional footnote to his manuscript. Although I read his mountain of research materials and multiple drafts of many sections, I did not construct any new chapters from his outlines and notes. Jackson's social-historical and psychological insights into the Myrdals are inimitable, and no one else, however deeply immersed in the sources, could reproduce his thought process and mode of expression sufficiently to complete the book he had conceived. Instead, I have taken a manuscript he did write, which summarizes the years between 1922 and 1940, and turned it into a transitional chapter. What the finished work lacks in comprehensiveness, it makes up for in its depth and clear focus on the intersection between the personal and the political in the intertwined, yet individual lives of these epoch-making social reformers.

I am deeply grateful to Rachida Chbihi Jackson for entrusting me with the task of preparing her late husband's manuscript for publication and to his friend and counsel, Stewart Fisher, for his guidance and support. Lars Gogman and the rest of the staff at the Swedish Labour Movement's Archives and Library as well as Arne Fetveit of Oslo, Norway, provided generous assistance as I assembled the illustrations. At Routledge, Max Novick offered expert advice and responded rapidly to my questions, despite the adverse circumstances we were all working under in 2020. Finally, I am personally indebted to Lena Sommestad, a Swedish feminist, economic historian, and policy maker, for her insights into recent debates about the Myrdals and the postwar welfare state.

Grey Osterud
Needham, Massachusetts
2020

1 Unsparing Honesty

On the night of February 20, 1950, Gunnar Myrdal sat at his desk in Geneva and wept. He had just received word of the death of his closest friend from secondary school and university, the chemist and novelist Fritz Thorén, with whom he had had little contact during the previous decade. This shock led him to reflect on his early life in a handwritten letter to his wife, Alva Myrdal, who was living in New York. At 51, Gunnar directed the United Nations Economic Commission for Europe, charged with rebuilding the European economy and encouraging trade between the Soviet bloc and the West. Alva headed the United Nations Department of Social Affairs, which addressed the needs of children and women living in poverty amidst the aftermath of war. Together they had contributed important ideas to the formation of the Swedish welfare state in the 1930s. Now, as Gunnar and Alva pursued careers on different continents, their relationship had taken a new turn. Without Alva at his side and with the future of their marriage unclear, Gunnar felt peculiarly alone as he picked up the pen to capture the emotions he felt. (G to A, Feb. 20, 1950)

To Gunnar, the death of his old friend symbolized the loss of his own youth, and he sensed that a very deep-rooted part of himself had been severed and was now decaying.

> A personality is constructed like a shell, like a suit of armor, and one manages ever greater things. But inside one remains frozen and sad. I am crying tonight for the first time in many years. . . . I had forgotten so much! If I had the time, I would like to shut myself away for a week and think about . . . myself. It is such a macabre pleasure to brood on one's youth. What has gone wrong and what turned out right.

Suddenly terrified of being alone with these powerful memories, he blurted out: "Alva, I am so lonely here. . . . Alva, dearest, you won't abandon me, will you?"

Why was it such a "macabre pleasure to brood" about his youth? What memories had he repressed in his rise from his parents' cottage in the rural province of Dalarna to his position of worldwide prominence? Why does a man describe his personality as a "suit of armor" inside of which he remains "frozen?" What hidden side of his divided self had Fritz seen that no one else but Alva had glimpsed?

As Gunnar contemplated these vivid images from his youth, his early life seemed cut off from the professional and public persona he had fashioned as a young economist in the 1920s, an economic advisor to Sweden's Social Democratic government in the 1930s, an internationally known expert on race relations and racism in the early 1940s, Sweden's Minister of Trade in 1945–1946, and then director of a major UN commission during the early years of the Cold War. "I would like to write my memoirs," he told Alva, but not about his public activities. Instead, he was focused on the "images" of the past "that continually pop up about the boy with a hip injury, and the girls, and the books and the dream" of being a "lawyer, handwriting, Father [underlined three times], Elsa [his sister], Stockholm, . . . the cold streets, yes . . . everything that is important and small and frightening."

He was also tempted to write about "you [Alva] who were also a bit frightening but more and more the opposite." At first, Gunnar remembered, he had been "scared of life," but then "indifferent." When does a person "live fully," he wondered, and "what does it mean?" "What is truth and what is illusion?" Having lived through two world wars in Sweden and America, he asked, "What [is] an ideal which you are really prepared to—not die [for] because I am not willing to die for anything—but work for?" How does one distinguish "'honest logic' from . . . opportunism?" "And how does it all come together to form a fate?"

"What am I frightened of?" Gunnar wondered. On reflection, "mostly childish things, memories of fear. Everything is so complicated to work out. Much more complicated than all my books." Gunnar nervously reassured his wife that he "will soon be normal again." But "it feels so good for a depressive like me to cry. It is horrible to be alone."

Gunnar Myrdal never wrote his memoirs. Until his early 80s, he strove to keep up the public persona of a wide-ranging social scientist engaging in global public policy debates. Over a decade after his death, his personal papers were opened to reveal some of the conflicts and self-doubts that he had learned to repress.

We do not have a written response to these anxious reflections from Alva Myrdal, but the couple discussed these memories in phone calls between Geneva and New York. The daughter of a family with roots in rural Sweden and in the working class, Alva was born in 1902. They moved many times before she was 12, as her father struggled to lift them out of poverty. Alva had to leave school at 14 because there was no high school for girls in the town where she lived. She was working as a secretary at age 17 in June 1919, when Gunnar, age 20, and two other Stockholm University students on a summer bicycle trip stopped at her family's farm. The bond between the two was immediate and transformative for both and, despite chronic stresses and serious crises, lasted for 66 years.

They were passionately attracted to each other in spite of their differences in class background, education, and politics. Although both were the children of builders, Gunnar's father had become a successful contractor in Stockholm, while Alva's father had been a farm worker, clerk and bookkeeper, life insurance salesman, cement mixer, home builder, and farmer. When they met, Alva's and Gunnar's political outlooks differed sharply. Her father was an ardent Social Democrat. While Alva worked as a secretary, she dreamed of leading a life of service to humanity. His bourgeois father was quite conservative. As a law student, Gunnar considered himself an intellectual aristocrat and professed disdain for the uneducated masses.

Both Alva and Gunnar had grown up in unhappy families, considered themselves rebels against conventional Swedish society, and studied the social sciences in order to enable people to live happier and more productive lives. During the first year of their relationship, they wrote to each other constantly, both about their voracious reading and about themselves. They discussed psychology, analyzed each other, and even hoped to achieve a catharsis by correspondence during times of personal crisis. Although the youthful Gunnar believed men to be superior in intellectual capacity, he quickly became dependent on Alva, who served as both his debating partner and his counselor. While still a teenager, she came to function as a kind of therapist for Gunnar, whose extraordinary egotism, brilliance, and creativity were sometimes derailed by periods of paralyzing depression, anxiety, and fear. A university student 3 years older than Alva, Gunnar initially dominated their intellectual discussions, but Alva learned to be the strong one in the relationship, to listen sympathetically to Gunnar's painful descriptions of psychological torment, build his self-confidence, and restore him to good health.

As the two young people discussed how to live their lives and how to find an ethical basis for decision making in an era when relativism had upended traditional moral values, honesty emerged as their highest value. If they could remain honest with each other, they believed, they could overcome personal difficulties and respond to changes in each other's lives. Gunnar helped Alva take herself seriously as an intellectual and encouraged her efforts to complete a college-preparatory course and enroll in Stockholm University. After her graduation in 1924, they married. Gunnar pursued a PhD in economics, while Alva studied psychology in Uppsala and cared for their son Jan, born in 1927. Although they were not politically active during the 1920s, Gunnar managed to pull Alva away from her Social Democratic moorings into the intellectual elite, where social scientific expertise was more respected than democratic principles. Over time, however, her egalitarian and humanitarian outlook had an equally profound impact on Gunnar.

An important turning point in their lives came in 1929–1930, when Gunnar and Alva spent a year in the United States as Rockefeller fellows, visiting leading universities and immersing themselves in recent interdisciplinary social scientific research. Alva laid the foundation for a career as a child psychologist and educator, although she acceded to Gunnar's demand that they leave their son with his parents during his second year. Her exposure to new work on early childhood development, psychoanalysis, Boasian anthropology, Chicago sociology, and John Dewey's educational thought gave her new tools for understanding how cultural and environmental influences shape personality, gender, and family life. Although national politics in the United States was still dominated by conservative Republicans, the Myrdals were impressed by the continuation of progressive reforms at the state and local levels and by the role that applied social science research played in them. Glimpsing new possibilities for social engineering, the young Swedes decided to become politically active when they returned home.

In Sweden, the Myrdals emerged as prominent Social Democratic intellectuals and architects of the welfare state during the 1930s. Gunnar became a leading economist of the Stockholm School and a key author of the Social Democrats' "Crisis Program," which helped pull the country out of the depression. Alva helped to design apartment buildings with communal kitchens and daycare, enabling women to work outside the home and spend less time on housework. She founded a training school for preschool teachers and taught parenting.

The Myrdals were seen as heralds of modernity, advocates of a forward-looking, scientifically based form of social engineering designed to rationalize the family and childrearing, balance gainful work and family responsibilities in women's lives, and provide greater equality of opportunity to all Swedes. In 1934 Alva and Gunnar coauthored a bestselling book, *Kris i befolkningsfrågan* (*Crisis in the Population Question*), which challenged Swedes to rethink social policy regarding birth control, education, and housing and played a formative role in the making of the Swedish welfare state. The national debate also brought unprecedented public attacks on the Myrdals, which had the effect of strengthening their professional partnership, which Gunnar liked to call "the firm" of "AGM."

Despite Alva's impressive achievements, she was held back in her professional development by class and gender barriers in higher education and public life. Moreover, she assumed far more of the responsibility for raising their three children than her husband. It was not until her early 30s that Alva came to the realization that much of what she had learned about the biological differences in the abilities and temperaments of men and women was bunk. "Where does 'femininity' come from?" she asked.

> Sociologists and anthropologists trace the division of labor in primitive societies to notions of women's "impurity," such as the Christian idea of sin. Traditional concepts of "femininity" are rooted in

> women's economic dependency on men and kept alive in women's "psyche" by an "inferiority complex" which actually is the background to all ideas of "femininity."

"The woman," she concluded, was largely a social construction conditioned by centuries of male-dominated socialization. In fact, "the woman as she really is does not exist. We don't know her. We will have to discover her."[1]

The following year, in a speech to a Social Democratic youth group, she compared women to various "minorities," including Negroes, Jews, the poor, and the unemployed, and insisted that their behavior is shaped by socialization, not determined by nature. Paradoxically, she observed, women are not a minority. "Why isn't this considered a 'man's problem' or a 'masculinity problem'?" One answer she offered was that women had unconsciously accepted the subordination that had been forced on them. A second reason was the many social divisions among women, such as "home-makers versus working women, rural versus urban," which are exacerbated by ideological differences among political parties.[2]

From this point on, Alva became a significant figure in the women's movement in Sweden. She was already renowned as a developmental psychologist, educator, and family policy reformer, which made her especially effective. Working both within the Social Democratic Party and in all-women's organizations, Alva sharpened her ability to think strategically and plan long-term policy changes that would advance the status of women in many areas of life. She learned to build coalitions with women from other political parties, uniting women of all classes to achieve common goals. What new qualities did Alva discover in herself as she plunged into the feminist movement? How did it affect the firm of AGM, and did she see her marriage to Gunnar in a different light?

While Gunnar won election to the upper house of the Swedish parliament, became a governor of the Bank of Sweden, and served on royal commissions on Population and Agriculture, Alva—like many women who actively addressed social questions—was not elected or appointed to an important public office. At the age of 36, she could look forward to continued success as a feminist writer, speaker, and educator, but the Social Democratic Party leadership was not interested in elevating her to a position with significant power.

In the fall of 1938, the Myrdals, with their children, returned to the United States at the invitation of the Carnegie Corporation of New York. This major philanthropic foundation commissioned Gunnar to lead an "unbiased" investigation into America's "Negro problem" and supported Alva's work on an English-language book on the Swedish experiment in social welfare and family policy.[3] In a previous book, I have told the story of Gunnar Myrdal's immersion in the issue of race, his creation of an interracial staff of social investigators representing several major points of view, and his production of a landmark study, *An American Dilemma* (1944), which was the key work in shaping postwar liberal thinking about race relations and framing the issue of civil rights as a problem "in the heart of the American."[4]

This study takes a closer look at both Alva and Gunnar as intellectuals and political reformers in Sweden and the United States. Inspired by their commitment to the human and social sciences and their willingness to scrutinize themselves as well as their society, it focuses on the psychological dynamics of their marriage and their evolving views of how the social sciences can enable men and women to overcome the conditioning of race, gender, and class to achieve a more rational, equal, and modern way of living in which each person is free to develop their special talents and cooperate with others to enrich our common life.

I draw on a treasure trove of personal letters between Alva and Gunnar and their unpublished autobiographical writings, as well as oral history interviews, to explore their family backgrounds and the shaping of their personalities in early twentieth-century Sweden. Indeed, this book was made possible by the remarkable commitment of Gunnar and Alva Myrdal to collecting and preserving their correspondence and manuscripts. In order to make these documents available to future researchers, they donated them to the Arbetarrörelsens Arkiv och Bibliotek (Swedish Labour Movement's Archive and Library), which has organized and catalogued them and offers valuable assistance to scholars. The Myrdals' personal papers, including an extensive collection of letters they exchanged from their meeting in 1919 to Alva's death in 1986, became available in 2000, 13 years after Gunnar's death. Subsequently more material has been added by their families. This extraordinary collection was assembled because Gunnar thought that we need to know more about the values, life experiences, and biases that social scientists bring to their interpretations of the world.

Tracing the development Alva and Gunnar's relationship from 1919 to the end of the Second World War, this book explores their effort to forge an honest and equal partnership as husband and wife and the intellectual and emotional dimensions of their "unsparing honesty."[5] The psychological interdependency of Alva and Gunnar both furthered and limited their careers. In their lives, the personal and the political were inseparable; Alva, especially, staked her own life, as well as her marriage, on this experiment in gender equality. Together and as individuals, the Myrdals brought a unique perspective to the study of modern families and child development, the shaping of the Swedish welfare state, the critical analysis of race relations in the United States, the reform of gender and class in Sweden, and the resistance to the threat posed by Nazi Germany to the democratic values they espoused.

This dual biography devotes considerable attention to the personal crises between Alva and Gunnar in 1940–1945 that brought to a head tensions long simmering beneath the surface of the marriage and affected his work on American race relations as well as her work on gender and the family in Sweden. How was Gunnar able to overcome cycles of anxiety and depression, look deeply into complex issues of race, economics, and society, and summon the willed optimism necessary to offer policy solutions to seemingly intractable social problems? How did his doubts about his self-worth drive him to a frenzied perfectionism in his social scientific research and writing? Both of the Myrdals emerged from the crisis as stronger public intellectuals, more confident in their contributions to national and international debates, but many interpersonal issues—although explored exhaustively in intense dialogue—remained unresolved.

During the spring and summer of 1941, without Alva at his side, Gunnar had difficulty writing his "big book" on race relations in America and fell into a severe depression. In increasingly frantic letters, he badgered his wife to do her "duty," leave the children with relatives, and undertake the risky wartime journey to the United States. Alva fought back with a devastating critique of Gunnar's dominance in their relationship, and a full-scale marital crisis ensued. In daily letters back and forth across the Atlantic, the Myrdals relived their 22-year relationship, explored the moral issues it involved, analyzed their current crisis in relentless psychological detail, and discussed whether they would continue their marriage.

While he was working on *An American Dilemma*, Gunnar wrote long letters to Alva in which he ruminated on his life, his faults, his philosophy, and his ideas. Fearing that his personality was disintegrating, he envisioned his study of American Negroes as his final redeeming mission. "From the first page to the last it is about just me and us and my fateful life dilemma," he confessed. In its analysis of racial inequality in a democracy with egalitarian ideals, it exemplified "humanity's elemental tragedy: that good people turn life into a pure hell when they live . . . in families and in society." (G to A, July 26, 1941) After two months of psychotherapy by letter, Alva Myrdal felt that the "intoxicating honesty" of their correspondence had cleared the air and set out on a dangerous journey to join him in the United States.

A crucial period of introspection for Alva came in 1944, when Gunnar, having published *An American Dilemma* in January, took on a major role in planning Sweden's postwar economy and returned to parliament. Alva, whose parents had died the previous year, wrote three unpublished manuscripts that have hitherto remained unknown. The first two were written simultaneously from April to June: an autobiography that explores the psychological dimensions of her childhood and youth to age 17, when she met Gunnar; and a dream diary that she kept each morning. Her reflections on her family, her friendships, and the process of growing up shed light on the sense she made of herself and her relationships with others. The record of Alva's dreams, which range from childhood memories to surreal, cinematic vignettes of her marriage and her political career in the Social Democratic Party, provides a unique window on the imagination of the 42-year-old feminist activist, wife, and mother.

The third manuscript in the 1944 trilogy is a private journal that Alva kept for three weeks in December. Like a movie camera, it records Gunnar's words and gestures at a party, and Alva compares herself to the women fawning over him. Alva asks herself how she could stay in a marriage with a man whose extraordinary demands drained so much emotional energy from her relationships with her children and from her own work. She then confronts a list of four alternatives she gives herself: divorce, separation, an open marriage, or plodding on in her relationship with Gunnar. But the world would not stand still long enough for her to give much attention to these options. When she completed the journal in December 1944, the war in Europe was entering its final phase.

As Gunnar planned Sweden's postwar economy, Alva wrote articles about reforming Swedish public education, advocated a vast campaign of building apartments for working families, and advanced ideas for improving the status of women in the labor force. Working with leaders of women's organizations in Sweden, the United States, and Britain, she drew up plans to defend the gains that women had made in the work force during the war, knowing that if women did not get in on the ground floor of postwar planning they would have no chance of making permanent improvements in their situation. Alva had also contributed numerous articles on international relations to Swedish magazines and newspapers since 1938, adding to her portfolio an expertise on foreign policy to complement her achievements as an advocate for domestic reform. When the Social Democrats won an outright majority in the first parliamentary election after the war's end and Gunnar was appointed Minister of Trade, the couple saw unprecedented opportunities for each of them to be effective in expanding Sweden's social democratic welfare state and to contribute to the shaping of a more just international order.

In an address in 1972, Gunnar complained to a group of sociologists that there had been much more research on the lives of businessmen, workers, politicians, criminals, and prostitutes than on social scientists. He suggested that scholars should not only investigate the breadth or narrowness of social scientists' training, their "reading habits," and the "scope of their social contacts," interests, and biases, but also examine how their research is "irrationally conditioned." Observing that most of the great economists, such as Smith, Marx, Mill, and Keynes, were "strikingly idiosyncratic" personalities, he envisioned "a large field for intensive psychological research, which must, however, situate individual social scientists in the social setting where they lived and worked." This lacuna cannot be excused on the grounds that these materials are inaccessible, since "the corpus delicti, our writings, is on the table." "And for the rest, it should not be more difficult to get at the other forces influencing us in our work besides our intention to seek true knowledge."[6]

Alva was keenly aware that her own life story illuminated painful issues that faced women in the twentieth century who plunged into public life and intellectual debate while carrying the burden of providing emotional support for a husband and caring for children. We have a glimpse of an extraordinary couple, both born in modest circumstances, who were engaged in some of the twentieth century's most important issues. They are the only husband and wife ever to win Nobel prizes independently in different fields. By the time this book ends, Alva and Gunnar had each found their own separate path.

Although Gunnar was 3 years older, my narrative begins with Alva's family, which in its struggle against poverty and its involvement with popular social movements is representative of Swedish social and political history during the late nineteenth and early twentieth centuries. Alva's family history helps to crystallize many of the issues with which the couple contended during their careers. While Gunnar's father also began in poverty, Gunnar was educated for membership in Sweden's small leadership class, which found the intellectual ground shifting under its feet during and after the First World War and encountered fierce resistance from below as the Social Democrats, with strong links to the growing trade union movement, eclipsed the Conservatives and Liberals as the nation's largest political party. The Myrdals established themselves as leading intellectuals in this modern movement for greater equality, and their success in Sweden led to their confrontation with even more profound challenges in other parts of the world.

Notes

1 Alva Myrdal, Uppfostrad till "akta kvinnlighet."
2 Alva Myrdal, Moderna kvinnoproblem.
3 Alva Myrdal, *Nation and Family.*
4 Jackson, *Gunnar Myrdal.*
5 Alva and Gunnar's commitment to unsparing honesty has also struck others: see Hederberg, *Sanningen, inget annat än sanningen.*
6 Gunnar Myrdal, How scientific are the social sciences? See also Lyon, Use of biographical material in intellectual history.

References

Alva and Gunnar Myrdal's Collection (AGMA). Arbetarrörelsens Arkiv och Bibliotek (Swedish Labour Movement's Archives and Library). Stockholm, Sweden.

Alva Myrdal's published works, 2.1

Alva Myrdal. Uppfostrad till "akta kvinnlighet" (Socialized to protect "femininity"). *Idun*, no. 8 (1934).

Alva Myrdal's manuscripts, 2.3

Alva Myrdal. Moderna kvinnoproblem (Modern women's issues). Manuscript of lecture delivered to Social Democratic Party youth group, Jan. 13, 1935.

Correspondence between Alva and Gunnar Myrdal, 3.3

[Letters cited as A to G or G to A, date]

Alva and Gunnar Myrdal's Published Works

Myrdal, Alva. *Nation and Family: The Swedish Experiment in Democratic Family and Population Policy*. New York: Harper & Bros., 1941.

Myrdal, Alva, and Gunnar Myrdal. *Kris i befolkningsfrågan* (*Crisis in the Population Question*). Stockholm: Bonniers, 1934.

Myrdal, Gunnar, with the assistance of Richard Sterner and Arnold Rose. *An American Dilemma: The Negro Problem and Modern Democracy*. New York: Harper and Row, 1944.

Myrdal, Gunnar. How scientific are the social sciences? Gordon Allport Memorial Lecture, Harvard University, November 4, 1972. *Journal of Social Issues* 28, no. 4 (Fall 1972): 151–170.

Published Sources

Hederberg, Hans. *Sanningen, inget annat än sanningen: Sex decennier ur Alva & Gunnar Myrdals liv*. Stockholm: Atlantis, 2004.

Jackson, Walter A. *Gunnar Myrdal and America's Conscience: Social Engineering and Racial Liberalism, 1938–1987*. Chapel Hill: University of North Carolina Press, 1990.

Lyon, E. Stina. The use of biographical material in intellectual history: Writing about Alva and Gunnar Myrdal's contributions to sociology. *International Journal of Social Research Methodology* 7, no. 4 (2004): 323–343. htpps://doi.org.10.1080.1364557092000046671

Part I

Becoming Alva, Becoming Gunnar

2 Alva's Family on the Edge of Poverty

Remarkably, Alva emerged from a background that did not nurture young women's aspirations, support their education, or offer them models of achievement. Born in Uppsala on January 31, 1902, she was the first child of a young couple from rural Sweden who were struggling to gain a foothold in the expanding industrial economy. The Industrial Revolution had come to Sweden relatively late, but the urbanization that followed was phenomenally rapid. Stockholm's population tripled between 1870 and 1900. Uppsala, a commercial center north of Stockholm, was home to the country's oldest cathedral and its oldest university. As manufacturing took hold, it attracted numerous migrants from the countryside. The cityscape was marked by a deep division between the cathedral, castle, and university buildings on the west side of the Fyris River, and the railroad, factories, and crowded wooden housing where the working class lived on the east side.

Sweden remained a rigidly hierarchical society, and fewer than 10 percent of adults could vote in parliamentary elections. Although the country had achieved mass literacy by the mid-nineteenth century, only a small proportion of young men were able to attend the college preparatory schools called *gymnasium*. But there were no gymnasiums for young women, so only a handful of women could be admitted to university. A small proportion of school teachers were women, and most other white collar and professional occupations were closed to them. The majority of wage-earning women toiled as domestic servants. Factory jobs were open to women in some industries, but paid roughly half of the low wages men earned.

Albert and Lowa Jansson, Alva's parents, had lived in Uppsala for less than two years when Alva was born. They rented an apartment with Albert's cousin in a new building near the city center, which was a great improvement over the squalid conditions elsewhere. Albert Jansson arrived with great optimism about the prospects for both his family and the nation. Although poor people faced the ups and downs of the market economy without any government system of social services or unemployment insurance, the Janssons' neighborhood included the offices of self-help and voluntary associations that served the working class. The temperance, cooperative, and labor movements had gained a mass following. A gathering place for union meetings called the People's House was under construction nearby. The Uppsala Workers' Institute, founded in 1883, sponsored lectures on politics and economics. By 1900, study circles had been fostered by the labor movement and Social Democratic Party, which eventually coalesced into a national adult education program.[1]

After the founding of the Social Democratic Party in 1889 and the national trade union confederation in 1898, the workers' movement became independent of middle-class reformers. Demands for universal male suffrage moved to the center of political discourse. As Sweden's Conservative government resisted fiercely, the debate became more polarized and workers' class consciousness intensified. The People's Parliament, formed in 1892, organized alternative parliamentary elections open to all adult men, demonstrating their determination to win the right to vote. At a national meeting protesting the extension of military conscription in 1895, Hjalmar Branting, who led the Social Democrats from 1892 to 1924, addressed the People's Parliament at a hall in Uppsala, contrasting the privileged *överklass*, centered in the business elite, large landowners, church hierarchy, and university, with the *underklass*, the working poor, and sought a voice in government for those who were disfranchised but subject to the military draft.[2]

Alva's father participated enthusiastically in the culture of mutual aid and self-education promoted by popular movements. He had been active in the Good Templars, Sweden's largest temperance organization, since his teenage years. Unable to continue his education beyond elementary school, he was determined to educate himself. In workingmen's libraries he read books by Karl Marx, Peter Kropotkin, and other socialists and anarchists, which offered a radical alternative to the conservative, religious, and patriotic history he was taught in school.[3]

Albert Jansson sold life insurance to working men, many of whom had grown up in rural poverty. The son of a blacksmith in Västmanland, the county west of Uppsala, he had started working as a farm laborer at 14, then became a store clerk and bookkeeper. Albert's father had died young, leaving his widow and children only a small house and a few possessions, so Albert understood first-hand the fragility of life and the needs of working-class families. Private life insurance was well beyond the means of working people. The Swedish Workers' Security Insurance Company, established in 1899, charged low premiums for basic benefits. Albert sold policies, collected premiums, and investigated claims. It is doubtful that he made much money, since the city had many other insurance agents.[4] This white collar job gave him a comprehensive view of the problems that urban working-class families encountered. He became a Social Democrat and struggled for a fairer society for all.

Lowa Larsson Jansson, Albert's wife, was the only surviving child of a family that owned a small farm in Södermanland, the county immediately west of Stockholm and south of Lake Mälaren. An attractive, well-dressed woman, she had no formal education beyond elementary school. After her mother died in childbirth when she was 9, she devoted herself to raising her younger siblings, Anna and Edvard. Lowa loved sewing and had been trained by a seamstress in Eskilstuna, the nearby small town, but she did not want to earn her living by plying her needle. She had escaped life on the farm by marrying Albert, and she expected her husband to support her and their baby. When she read the city's newspaper, she saw advertisements for many consumer goods—for those who could afford them. The liberal newspaper proclaimed its "free-thinking and democratic principles," but included little of interest to working people.[5]

Lowa's married life had begun in the shadow of death. Her beloved sister Anna succumbed to tuberculosis only 12 days before Lowa and Albert's wedding. The couple decided to go ahead with the ceremony, but the bride wore her black mourning dress. Just six weeks before she expected her baby, her brother Edvard died during his military service. Lowa had shaped her identity around nurturing her siblings. Now they were both gone; only her father and paternal grandmother remained. Doubly bereft, Lowa was extremely apprehensive about giving birth for the first time.[6]

Albert and Lowa had hoped for a son, but they rejoiced at the birth of a healthy daughter. Her name, which combined the first syllable of Albert's name with the last syllable of Lowa's, symbolized the new beginning for their family (see Figure 2.1).

Alva's parents had quite different personalities, opinions, and tastes. It took a long time before their daughter could comprehend the class, gender, and political tensions in the family or see her family in relation to Swedish society as a whole. Eventually she came to understand the world of her parents and the roots of her childhood experiences in the stories of two farming families in Södermanland and Västmanland. The history of these families in the century before her birth encapsulates many of the social issues for which Alva would struggle to find policy solutions: the class system; the vulnerability of working families—especially women and children—in the new capitalist agricultural and industrial economy; inadequate housing; and women's lack of educational opportunities, access to birth control, and the right to vote.

In Search of Livelihoods

The nineteenth century brought downward mobility for many rural Swedes whose families lost their land or were unable to provide land for their children. The population soared after 1800, as mortality declined first among infants and then among adults. The causes of this increase in

Figure 2.1 Lowa, Albert, and Alva Jansson (later Reimer), circa 1902. Studio portrait by Axel Wester, Eskilstuna. Courtesy of Alva and Gunnar Myrdal's Collection, Arbetarrörelsens Arkiv och Bibliotek, Stockholm, Sweden.

life expectancy included agricultural improvements, potato cultivation, vaccination against smallpox, better hygiene, and the long peace after the Napoleonic wars. In 1800, land ownership was more widely distributed in Sweden than in many other parts of Europe, where large estates worked by peasants and laborers were the norm. But the gap between those with land and the landless widened in Sweden as well. Many farmers increased the amount of land they cultivated by clearing forests, draining swamps, and converting meadows and pastures to fields. Some raised productivity by taking advantage of legal reforms that encouraged the consolidation of small plots of land in open, common fields into contiguous, privately owned and separately cultivated farms. The property rights of small landowners were strengthened by Sweden's parliament, the Riksdag.[7]

For those who did not inherit land, the prospects were bleak. Many young men joined the migratory class of annual or seasonal farm laborers. Others eked out a livelihood as tenants, artisans, loggers and lumbermen, or laborers in the mines and ironworks that dotted the countryside. Young women found jobs mainly as servants and were expected to work in the barn and the fields as well as the dairy and the house. Some young men and women moved to small towns and cities, but there were few large factories, and employment for the unskilled was uncertain. In these circumstances, many could not afford to marry, so illegitimacy and prostitution became more common, especially in Stockholm. A wave of migration to North America that had begun in the 1840s became a flood in the late nineteenth century. By 1900, one-fifth of the Swedish population had emigrated in a massive effort to escape rural and urban poverty.

In the nineteenth century, large landowners had evicted tenants in order to enlarge the estates they cultivated with hired labor. Although the landless population grew, landowners did not always have enough workers at their disposal during planting and harvest seasons. They worried about controlling large numbers of migratory workers and the social disorder that might arise from masses of unsettled people. As a solution to this perceived crisis, they introduced the *statare* system, hiring married couples to work for them year round. *Statare* lived on the estate, often in barracks-like buildings, and were paid mostly in kind rather than in cash. Married women in *statare* families were required to work in the estate's dairy and fields. Although rising from this class was very difficult, the system enabled young couples to marry and contributed to the rapid growth of the rural labor force. By the mid-nineteenth century, the *statare* system had become common in the thickly settled counties of east-central Sweden that surrounded Stockholm and Lake Mälaren. *Statare* worked on annual contracts, which usually expired on October 1 and could not be broken during the rest of the year. During the first week of October, the roads were clogged with wagonloads of families fleeing bad conditions and seeking better situations somewhere else.[8]

The situation of other agricultural workers was no better. Tenants on estates and large farms lacked secure contracts and could easily be dispossessed. They usually had access to barely enough land for a small garden and performed seasonal or day labor for their landlord. Although agricultural productivity increased over the course of the nineteenth century, harvest failures led to famines. During Alva's childhood, older people who could remember the 1860s told stories of starving children and families wandering in search of work.

Alva's mother's family, the Larssons, had managed to hold onto their small farm through the many economic crises of the nineteenth century. Alva's father's family, the Janssons, was less fortunate. By the middle of the century they were landless and faced the difficult task of finding work in a rural economy increasingly dominated by commercial agricultural estates.

The stories Alva knew about her father's family begin with her great-great grandparents. Jan Jansson, born in 1793, married Stina Cajsa Larsdotter, a widow eight years his senior. Stina had inherited a small farm after the death of her father, and under Swedish law Jan became the manager of his wife's property. Jan was regarded with respect in the community, but he, Stina, and their three children worked the land by themselves. Gustaf Jansson, their middle child and oldest son, was Alva's great-grandfather. At the age of 20, he left home and worked as a wagon driver among 20 farm employees supervised by the leaseholder on a nearby estate. In 1846 Gustaf married Anna Maria Leisted, the daughter of a farm worker. The newlyweds moved back to his father's farm, where two sons were born. In 1853 they moved west to Västmanland in the heart of Sweden's *Bergslagen*, a region known for mining, charcoal burning, iron works, timber, and handicrafts. Here Gustaf and Anna Maria had their third and last child, a daughter.[9]

Gustaf became the foreman and then manager of a commercial farm owned by Adolph Zethelius, a wealthy Stockholm businessman who owned several ironworks and estates. In 1872, ownership of these enterprises passed from the family to a corporation. Jansson supervised roughly 70 people, including tenants, laborers, and their families. He managed the estate for 30 years, an unusually long tenure, and his family was proud of his skill as a "forward-looking" agriculturalist, draining swamps, bringing new land under cultivation, and increasing productivity, as well as buying, fattening, and selling steers for slaughter. For all his achievements, the corporation awarded Gustaf a medal. Yet he never owned land himself and left only a small estate at his death in 1903. His descendants remembered him as a gruff, tight-fisted patriarch, nicknamed "Upsala gubben," the old man of Upsala farm.[10]

Fredrik Jansson, Gustaf's eldest son, was born in 1847. He left the farm when he was 17 and went to work on a much larger estate with an impressive manor house that had been owned by noble and wealthy families before Zethelius purchased it. His younger brother, Albert, followed him to the estate village a few years later. The place was dominated by its paternalistic landlord, who owned his employees' housing and tried to instill industrial work discipline. Although Fredrik learned the blacksmith's trade, he did not find his feet financially or socially. During his late teens he got into trouble with the law and moved to a nearby city, then tried his hand at factory work in his native parish. He returned to the farm his father managed in 1866. Fredrik worked there as a blacksmith until 1873, when he married a young woman from a neighboring parish and took a job as a smith on the vicarage estate in the tiny hamlet of Munktorp.[11]

Anna Sofia Jansdotter, Fredrik's wife, came from a poor family that had lived in the parish for three generations. Her grandfather, Jan Erik Söder, was born in 1811 to an unwed servant in Västerås. Four years later, Jan Erik's mother married a man from Munktorp and moved to the parish with her son. After an unsuccessful apprenticeship, Jan Erik Söder became a soldier but never had to fight. When he retired on a small pension, he served as the church watchman and died in 1870, leaving a minuscule estate. He and his first wife, Christina Larsdotter, had eight children, five of whom lived to maturity. The second-oldest, Jan Erik Ersson, was born in 1835 and was a 19-year-old farm worker when he had a daughter out of wedlock with Sofia Louisa Anderssdotter, a young woman in the village. Sofia's father was not sure if the lad could support his daughter and grandchild, so he made them wait to marry until Jan Erik reached the age of 21. Sofia Louisa and her baby, Anna Sofia, lived with her parents for three years.[12]

After marrying in 1857, Jan Erik Ersson, Sofia Louisa, and their daughter moved to a cottage on a nearby estate, where Jan Erik was employed as a wagon driver by Henrik Sebastian Tham, an aristocrat who had served in the cavalry. They lost an infant in 1859, and Sofia remembered bitterly that Tham had said it was not suitable for a simple family to have such a fine funeral. Three years later they rented a farm on the estate, where they lived for more than 35 years; Sofia Louisa stayed on after her husband's death in 1898. The couple had nine children, but only three lived to adulthood. In 1873 Jan Erik asked the pastor to give his new son-in-law, Fredrik Jansson, a job as blacksmith. Fredrik and Anna Sophia settled down in a small house next to the forge, 50 meters from the church and even closer to the pastor's elegant mansion.[13] But the blacksmith's income from the vicarage estate was meager and irregular, so Fredrik sought other customers as well.

Munktorp consisted of the vicarage, a few small houses, and a general store on the pastor's large estate. In addition to their religious duties, pastors of the Church of Sweden were civil servants and employers. Most of their income came from the grain their farms produced, as well as from church taxes that farmers generally paid in kind. The pastor at Munktorp enjoyed considerable secular power as well as clerical authority. His income placed him in the top 10 percent of men in the parish. He employed an assistant minister, a farm manager, and a teacher for the elementary school, and often served on the parish council that oversaw local government. All pastors in Sweden conducted an annual census, visiting each household in the parish and recording the name, age, and sex of each inhabitant, as well as their degree of literacy, knowledge of

Luther's catechism, church attendance, and moral reputation. The pastor at Munktorp had a relatively peaceful tenure from his arrival in 1859 until his death in 1888. Dissenters were few, and he felt secure enough to allow itinerant evangelists from free churches to preach in his parish. There were a few signs that people resented his exercise of authority, although some parishioners complained to the diocese that he had not consulted them sufficiently about school affairs.[14]

Fredrick and Anna Sofia had three children, the second of whom was Alva's father, Albert Jansson, born on December 20, 1876, and named for Fredrik's brother. Anna Sofia, a strong and sturdy woman, sometimes worked at the vicarage as a domestic and agricultural laborer, and the children were expected to go to work as soon as they finished elementary school. The fondest memory of Albert's childhood was the summer of 1883, which he spent with his grandfather on Upsala farm. The 6-year-old loved playing in the fields, roaming the woods, and taking part in the harvest. During that summer Albert dreamed of becoming an independent farmer. As he later wrote in a short memoir, Albert thought that "the highest and best I could wish for in life would be to own land and be able to bring forth food for humanity." "But," he wondered, "how would that come to be for one as little and poor as I felt myself to be?" Those childhood memories and his dream of a better life sustained him throughout his life.[15]

In Munktorp, Fredrik was no longer under the capitalist labor discipline of the Zethelius family or the corporation; instead, he had to defer to the Church of Sweden. As the only blacksmith in a farming area, he had no working-class community or labor movement to offer him support or a sense of solidarity. Fredrik was a strong and proud man. Hammering at the forge was hot work, and smiths often drank beer while working; sometimes they received part of their pay in locally distilled alcoholic spirits. Drinking was an important part of workingmen's culture of masculinity.[16]

A Working-Class Family in Crisis

After eight years in Munktorp, Fredrik decided to try his luck in the nearby city of Västerås, which had a growing number of metal works, and in 1881 the family moved to an apartment in a working-class district. At first Fredrik worked for a manufacturer; then he took a job as a blacksmith on a large estate in a neighboring parish. At the end of the summer of 1883, Fredrik lost that position. The number of jobs in iron works was declining, since many small foundries closed as production was centralized.[17] Fredrik returned to Munktorp, where he resumed his trade as the blacksmith on the vicarage estate.

Anna Sofia did not want to move back to the hamlet, so she and the children stayed in their apartment in Västerås, whose lease did not expire until February 1, 1884. Like many poor women who managed the family budget, Anna Sofia took in a boarder to help pay the rent. Since the vast majority of working-class apartments at that time consisted of only one room and a kitchen, taking in a boarder could mean a loss of privacy. Although this practice did not imply any sexual relationship between landlady and boarder, that was what Fredrik suspected when he returned to find a coachman named Pettersson living there. One night in late November 1883, a neighbor heard the enraged Fredrik yell at his wife: "Get out of here!" "Go to hell and take your coachman with you." The blacksmith threw Anna Sofia and the three children out of the apartment with the intention of taking them back to Munktorp, and the neighbor found 6-year-old Albert, his older brother Theodor, and his younger sister Mimmi crying on the front porch while Fredrik and Anna Sofia quarreled. Fredrik was so furious at his wife that he neglected to dress the children before pushing them out the door, and they sat on the porch in their nightclothes frightened, freezing, and ashamed in front of the neighbors. It was an experience that none of the children would ever forget.[18]

Fredrik went back to his forge in Munktorp, but Anna Sofia adamantly refused go with him. After the Janssons' lease expired, Anna Sofia and the children temporarily moved in with their upstairs neighbors, the Björkholm family. Fredrik returned to Västerås on February 11. According to witnesses, he again accused his wife of adultery and charged that she had pawned all their belongings. When Anna Sofia replied in a manner that was described as verbally abusive, Fredrik threatened to kill her. During this visit he lodged with a friend named Eriksson. The following day Anna Sofia came to visit Fredrik at the Erikssons' apartment. They had another loud argument, and he pushed her so hard that she fell against a chest of drawers and onto the floor. With no male relatives of her own nearby to protect her from her abusive husband, Anna Sofia filed a complaint against Fredrik for "manhandling" her, an unusual step for a woman to take at that time.[19] The case was heard in court in Västerås on February 24, 1884.

The judge pointed out at the beginning of the trial that, according to the parish records, the couple had already been warned twice after domestic arguments. Confronting Fredrick in court, Anna Sofia Jansson charged that on November 20, 1883 and on February 12, 1884, he had pushed her to the floor, kicked her, and gripped her by the throat while threatening that if she tried to return to Munktorp he would "bump her off." Testifying in his own defense, Fredrik denied manhandling or threatening his wife and stated that she had behaved abusively and provocatively. He admitted that he had told her to get out, warned her that if she did not do as he said he would throw her out, and gripped her by the arm and grabbed ahold of her coat. But, he insisted, she had thrown herself to the floor. He argued that the quarrel between them was mainly due to the fact that, against his will, his wife had a male boarder staying in their home since October 24. Although Sofia claimed that she made money by letting him stay on, Fredrik alleged that the man had never paid anything for the privilege. Instead, the blacksmith insisted that the relationship between his wife and the coachman had been sexual.

The Björkholms testified that they had heard loud arguments between the Janssons on November 20 and February 11 and that Fredrik had threatened to kill his wife. Mrs. Eriksson was the only witness to the February 12 altercation. She confirmed that Fredrik had accused his wife of adultery and that when Anna Sofia had responded "provocatively and peevishly," he had told her to leave. There was a scuffle between them and Anna Sofia had fallen, but Mrs. Eriksson said she was not sure of the details.

Under questioning from the judge, Fredrik admitted that on February 12, having been provoked by his wife, he had pushed her hard enough to make her fall on the floor, but he denied all other accusations. The judge then convicted the blacksmith of manhandling his wife. Since she was not injured, he sentenced Fredrik to a month in Västerås jail. Although alcohol is not mentioned in the trial, it may have played a role in his behavior. The judge did not investigate the allegation of adultery, as Fredrik had not filed countercharges against his wife in a suit for divorce, and neither party called Pettersson to testify.

The family was reunited at Munktorp vicarage after Fredrik was released from jail, and there were no more reports of violence. Court and church records do not give any indication of why Anna Sofia, after accusing her husband of domestic violence and testifying in court against him, reconciled with him after he had served his sentence. Perhaps she felt he had been put on notice that, if his behavior were repeated, he would suffer a more severe punishment. To be sure, there were few options open to poor women at that time: Anna Sofia needed a home for herself and the three children, and Fredrik's income, however scanty, supplemented her own meager earnings. Anna Sofia's parents were still tenant farmers in Munktorp parish. She may have found emotional support from them and from others in the community, but no financial help was forthcoming. Fredrik and Anna Sofia were able to buy a small, two-story house on the estate; they lived on the second floor and rented out the first floor to the store. The smith remained under the watchful eye of the pastor, who recorded Fredrik's jail term in the annual church census in 1884 but did not make any comments about his character in subsequent years.[20]

As a child, Albert found a refuge from his parents' troubles at the elementary school in Munktorp's church. The Church of Sweden had taken a strong interest in basic education since the Reformation, encouraging all believers to learn to read the Bible and Luther's catechism. In 1842 the Riksdag had passed a law requiring every parish to maintain an elementary school, and in 1882 seven years of schooling was made compulsory.

When Albert entered school in the mid-1880s, however, children from the working class still felt like outsiders, as their teachers considered themselves socially superior to pupils from poor families. Albert's thirst for learning led him to excel; he received all As and Bs and did especially well in math. As he neared the end of elementary school, he and three of his classmates charged ahead of the others, and his new teacher offered them extra instruction until he had taught them all the math he knew. Albert's three classmates, the sons of the teacher and of wealthy farmers, continued their studies, and two eventually earned PhDs. But Albert had no opportunity for further education because of his parents' poverty. As he later remembered, he did not question his duty to help support the family and was not upset about leaving school at the time.[21]

Albert resolved to be a different sort of man than his father. His mother made all the children promise never to touch alcohol. He grew into an austere and earnest man, setting a high moral standard for the family. A taciturn, self-controlled father and devoted husband, Albert stressed the importance of sobriety and sexual propriety as well as honesty and social justice. He never told his children about his father's conviction for domestic violence or his accusation of adultery against his mother. Alva and his other children did not find out about this family conflict until long after his death. But this childhood trauma and the shame that Fredrik's lack of self-control brought on the family were important in shaping Albert's personality and conduct. He supported women's equality in the workplace, the labor movement, politics, and education, and he encouraged Alva's intellectual and political interests. In her eyes, however, he seemed overly deferential to Lowa; she found her mother too demanding and her father too compliant. Albert and Lowa frequently had trouble paying the rent, but they did not take boarders; only relatives and an occasional servant girl lived with the family as they sought to maintain their respectability. Many years later, when the widowed Anna Sofia considered moving in with a local policeman with whom she had a romantic relationship, Albert and Mimmi vehemently opposed the idea, fearing that people might cast aspersions on their mother's sexual morality and damage her reputation—and, by extension, their own.[22]

Albert worked for his maternal grandfather and then got a job as a farm hand at the vicarage estate where his mother and father worked. He was in for a shock as he shoveled manure in the barn, harvested grain, and drove a horse and wagon. He resented being treated "like just a servant" and came to see the Church of Sweden as part of the class hierarchy that oppressed ordinary people.[23]

Class Consciousness and Popular Movements

Albert's acute consciousness of class distinctions was widely shared during the early 1890s. Skilled workers had organized local unions as early as the 1840s, and in the 1880s both skilled and unskilled workers founded national unions on an industry-wide basis. The commercialization of agriculture created a large class of landless laborers and spurred massive migration to industrial cities. Class consciousness grew rapidly, uniting factory workers in cities and towns with miners, iron workers, and farm laborers in the countryside. A strike by sawmill workers in the northern town of Sundsvall in 1879 attracted widespread public attention. Although the employers crushed the strike, the workers held out for two months and aroused great sympathy throughout the country.[24]

The socialist movement came to Sweden in the early 1880s, led by the fiery agitator August Palm, a Swede who had been apprenticed to a tailor at the age of 9 and then worked in Denmark and Germany, where he became a union member and a socialist. Although he was committed to achieving socialism by democratic means, his critique of capitalism, the state, the bureaucracy, the military, and the Church of Sweden in his newspaper *Socialdemokraten* made him many enemies. Imprisoned for his inflammatory attacks on the government and state church, Palm orchestrated the socialist congress at which the Swedish Social Democratic Party was founded in 1889. By 1892 party leadership had passed to Hjalmar Branting, a masterful tactician and clever orator who led the working-class movement as it grew into Sweden's first mass-based political party. No Social Democrats were represented in the Riksdag until 1896 because of restrictive property qualifications for voting. In the 1890s Liberals and Social Democrats collaborated to campaign for universal male suffrage. Landowning farmers, many of whom supported the Liberals, had long been represented in local governments and in parliament.[25]

Local grievances drove national trends. In Munktorp, Albert Jansson tangled with the new pastor, Johan Erik Ekblom, his employer on the vicarage estate. When Fredrik and other farm workers took his measure, they saw a 47-year-old cleric with an imperious manner and very conservative politics. In a memorial tribute written after his death, Ekblom's daughter explained her father's rigid personality and controversial career by recounting his impoverished and lonely childhood. After studying theology at Uppsala University, he became a pastor in a remote village in Dalarna.[26] From that experience, Ekblom retained an idealized picture of the "traditional" Swedish village as a unified community of hard-working farmers, untouched by the free churches, reform, and labor radicalism that swept through rural Sweden in subsequent decades.

Ekblom found Västmanland distressingly different from the Dalecarlian village he romanticized. Mines and iron works provided fertile soil for the labor and socialist movements. The market economy made life insecure for farm workers, especially on large estates. Ekblom was a fierce opponent of the free churches and the anticlerical socialist movement, which threatened to undermine the pastor's authority. He had little patience with those who urged him to compromise and plenty of support from those above him in the church hierarchy. At an 1892 meeting of clergymen, Ekblom's bishop declared that "every kind of belief in God is incompatible with social democracy."[27]

At 15, all the children living in the parish were expected to attend confirmation class, where they memorized passages from the Bible and Luther's catechism. Looking back at the age of 66, Albert regretted his decision to go through with his confirmation despite his serious doubts about the divinity of Jesus. But the family depended upon the vicarage for much of its income and the young assistant pastor who taught the class seemed like a nice man, so Albert concentrated on the discussions of ethical questions and tried to ignore the rest. At the ceremony, he remained silent during the profession of faith but took communion. Remembering that day as "the unhappiest I have ever experienced," he regretted not having had the courage or honesty to refuse to take part. The remorse Albert felt drove him to think more deeply about religion, and he concluded that he did not believe in a God who personally punished and forgave. In his view, Jesus was a good man, but the "so-called Christian faith as it was preached then" was "idolatry." Eventually, Albert called himself an atheist.[28]

During his teen years, Albert worked full-time and rarely had a chance to indulge his love of reading. He read the newspapers to which his father subscribed, including *Bärgslagsbladet*, a radical weekly that took its name from the mining and ironmaking region. "To read *Bärgslagsbladet* was to be seen by the conservatives as a bad person, a *nihilist*," Albert recalled. He received his first impressions of politics and class conflict at the age of 15 when he heard a speech by Alfred Stärner, the paper's editor, during the 1892 parliamentary election campaign. Stärner helped to organize the People's Parliament, which held a six-day meeting in Stockholm with speeches, demonstrations, and songs to demand universal male suffrage and rights for working people, ideas that most of the candidates for the official Riksdag would not even consider. By the fall of 1892, 13,200 men had registered to vote in this alternative election. The People's Parliament united Liberal reformers such as Stärner with leaders of the nascent Social Democratic Party such as Branting. Stärner had participated in the mass mobilizations of late nineteenth-century Sweden, including the temperance, cooperative, and labor movements. He supported proposals for universal medical and life insurance, pensions, and the building of houses which poor families would own. But in the 1890s he was best known as an advocate of universal suffrage for adult men. He began his speeches by addressing his audience as "honored Swedish citizens without the rights of citizenship." Local authorities barred him from lecture halls, theaters, and churches, forcing him to hold outdoor rallies that often attracted crowds. Stärner leavened his lectures with dramatic gestures and funny stories and punctuated his speeches with song. When law enforcement officers tried to stop his meetings and hecklers paid by business owners sought to disrupt them, he used his wit to make the policemen and hecklers the subject of the audience's derision. Writing about these events in *Bärgslagsbladet*, he denounced all attempts at intimidation and portrayed the universal suffrage movement as unstoppable.[29]

Fredrik Jansson joined the People's Parliament movement and helped prepare for a speech by Stärner in Munktorp. But when he put up posters around the village announcing the event, Ekblom tore them down. The enraged clergyman even came onto the porch of the little house that Fredrik owned and tore down a poster the blacksmith had nailed to the door. Two generations later, parishioners still told the story of this astonishing event. "It is understandable that blessings were not exactly what my father called down upon the pastor," Albert later wrote.[30]

Fredrik died in 1893 at the age of 46, his health broken by too much drink and bad working conditions in the drafty forge. His father, Gustaf Jansson, his estate's largest creditor, was the court-appointed guardian of the children, but he declined to offer any further support to his quarrelsome daughter-in-law beyond her life tenancy of the house. Albert, then 16, remembered the humiliation of seeing his family's household goods sold at auction. To escape being a farm servant, he tried to earn a living in commerce. He scraped together enough money to take a short course at Köping's Practical Bookkeeping School, from which he graduated "with distinction" in 1893.[31]

Two years later Albert moved to Eskilstuna, a city of 13,000 inhabitants, where he clerked and kept the books in several stores. But he retained a deep love of the land. He idolized Rousseau's independent, landowning, and self-sufficient farmer, whose life he imagined as the antithesis of the vassalage of the farm worker on an estate. He was disappointed by conditions in Eskilstuna, however. It had been granted the prerogatives of a "free city" in 1771 in order to facilitate the capitalist manufacture of iron products and attract both investment and labor. Artisanal production was transformed by a specialized division of labor. The influx of smiths meant that wages were very low, while successful merchants became rich. The rapid increase in the population of workingmen also created a gender imbalance in the city.[32]

In Eskilstuna, Albert was active in the International Order of Good Templars. This temperance organization sought to provide an all-encompassing social environment for men that served as an alternative to the saloon. At a time when alcoholism helped to keep families in poverty and led men to neglect and abuse their wives and children, the movement encouraged poor men to develop habits of hard work, thrift, and mutual aid. Good Templar halls were places where ordinary men could make friends. Many workingmen gained valuable experience in conducting meetings, developing skills in democratic decision making that they carried into the labor movement. Temperance groups provided a forum where men were free to express political ideas they could not yet proclaim in public.

Because the Good Templars nurtured trust, young men like Albert could find work with lodge brothers. Letters of recommendation from former employers invariably describe him as a non-drinker as well as a competent and hard-working young man. The temperance movement reinforced Albert's critical view of the Swedish state, which operated the distillery industry as a state monopoly. The second-largest source of revenue for Eskilstuna came from the sale of alcoholic beverages. Albert's membership in the Templars led to his involvement in other popular movements. He participated in founding the national cooperative organization in 1899, and soon identified himself as a socialist.[33]

When so many Swedes no longer belonged to a village community but migrated from one place to another in search of employment, these popular movements offered a sense of solidarity. Over the next two decades Albert moved frequently and changed his occupation several times, but he found a home in organizations that fused a doctrine of self-help with a program of community-building and political reform.[34] Although he read Marx, Albert did not see himself as a member of a proletariat whose revolutionary sentiments were a reaction to their exploitation and an expression of the class consciousness they developed in the workplace. Rather, he thought that Swedish farmers and workers were reclaiming a dignity and independence they had recently enjoyed in rural communities, building on traditions of democracy, independence, and mutual aid and demanding full citizenship rights. Jean-Jacques Rousseau, who had declared in *The Social Contract* (1782) that "all men are born equally free," was a great hero to Albert, as to other European workingmen. Rousseau's pastoral ideal and his postulate that people should dismantle artificial hierarchies and recover an earlier "state of nature" that had been denied to them by kings, nobles, and bishops resonated deeply with Albert's own experiences and perspective.

Between the ages of 16 and 22, Albert kept a journal in which he wrote satirical poems that expressed his radical opinions. He began the journal in Munktorp a year after the death of his father and continued it in Eskilstuna through his courtship of Lowa Larsson, who kept a notebook of her own. Most of Albert's political poems were adapted from well-known ballads and verses, with the words changed to fit his personal circumstances and contemporary events. This poetry offers a rare glimpse of an angry young man who channeled his rage into idealistic social movements that aimed at the long-term betterment of working people's lives.[35]

Albert's antireligious and antibourgeois sentiments were shared by the leaders of the Social Democratic Party, who saw the state church as a major source of support for the ruling class and its most significant propaganda instrument. Christian theology had been under assault from Swedish intellectuals since mid-century, and many interpreted the Darwinian revolution as heralding a process of social evolution in which religion was no longer necessary. The prominent socialist Axel Danielsson argued that the ruling class wanted workers to bow down "before the lying priest, who poisons your soul . . . and keeps you in animal ignorance of yourself, nature, and its laws." Christopher Isaac Huerlin's "Catechism," which was widely used in socialist propaganda, asked, "What is a clergyman?" and answered mockingly: "He is the highest paid civil servant in a community. He preaches self-denial [and] how man shall work six days in the week and rest on the seventh. He himself rests six days in the week and speaks deliberate untruths on the seventh. A hypocrite dressed in a masquerade costume!" Branting spoke more tactfully, as he wanted to bring workers from the free churches into the socialist fold. Realizing that these lay-led groups had led many poor Swedes to question both civic and clerical authority, he promoted more active participation by workingmen in church leadership and encouraged each individual to interpret the Bible for himself. While he respected individual freedom of conscience, Branting held that religion was incompatible with a high degree of knowledge and predicted that the rise of science would lead to a progressive decline in religious belief and practice.[36]

For Albert Jansson, capitalism, the state, the church, and alcohol conspired to trap workers in a life of wage slavery. Temperance was a prominent theme in his poetry. His most compelling political poem is a satire of the Conservative prime minister who sought to lengthen the term of universal military service as part of Sweden's buildup against the Russians to the east and the restive Norwegians to the west, as well as to facilitate the repression of radical workers at home. Social Democrats and some Liberals argued that young men required to serve in the military should also be allowed to vote. Albert, who did his military service two years after writing the poem, lampooned the prime minister who would send poor boys to fight for a country in which they had no voice.[37]

As Albert continued his education in workers' study circles and libraries, he encountered others with similar interests and convictions. Like many of his generation, he was fascinated by the promise of new technology and hoped that it would be used for the betterment of humanity, not for private profit. Although the government of Sweden remained in the hands of the upper class in the 1890s, he believed that the temperance, cooperative, and labor movements would forge a socialist society and transform everyday life for the vast majority of Swedish men and women. To the end of his life in 1943, Albert steadfastly maintained his faith that "the good" would triumph over evil and his conviction that serving "the good" was the highest goal of life.[38]

Lowa and Albert

During his first five years in Eskilstuna, Albert met, courted, and married Lowa Larsson, who was a year younger than he. She was the daughter of Lars Erik Jonsson and the late Anna Sofia Jonsson, who owned and lived on Slagsta farm outside the small town. Lowa was a beautiful and sociable girl who hoped to leave the countryside and move to a city. Albert, despite his rural origins and radical political opinions, won her with his handsome good looks, quiet charm, sense of humor, modesty, and strong character. The young clerk was ambitious and hard-working. He wrote poetry for Lowa, which he recorded in a notebook of poems she kept.[39]

Albert was aware that he was marrying into a family that was a step above his parents on the economic ladder. Lowa's father's family had owned land in Södermanland for at least six generations. The women in her family passed down stories about Brita Andersdotter, a remarkable woman who had been born into a landowning family near Eskilstuna in 1767. Brita had inherited one-quarter of her father's farm and had increased her wealth by surviving two husbands, both of whom were connected with the flourishing iron industry. She was the mother of two surviving children by her first husband, Eric Jonsson, and three children by her second husband, Erik Moberg. Brita's eldest daughter, Maria Jonsson, married an iron merchant, Erik Södermark, who bought Slagsta farm in 1812.[40]

During her second marriage Brita and her husband's household included her two children, his children by his deceased first wife, and three children of their own, as well as his apprentices. After his death in 1819, she continued to live with their youngest daughter in the house and held an interest in her late husband's business, which was managed by a son-in-law. After the daughter married, Brita sold her interest in the business and retired to the country. She lived to be 88 and was remembered by her descendants as a clever and forceful woman. Brita sold the farm she had inherited from her parents, and at her death in 1855 she left an impressive estate worth far more than her second husband had left her at his death 36 years earlier. In an era when married women had few rights, a widow could act independently and increase her wealth if she was a good manager.[41]

Brita's granddaughter, Kristina Lovisa Södermark (1830–1905), married Jonas Larsson, and they farmed Slagsta, which Kristina had inherited from her mother, Maria. The farm was passed on to their son, Lars Erik Jonsson (1854–1921), and eventually to Alva's mother, Lowa. Slagsta farm remained in the family for five generations. The family's modest wealth had been handed down by three generations of women before passing to Lowa's father and then to Lowa. Lowa's paternal grandmother, Kristina Lovisa Södermark, took her place in this long line of strong women. Her great-granddaughter described her as "tall, slender, organized, dominant, proud." Because Kristina Lovisa and her husband lived on her family's land, she was listed in the church records under her own last name, Södermark, until her husband's death, when she is referred to as "the widow Jonsson."

This family pattern was unusual in the patriarchal society of Sweden at the time: over five generations, four women inherited and owned the farm, although its management was sometimes shared with their husbands.[42]

Lowa's inheritance of Slagsta farm came at a great price: she was her father's only surviving child. This turn of events was unforeseeable when Albert was courting Lowa. At that point Lowa was one of three children of the owner of a small but productive family farm. Lars Erik, while respected as a hard-working farmer, had little formal education and stood outside the local economic, political, and social elite.

In her late teens and early 20s, Lowa tried to project a pleasant personality and cheerful demeanor, but her life had already been marked by tragedy. Born in 1877, the oldest of three surviving children, she had grown up in an extended family at Slagsta. Her mother, Anna Sophia, died in childbirth on her 31st birthday in 1881, and the infant also died. Lars Erik was devastated by the loss of his beloved wife, whom he mourned as "the lily of the valley." Her picture remained enshrined in the Janssons' living room: a beautiful young woman clad in mourning clothes, with braided hair, wearing a large cross on her breast. Lars Erik often spoke of how kind and gentle she had been. Lowa had to absorb this loss at the age of 9; her brother was 7, and her sister was 6. Lowa took it upon herself to help raise her younger siblings and perform many household tasks.[43] These concerns did not leave much time for anything else.

During her childhood the household included Lars Erik's parents, a maternal uncle officially classified as a pauper, and Lars Erik's younger brother, Leonard. Lowa formed a close bond with Leonard, an affectionate youth who was only 11 years her senior. To Lowa, he seemed more like an older brother who needed her care and devotion than an uncle. Although able to work, Leonard was mentally slow, and the church census of 1896 characterized him as a dependent "child," an unusual designation for a man of 28. His parents feared he would not be able to manage as an independent farmer, so in 1896 they settled a sum of money on him. Leonard set off for America, leaving his elder brother to inherit the farm. It was a long time before anyone in the family heard from Leonard again.[44]

The 18-year-old Lowa brought this tragic history and sense of vulnerability to her relationship with Albert. Like many Swedish girls at the time, Lowa kept a notebook in which she, her siblings, and her friends occasionally entered verses and maxims. Through this collection of poems, some copied from magazines and others based on traditional ballads, Lowa tried to cultivate her sensibility and develop a fortitude that would enable her to face life's sorrows. Her sister Anna and other girls contributed poems that expressed the usual concerns of teenage girls, wondering what love would be like, what kind of man they would marry, and what sort of life they would lead as adults.[45]

Albert began writing poems in Lowa's book in the fall of 1896, offering "kisses" and speaking of the love he felt in his heart, which he described as "nature's greatest mystery." In the spring of 1897 he pledged his devotion in classic Romantic fashion: "If my love flees, then perhaps I will wish to die." On the whole, however, his poems express his optimism about the new way of life he hoped they would enjoy. Albert's radical, anti-establishment political convictions were clear in a whimsical autobiographical poem that he wrote for her.[46] The Larssons, like many Swedes who owned small farms, favored the Liberal Party rather than the Social Democrats. But this did not pose a barrier to marriage. Indeed, the Liberals and Social Democrats often formed coalitions before World War I, and both parties supported universal male suffrage, pension reform, and a leaner defense budget.

Lowa's sister, brother, and friends offered their sympathy and encouragement by inscribing verses in her book about the importance of love and the difficulties lovers often face. Lowa let Albert's early poems go unanswered; after all, a proper girl was supposed to be coy. When she began to respond to his poems, she asked herself whether she could find not only the love, but also the "faith" and "hope" she needed in order to love. While references to love as an anchor amidst life's trials are a romantic convention, the poems Lowa entered contain a striking number of allusions to death, loss, and sorrow.

After three and a half years of courtship, Lowa accepted Albert's proposal, and they were married on April 15, 1900. Three years earlier, Anna had intended to reassure her sister by writing in her notebook: "Memory is the one paradise/ From which we could not be driven."[47] Lowa was mournful while leafing through the poetry book, reading the loving poems from Albert alongside the words from her younger sister whose death cast a pall over their wedding.

Alva's Advent

The differences in Albert's and Lowa's outlooks gave rise to a dispute that became a family legend. According to the story, Alva's socialist and atheist father had resisted her mother's desperate desire to have Alva baptized, and he did not give in until their daughter was 2 years old. For Lowa, still stricken with grief over her brother Edvard's death a few weeks before her daughter's birth, Alva's baptism was a symbol of renewal for the Larssons as well as the joyous beginning of her own family. Baptism in the Church of Sweden was also a marker of respectability for an upwardly mobile family eager to secure a place in the middle class. For Albert, on the contrary, the ritual raised the prospect of his having to perjure himself by promising to bring up his daughter in the church. Baptism in Uppsala's medieval cathedral was often reserved for the children of the upper class, with poor families shunted off to another location where many children were baptized at the same time. The legend contains a kernel of truth: it bespeaks an unresolved tension between Albert and Lowa, a failure to reach accord on fundamental issues that included, but went beyond, religion. On the question of baptism, however, the grief-stricken mother got her way: Alva was baptized on February 21, 1902, three weeks after her birth, by a pastor on the staff of the cathedral who was known for his ministry to the working class.[48]

Baptism did not wash away Lowa's fears for the health of her newborn daughter. Death had stalked the Larsson family for so long, and the recent loss of her two siblings had been so traumatic, that Lowa developed a neurotic fear of bacterial infection. She felt that she had failed to protect her younger sister and brother and suspected that she was carrying tuberculosis herself. Terrified that she might infect the newborn, she never kissed or hugged her baby. A degree of physical reserve was common in early twentieth-century Sweden; when babies cried, most mothers would let them cry rather than pick them up to comfort them. But Lowa's distance was different in kind as well as degree. Her fear that she might transmit this deadly disease kept her from demonstrating any physical affection to her children or grandchildren. She was also obsessed with cleanliness. Her generation was the first to learn that diseases were transmitted by germs, giving new impetus to campaigns for municipal sanitation and concern about dirty households. Through the family' many moves, Lowa devoted much of her energy to meticulous, endless housecleaning. Her fears were expressed in a certain self-preoccupation as well: Lowa frequently referred to her "weak lungs" and complained of feeling tired. Eventually her pleas of ill-health justified her retreat from her growing family. Despite her hope that Alva's birth would be a new beginning, Lowa was burdened by many anxieties as she became a mother.

Notes

All translations of manuscripts by Alva Myrdal and Albert Reimer were done by the author.

1 Lundberg, *Uppsalas byggnader*, 111; Bergold, *Uppsala*; Bergqvist, *Arbetarrörelsen i Uppsala*, 40–79; Ullenhag, *Industriell utveckling och demokratisering*. For a visual record, see http://www.uppsalaindustriminnesforening.se
2 Kléen, Profiler från Folkriksdagen 1896.
3 Bok, *Alva Myrdal*, 17–20.
4 *Upsala Nya Tidning*, 2 Jan., 30 Jan., 1 Feb. 1902. Stockholms Mantalsläng, 1903, Stockholms Stadsarkiv. Landén, *Försäkrings-funktionärernas förbund*, 15–32. Jansson, GA, Inspektör, St Persgatan 28, *Adress-Kalendar för Uppsala stad, år 1902* (Uppsala: Edv. Berlings Boktryckerie, 1902), 54.
5 Hirschfeldt, *Upsala Nya Tidning.*
6 Bok, *Alva Myrdal*, 20–21.
7 On demography, see Boucekkine, de la Croix, and Licandro, Early mortality declines; de la Croix, Lindh, and Malmberg, Demographic change and economic growth in Sweden. For economic history, see Magnusson, *Economic*

History of Sweden; Schön, *Economic History of Modern Sweden*; Gadd, The agricultural revolution in Sweden, 1700–1870; Morell, Agriculture in industrial society, 1870–1945; Flygare, Swedish smallholdings.

8 Eriksson and Rogers, *Rural Labor and Population Change*.

9 Alva Myrdal, Släkten, AGMA.

10 Albert Reimer, Uttkast till självbiografi, AGMA. On Zethelius and Surahammar, see *Nordisk familjebok* (Stockholm, 1922), 743, 767–770; *Svenska orter* III, 1255–1256; Andersson, *Surahammars bruks historia*. Gustaf Jansson, Estate Record, Snefringe Härad H.T. 1903, Bouppteckning Prot. No. 7, Landsarkivet i Uppsala. Holst, interview.

11 Reimer, Uttkast till självbiografi. In och Utflyttnings längd, 1862–1882, Härads kyrkoarkiv AI:18, p. 63, Köpingsstadsförsamling AI:20, p. 311, Landsarkivet i Uppsala.

12 Lådberger, Albert Reimers morfars far, AGMA. Munktorp Födelse och Dopbok, 1854–60, C:7, Anna Sofia, birth 103 in 1854, 286:); Munktorp Husförhörslängd, 1857–1863, Landsarkivet i Uppsala. Persson, interview. See also Bok, *Alva Myrdal*, 16–17.

13 Lådberger, Albert Reimers morfars far; Persson, interview.

14 Svensson, Biographical timeline, Erik Jonas Nordenson; Royal decree concerning compensation of Munktorp parish priest, July 5, 1867, 0111:1, Landsarkivet i Uppsala.

15 Alva Myrdal, Släkten; Jansson, Mit Lif, 1876–1896, AGMA; Reimer, Uttkast till självbiografi; Bok, *Alva Myrdal*, 17.

16 Horsell, *Borgare, smeder och änkor*.

17 Nordstrom, *History of Sweden*, 77.

18 Västerås *Folkblad*, 13 December 1934, 41. Anna Sofia Jansson vs. Fredrik Theodor Jansson. All subsequent quotations in this section are from this court transcript. Annika Reimer, personal communications; Fölster, interview, May 6, 2011.

19 On the legal subordination of women to their fathers and husbands, see Sjöberg, Mellan far och make.

20 Västerås Flyttningsbetyg, Feb. 12, 1884; Munktorps Kyrkoförhörning, 1884, Landsarkivet i Uppsala.

21 Nordstrom, *History of Sweden*, 83. Reimer, Uttkast till självbiografi; Jansson, Mitt Lif, 1877–1896.

22 See letter from Alva to Per Sundberg, April 29, 1918, AGMA. When Albert and Lowa Jansson moved to Bellmansgatan 23, Stockholm Söder, in 1902, they listed Albert's brother, Karl Theodor Jansson Reimer, as a boarder. When they had three children, Albert and Lowa had a series of young female servants to help with the childcare and cleaning. Uppgift till 1903 års mantalsskrifning i Stockholms stad och Maria församling, Stockholms Stadsarkivet. Bok, *Alva Myrdal*, 17; Fölster, interview, Dec. 11, 2007.

23 Albert Jansson's transcript from Munktorp's Folkskole, December 1, 1890, in Albert Reimer's Betyg; Reimer, Uttkast till självbiografi.

24 Bäkström, *Arbetarrörelsen i Sverige*; Ekdahl and Olsson, *Klass i rörelse*.

25 Nordstrom, *History of Sweden*, 74–79; Scott, *Sweden*, 404–405, 413–417, 433–437; Therborn, A unique chapter in the history of democracy; Tilton, *Political Theory of Swedish Social Democracy*.

26 Wik, Memorial; Svensson, biographical timeline of Johan Erik Ekblom.

27 Wik, Memorial; Bexell, *Sveriges kyrkohistoria*, vol. 7: *Folkväckelsens och krykoförnyelsens tid*, 175.

28 Reimer, Uttkast till självbiografi.

29 Björnänger, *Bärgslagsbladet*, 8–22; Mral, En vanlig agitations-kampajn i Bergslagen, 1895–96.

30 Reimer, Uttkast till självbiografi. Alfred Stärner, *Svenska män och kvinnor*, vol. 7, 312.
31 Fredrik Jansson, Inventory of property after death, 1893, Snevringe häradsrättsarkiv, Landsarkivet i Uppsala. Certificate of graduation, Praktiska Bokhålebskola, Köping, April 18, 1893, in Albert Reimer's Betyg, AGMA.
32 Horsell, *Borgare, smeder och änkor*.
33 Certificate from Praktiska Bokhålleniskola, Köping, April 18, 1893, and Good Templars membership and letters of recommendation, in Albert Reimer's Betyg. Johansson and Johansson, *Eskilstuna i våra hjärtan*, 52.
34 Hansson, *Svenska folkrörelser*.
35 For poems critical of church and state, see Albert Jansson's notebooks, and Jansson, Mitt Lif: 1877–1896.
36 Frängsmyr, *Svensk Idéhistoria*, vol. 2; Tingsten, *Swedish Social Democrats*, 587–596.
37 Krigssång för Boströmska lantvänet, in Albert Jansson's notebooks.
38 Reimer, Uttkast till självbiografi; Albert Reimer's Betyg. Fölster, interview, Dec. 11, 2007. See also Hirdman, *Det tänkande hjärtat*, 18–19. On the ideology of Albert's generation of Swedish workers, see Ambjörnsson, *Den skötsamme arbetaren*.
39 Larsson, Pösie, AGMA.
40 Lådberger, Vår mormor Lovisa Reimers farmors mormor.
41 Lådberger, Vår mormor Lovisa Reimers farmors mormor; Alva Myrdal, Släkten.
42 Thim, Anna-Sofia Larsson och hennes systrar, 1866–1950. On daughters' inheritance of farms, see Ågren, *Domestic Secrets*; Holmlund, From formal to female property rights; Holmlund, *Jorden vi ärvde*; Flygare, Family land.
43 Husförhörning för Kloster, 1883–87, Slagsta on 336, Landsarkivet i Uppsala.
44 Klosters Församlings Husförhörs bok, 1893–97, 655, Landsarkivet i Uppsala.
45 Larsson, Pösie. Although the poems that Albert wrote in Lowa's book of poetry were his original compositions, as their autobiographical details attest, many of the poems contributed by her family members and friends were copied from published sources, in keeping with customary practice for commonplace books.
46 Jansson, in Larsson, Pösie, p. 19; Jansson, Mitt Lif, 1877–1896.
47 Larsson, Pösie.
48 Fölster, interview, May 6, 2011; Svensson, interview. Uppsala Domkyrkans Födelsebok och Dopbok, A II.a.a, vol. 6, Landsarkivet i Uppsala.

References

Alva and Gunnar Myrdal's Collection (AGMA). Arbetarrörelsens Arkiv och Bibliotek (Swedish Labour Movement's Archives and Library). Stockholm, Sweden.

Alva Myrdal's personal documents, 1.1

Albert Reimer, Uttkast till självbiografi (Sketch of an autobiography), 1943.

Alva Myrdal, Släkten (Genealogy).

Alva Myrdal's correspondence, 3.1

Letter to Per Sundberg, April 29, 1918.

Alva Myrdal's family and kin, 6.3

Albert Reimer's Betyg (Transcripts).

Albert Jansson's Anteckningsböcker (Notebooks).

Albert Jansson, Mit Lif (My Life), 1876–1896, poem written Sept. 23–24, 1896, in Lowa Larsson, Pösie (Poetry book).
Lowa Larsson, Pösie (Poetry book).

Manuscripts

Jansson, Anna Sofia, vs. Fredrik Theodor Jansson. Tingsprotokoll (District court records), Västerås rådhusrätt. Feb. 25, 1884. Landsarkivet i Uppsala.
Kléen, Emil. Profiler från Folkriksdagen 1896. Manuscript. Carolina Rediviva Library, Uppsala University.
Lådberger, Ulla. Albert Reimers morfars far (Albert Reimer's maternal great-grandfather). Manuscript in possession of Gunnel Holst.
Lådberger, Ulla. Vår mormor Lovisa Reimers farmors mormor (Our maternal grandmother Lovisa Reimer's paternal grandmother). Manuscript in possession of Gunnel Holst.
Svensson, Inge. Biographical timeline of Johan Erik Ekblom. Copy of manuscript in possession of Walter Jackson.

Interviews

Fölster, Kaj. Interviews with Walter Jackson. Stockholm, Dec. 11, 2007; May 6, 2011.
Holst, Gunnel. Interview with Walter Jackson. July 2008.
Persson, Anne-Marie. Interviews with Walter Jackson. Stockholm, May 30, 2011; June 2011.
Reimer, Annika. Personal communication with Walter Jackson, May 27–28, 2012.
Svensson, Inge. Interview with Walter Jackson.

Published Sources

Ågren, Maria. *Domestic Secrets: Women and Property in Sweden, 1600–1857.* Chapel Hill: University of North Carolina Press, 2009.
Ambjörnsson, Ronny V. *Den skötsamme arbetaren: Idéer och ideal i ett norrländskt sågverkssamhälle, 1880–1930.* Stockholm, 1988.
Andersson, Fritz. *Surahammars bruks historia: aktiebolagstiden 1883–1908.* Surahammar: Surahammar bruks AB, 1963.
Bäkström, Knut. *Arbetarrörelsen i Sverige.* Stockholm: Arbetarkultur, 1967.
Bergold, Carl Erik. *Uppsala: Stadsbyggande 1900–1960*, vol. 6 of *Uppsala stads historia.* Uppsala: Almqvist & Wiksell, 1989.
Bergqvist, Bertil. *Arbetarrörelsen i Uppsala*, vol. 10 of *Uppsala stads historia.* Uppsala: Stadsarkivet, 1992.
Bexell, Oloph. *Sveriges kyrkohistoria*, vol. 7, *Folkväckelsens och krykoförnyelsens tid.* Stockholm: Verbum Förlag, 2003.
Björnänger, Oskar. *Bärgslagsbladet hundra år.* Köping: VLT Press, 1990.
Bok, Sissela. *Alva Myrdal: A Daughter's Memoir.* Reading, MA: Addison-Wesley, 1991.
Boucekkine, Raouf, David de la Croix, and Omar Licandro. Early mortality declines at the dawn of modern growth. *Scandinavian Journal of Economics* 105 (2003): 401–418.

de la Croix, David, Thomas Lindh, and Bo Malmberg. Demographic change and economic growth in Sweden: 1750–2005. *Journal of Macroeconomics* 31 (2009): 132–148.

Ekdahl, Lars, and Lars Olsson. *Klass i rörelse: Arbetarrörelsen i svensk samhällsutveckling*. Stockholm: Arbetarrörelsens arkiv och bibliotek, 2002.

Eriksson, Ingrid, and John Rogers. *Rural Labor and Population Change: Social and Demographic Developments in East-central Sweden during the Nineteenth Century*. Uppsala: Acta Universitatis Upsaliensis, Studia Historica Upsaliensis 100, 1978.

Flygare, Iréne A. Swedish smallholdings: An enduring element of the countryside. In *Agriculture and Forestry in Sweden since 1900*, ed. Hans Antonson and Ulf Jansson, 74–92. Stockholm: Royal Swedish Academy of Agriculture and Forestry, 2011.

Flygare, Iréne. Family land: Generational succession and property transfer in two Swedish agricultural areas from 1870 to 2009. *Ethnologica Scandinavica* 42 (2012): 86–100.

Frängsmyr, Tore. *Svensk Idéhistoria*, vol. 2. Stockholm: Natur och Kultur, 2000.

Gadd, Carl-Johan. The agricultural revolution in Sweden, 1700–1870. In *The Agrarian History of Sweden*, ed. Janken Myrdal and Mats Morrell, 118–164. Lund: Nordic Academic Press, 2011.

Hansson, Sigfrid. *Svenska folkrörelser*. Stockholm: Lindfors, 1936.

Hirdman, Yvonne. *Det tänkande hjärtat: Boken om Alva Myrdal*. Stockholm: Ordfront, 2006.

Hirschfeldt, Lennart. *Upsala Nya Tidning: Nyhetsorgan och opinionsbildare 1890–1959*, 2 vols. Uppsala: Uppsala Nya Tidning, 1987 and 1988.

Holmlund, Sofia. *Jorden vi ärvde: Arvsöverlåtelser och familjestrategier på den uppländska landsbygden 1810–1930*. Stockholm: Acta Universitatis Stockholmiensis 88, 2007.

Holmlund, Sofia. From formal to female property rights: Gender and inheritance of landed property in Estuna, Sweden, 1820–1845. In *Gender Regimes, Citizen Participation, and Rural Restructuring*, ed. Ildikó Astzalas Morell and Bettina B. Bock, 239–260. Amsterdam: Elsevier/JAI Press, 2008.

Horsell, Ann. *Borgare, smeder och änkor: Ekonomi och befolkning i Eskilstuna gamla stad och Fristad, 1750–1850*. Uppsala: Acta Universitatis Upsaliensis, 1983.

Johansson, Hans, and Gun Johansson, eds. *Eskilstuna i våra hjärtan: Hundra år av minnen, beslut och utveckling*. Eskilstuna: Arbetshistorika rådet i Eskilstuna/Tuna Tryck, 1999.

Landén, L.H., ed. *Försäkrings-funktionärernas förbund: Minnesskrift till de förbundets tjugofemårsjubileum*. Stockholm: Förbi, 1943.

Lundberg, Kerstin, ed. *Uppsalas byggnader*. Uppsala: Uppsala kommun, 1992.

Magnusson, Lars. *An Economic History of Sweden*. New York: Routledge, 2000.

Morell, Mats. Agriculture in industrial society, 1870–1945. In *The Agrarian History of Sweden*, ed. Janken Myrdal and Mats Morrell, 165–213. Lund: Nordic Academic Press, 2011.

Mral, Birgitte. En vanlig agitations-kampajn i Bergslagen, 1895–96. In *Arbetarrörelsen och Språket*, ed. Kurt Johanssonk, 50–90. Stockholm: Carlssons, 1996.

Nordstrom, Byron J. *The History of Sweden*. Westport, CT: Greenwood Press, 2002.

Schön, Lennart. *An Economic History of Modern Sweden*. Abingdon: Routledge, 2012.

Scott, Franklin D. *Sweden: The Nation's History*. Carbondale: Southern Illinois University Press, 1988.

Sjöberg, Marja Taussig. Mellan far och make: Ägandet, arvet och kvinnorna. In *Brytta, bygga, bo: Svensk Historia Underifrån*, ed. Gunnar Broberg, Ulla Wikander and Klas Åmark, vol. 2, 51–71. Stockholm: Ordfont, 1994.

Svenska män och kvinnor, ed. Nils Bohman and Torsten Dahl. Stockholm: Bonniers, 1954.

Svenska orter III. Stockholm, 1934.

Therborn, Göran. A unique chapter in the history of democracy: The Social Democrats in Sweden. In *Creating Social Democracy: A Century of the Labor Party in Sweden*, ed. Klaus Misgeld, Karl Molin, and Klas Åmark, 1–34. University Park: Pennsylvania State University Press, 1992.

Thim, Olle. Anna-Sofia Larsson och hennes systrar, 1866–1950. In *I samhaellets utkant: Ur Stockholms sociala historia*, 111–120. Stockholm: Tidens, 1989.

Tilton, Timothy. *The Political Theory of Swedish Social Democracy*. Oxford: Oxford University Press, 1990.

Tingsten, Herbert. *The Swedish Social Democrats: Their Ideological Development*. (1941) Totawa, NJ: Bedminster Press, 1973.

Ullenhag, Kersti. *Industriell utveckling och demokratisering, 1862–1911*, vol. 5 of *Uppsala stads historia*. Uppsala: Almqvist & Wiksell, 1984.

Wik, Karin Ekblom. Memorial in *Julbok för Västerås Stift* (1922), 26–35.

3 Alva in the Family Crucible

Sweden's capital city pulsed with class conflict in November 1902, when Albert, Lowa, and 9-month-old Alva moved to a new apartment building in Södermalm, a working-class district in Stockholm. As the labor movement challenged the upper class's monopoly on political power, Söder was a stronghold of labor. Just seven months earlier, the Social Democratic Party and the trade union confederation (LO) had staged the largest mass march in the country's history and a three-day general strike to demand manhood suffrage.

At first, Albert continued working for the insurance company. The family had two lodgers: Albert's older brother, Theodor Jansson Reimer, who worked as a night watchman, and Lowa's younger cousin, Nils Södermark, a store assistant.[1] Like many Swedes who moved from the country to the city, Theodor had taken a new surname, Reimer, to establish an individual identity in a metropolis with thousands of people with the patronymic Jansson. Albert soon adopted it as well.

Södermalm is an island immediately south of Gamla Stan, which formed the city's medieval core. Here stood the royal palace, cathedral, and parliament building, surrounded by narrow cobblestone streets lined with three- and four-story houses that dated from the seventeenth century. At the turn of the twentieth century, Söder was connected to the rest of the city by a bridge and ferries. One of its hilltops offered a panoramic view. To the west lay Kungsholm, another island crammed with poor people, and Långholm, which held a prison. An industrial district lay to the south, on a peninsula of the mainland. Further north on the mainland was Norrmalm, which contained the city's rapidly expanding central business district, the train station, and distinct neighborhoods for the wealthy, the middle class, and the far more numerous working class. Across the harbor to the east lay the beautiful wooded island of Djursholm, where the amusement park Skansen had recently opened. To the southeast, a vast salt water estuary dotted with hundreds of small islands linked Stockholm to the Baltic.

For most of the nineteenth century Söder had been a world apart from central Stockholm, with some of the city's worst slums and most dire poverty. Its narrow streets and alleys were packed with migrants from the countryside who tried to piece together a living from seasonal factory work, casual labor on the docks, handicrafts, and domestic service. The textile factories, tobacco workshops, glassworks, and canneries all paid low and irregular wages. Multiple families crowded into small apartments; privacy was an unthinkable luxury. Most houses were one- or two-story wooden shacks without indoor plumbing. People walked to work on muddy streets, stepping around garbage and horse manure. Cholera, diphtheria, and tuberculosis ravaged poor neighborhoods.[2]

In the mid-nineteenth century, Stockholm, especially Söder, had a high rate of illegitimacy; more than half of all children were born to unmarried women. Not all of these children were raised only by their mothers, however; many working-class couples had what were called Stockholm marriages. They did not see the point of scraping together the money necessary to post the banns, obtain a marriage license, and pay the pastor, who was often a distant figure with little sympathy for the poor. Small children were generally looked after by older siblings. They subsisted on inadequate diets, and many succumbed to disease because of malnutrition and lack of sanitation. Many poor women had to give up their children because they were unable to support them. Most orphans lived with foster families who took in poor children for money, although a few were sent to orphanages run by middle-class philanthropists. Foreign visitors observed that the city had thousands of prostitutes and that the authorities rarely interfered with their business. In addition, young women turned to the sex trade on a seasonal or part-time basis because of factory layoffs or inadequate earnings from their jobs.[3]

By the turn of the twentieth century, new housing was being built in Söder and sanitation and public health services had improved, but poverty and overcrowding persisted. In a disciplined, long-term effort to change their circumstances, Stockholm's workers organized to fight for higher wages and the right to vote.

In the spring of 1902, the labor movement was strong enough to press its demands for the eight-hour day, unemployment insurance, old age pensions, no extension of the military draft, and the elimination of property requirements for male voters. Although its platform called for public ownership of industry, the Social Democratic Party, which had only a handful of seats in the Riksdag, worked with the Liberals in support of these crucial reforms. While Conservatives and Liberals in parliament prepared to debate a bill to extend the right to vote in the lower chamber to more, but not yet all, adult men, Hjalmar Branting called a national meeting of Social Democrats and union members, which was held in Stockholm on April 20, 1902. Twenty thousand people assembled in a field on the eastern outskirts of the city to hear Branting demand universal suffrage and then marched through the capital. As they made their way through central Stockholm, saber-wielding cavalry tried to turn them back, but most of the marchers managed to get past the police line and reach the People's House, where Branting and union leaders summed up their case for suffrage before an angry but exhilarated mass meeting.[4]

The national trade union organization (LO) called a general strike for May 15, the day the Riksdag began its debate on the right to vote. Throughout the country, 110,000 workers stopped work for three days, an unprecedented event in Swedish history. The Social Democratic Party paper described the stillness that descended over the city when the workers laid down their tools:

> Over the whole city lay a quiet, reverent holiday atmosphere. As if by a stroke of magic the large factories' clatter and roar was silenced, the steam whistle's shrieking, jarring sound was muted, and the streetcar's beloved clanging bell and the rattle of its wheels against the stone streets were hushed. As if by a stroke of magic thousands of workers dressed in their best Sunday clothes were called forth—all these battalions of work-hardened sons of labor were assembled wherever the red banner was flying.

The political general strike was a vivid demonstration of working people's collective power, not least to the participants themselves.[5]

The Riksdag refused to give in to the suffrage reformers' demands, but the unrest shook the government. In response to workers' growing mobilization, businessmen formed the Swedish Employers' Federation (SAF) as a counterweight to the LO. Capital and labor both developed stronger and more centralized organizations.[6] Despite the lack of immediate political gains, workers realized the strength that lay in unity. They could make their voices heard and broaden the political dialogue.

In Söder, Albert found himself surrounded by people who shared his socialist beliefs and aspirations for a more just society. Albert and Lowa were able to shield their daughter from the city's worst threats. Lowa kept the apartment hyper-clean. With two male relatives contributing to the rent, they lived better than most of their neighbors. But what about the future? Albert wondered whether he could earn enough to support Lowa, Alva, and the other children they hoped to have. Not many workingmen in Söder were able to afford life insurance, even with the low premiums charged by the company.

"Home was not a place"

Alva's family moved at least ten times before she was 12, as her parents' financial problems constantly interfered with their perennial hopes of living in a better neighborhood. After six months in Söder, the family moved to Albert's mother's apartment in Munktorp and stayed there from May to the end of August 1903. Many Swedes returned to their rural homes or visited relatives in the country during the summer to help with the farm work. Lowa was unhappy about crowding into the living quarters over the store in this isolated hamlet, but financial exigencies made it unavoidable. Anna Sofia turned over her extra bedroom, which she usually rented to an unmarried schoolteacher or domestic worker, to her son, daughter-in-law, and granddaughter. When the pastor came down from his manse to interview the family for the annual church census in July 1903, Albert proudly listed his profession as "life insurance inspector." Ekblom gave good marks to Anna Sofia and Lowa for their knowledge of the Bible and catechism, but found Albert sadly deficient in "Christian learning."[7]

In September 1903 the family returned to Stockholm, this time to the Vasastan neighborhood north of the central train station. It had a mix of middle-class and working-class residents and more new apartment buildings than Söder. Here Albert began a career in construction. Initially listed in the census as a cement mixer, he soon became a subcontractor and then an independent contractor. Always on the move, the family next took up residence in Norrmalm, closer to the city center.

A second daughter, Rut, was born on April 1, 1904. The sisters, only two years apart in age, formed a close, lifelong bond as they navigated between two parents whose relationship became increasingly strained and took responsibility for three younger siblings who claimed much of their time and attention. For most of their childhood and adolescence, the sisters shared a double bed. In contrast to their parents, they were physically affectionate, comforting and caressing each other, and curling up together when it was cold.[8] Rut grew into a cheerful, outgoing young woman whose interpersonal skills Alva came to admire.

On April 24, 1906, when Alva was 4 and Rut 2, their brother Folke was born. Lowa and Albert were overjoyed at the birth of a son, and Alva and Rut delighted in playing with the baby. But the sisters soon realized that their younger brother, nicknamed "the Golden Dumpling," was entitled to many privileges that had been denied to his older sisters.[9] A photograph of the three children from that year (see Figure 3.1) shows Alva and Rut in matching dresses that Lowa had sewn for them, while the infant Folke is decked out in elaborate plumage. Alva looks doubtfully past the camera.

During these years, Alva began to experience what she later called a painful sense of "isolation" from her family. As an adult, she remembered having felt intense hunger. Although the family was not impoverished, the children were served small portions, and Alva was admonished not to be so "greedy." Lowa followed physicians' advice to give each child the same amount of food at the same times every day. But Alva's hunger was as much emotional as physical. Her parents' attention was centered on Folke, and Rut was cheerful and eager to join in family activities. Alva later recalled that at age 4, she had overheard Lowa describe her as "sullen," and after that she had a less open relationship with her mother.[10]

Figure 3.1 From left to right: Alva, Folke, and Rut, circa 1906. Studio portrait by Tor Sandels, Stockholm. Courtesy of Alva and Gunnar Myrdal's Collection, Arbetarrörelsens Arkiv och Bibliotek, Stockholm, Sweden.

The births of Rut and Folke and Alva's observations of playmates' families made her realize how different her mother was from other mothers. Lowa's fear that she might be carrying tuberculosis meant that she did not hug or kiss her children. She demanded immediate obedience on even the smallest matters and tried to exert strict control over their behavior. Yet she frequently retired to her bed, explaining that she felt ill, and did not discipline the children consistently. The unusual patterns within the Reimer family were initially obscured by Alva's guilt over not meeting her mother's expectations. In retrospect, however, Lowa's emotional aloofness, lack of physical expressions of affection, and insistence on control stood out.

In the summer of 1906, when Alva was 4½, the family rented a vacation cottage on Lake Mälaren. Here, she recalled, she first experienced "the absolute loneliness of the individual." "I sat on a tree stump" and "suddenly knew that I was alone." This terrible feeling of "homelessness" was intensified by the family's frequent moves. "Home was not a place" (14). Alva realized in retrospect that she had never had "that in-the-womb sense of security." "New rooms, new streets, new schools, and new friends" required constant adaptation (18). She experienced her parents' conflicts as a recurring drama enacted in one setting after another. While she gained many social skills from her interaction with Rut and their three younger siblings, she had to think about how to make things right and put the needs of others ahead of her own.

Albert was strong, steady, and affectionate, and he read to the children and tucked them in at bedtime. But he was away at work all day, and his attention did not assuage Alva's sense of isolation. It was not until she was old enough to read and take an interest in ideas and politics that Alva grew close to her father. In contrast to his own father, Albert kept a tight rein on his emotions. When combined with Lowa's undemonstrative personality, the result was a minimum of spontaneity or free expression of feelings in the family. Albert had "strict principles" of child-raising and usually disciplined the children. Alva recalled being spanked several times, usually for saying impudent things or staying outside too long. On one particularly painful occasion she was spanked for saying something like "stupid mommy"; she "wanted to go out into the woods and scream until they felt ashamed of having hurt me." When she looked back on those experiences in an autobiography written when she was 42, Alva insisted that these spankings were uncalled for, although spanking was a common form of discipline at the time. She regarded her parents' method of punishment as particularly damaging because it "denied me permission to be really angry, tell them when I felt unjustly treated. I was supposed to repress everything and show a 'nice' face. It became a matter of duty" (17).

This estrangement from her parents only deepened Alva's sense of guilt. While she was becoming more self-sufficient, mastering many household duties, and learning to keep everything spotlessly clean, she felt a nagging sense of never doing enough, as well as guilt over not loving her mother enough. When she was only 6, Alva remembered, she was "peering into the soul's landscape" and not liking what she saw.[11]

Albert Jansson Reimer worked at various building sites to gain experience in different trades, and in March 1907 the family moved to Altuna, a town north of Stockholm, where they lived for nine months in a house that Albert was renovating. Lowa's uncle Leonard, to whom she had been close at Slagsta, came to live with them for a few months. Although Alva's memories of childhood focused sharply on her nuclear family, especially the tensions between her parents, Lowa and Albert took in relatives and employed servants at various times. They remained in contact with their extended families and sometimes received help from them. Alva's parents were embedded in a kin network that served as their primary safety net, as was true for many working families. Assistance from relatives helped to cushion the privations caused by periodic economic downturns and dislocations.[12]

At the end of 1907, Albert, Lowa, and the three children moved back to Söder. The large, modern apartment seemed luxurious to Alva because it had a dining room, electric lights, and an office for Albert.[13] Although Leonard remained in Altuna, the young woman who served in the household accompanied the family to Stockholm. On May 4, 1909, Lowa gave birth to her fourth child, Maj, who seemed sickly and required much attention. Maj became Lowa's favorite and was beloved by Alva and Rut, but her arrival meant more work for them at home.

The building where the Reimers lived was on a steep hill near a park that offered a spectacular view of the city. The prospect was famously captured in the opening lines of Strindberg's 1879 novel, *The Red Room*, but the tale soon descends into a thicket of human follies and sorrows, including poverty, greed, bourgeois hypocrisy, and political chicanery—all of which were still flourishing when the Reimers arrived 28 years later. The rebuilding of the district left it clearly stratified by class. While a new streetcar line connected Söder to the city's commercial center, factories, impoverished workers, and ramshackle wooden housing remained, in stark contrast to the Reimers' hard-won prosperity.[14]

The Great Strike of 1909 and the Election of 1911

After a period of rapid expansion from 1904 to 1907, the Swedish economy began to contract, construction slowed, and workers endured painful wage cuts. A cost of living survey detailed the growing poverty in Stockholm, and there was public discussion of meals for school children and other measures to help poor families.[15] The Riksdag took little action. The ruling Conservatives worried that government assistance would weaken family ties and lead to moral decline, while some Liberals feared that social welfare measures would restrict individual freedoms.

Opposition stirred among the 90 percent of adult men and women who remained ineligible to vote. The trade union confederation (LO) demanded collective bargaining and higher wages. As tensions with the Swedish Employers' Federation (SAF) heightened, the working class intensified its drive for universal male suffrage. When negotiations between LO and SAF stalled in the summer of 1909, the unions planned a general strike with both economic and political demands. The SAF calculated that the employers could outlast the unions and imposed a nationwide lockout on August 2. The unions responded with a general strike two days later. The Great Strike of 1909, as it came to be known, was the largest ever attempted in Sweden and attracted worldwide attention.[16]

As a small, independent building contractor, Albert now had employees of his own. He ran his business from his office, a separate space where he could work undisturbed and he could gather with other men for cigars and conversation. In most petit bourgeois homes, this was the only room that children rarely entered, but Alva was an exception. She loved to be with her father, and every Thursday she helped him check the money in the workers' pay envelopes. She remembered that he was fair, and even generous to those who needed money. Although Albert's role as a contractor complicated his class position, his loyalties remained uncompromised. As a Social Democrat, he strongly supported the labor movement. Alva recalled having been "proud" of her father for "siding with his own workers against his own interest as an employer." Söder, which was disproportionately affected by wage cuts, unemployment, and the factory lockout, was one of the strongest centers of resistance. As the strike escalated, employers panicked. Alva remembered hearing a contractor friend of her father's exclaim that he "would shoot himself if the strike did not end soon" (16).

In the midst of this intense class conflict, the 7½-year-old was confused about where her family stood in the class system. Lowa strove to provide her children with a proper, middle-class upbringing and kept their apartment nicely furnished. Rut later recalled that she sewed beautiful dresses for her daughters, and the neighbors used to say that the "Reimers always go in style." "We were supposed to be refined," Alva remembered. Noticing that her mother would deliberately alter her voice when she was speaking with "high class" people, she found this anxious pretentiousness disturbing. Alva gradually came to understand that social status was what Lowa valued most highly. She also realized that her father did not share her mother's attitudes. He wanted his family to be comfortable, but he was committed to universal suffrage, public ownership of large corporations, and social equality. Alva noticed the differences in living standards in Söder while visiting the homes of schoolmates who were poor. The disparity between her family and other families in the neighborhood "embarrassed" her, and she felt sympathy for poor children and began to identify with those who were unfairly treated.[17]

The Great Strike was an unprecedented assertion of working-class power. On September 1, 1909, 30,000 people assembled in Stockholm demanding higher wages and the right to vote. Some of the Young Socialist radicals in the Social Democratic Party and the union movement hoped that a revolutionary moment was at hand, but the leadership of the LO and the Social Democrats was more cautious. They tried to stay within the limits of the law and exempted workers involved in public health and safety from the strike in an effort to avoid antagonizing public opinion. Since the railroad workers and shippers stayed on the job, mining companies and manufacturers of export products could send their excess inventories to market even while their workers were on strike. The unions' treasuries were depleted within a month, and strikers began to drift back to work in September. By December, the general strike had ended in a major defeat, and LO membership fell by half. But the labor movement learned some useful lessons, and LO membership recovered within a decade.[18]

The suffrage question had continued to be the subject of parliamentary wrangling between Liberals and Conservatives, with the small Social Democratic caucus in the Riksdag playing a minor role. In the election of 1908, however, the number of Social Democrats increased almost threefold. The Conservatives and Liberals, neither of which had a majority, negotiated a suffrage reform bill. These maneuverings continued throughout the Great Strike, but once it was over the compromise bill was passed. All men over 24 were allowed to vote for the lower house provided they had completed their military service and paid taxes. The Conservatives ensured continued elite control of the upper house by introducing suffrage for a minority of affluent women as well as propertied men, adding income requirements, and instituting a system of plural voting that allotted votes to men and women roughly corresponding to their wealth. Voting for the upper house had more in common with the shareholder elections of modern corporations than with political democracy. Conservatives also insisted on a system of proportional representation for both houses, ensuring that they would win some seats even in districts where they were outvoted by the Liberals and Social Democrats.[19]

The 1911 parliamentary election began a significant shift of power. The electorate for the lower house doubled from 9.5 percent to 19 percent of the adult population. The Liberals won a plurality but not a majority, and Social Democrats tied Conservatives for second place. The Liberal leader returned as prime minister, while the Social Democrats supported his government but declined to serve in the cabinet. The Liberals passed a few reforms, establishing a social welfare board and old age pensions. The maddening electoral system and the slow pace of social reform drove most working-class Swedes into the ranks of the Social Democrats, and during the First World War it surpassed the Liberals. Closely allied to the union movement, the party grew quickly and increased its participation in local government.[20]

Albert Reimer, whose earliest memory of politics was of his father campaigning for universal male suffrage through the People's Parliament movement in 1892, was able to vote for the first time in 1911. He became involved in local government, where he was able to have some impact. Lowa, like the majority of Swedish women, remained disfranchised.

Schooling

Alva started school at age 7½ as the Great Strike of 1909 was winding down. She liked to sing and talk with other children, but she would fall silent whenever an adult entered the room, not wanting to stand out or attract attention. The first-grader suffered acute "anxiety and shame" when she lost a book that a classmate had loaned her. Alva was walking home from school with her friend, Karin, when she offered to carry Karin's book in her bag. After the two girls parted, Alva realized that she had forgotten to return the book. She was suddenly seized with terror that her mother would "nag me for being careless." So Alva hid the book under the porch of the house opposite theirs. When she went back the next morning to fetch the book, it was gone! Alva feared a "catastrophe" if her mother or father learned of this transgression. Afraid of being punished, she made up a story that a little elf had stolen it and carried it up the chimney. When her teacher reprimanded her in front of the class for telling a lie, Alva was filled with anxiety and humiliation. Those emotions stayed with her for a long time after her teacher meted out the customary punishment, beating her with a birch branch in front of the other children. She also felt awful that she had gotten her friend into trouble.[21] Karin came from a poor family, and school was an unfamiliar environment for her, as for Alva.

Albert made sure that Alva did not forget this lesson on the importance of truthfulness. On the few occasions when she lied, she felt overwhelmed by guilt, even if it involved something as trivial as taking a lump of sugar. At 18, Alva remembered that fear was the dominant emotion during her childhood. Her inability to tell the truth had set in motion a chain of consequences beyond the comprehension of a 7-year-old: angry parents and teacher, humiliation before her peers, the shame of causing embarrassment to a friend, and a guilty conscience that lasted well into her adolescence. Alva told this story to her children to underline the value of honesty.[22]

Soon the Reimer family moved to the Vasastan neighborhood in the Norrmalm district where they had lived briefly six years earlier. It had more new construction and less poverty than Söder, and Lowa had help from a live-in servant. The chastened Alva attended a new school, but she was haunted by fear that teachers there knew about her lying and she had been stigmatized as a bad girl. Trying to avoid attracting attention, Alva made no close friends. On the playground she often stood alone, afraid to make the first move to join in games and wondering whether the other girls would accept her. Academically she remained an underachiever; bored with school, she had no ambition and did not try to be the best at anything.[23]

When her younger sisters and brother were born, Alva had accepted these additions to the family without asking any questions about where babies came from. After all, she was accustomed to seeing her mother retire to her bed. In December 1912, as the family prepared for yet another move, Alva and her siblings were sent outdoors to play in the freezing weather, which Lowa believed was good for the children's health. Finally Albert summoned the children back into the apartment for a solemn announcement: Lowa had given birth to her fifth child, Stig. Although Alva was only a few weeks away from her 11th birthday, she had not been told that her mother was expecting. She feared that her mother's fragile health would be imperiled by another child and wondered if the babies would ever stop coming. But the shock of her parents' not confiding in her made Alva angry. After all, they expected her to assume greater responsibilities at home, yet they had kept Lowa's pregnancy a secret (23–26).

In reaction to her parents' deception, Alva tried to deny Stig's existence. When the Reimers moved to a new neighborhood, she told her classmates that the family had only four children, even after a schoolmate saw Lowa pushing a baby carriage. Alva's parents were puzzled by this denial, not realizing that the problem was her resentment over not having been trusted with the truth. After six months of responding to this deception by lying, Alva gave up this fiction. Stig was too cute, and she was won over by his sweet disposition (25–27).

The birth of her fifth child left Lowa exhausted, and she refused to have any more. She continued to complain about her "weak lungs," and her periods of indisposition became more frequent. Alva recalled that her mother "closed herself in her room" and, from this time until the end of her life, would spend half of every day in bed. Other relatives said this was an exaggeration. But Lowa sometimes found family responsibilities overwhelming and went away to rest homes.[24]

As Alva entered puberty, she encountered a confusing array of signals as to how she should behave. She was expected to play outside and to clean the house meticulously, both for the sake of good health. She was supposed to exercise some independence of judgment, yet she was bound by a daunting set of restrictions and responsibilities. Albert strictly enforced the rules for his five children, admonishing them to do their part because of their mother's poor health. "Papa is hard, mamma impossible," Alva and Rut used to say (18).

In January 1913 the family relocated to Älvsjö, a suburb south of Stockholm, where Albert joined his favorite uncle in the construction business. His cousin Carl Bernhard Reimer, who had been living with Albert and Lowa in Uppsala at the time of Alva's birth, had also moved there. In addition to building houses for profit for private owners, Albert became active in a local cooperative building association, serving on its board of directors and building houses at cost for the coop as part of the state-subsidized home ownership program. At the age of 11, Alva learned about politics by hiding under her parents' dining room table during meetings of the co-op board and listening to the political conversations.[25]

At her new school in Älvsjö, Alva began to make friends. She was full of ideas but, in contrast to most girls, was not interested in dolls. At home, she preferred reading her father's books in his office, finding a secret hiding place between his desk and the window where she could read undisturbed. The books that she sneaked out of her father's locked bookcase reflected Albert's range of interests. Most treated socialist theory, but his library included the works of Zola and Strindberg. Alva later claimed to have read them by the age of 11, although she admitted that she had not understood them very well (30). This dose of literary realism was not complemented by the romantic novels that young girls often read.

While Alva enjoyed the time spent with her father, she still felt "completely alone" at home. She carried with her the "traumatic memory" of the lost book and believed that she had much to "be ashamed of," yet she began to nurse the hope that she had a "secret destiny." Sometimes she felt a "perfectionist frenzy," a restless stirring in reaction to her sense of guilt, but it did not prompt her to try harder in school. Her inner striving for excellence was held in check by a sinking sense of defeat. Reacting to parental authority at home and peer pressure at school, she brooded constantly about herself. Looking back with the eyes of a child psychologist, the middle-aged Alva thought that her need to differentiate herself from her parents and to understand her unique experience and personality was paramount. As for sex, she understood little. Stig's birth had piqued her interest in reproduction, but the subject remained largely a mystery. She and Rut would play mommy and baby, taking turns with one stuffing a pillow under her dress and "giving birth" to the other. At first Alva did not see any connection between her genitals and reproduction, but she did sense that her body was beginning to change (27).

As she sought new friends, Alva tried not to stand out as the best student in her class. She wanted to be accepted by a clique of girls who were smart but did not compete with each other. Alva did not want to be either "above" or "below" her friends, whether it had to do with clothes, homes, or "brains." "From the whole of childhood up to puberty," she later wrote, "I had an immeasurable desire to be like the others. I did not stand up for my own views (and needs). I denied them willingly, without pride" (10, 23).

Fortunately, Alva encountered a teacher who stimulated her intellectual development. A recent graduate of a teacher-training college, Per Sundberg was only 24 years old when he taught Alva. She was drawn to his warm, open, and "honest" character and sensed his vulnerability as a new teacher struggling to develop his own style in the classroom. Sundberg became the first non-parental authority figure in her life. He helped to awaken her interest in ideas, encouraged her voracious reading, and allowed her feel less alone. She dreamed about doing great things, becoming a police officer, a general, a dictator, a doctor, a priest, a missionary, a newspaper editor, or a poet (69–70).[26] At the age of 11, in an all-girls' school, she did not understand that most of these avenues were closed to her. Although Per Sundberg may not have known about Alva's secret ambitions, he did not try to limit the horizons of his students or socialize them into conventional femininity.

Accustomed to moving frequently and open to change, Alva envisioned a life in motion. Books about male adventurers particularly fascinated her: Mark Twain's *Huckleberry Finn*; Henrik Ibsen's *Peer Gynt*;

and the novels of Jules Verne. Alva dreamed about escaping the house and embarking on a great exploration of the wider world. Although she sought to be like the other girls at school, in the world of her imagination she identified with male heroes. Looking back in later years, she considered the family's 18 months in Älvsjö as a transitional period between childhood and adolescence (14–15).[27] She had begun to overcome her sense of loneliness, and her imagination had been able to roam freely without the intrusion of more difficult concerns posed by the transition to adult womanhood.

Adolescence at Slagsta Farm

In March 1914, tragedy again struck Lowa's family. After many years as a widower, her father, Lars Erik Larsson, had remarried in 1905, a few months after the death of his elderly mother and five years after Lowa had married and left home. His second wife, Carolina Charlotte Lindberg, called Lina, was a widow who had lived in the parish for five years. She brought with her to Slagsta a daughter from her first marriage, Hilda Maria, then 17. In 1911, at age 23, Hilda Maria had given birth to an illegitimate son, Gösta. Two years later she had become engaged to the reputed father of the boy. The banns were published, but he broke off the engagement before the wedding. Ten days later, Hilda Maria and her 2-year-old son moved away. Lina could not bear the shame and suffering that followed, and she committed suicide four months later.[28]

Lowa Reimer was her father's only surviving close relative, and Lars Erik invited his daughter and son-in-law to move back to Slagsta, with the prospect of Albert taking over management of the farm. Lowa had begun to settle into Älvsjö, where her husband was making a good living. She was not eager to return to her childhood home, which was filled with memories of loss, but felt unable to refuse her father's offer. Four months after Lina's suicide, Albert, Lowa, and their five children arrived at Slagsta. Lowa did not tell Alva and the other children that Lina had committed suicide, nor did they learn the story of Lina's daughter and illegitimate grandson. For Albert, in contrast, the sad circumstances in his wife's family offered the opportunity of a lifetime. At last he could fulfill his boyhood dream of becoming an independent farmer and living in accord with Rousseau's pastoral ideal. He promised to build the family a new house and relished teaching his children how to farm.[29]

Alva, then 12, had grown up in the city. She expected life on the farm to be one long summer holiday, but the very first morning her grandfather awakened Alva and Rut at seven o'clock and sent them to remove stones from a field. Lars Erik, like Albert, believed in the sacredness of labor and had no doubt that a farm upbringing was best for children. Like most rural girls, the two sisters did all kinds of agricultural work, both outdoors and in the barn and dairy. Alva and Rut also cooked, cleaned, did laundry, and looked after the younger children. Rut became quite good at milking, but Alva steadfastly resisted. She hated her chores and never adapted to life on the farm (36–38, 40).[30]

For five years, before their new house was completed, Alva's family crowded into the small farmhouse, which housed three adults, five children, and usually a servant. From age 12 to 17, Alva had to sleep in the kitchen on a sofa bed with her two sisters and was awakened every morning by her grandfather shaving in front of a mirror before breakfast. She hid her head under the covers and pretended to be asleep rather than suffer the embarrassment of acknowledging her lack of privacy. Accustomed to a modern bathroom, Alva had to adjust to using an outside privy and washing her hair in the kitchen sink. At night, after Maj had fallen asleep, Alva and Rut would listen to their parents arguing through the paper-thin wall that separated the kitchen from Albert and Lowa's bedroom. Their quarrels were always about money and sex. In these overcrowded conditions, the marriage suffered badly. In retrospect, Alva saw her home as a "really Strindbergesque family inferno, marked by sexual repression and arguments over money" (18–19, 34–35, 39, 47–49).[31]

Albert clung to the frugal habits he had been forced to adopt during his childhood. He kept tight control over the money that he earned, and Lowa had to ask him even for small sums when she needed something for the house or the children. Since her husband was the sole breadwinner, Lowa rebuked him for devoting so much time to building houses for the cooperative association instead of concentrating on profit-making contracts. To Albert's dismay, his wife, who received small inheritances from various relatives from time to time, usually spent the money on fine fabrics which she sewed into beautiful dresses for herself and her daughters instead of saving for a rainy day.[32] Lowa's prospective inheritance of her father's farm gave her some leverage in relation to her husband.

By listening to her parents' arguments, Alva sensed the differences in how men and women staked their claims to a family's resources and the language they used to assert their distinct interests. She also became more aware of the political differences between her parents. Although the Social Democrats had become Sweden's largest party, Lowa continued to support the Liberals, who won votes from many owners of small farms as well as from some business leaders. She subscribed to the Liberal newspaper, while Albert had the Social Democratic paper delivered to their home every morning. Alva began to understand the power of class backgrounds in shaping political perspectives (30).[33]

Alva had little direct exposure to the women's movement, which was fragmented along class lines and did not receive much coverage in either newspaper, although the Social Democrats had an active women's organization with a local chapter in Eskilstuna. Alva read books by middle-class feminists such as Ellen Key and newspaper accounts of the parliamentary discussions of women's suffrage, and her father supported giving women the vote as the final step in Sweden's movement toward democracy. But she did not yet connect the political debate over women's rights with personal or family issues.

Listening through the wall, Alva and Rut learned that Lowa no longer wanted to have sexual relations with her husband because she felt unable to cope with any more children. The picture of Lowa's mother, who had died when Lowa was 9, hung in the living room as a daily reminder of the risks of childbirth. "Go to prostitutes if you must, but I can't have any more children," the sisters overheard Lowa telling Albert. Albert protested that sleeping with prostitutes would be completely against his principles and said he wanted to resume their marital relations. But Lowa held firm. Five children were enough. She believed that her health was fragile. Birth control was not available. And she could afford to engage in a little rhetorical hyperbole because she knew that her husband would not resort to other women, burdened as he was by the knowledge that his mother and great-grandfather had been born out of wedlock and by the memories of his father's public accusations of adultery against his mother.[34]

As Alva reached puberty and sought to understand her own sexuality, her parents' conflicts complicated matters. She had grown closer to her father, and during her teenage years when the family crowded into her grandfather's house her sense of rivalry with her mother for Albert's attention became more intense. The ultra-hygienic Lowa was not helpful when Alva began to menstruate at the age of 13 years and 9 months. By this time Alva had developed habits of secrecy, responding to Lowa's emotional distance and need for control by claiming some space of her own. She tried to conceal her period from her mother, but its signs inevitably appeared. Yet she took pride in the bodily manifestations of puberty. The teenager knew that she wanted children of her own someday, but so much embarrassment surrounded the subject of sexuality and Lowa said so little about reproduction to her daughter that Alva was not clear about sexual relations. Sex education was also absent from the curriculum in her all-girls' school. Under the circumstances, Alva naturally wondered about women's inability to control their own childbearing (24).

Alva and Albert often talked about books and ideas, but on more personal matters there was silence between father and daughter. Albert's reticence was due in part to his sense of propriety, but there were many things about his own family background that he did not want to reveal. Albert rarely asked intrusive questions, but he relied on Alva to be truthful about where she had been and what she had been doing. She was punished occasionally for staying out beyond a specified time. Her parents worried that she was secretly seeing boys, but her time away from the house was actually spent in more innocent pursuits (17).

During her teenage years, Alva firmly believed that her father could have been a great man if her mother had been more supportive, and she pitied him for having to spend so much time coping with a cold and neglectful wife. In her view, Lowa was an irritable hypochondriac. Alva could not abide her mother's weakness, her sense of martyrdom, and her incapacity to raise her children and perform basic household tasks. She resented the fact that Lowa constantly imposed restrictions on her, did not understand her, and seemed so different from other mothers. For her part, Lowa could not comprehend why her daughter was so rebellious and chafed at doing household chores that were light by comparison with the burden that she herself had borne in childhood. She worried that Alva's grandiose ambitions were so ridiculous that they would come crashing down upon her head when she realized that they were unattainable. A mother had the duty to prepare her daughter for life in the real world, not in the realm of fantasy (47–48).[35]

As an adolescent, Alva did not understand the strict limits society placed on women or comprehend the toll that bearing five children had taken on Lowa. She did not realize that her mother's cycles of anxiety, depression, breakdown, and recovery at rest homes could be attributed to anything other than a lack of will and fortitude. Alva tried to steel herself against any "weakness" of the sort that she saw in Lowa. In addition to her dreams of accomplishing great things and winning public recognition, Alva began to read romantic novels and fantasized about finding a young man to whom she would devote herself as she believed Lowa had been incapable of doing with her father.[36] While her ambition for achievement seemed "masculine" and her romantic dreams "feminine," she hoped it would be possible to reconcile the two. Her conflict with her mother peaked when she was 15. It remained one of the central dynamics of the household, but Alva learned to defuse tensions by developing self-control and conspired with Rut to avoid triggering her mother's anxieties. Lowa's absences at rest homes now seemed a blessing in disguise, providing Alva with opportunities to escape the house. She developed other interests that eased some of her feeling of constant tension with her mother.

Alva's love of reading was the most important redeeming feature of these years. Indulging her intellectual interests gave her a realm of freedom in which she could decide things for herself. No one could tell her what to like or dislike. Even if she did not understand everything she read, the effort to develop her own opinions mattered. Alva's interest in politics intensified. She had listened to political discussions at the time of the Great Strike. Now she started to follow world and national affairs through the two daily newspapers that were delivered to Slagsta and compared their social democratic and liberal perspectives. As she discussed politics with Albert, Alva's identification with her father deepened. She admired his activism and ideals, and especially valued his integrity. She realized that many people in Eskilstuna thought him too radical when she heard some children shout "Socialist!" to insult Alva and her siblings.

Once she overheard a man say, "Reimer may be a Social Democrat but at least he is honest." After that, Alva was ready to "share his martyrdom for a just cause." The farmhouse may have been claustrophobic and her mother's rules constricting, but books and politics inspired her hope for what she later called an "expansion" of the self.

Alva drew strength from her relationship with Rut. Like the Biblical figure for whom she had been named, Rut was willing to sacrifice much for others. While Alva resented the time she had to spend on farm chores, housework, and childcare, Rut thrived as the daughter both her parents could rely on. She was devoted to her older sister and did not complain when her workload was greater than Alva's. Rut also enjoyed a closer relationship with their mother. As a teenager, she too chafed under Lowa's rules, restrictions, and demands for cleanliness and order, but Rut shared her mother's love of sewing and spent many happy hours with her learning to make fashionable clothes. She did much of the work of preparing meals and teas so Lowa could entertain relatives and neighbors. Rut was sometimes able to head off conflict and bring the family together. She also became popular in the community, and as a teenager seemed more comfortable in the company of boys than her older sister did (31).[37]

The two sisters took very different memories away from their childhood and adolescent years. Alva continued to puzzle over why her family seemed so different from the way families were supposed to be. She began reading books about psychology as a teenager. When Pastor Wilhelm Andeer, who confirmed both sisters, suggested to Albert that Rut as well as Alva should have a gymnasium education, Albert said no: Rut was needed at home. She accepted the decision. Rut eventually married a well-respected farmer in rural Västmanland. To her children and grandchildren, she passed on only happy memories of the Reimers and did not regard the family in which she had grown up as abnormal or dysfunctional. In private conversations with her daughters long after Lowa's death, Alva ridiculed her mother for keeping a silver snuff box full of small pieces of paper containing maxims about life that she pulled out to read in times of adversity. Rut, in contrast, cherished the little box full of traditional wisdom and passed it on to one of her daughters as a family keepsake.[38]

Alva was happier at school than she was at home. During her first year in Eskilstuna, she was a star. She wrote essays that her teacher read aloud to the class, and she enjoyed being praised for her work. This success gave Alva the self-confidence to protest her parents' "exploitation" of her labor. She contended that she had been assigned an excessive number of chores on the farm and in the house and that her workload was detrimental to her studies. Although her parents did not reduce her duties, Rut started doing some of Alva's tasks in the fields so that her sister could hide in an outbuilding and read (32). Alva's academic success did not impair her ability to find a few good friends. She stood out a little with her Stockholm dialect and nice clothes, but she made friends with three or four of the "top girls" in her class. They even formed a girls' club named for the great Swedish botanist Linnaeus, with its own badge and secret rituals. In contrast to her loneliness at previous schools, Alva felt a sense of belonging (40).

Not long after the family moved to Slagsta, Alva formed the closest friendship of her youth. Märta Fredriksson, who was just a year older, was the daughter of a modest, hard-working farm family that lived near the Reimers. The girls shared a love of reading and spent hours browsing in a bookstore in a nearby town. They enjoyed singing together, and their conversations were filled with laughter. Above all, they reached a level of trust that Alva had never experienced with anyone. The two were kindred spirits, keepers of each other's secrets. Alva regarded Märta as more fragile, melancholic, and subtle; she saw herself as more concerned with social and political questions, an organizer and planner. But she rarely made comparisons, as she and Märta never competed with one another. Their striking affinity and spontaneous exploration of new worlds together were what counted.

To her former teacher, Per Sundberg, Alva wrote at the age of 15:

> Märta is closer to me even than my own siblings. . . . You may find that it is wrong for me to think so, but then you do not know Märta nor the great difference between her and my siblings. But I feel, also, the responsibility that comes with having a friend, and such a friend.

Above all, Alva could relax with Märta, who was a good listener and understood her. "Never have I found a person who 'suits' me as well as Märta," she wrote at 18.[39]

With Märta to confide in, Alva could undergo the physical and emotional changes of adolescence with greater confidence. She was leaving childhood behind and would soon be free of her mother's restrictions and able to make more of her own decisions. Märta encouraged her to look for the reasons why the family was so unhappy, rather than blaming herself. Alva and Märta agreed that both sets of parents had failed to bring them up at all, and therefore they would have to "bring themselves up." Above all, they aimed at "honesty." They developed a passionate interest in psychology, influenced by a series of lectures on "The Psychology of Everyday Life" given by Pastor Andeer, who had recently returned from the United States, where G. Stanley Hall had begun to explore the new concept of adolescence.[40]

At 15, Alva confided to Märta that she "hated" her mother and considered Lowa's behavior "hysterical." She did not realize that her mother's periodic collapses might be viewed, in part, as involuntary protests against what Alva would later call "domestic slavery" (48). Holding her children at arms' length and abstaining from sex with her husband after the age of 35 also took their toll. What bothered Alva was her mother's inability to see herself in perspective, to realize the connection between her life of suffering and broader social conditions. But to make those connections and take the first steps toward a healthy and loving life would require a broader education, greater self-understanding, and a strong will to change. The refractory daughter believed that her mother lacked all these capacities.

Instead, Alva observed, her tired and irritable mother perked up in the presence of adult friends in a way that seemed artificial. With guests in the house, Lowa told little white lies and was boastful. Her values were utterly conventional, even false. In Alva's eyes, Lowa was materialistic, house-proud, petty, and banal. Her rebellious daughter's effort to "bring herself up" was intended to distance herself from her mother's personality, which she feared would stifle her own development. In Märta she had a ready audience for these assertions, as well as a resolute partner in declaring independence (42–48).

Alva finished elementary school at age 14½. For over 90 percent of Swedish youth, this was the end of formal education. Some might take a brief training course in a trade school, while others might participate in a reading and discussion circle at church, in the temperance movement, the union, or a women's club. As they sought to build their democracy and improve their own life chances, Swedish workers and farmers enjoyed almost universal literacy, but the state's responsibility stopped with elementary school. No further education was available to Alva in Eskilstuna. The town's gymnasium was for boys only, and Lowa was adamantly opposed to her leaving home to continue her studies. Alva saw this decision as the denial of a right she had previously taken for granted. When they lived in Stockholm, Albert had promised her that she could attend gymnasium while living at home (34–35).

Since this avenue was closed, Alva enrolled in a commercial school, as her father had done 20 years earlier. Her year-long vocational course taught her typing, shorthand, and accounting. The only part of the curriculum she enjoyed was the opportunity to study English with Pastor Andeer. At the end of this short course Alva had not mastered English pronunciation, but reading English gave her access to a wider range of books. Then she began work at the Eskilstuna town clerk's office, where she was known for her speed on the adding machine. The routine was boring, but Alva was thrilled to earn money. She spent some of her salary on books and saved the rest in the hope of attending gymnasium in Stockholm. Although Lowa was implacably opposed, she could discuss the prospect with her father. Secretly, she sent for an application form for a student loan, but when Lowa found out she tore the form to pieces, accusing Alva of trying to raise herself above the family. So the plan came to nothing. But Alva refused to give up.

Notes

All translations of Alva's and others' manuscripts were done by the author. These passages may differ from the English-language versions quoted in other publications. What Alva wrote in longhand is often difficult to decipher, with abbreviations for common words and dashes instead of more precise punctuation. Transcribing and translating them necessarily involves matters of interpretation.

1 Uppgift till 1903 års mantalsskriftning i Stockholms stad och Maria församling, kvarteret Paris, 23 Bellmansgatan, 15 roten, Stockholms stadsarkivet. Södermark was the maiden name of Lowa's grandmother, Kristina Lovisa.
2 Hellbom and Gullers, *Stockholm*; Band, *Bekvämlighetsrevolutionen*; Stockholms Stadsmuseum, *Portraits of a City*; Norstedts Rabén multimedia, Söder i våra hjärten.
3 On "Stockholm marriages," single motherhood, prostitution, and orphanages, see Matovic, *Stockholmsäktenskap*; Svanström, Prostitution in Stockholm; Söderlind, *Barnhem för flickor.*
4 Ståhl, *Möten och människor i Folkets Hus och Folkets Park*, 65.
5 Cederqvist, *Arbetare i strejk*; *Social Demokraten*, 20 May 1902.
6 Nordin, *Fackförenings-rörelsen i Sverige*, vol. 1, 131; Scott, *Sweden*, 415; Schiller, *Storstrejken 1909*, 2–3.
7 Munktorp Församlingsbok 1896–1909, 8, IIa:1, Landsarkivet i Uppsala.
8 Alva Myrdal, Autobiographical notes.
9 Bok, *Alva Myrdal*, 23.
10 Alva Myrdal, Autobiographical notes. Alva Myrdal, Självsbiografi, 14–16, AGMA. All page numbers in parentheses in the text refer to Alva's Självsbiografi, while the numbered notes refer to other sources.
11 Alva also described her childhood feelings in her letters to Gunnar: A to G, July 12 and 18, Sept. 27, and Oct. 2, 1920, AGMA.
12 Altuna Församlingsbok, 1901–11, p. 42, Landsarkivet i Uppsala.
13 Bok, *Alva Myrdal*, 24.
14 Norstedts Rabén multimedia, Söder i våra hjärten.
15 Perlinge, *Bubblan som sprack*; Hirdman, *Magfrågan*, 207–208.
16 Schiller, *Storstrejken*; Nordstrom, *History of Sweden*, 80–81.
17 Westerberg, Berättelse; Alva Myrdal, Autobiographical notes.
18 Schiller, *Storstrejken*; Nordstrom, *History of Sweden*, 81.
19 Scott, *Sweden*, 406–408.
20 Scott, *Sweden*, 427–432.
21 Alva told the whole story in her Självsbiografi, 1–8. See also A to G, Sept. 27, 1920.
22 Fölster, interview, 2008.
23 Gustaf Albert Reimer, Mantalslängd, 1910, and Mantalsuppgift, 1910, Stockholms Stadsarkiv. Bok, *Alva Myrdal*, 25; Fölster, interview, 2010.
24 Bok, *Alva Myrdal*, 26; Holst, interview.
25 On Carl Bernhard Jansson/Reimer, see Uppsala Fastighetslängt 1900–06, 3290; Bok, *Alva Myrdal*, 26. On government-subsidized programs to help working families build and buy their own homes both in cities and on rural smallholdings, see Edling, *Det fosterländska hemmet.*
26 Although Alva had not told her family about these ambitions, she disclosed them to Gunnar two months into their relationship: A to G, August 29, 1919.
27 Alva to Per Sundberg, Feb. 24, 1918, Christmas 1918, AGMA; A to G, August 29, 1919; Bok, *Alva Myrdal*, 7–8, 29–30.
28 Persson, interview.
29 Persson, interview; Fölster, interview, 2007.

30 Westerberg, Berätellse. On farm women's work, see Morell, Agriculture in industrial society, 1970–1945, 172–177; Flygare, Women and men, 223–225; Sommestad, Agrarian Women.
31 Bok, *Alva Myrdal*, 24–28, 32–33; Fölster, interview, 2011.
32 Fölster, interview, 2011.
33 Fölster, interview, 2011.
34 Fölster, interview, 2011.
35 Alva to Per Sundberg, April 29, 1918; Hirdman, *Alva Myrdal*, 10; Bok, *Alva Myrdal*, 40, 45–46; Fölster, interview, 2011.
36 Bok, *Alva Myrdal*, 37–40; Alva Myrdal, Autobiographical notes.
37 Westerberg, Berättelse; Bok, *Alva Myrdal*, 30–31; Fölster, interview, 2011; Holst, interview; Vinterhed, interview.
38 Westerberg, Berättelse; Bok, *Alva Myrdal*, 81; Fölster, interview; Holst, interview; Vinterhed, interview.
39 A to G, July 12, 1920; Bok, *Alva Myrdal*, 38–39; Fetveit, interview.
40 Alva Myrdal: En romantisk rationalist, AGMA. Carl Vilhelm Andeer read G. Stanley Hall's *Adolescence* (1904).

References

Alva and Gunnar Myrdal's Collection (AGMA). *Arbetarrörelsens Arkiv och Bibliotek* (Swedish Labour Movement's Archive and Library). Stockholm, Sweden.
Alva Myrdal's personal documents, 1.1
Alva Myrdal. Själsbiografi (Biography of the psyche). 1944.
Alva Myrdal's published works, 2.1
Myrdal, Alva. Alva Myrdal: En romantisk rationalist (A romantic rationalist). *Afton Tidning*, 12 July 1943.
Alva Myrdal's correspondence, 3.1
Correspondence between Alva and Per Sundberg, 1916–1918.
Correspondence between Alva and Gunnar Myrdal, 3.3
[Identified as A to G or G to A, with date or letter number.]

Manuscripts

Myrdal, Alva. Autobiographical notes, Geneva, June 1973, written at the request of Sissela. Original in possession of Sissela Bok.

Westerberg, Rut Reimer. Berättelse, recollections written at Alva's request, circa 1958.

Interviews

Fetveit, Arne. Interview with Walter Jackson. Oslo, 2008.

Fölster, Kaj. Interviews with Walter Jackson. Stockholm, Dec. 11, 2007; 2008; 2010.

Holst, Gunnel. Interview with Walter Jackson. July 2008.

Persson, Anne-Marie. Interviews with Walter Jackson. Stockholm, May 30 and June, 2011.

Vinterhed, Kerstin. Interview by Walter Jackson.

Published Sources

Band, Dansk. *Bekvämlighetsrevolutionen: Stockholmshushållen och miljön under 150 år*. Stockholm: Stockholmia, 2008.

Bok, Sissela. *Alva Myrdal: A Daughter's Memoir.* Reading, MA: Addison-Wesley, 1991.

Cederqvist, Jane. *Arbetare i strejk. Studier rörande arbetarnas politiska mobilisering under industrialismens genombrott: Stockholm, 1850–1909.* Stockholm: Stockholmia, 1980.

Edling, Nils. *Det fosterländska hemmet: Egnahemspolitik, småbruk och hemidiologi kring sekelskiftet 1900.* Stockholm: Carlsson, 1996.

Flygare, Iréne. Women and men. In Mats Morell, Agriculture in industrial society, 1870–1945, 223–225. In *The Agrarian History of Sweden*, ed. Janken Myrdal and Mats Morrell. Lund: Nordic Academic Press, 2011.

Hellbom, Thorleif, and Peter Gullers. *Stockholm: Om livet på torgen.* Uppsala: Gullers Bild, 1996.

Hirdman, Yvonne. *Magfrågan: Mat som mål och medel i Stockholm, 1870–1920.* Stockholm: Raben & Sjögren, 1983.

Hirdman, Yvonne. *Det tänkande hjärtat: Boken om Alva Myrdal.* Stockholm: Ordfront, 2006. English-language version, *Alva Myrdal: The Passionate Mind*, trans. Linda Scheck. Bloomington: Indiana University Press, 2008.

Matovic, Margareta R. *Stockholmsäktenskap: Familjebildning och partnerval i Stockholm, 1850–1890.* Stockholm: Stockholmia, 1984.

Morell, Mats. Agriculture in industrial society, 1870–1945. In *The Agrarian History of Sweden*, ed. Janken Myrdal and Mats Morrell, 165–213. Lund: Nordic Academic Press, 2011.

Nordin, Rune. *Fackförenings-rörelsen i Sverige*, vol. 1. Stockholm: Prisma, 1981.

Nordstrom, Byron J. *The History of Sweden.* Westport, CT: Greenwood Press, 2002.

Norstedts Rabén multimedia. Söder i våra hjärten: Människor och miljöer i Stockholm 1870–1930. 1998.

Perlinge, Anders. *Bubblan som sprack: Byggboomen i Stockholm 1896–1908.* Stockholm: Stockholmia, 2012.

Schiller, Berndt. *Storstrejken 1909: Förhistoria och orsaker.* Göteborg: Akademiförlaget, 1967.

Scott, Franklin D. *Sweden: The Nation's History.* Carbondale: Southern Illinois University Press, 1988.

Söderlind, Ingrid. *Barnhem för flickor: Barn, familj, och institutionsliv i Stockholm, 1870–1920.* Stockholm: Stockholmia, 1999.

Sommestad, Lena. *Agrarian Women, the Gender of Dairy Work, and the Two-Breadwinner Model in the Swedish Welfare State*, ed. and trans. Grey Osterud. London and New York: Routledge, 2019.

Ståhl, Margareta. *Möten och människor i Folkets Hus och Folkets Park.* Stockholm: Atlas, 2005.

Stockholms Stadsmuseum. *Portraits of a City: An Urban Anthology.* Stockholm: Stockholmia, 2004.

Svanström, Yvonne. Prostitution in Stockholm: Continuity and change. In *Selling Sex in the City: A Global History of Prostitution, 1600s–2000s*, ed. Magaly Rodríguez García, Lex Heerma van Voss, and Elise Nederveen Meerkerk, 201–229. Leiden: Brill, 2017.

4 Alva and the Great Hunger

During Alva's first two years near Eskilstuna, 1914–1916, the Reimer family lived quietly on their farm as the Great War raged across Europe. Sweden remained neutral, but increased its trade with Germany, and farm incomes rose along with food prices. Lowa enjoyed sewing as a respite from her troubles. Albert constructed a number of houses in the locality, including some for the cooperative movement. He held on to his vision of lifting up his own family while helping his less fortunate neighbors and participating in the social democratic movement.

In the cities, working-class Swedes had a much harder time. The construction industry slowed, and investors hesitated to put capital into new enterprises. Exports to Britain and other western European countries slumped because of the British blockade. During the last two years of the war, as the price of grain soared, Swedes suffered severe food shortages. The government introduced rationing in the summer of 1916. Since Sweden had not been affected by war for a century, this necessary measure met widespread resistance. Farmers who had always stored up grain for the long winter regarded it as a threat to their survival. The black market allowed middlemen to get rich quickly. War profiteers were contemptuously labeled "goulash barons" after those who sold canned meat to the German army. After Germany's resumption of unrestricted submarine warfare in January 1917 stopped virtually all imports to Sweden from the west, the food crisis became acute. Farmers withheld milk from the market and made their own butter. A potato shortage contributed to widespread hunger. Government efforts to impose price ceilings were a dismal failure.[1] Farmers were not organized into a single group, so it was difficult for the government to negotiate with them.

In the fall of 1916, thousands of unemployed people left the cities to roam the countryside in search of food. In the winter and spring of 1917, protest demonstrations spread. Social Democrats blamed the wartime coalition's prime minister, Hjalmar Hammarskjöld, whom leftists called "Hungerskjöld." He resigned in March, and the Conservatives formed a caretaker government to prepare for parliamentary elections. In Russia, which had long been regarded as Sweden's most powerful enemy, a popular revolution toppled the czar, raising the hopes of workers in Sweden and especially in Finland, which had been occupied by Russia for over a century. In April, thousands of people participated in hunger marches in Swedish cities, and a few bread riots broke out. Many young Socialists split with the party of Branting to form the Left Socialist Party, which soon allied with the Communists.[2]

As May Day approached, the government tightened security. Dubious about the loyalty of army conscripts, it replaced the regular troops in Stockholm with regiments from rural areas. Right-wing university students organized a civil guard to help keep order if soldiers defected to the protestors. The Left Socialists wanted to organize a general strike, but trade union leaders were cautious after the failure of the Great Strike of 1909. On May 4, a hunger demonstration in Söder turned into a confrontation between the people and the police, and some protestors threw stones at the officers. The streets were not cleared until 11:30 that night. Seventeen people, including five women, were arrested. The next day, thousands of workers responded to a call from the Left Socialists to gather in front of the Riksdag while Branting, the parliamentary leader of the Social Democrats, questioned the prime minister inside. Mounted police wielding sabers drove the demonstrators away, and the furious crowd reassembled in front of the People's House, where Branting pleaded with them to wait for the November elections, after which he hoped the suffrage question would finally be settled. Ten thousand workers assembled in Söder to express their outrage, but the trade union and party leadership would not call a general strike.[3]

In October 1917, the Bolsheviks seized power in Russia, raising the stakes for Sweden's election. As Branting hoped, it was a great breakthrough for the Social Democrats, which became the largest party in the lower chamber of parliament. Liberals formed a government with Social Democratic support, although the party declined to serve in the cabinet. After the Liberal–Social Democratic victory, the king made no serious attempt to interfere with parliamentary government.

These political dramas were acted out in miniature within the Reimer household. Albert Reimer served on Eskilstuna's committee in charge of rationing, which enforced the law at a time when hoarding, fraud, and profiteering on the black market were widespread. Most workingmen and many small farmers had only been able to vote in parliamentary elections for six years, and it was important for Social Democrats serving in government to establish a reputation for honesty when the upper class still regarded universal manhood suffrage with fear and anticipated incompetence and corruption on the part of officials chosen by newly enfranchised voters. A crisis erupted in the Reimer home when Lowa admitted to Albert that she had held back a little grain to ensure that her children did not go hungry. When she tearfully asked how he could stand to let his children suffer, he replied: "What is more important, that the children's bellies should be full, or that they should learn about justice?" He turned this incident into a lesson in honesty and civic ethics for his children.[4]

Spiritual Struggle

In the summer of 1916, Alva's best friend Märta began preparing for confirmation in the Church of Sweden. The confirmation process, which usually came just as young people were leaving elementary school, marked an important step in the passage from childhood to adulthood. For intelligent and sensitive girls who had completed their formal schooling, confirmation classes and church youth groups provided one of the few

Figure 4.1 Märta Fredriksson, at an outing of a youth temperance group, Eskilstuna, 1919. Courtesy of Arne Fetveit.

Figure 4.2 Alva Reimer, Eskilstuna, circa 1918–1919. Courtesy of Alva and Gunnar Myrdal's Collection, Arbetarrörelsens Arkiv och Bibliotek, Stockholm, Sweden.

socially sanctioned venues for self-exploration, as well as a chance to get out of their conflict-filled homes. Looking into one's soul and considering ultimate questions allowed, even facilitated, the expression of feelings and thoughts in defiance of the adults who usually demanded silent obedience. Young people had an opportunity to ask their parents, teachers, and pastors why the world is as it is, why good and evil coexist, and how faith affects a person's life and relationships with others. For the first time in many adolescents' lives, the focus of the family shifted from their parents to them—if only briefly. The young person's beliefs mattered in the eyes of the community. Each individual had to declare her own faith in God and adherence to church teaching.

For some teenagers, confirmation class was merely another chore; memorizing large parts of Luther's shorter catechism had little relevance to their lives. But Alva chose to embark upon this inquiry. She had many questions about Christian theology and Biblical teachings. Her father had rejected religion for reason and replaced the hope for spiritual redemption with the prospect of human improvement and social transformation. Firm in his own views but supporting liberty of conscience, Albert did not hinder his daughter's spiritual exploration. Alva was not impressed by her mother's formulaic adherence to Christianity. As she saw it, Lowa found comfort in reciting prayers at times of distress but otherwise showed no emotional investment in her faith. While Lowa, fearing a repetition of tragedy, had sought to deaden feeling, Alva looked inside and tried to give expression to her deepest emotions.

Alva joined Märta in attending confirmation classes, although she was unsure about joining the church. Previously Alva had proclaimed herself a "freethinker," a label she adopted in her struggle to establish an identity outside of her mother's control and align herself with her father. Now she probed her own ideas and emotions. Märta and Alva shared a "religious brooding," as well as a "defiant rejection of the petit bourgeoisie and yearning for a great and noble life." The girls bicycled to a variety of free churches that offered alternatives to the established church. Alva accepted the challenge of forming her own beliefs independently of her parents and friends. Would she reject religion altogether, as her father had done, join Märta and other friends in being confirmed as a Lutheran, or pursue a spiritual life outside the state church? Each choice would put her at odds with one of her parents as she struggled to define herself.[5]

The process of introspection made Alva aware of her drive to develop her own personality. It represented a reframing of the conflict with her mother that she had articulated to Märta in blunt, personal terms. While other adolescent girls experienced similar tensions with their mothers, Alva tried to understand these emotions. She no longer merely observed her parents' religious differences, but sought her own ground. Nor did she go along with the confirmation process merely to be accepted by her peers. Despite her unusually forthright and confrontational stance, Alva engaged in disciplined self-examination. Confirmation required her to take responsibility for herself. If she could bring herself to believe in God, Alva would have to explain her strengths and weaknesses to the ultimate authority. Even if she could not, she still had to consider how she measured up in a cosmic perspective rather than within the microcosm of her family.

The confirmation ritual, which took place before the congregation after a period of soul-searching, required young persons to consider themselves in social context. At this time, the Lutheran Church of Sweden was seriously challenged by adherents of alternative denominations, scientists and intellectuals, and many socialists. At first Alva's religious inquiry combined reading the Bible with forays into the writings of secular authors. She attended confirmation classes taught by Pastor Andeer, as well as the English classes he taught at night. Alva often stayed after class for discussions with the pastor. Sometimes they had debates about religion, with the student taking the role of "confirmed atheist." That stance did not represent a settled opinion, however. She remained an earnest inquirer into the Christian faith for two years.[6]

As her conflict with her mother peaked, Alva confronted her long-festering guilt feelings, which went far beyond her sense of unworthiness over her resistance to performing her assigned tasks in the house and on the farm. Her conscience troubled her because she was unable to love her mother as she thought a good daughter should. She was so terrified by the sense of her own guilt that she fell into a "spiritual abyss." For as long as she could remember, Alva had always been conscious of her insignificance. Only rarely had she overcome a deep sense of personal isolation. Now she feared that she did not fit in anywhere—at home, at school, or in the community. A self-described "perfectionist," she was acutely aware of every sin she had ever committed. Was it possible, she asked herself, to burn away all her impurities and find forgiveness, peace, and harmony in this discordant world through Christian faith?[7]

A Mentor's Fusion of Spiritual Inquiry and Social Reform

During this process of internal crisis and growth, Alva turned for advice to her former teacher, Per Sundberg, with whom she began a soul-searching correspondence in August 1916. Alva admired his unusual combination of a warm, affectionate personality, a questioning spiritual temperament, and a rigorous intellect. She hoped that he would understand her more fully than her family.

Sundberg's lasting influence on Alva makes his life and work worthy of attention. Born into a carpenter's family in Stockholm in 1889, he had known hard times and observed abject poverty when he visited the homes of other working-class families. Per had done well in school, but his studies put him amidst boys from upper- and middle-class families who ostracized him, and this experience of class differences awakened his social conscience. He suffered through emotional as well as intellectual crises as an adolescent. After doubting everything, he emerged strengthened and anchored by personal faith and a serene temperament. For some years, he remained a member of the Church of Sweden but eschewed doctrinal and institutional controversies, focusing instead on spirituality. Upon graduating from Stockholm's prestigious Norra Real gymnasium, where he was one of only a few students from the working class, Sundberg passed up the opportunity for a university education. Instead, he chose elementary school teaching as his vocation and graduated from teacher training college in 1911. He began his career at the elementary school in

Älvsjö. During summer vacations, Sundberg earned money as a factory worker and timber-cutter, traveling in Sweden and Germany where he met people with a wide range of opinions. He loved nature, and his wanderings in the countryside helped nurture his faith. While he was teaching, he read widely in philosophy, literature, and politics.[8]

During his early years as a school teacher, Per Sundberg came under the influence of the Christian social reformer Natanæl Beskow and volunteered to help at Birkagården, Beskow's settlement house in a poor neighborhood of Stockholm. Here the elements of his life's work came together: an approach to teaching children that linked academic skills to emotional and moral development; wide-ranging education for working-class adults; and religion as a spiritual bond among people working toward human betterment. Sundberg taught "street children" who came to live at the settlement, organized study circles that brought university and college students together with working-class youth, and invited impoverished families to the settlement house for "family evenings." Cooperating with the unions' adult education association, he helped Birkagården evolve into a "people's high school" for adults. Sharing his love of learning with others from a background similar to his own, he no longer felt estranged from his working-class roots.[9]

Immersing himself in this Christian settlement house fueled Sundberg's intellectual growth. Beskow, who came from an upper-class family, fused theological liberalism and the social gospel with intense personal piety. He studied theology at Uppsala University in the 1880s, intending to become a minister and missionary, but had enough doubts to forego ordination. Inspired by the Christian socialists, he visited Toynbee Hall, a settlement house in London's impoverished East End. At the turn of the twentieth century, Sweden had no settlement houses, so Beskow and social worker Ebba Pauli established Birkagården in a working-class neighborhood in Vasastan in 1912. The reformers sought to avoid the paternalistic tone of earlier philanthropic and home mission efforts and involved working-class people in directing their own education. A magnetic and inspirational teacher, Beskow gathered a circle of idealistic young reformers at Birkagården, including Per Sundberg.[10]

World War I was a turning point for Beskow and Sundberg. Like progressive reformers on both sides of the Atlantic, they had believed that education, scientific and technological progress, and democracy would lead to international cooperation. Swedish Social Democrats had looked to their German brothers for leadership and fraternal support through the Second International, but their German, French, and British counterparts had all fallen in line behind their governments at the outbreak of war. In neutral Sweden, the conflagration fueled skepticism about social amelioration. Beskow, Sundberg, and their circle observed the war with growing horror at the immense scale of the killing and the inability of existing institutions to stop it. They helped refugees who fled to Sweden and aided unemployed Swedes. The Great War pushed both men toward radical pacifism. Afterwards, Beskow joined the International Fellowship of Reconciliation and wrote hymns that emphasized pacifism and social justice with the theme of "unity in diversity." Sundberg's spiritual journey also led him to pacifism, and he eventually joined Sweden's small Quaker organization.[11]

When he began answering Alva's earnest inquiries in August 1916, Sundberg proved to be a good listener. He responded to Alva's questions, allowing her to focus the discussion on her spiritual and emotional crisis, and rarely alluded to himself.

A Dialogue with her Teacher and Herself

To Alva, her former teacher resembled her father in his political idealism and served as a bridge between Albert's staunch secularism and the emotional search for a personal relationship with God that Märta and others in her circle sought in their confirmation class. Alva wrote frankly to Sundberg about both her doubts on matters of doctrine and her strongly felt need for faith. While Albert had struggled to free himself from religion, his daughter desperately searched for a God to whom her proud nature could submit in good conscience. In God, she found a more worthy adversary than Lowa, and her hostility to her mother began to subside. While describing her struggle with religion in her letters to her former teacher, she revealed much about herself.

Twelve years her senior, Per Sundberg became her mentor and confidant. Although she may not have admitted it to herself at the time, Alva had a schoolgirl crush on her former teacher. As she opened up to him about her emotional life, his opinion of her mattered more and more. Where she found the privacy to write such well-crafted letters in her grandmother's crowded farmhouse is not clear, but she poured everything into them.[12]

Alva began by telling Sundberg about her schooling, bragging about her good grades and expressing the hope that eventually she would be able to continue her education. She talked about her reading, including literary realists, especially Zola and Strindberg, and philosophers, especially Voltaire and Schopenhauer. The only woman writer who attracted Alva's attention was the Swedish feminist Ellen Key, whose writings combined a revaluation of what she deemed essentially feminine qualities such as maternal nurturing with radical demands for personal independence. (Aug. 5, Sept. 23, and Dec. 23, 1916)[13] In July 1917, Alva was relieved to complete her "horrid" commercial school course. Its only redeeming value was learning to read English. Among British philosophers, Alva especially liked John Stuart Mill, a utilitarian and supporter of women's rights who collaborated with his wife, Harriet Taylor, on *The Subjection of Women*. Sundberg suggested some of his favorite writers, including Tolstoy, and sent books to a neighbor's home for her to read without her parents' knowledge. His renewed interest helped Alva to feel that her education was not over.

After a year's correspondence, at the age of 15, Alva took the bold step of writing to Sundberg about her personality. She revealed that her friends said she had very strong feelings on most subjects. They saw her as "honest, . . . extremely self-controlled," and "most of all, my own person." Alva was particularly pleased with that compliment, because "ever since I read Peer Gynt, I have been wondering if I were my own person." Others considered her open-minded and "generally free of prejudice," which she had striven for. Although she would never have admitted it to her parents, Alva confessed to her teacher that she had always been "stubborn," but now she considered herself "strong-willed." (July 8, 1917)

Per Sundberg responded to his "dear friend's" religious questions with respect, sympathy, and support. He admitted that he himself had struggled with the question of the divinity of Christ. "But I do think that we allow this as well as most theoretical issues to cause us too much suffering. After all, life is not theoretical." Instead, life must be completely and fully lived. Sundberg alluded to the poetry in the Bible: "I wish I had the gift of singing 'The Song of Songs' of life. The art of living is probably that of living life as unmediated as possible." He suggested that a new understanding of Jesus was being formulated amidst the current intellectual and social upheaval; Christians must go beyond dogmas to perceive his struggle against falsehoods and injustice and his support for the weak and oppressed. He underlined the importance of an experiential approach to God: "We should be standing in the rushing stream of life and let its power flow all around us. . . . His power and the rapture in our soul is life." This approach "allows us greater freedom and openness towards all things human and divine wherever we find them." It made the lives of young people lighter and freer than they had been "during the intellectual phase that has now been left behind," the effort late nineteenth-century Swedes had made to reconcile Scripture with Biblical criticism, Darwin, and materialism. (July 29, 1917)

After reflection and encouragement from Per Sundberg, Alva decided to join Märta in being confirmed in the Church of Sweden at the end of the summer of 1917. She wrote her teacher that she had enjoyed the church seminars, particularly one on "The Forgiveness of Sinners." Alva resonated to religious experience as part of her deep-seated quest for a quiet center amidst the discordant life at home and in the world around her. As the summer ended, she was filled by a sense of her own potential. (Aug. 12, 1917)

But doubts soon overtook her. Alva preferred philosophy to religion because she was able to accept some propositions and refute others. She especially admired the logic, honesty, and thoroughness of John Stuart Mill. The positivist August Comte, on the other hand, represented excessive theory and authoritarianism. No philosopher or religious thinker seemed to have all the answers. "In general, I am never satisfied, cannot be satisfied, do not want to be satisfied," she declared to Sundberg. (Aug. 12, 1917) "I am a free thinker," she proclaimed in a letter at Christmas 1917. Drawing on secular metaphors for God, Alva affirmed that she still believed in "a creative world spirit, power, the first molecule, God. . . . All this is one and the same." She had no interest in opposing religious dogmas, insisting that "harmony between all opposite points of view is the only truth" and disclaiming any fixed views because "we can only know one side of the infinitely complex and multifaceted truth." (Dec. 25, 1917)

Despite the unprecedented violence that was raging across Europe, Alva did not focus on mass slaughter as evidence of inexplicable evil. She was more concerned about social injustice in Sweden. Alva thought that the true conditions of the world were "obscured by cultural and social falsehoods." To the blind it might be "pleasant enough," but to the sighted, the world is an "inferno." On the eve of her 16th birthday, Alva expressed "despair" and "hatred for myself and the whole world." Feeling the burden of suffering that came with knowledge, she wondered how people accepted the lies that sustained and justified the social world around them. She mocked the stance of her conformist, self-pitying mother, which seemed to be: "Why we and no one else?" or "Why not we when everyone else?" Alva defiantly proclaimed her alternative: "Why not I when no one else?" But she found it hard to chart an independent course. "Why should I live?" she asked. "Sometimes I can go quite insane," she declared dramatically. "Once I even got as far as wondering how I could get my hands on father's revolver." "If I knew why [I should live], I would do something to reach that goal, whatever it may be. But I don't know why; no one does." (Jan. 13, 1918)

Alva tried to believe, but faith never came. One evening when she and a group of her friends attended a free church with the intention of criticizing it, the preacher singled them out and challenged them to accept divine salvation. She realized that she did not believe and never had. "If faith exists at all," Alva sighed, "it is not for me." She thought that faith is probably just a kind of ecstasy. She recognized that she had ignored many truths in her search for faith. Now she felt free from a foolish yearning. "I began to trust myself rather than God. But . . . I still am not happy." Her strongest feeling was of being "homeless." (Jan. 13, 1918)

Her predicament unresolved by either belief or unbelief, Alva found herself on the verge of despair. "I'm dying!" she exclaimed hyperbolically. "I never thought anyone could be as unhappy as I am now." She feared that she would have to stop thinking. Alva still felt enough attachment to the Christian tradition to worry that, if she did not stop questioning, she would be severely punished on a judgment day of her own making. But she found it impossible to lose herself in belief. She confessed that she was tempted to curse the day she had learned to read because all the challenges posed by philosophers had caused her so much pain. Yet she had almost come to love the suffering that reading and thinking caused her. Surely no one could go through life with such pain. But wanting to die would be cowardice. Then Alva asked herself what could be making her feel this way. She surmised that she was unduly focused on finding an absolute, and she felt weary of the struggle. (Feb. 24, 1918) On this cold winter night, panic enveloped this "self-controlled" young woman, and her usual self-confidence deserted her.

Per Sundberg, reading her letters in Stockholm, grew quite concerned about her psychological conflicts and replied immediately: "If only I could place a cool hand on your hot forehead and talk some calm and confidence into your soul! No one else can help us with those deepest experiences but we can perhaps hold each other's hands in new courage." He advised Alva to concentrate on practical work rather than abstract thought: "You have developed a psychic temperature and need to put your soul on a diet." He teacher acknowledged that he might sound unsympathetic, but work could be good, although bitter, medicine. Sundberg also recommended that she talk to her parents about her worries. (Feb. 26, 1918)

Alva fired back that she could not help having these strong feelings. She had tried working, reading "nice" books, and studying science on her own. But this was a spiritual crisis she had to get through, rather than avoid. "I long for faith," she confessed. "Not for God or anything similar, but to sink into and drown in a bottomless sea of faith, faith. I want to sacrifice myself, surrender with all my soul, but I am always held back by the off-putting image of god . . . that Christians worship." To reassure her mentor, Alva added that she was trying to study to stop herself from thinking about religion. She hoped to go to Stockholm and continue her education. "I want to be useful indirectly or on a grand scale," she affirmed; she could not be satisfied with humble pursuits. Alva had difficulty imagining a career in which she could find an outlet for her ambition and energy. "I cannot be a teacher, because I would suffocate and be suffocated." (March 5, 1918)

On the edge of an "abyss," Alva recognized the danger of too much self-absorption devoid of a sense of connection with others. Like her mentor, she sought to embed her struggle for identity in work for social betterment, but felt uncertain about her vocation because of class and gender barriers. Alva's turn from religious faith to self-cultivation followed a well-worn path traced by German and Swedish Romanticism, but her love of struggling with "hard" questions pushed her toward a more empirical approach to philosophy and psychology, in contrast to the philosophical idealism favored by most Romantic writers. She found herself in the predicament of many moderns who could not bring their soul into harmony with the universe because they found no God or perfect order in it. What, then, was the point of cultivating the soul, psyche, or personality?

A few days after receiving this letter, Sundberg penned a brief reply to let Alva know he was thinking of her during these difficult times. He stressed that the kind of struggle she was engaged in was necessary for a person's development because it helps us to grow and to understand the pain of others. He expressed the hope that Alva's emotional state would improve with the advent of spring. (March 17, 1918)

"Peace has overwhelmed me," Alva exulted on Good Friday. It was "an uneasy, apprehensive peace, but peace nonetheless." But this peace brought a "bad conscience" because she could not figure out why she felt at peace when she remained so out of kilter with the world. In contrast to a traditional Christian conversion, Alva's was a more mystical experience. She did not feel that this calmness was the "peace of God," but she reported feeling a sense of "vertigo," of looking down from the heights to which she had suddenly been lifted. "It is as if the angel of death has touched my face with a veil and left me in a kind of semi-sleep," Alva marveled. "But after death comes the angel of life and because of the contrast between them, the riches of Nirvana not yet enjoyed will turn into a pile of old clothes which I have yet to get past."[14]

"The real, true peace of god is harmonious growth," she believed. "Does such a thing even exist?" As soon as she began to think, doubt returned. She expressed the hope that "my faith will rise again and occupy my entire soul and never—in death or life—let its kingdom be taken over by the proletariat." Her choice of the metaphor of "the proletariat" to express the nagging doubts that assail the kingdom of the soul seems odd in view of her father's adherence to the socialist movement and Per Sundberg's roots in the working class and commitment to helping the poor. But Albert Reimer was a skilled craftsman and farmer, not a factory worker; his ideal of pastoral harmony and social equality was not based on an identification with the urban proletariat. Many contemporary intellectuals saw "the mob" as well as the establishment as enemies of individual creative genius. Alva often expressed her quest for individuality by separating herself from others who seemed so different from her. Despite her Good Friday experience, Alva admitted to herself and to Per Sundberg that she did not believe. Her inner world was full of contradictions. (Good Friday, 1918)

Two days later, on Easter Sunday 1918, Alva wrote that she regretted her inability to abandon herself to God. She was self-conscious about asking for help from Sundberg, since she realized that in interrogating God she had gone beyond what a 16-year-old girl was supposed to do, and her teacher had sent only a brief answer to her last letter. "Forgive me if I have upset you in any way," she ventured. Stricken with self-doubt and seeking reassurance, she wondered aloud whether "there [is] anything else, anything from the past, or do you quite simply dislike me?

Something is definitely wrong. Naturally, I would prefer for you to tell me what it is, but if that is not possible, all I can do is ask forgiveness." Alva testified that "you have helped me by providing an example of where a freer Christianity—or perhaps more correctly, perception of God—can lead. You have taught me to value it and I thank you." In a subsequent letter, Alva addressed Sundberg as "trusted friend." Recognizing his effort to come closer to God, Alva concluded that theories meant "less than nothing" and "experience of God is everything." (April 5, 1918) But on Easter Sunday, fearing that her personal confessions were unwelcome, she blurted out: "I really do not want you to dislike me. . . . And while I tell myself that it may not be so, I am still upset about there being something that cannot be talked about."

This was too much for Per Sundberg, and he issued a mild rebuke in a letter that has not survived. Concerned for some time about the growing intensity, confessional tone, and intimacy of her letters, he asked her not to address him with the familiar "du" (you). Alva sent an immediate apology, explaining that while she wanted to be honest and had confided in him, she had not forgotten her position in relation to him. (April 20, 1918) He graciously replied that "'Du' . . . is . . . a strange word. . . . Sometimes it is the key to the innermost secret of our soul. May we, independent of conventional barriers, use the words that open the gates to the spiritual world." Again choosing the metaphor of spring in the hope that Alva's dark night of the soul had passed, he recalled Jesus' words that faith is like a mustard seed sown in a field. "Not like lightning or an earthquake," but something that starts out small and has to be nurtured. "It is the eternal mystery," he concluded. (April 24, 1918)

If Per Sundberg had sought to suggest a more measured pace for Alva's quest for self-understanding, he was not successful. She had thought deeply about the spiritual and philosophical questions that were bothering her and earnestly pursued answers in her daring correspondence with him. Now she turned to some of the psychological issues that may have given urgency to these spiritual questions and exposed some of the guilt she felt as she contrasted her feelings with her supposed duties.

In a final letter, Alva sought to untangle her feelings toward her parents. "It upsets me, but—I don't like my mother at all. And neither does anyone else who knows her." "But I like my father too much. I love him first as my father . . . [and also] as a great poetic soul." Part of Alva's intense anger toward her mother stemmed from her belief that Lowa's constant demands, criticism, and illness had thwarted Albert's potential for self-realization. "If father were not married to mother, I know his spiritual strength would be very great. But he is bound by indissoluble ties." "To say it all," she gasped, "I don't see it as my duty to love a mother who is no mother at all. I value spiritual connections much more than legal ones, and all the duties I should have felt due to a mother are now passed on—doubled—to my father instead. Because he and I are spiritually as well as physically related." (April 29, 1918) As her faith in the Christian God ebbed, Alva associated her intense spirituality with Albert's quest for a just and harmonious society.

Only after she had confessed that she did not love her mother was Alva freed from the overwhelming sense of guilt and fear that had driven her to seek redemption in the Christian faith. Now Alva declared that sin is "nothing but imperfection," even suggesting that it "does not exist" as an independent force but is "only unhappiness." Words and actions were meaningless; in personal conduct, "intention is everything." Aware of her shifting moods and stances, Alva connected the state of her soul to the changing seasons. But while Sundberg saw spring as a time for planting the seed that would grow into faith, she cherished her intellectual questions and doubts and shouted defiantly: "May all the storms of autumn rage through our souls!" (April 29, 1918)

Alva's correspondence with Per Sundberg ends on April 29, 1918. Her former teacher, who had resonated with her pantheistic and socially progressive impulses, evidently felt that he should not hear further confessions about her feelings toward her parents. Sundberg sent Alva a note six months later inquiring about her well-being and inviting her to get in touch when she was in Stockholm (Nov. 5, 1918), but they did not meet again for 25 years, when she, then a well-known educator, spoke at the experimental school he had founded near Stockholm.

Many years later, Alva confided to her daughter Sissela that she had idolized Per Sundberg, but that, given the difference in age and their relationship as teacher and pupil, he had never really opened up to her. In retrospect, she saw him as "too much a completed man" and had resented his "distancing" himself from her. When she reread her youthful letters at the age of 70, Alva felt "ashamed at myself for being so calculating" in her efforts to impress him. "But it was never money or position or 'high class' that I was after," she insisted; "I just wanted to be myself."[15]

In 1919, Alva discovered the work of Sigmund Freud, where she found a psychological perspective on her intense love for her father and hostility to her mother, her adolescent need to define her own identity in contrast to the personalities of her parents, and her yearning for spiritual harmony and a feeling of peace in the midst of her family's repressed conflicts. She read new studies of the psychology of adolescence. Her outpourings to the young teacher and reformer had combined self-exploration and religious inquiry with elements of Romantic authors' exploration of the troubled soul and the idea that strength comes through suffering. Alva's revelations to Sundberg expose her desire to achieve intimacy through letters, her love of honesty and openness, and her daring pursuit of self-exploration. Her religious search was an important step in finding her own identity and separating herself from her parents. Her teacher's gentle encouragement strengthened Alva's conviction that there were intelligent, sensitive people, kindred spirits who would appreciate her questioning of religious dogma, her critique of the blind adherence to social conventions, and her passion for harmony.

Per Sundberg let her try out a variety of ideas, stances, and strategies forbidden in school and church and controversial at home. Although Alva's focus from age 14 to 16 was on the cultivation of her own soul, it is possible to glimpse hints of her later development as a reformer in her notion that sin is "imperfection" that can be cured by knowledge and her urge to help "blind" people see through the social lies around them. Instead of finding relief from her haunting feeling of guilt and sense of her own imperfection through God's forgiveness, she thought that human limitations can be remedied by education and self-understanding. From this religious crisis, Alva also carried forward a belief in the importance of emotional honesty and a powerful desire to reach concord with others.

In the fall of 1918 Alva had an intellectual "showdown" with Märta in which she proclaimed her unbelief.[16] Although Märta continued to be a professed Christian for a while longer, the two young women returned to their common ground: psychology, philosophy, literature, and their desire to do something to help others. Neither Alva nor Märta formulated her own struggle for independence in terms of feminism. Both chafed at the limits placed on them by the authority of parents, school, and bourgeois society and sought an "expansion of the self" through self-improvement and involvement with popular movements for social justice. Alva retained her passionate need for a feeling of spiritual connection to others, but she focused on questioning all preconceptions, finding rational solutions to problems, and understanding herself and others. Henceforth, much of the struggle within herself would be projected outward onto society.

Two years later, she looked back on this religious crisis as her "breakthrough year," an "epoch in my development," and marveled at "how many winding roads I traveled and how many unnecessary steps I forced myself to take." "I never can nor will forget how I once . . . longed to burn away all impurity and ugliness from my soul. I have never longed so strongly for purity, freedom, and harmony." This compulsion had driven her to intense self-observation and had led "of necessity" to emotional conflicts, from which she had gained self-knowledge.[17] Alva continued her quest for self-understanding, and her personality retained a perfectionist strain. Perfectionism without self-forgiveness would impose a heavy psychological burden on her as she came to expect more and more of herself and took on responsibility for others.

The Great Hunger

About this time, Alva began corresponding with Andreas Arnesen, a young Norwegian in his final year of gymnasium who was preparing to enter the University of Oslo. Simultaneously, Rut corresponded with another young Norwegian man. The sisters found their pen-pals through a youth club. For Alva, who had never been outside of Sweden, friendship with Andreas was an exciting opportunity to broaden her outlook. Like many idealistic young Swedes, she believed that strengthening the bonds of cooperation among the Scandinavian countries was a first step toward building a more peaceful world. She was also excited about embarking on a epistolary relationship with someone who might become a romantic interest. It was the first time she had found a young man near her own age with whom she could share her hopes and fears about how she might shape her life's mission in the world. Like Alva, Andreas had lost faith in Christian doctrine but felt a spiritual yearning to be useful to humanity, even if humans seemed to be unbearably cruel to each other.

Andreas was 3 years older and shared Alva's omnivorous appetite for philosophy, psychology, literature, and politics. In a letter to her in February 1919, he soberly contemplated the slaughter of the Great War and the unsettled politics of Europe three months after the armistice. Norway was in a political crisis for which he held both the left and the right responsible. Any hopes of Nordic unity had been dashed by the political and economic impact of the war. He was "skeptical" about talk of a League of Nations that would be able to prevent future wars. Immersing himself in Strindberg's *Advent*, he found that the author's dark vision of humanity now seemed even more prophetic than at the time of his death in 1912. Strindberg's genius, he contended, lay in his "grotesque" vision of "devilish, evil people who are there to torture each other. . . . They reap what they have sown." Andreas considered Alva a realist in her understanding that humans had created a hell on earth. "You are so right," he affirmed; "the world is evil. . . . Over the gates of hell, did it not say 'Abandon all hope here. There is no exit from here.'" Yet paradoxically, Strindberg had directed that a Latin inscription be carved on his tombstone: "O cross, our only hope," leaving his readers to wonder what possibilities for spirituality were left in a world dominated by what he had called "the dark powers."[18]

It was probably through Andreas that Alva came to read Johan Bojer's novel *The Great Hunger*, which had recently been translated into Swedish.[19] Bojer was a popular Norwegian writer born to an unwed mother in 1872 and raised by foster parents who were tenant farmers in the remote Lofoten Islands northwest of Trondheim. After working on a farm, he managed to get some secondary education in Oslo and turned to writing novels about the poor farmers and fisher folk in his native region. *The Great Hunger* is a Dickensian potboiler with a picaresque hero, Peer Holm, modeled primarily on the author but also bearing some resemblance to Ibsen's Peer Gynt. Hardworking, clever, and morally earnest, the young Peer feels a "great hunger" to do something important with his life. This desire is both spiritual and worldly. Peer thinks of becoming a pastor and serving the poor, but he also burns with the ambition to do great things and make a name for himself. He drifts to the capital and learns that his biological father has just died, having failed to acknowledge Peer in his will. After a few plot twists, he trains to become an engineer. Embracing science, technology, and engineering as a substitute for his lost religious faith, he leaves Norway and winds up in charge of building a great dam in Egypt that wins him wealth and renown. Like Peer Gynt, he gives up his wanderlust and returns to Norway to marry a sweet girl and settle down. But Peer Holm is bored by life as a gentleman farmer. Still burning with a passionate desire for achievement, he takes up the challenge of building a huge dam in the north of Norway. After many reverses and Herculean efforts, he completes the dam, which is a brilliant feat of engineering. But the project's enormous cost overruns drive Peer into bankruptcy, followed by a nervous breakdown. The ruined man returns to the Lofoten Islands and works a small farm with the help of his loyal wife and three children. He reluctantly sends his two older children to the capital to live with his wife's aunt so that they can receive an education as the others try to wrest a living from the rocky soil.

Then unimaginable disaster strikes and the Job-like ordeal is complete. Peer's youngest daughter is mauled to death by a vicious dog belonging to a neighbor who had ignored repeated warnings about the threat it posed. Driven to the "outermost point" of existence, Peer refuses the temptation to shake his fist at God and regard life as a cruel farce, but he also declines to shrink into a pitiful figure who accepts his loss as God's will and bends down in blind submission. He no longer believes in the Christian God but discovers "one little indomitable spark in me that began to glow all by itself . . . , the germ of an eternity of harmony" that links him to other people. At last Peer Holm knows that the "great hunger" he had felt was not to be a "creator in steel" or a pastor but to build within himself "a temple for the human spirit." While he rejects the idea of God, he comes to believe that a courageous individual can take actions that create spiritual bonds with other souls in a hostile universe. The next spring a terrible drought sets in and the farmers lose all their grain crop. The neighbor whose dog had killed Peer's daughter has no seed left and goes around begging, but people "hated the sight of him after what had happened" and talked of driving him from the parish. Silently, Peer gets up at two in the morning, takes his last half-bushel of barley, and sows his neighbor's field secretly so that no one would know who had done it.

Bojer's tale of ambition, suffering, and redemption through spiritual love struck a chord with 17-year-old Alva. In the next few years, she continued to allude to her great hunger for harmony and connection with other people despite her loss of religious faith and spoke of a desire to construct a temple within herself. The novel appealed to many young Scandinavians who were searching for a personal code of conduct or new spiritual language as they groped to comprehend the indifferent universe in which Europeans had used their advanced technologies to slaughter a generation of young men. *The Great Hunger* suggests that taking courageous action can generate spiritual bonds among people in a universe from which a living God is absent. Bojer's literary reputation did not last, but after World War II and the Holocaust pacifists quoted the lines that Peer Holm speaks at the end of the novel: "I went out and sowed the grain in my enemy's field, that God might exist."

In the spring of 1919, Alva looked anxiously to the future, wondering whether she would have the opportunity to do the great things she had secretly dreamed of and whether she would find a man who was strong enough in his own right to be able to share those ambitions. How could she get out of her parents' house and begin living her own life? Worried that, like her father, she might not have the means to continue her education, she struggled to save money in the hope of going to gymnasium and then university. Meanwhile she read widely, but only Märta shared her passion for ideas.[20]

Although Alva was intelligent and outwardly confident, she had always felt that her family was different from other families and that her emotions did not fit the norm for girls her age. She felt that Lowa had not been a nurturing mother. But Lowa's incapacities had forced Alva to be independent at an early age. She resented the housework, childcare, and farm work she had to do, but she learned to keep up a façade, cooperate with her father and Rut to avoid upsetting her mother, and carve out time for her own reading and reflection. Although she sometimes rebelled, she also learned skills of negotiation, problem-solving, and conflict resolution. Alva looked to her father and to Per Sundberg for a kind of idealism she did not find in her mother. Her father's ideology of socialism and cooperation put some limits on her strong ego, and she learned to channel her ambition through his social democratic ideology. Alva felt an emotional need to believe that she was serving others, a stance that made ambition among young women seem less dangerous to many people. Her drive for education, personal achievement, and self-fulfillment was filtered through gendered conventions as she tried to prepare herself for a life of independence and good works in a world where women were thought to be more spiritual, more cooperative, and more intuitive than men. Medicine appealed to her as a profession that would allow her to push against these limits and enable her to be a healer and community leader. Alva continued to feel a desire for harmony, reconciliation with others, unity with humankind, and oneness with nature.

As she sought to combine her urge to do something great with her belief in serving humanity, Alva wondered whether she could achieve something important in the world and also have the happy family life that had eluded her parents. She could not settle for an "ordinary" man, but worried that an extraordinary man might not find her worthy of his love. Yet Alva secretly dared to dream that there might be a brilliant young man of strong character who would join her in these adventures and help her to be a better mother to her own children than Lowa had been to her. Per Sundberg had raised her hopes of finding a kindred spirit, an educated man with a broad perspective. Dismayed by the prospects among the young men of Eskilstuna, she had taken the few opportunities that had come along to meet university-educated men. She and Rut had attended a ball with students from Stockholm's scientific and technological university. After several months of intense epistolary exchanges, Alva invited Andreas to visit her in Eskilstuna, and in the spring of 1919 he made plans to come. As she looked forward to his visit in the summer, she wondered whether he would be the man who would help her fulfill her extraordinary hopes.

Notes

All translations of Alva's manuscripts were done by the author. These passages may differ from the English-language versions quoted in other publications. What Alva wrote in longhand is often difficult to decipher, with abbreviations for common words and dashes instead of more precise punctuation. Transcribing and translating them necessarily involves matters of interpretation.

1 Hirdman, *Magfrågan*; Magnusson, *Economic History of Sweden*, 162–163.
2 Andræ, Swedish labor movement and the 1917–18 revolution; Andræ, *Revolt eller reform*, 62–67.
3 Scott, *Sweden*; Nordstrom, *History of Sweden*; Hirdman, *Magfrågan*.
4 Alva Myrdal, Självsbiografi, 30, AGMA; Bok, *Alva Myrdal*, 32; Fölster, interview.
5 Bok, *Alva Myrdal*, 41–43; Fölster, interview; Alva to Per Sundberg, Aug. 5, 1916, AGMA.
6 Alva Myrdal, Självsbiografi, 46, 52–53.
7 Alva discussed this time in her later letters to Gunnar: A to G, July 8, Sept. 27, and Oct. 1, 1920, AGMA.
8 Sundberg, interview; Sundberg, *Per Sundberg*; Björnhagen, *Pedagogiskt nytänkande*.
9 Björnhagen, *Pedagogiskt nytänkande*, 19–20.
10 Sjöholm, *Samvetets politik*, 302–406; Pauli, Fredrik Natanæl Beskow; Thysell, *Natanæl Beskow*.
11 Björnhagen, *Pedagogiskt nytänkande*, 21–26; Sjöholm, *Samvetets politik*, 51–79.
12 Alva Myrdal, Självsbiografi, 33. Bok, *Alva Myrdal*, 5–8; see also Bok, Alva Myrdal, an essay in which Sissela describes first reading her mother's letters to Per Sundberg after Alva's death. Alva's letters to Per Sundberg and his replies are identified by date in this section.
13 On Key, see De Angelis, Ellen Key; Lundell, Ellen Key and Swedish feminist views on motherhood. Although Key was a controversial figure among both liberal and labor feminists, her proposal for child allowances was highly influential. In the United States, Charlotte Perkins Gilman shared many of her views.
14 Alva was reading about Buddhism, and her letters to Sundberg contain several references to Nirvana. Her capitalization of God/god varied as she took different attitudes toward Christianity.
15 Alva Myrdal, Autobiographical notes.
16 Bok, *Alva Myrdal*, 42.

17 A to G, July 9, 1920.
18 Andreas Arneson to Alva Reimer, Feb. 1919.
19 Bojer, *Great Hunger*.
20 Märta Fredriksson and Andreas Arneson married in 1928, after a long courtship during which they worked as teachers in Sweden and Norway. Both stayed in touch with Alva as she embarked on her relationship with Gunnar. According to Märta's grandson, Arne Fetveit, Andreas earned a degree in psychology and specialized in treating persons with physical disabilities. He died in 1931, just three weeks after their daughter was born. Märta continued her career as an educator. As a feminist and activist, she focused on the poor and was involved in supporting Finnish orphans and the underground Norwegian resistance to Nazi occupation. The marriage of Alva's best friend to the first young man whom Alva took seriously suggests the affinities that she felt with both of them. The parallels between Märta's and Alva's careers also attest to their shared interests.

References

Alva and Gunnar Myrdal's Collection (AGMA). Arbetarrörelsens Arkiv och Bibliotek (Swedish Labour Movement's Archive and Library). Stockholm, Sweden.
Alva Myrdal's personal documents, 1.1
Alva Myrdal. Själsbiografi (Biography of the psyche). April–June 1944.
Alva Myrdal's correspondence, 3.1
Correspondence between Alva and Per Sundberg, 1916–1918.
Correspondence between Alva and Gunnar Myrdal, 3.3
[cited as: G to A or A to G, date and/or letter number]

Manuscripts

Arnesen, Andreas. Letter to Alva Reimer. Feb. 1919. In the possession of Dr. Arne Fetveit, Oslo.

Myrdal, Alva. Autobiographical notes, written at the request of Sissela. Geneva, June 1973. Original in possession of Sissela Bok.

Interviews

Fetveit, Arne. Interview with Walter Jackson. Oslo, 2008.

Fölster, Kaj. Interviews with Walter Jackson. Stockholm, Dec. 11, 2007; 2008; 2010; May 6, 2011.

Sundberg, Gunnar. Interview with Walter Jackson.

Published Sources

Andræ, Carl Göran. The Swedish labor movement and the 1917–18 revolution. In *Sweden's Development from Poverty to Affluence, 1750–1970*, ed. Steven Koblik, 232–253. Minneapolis: University of Minnesota Press, 1975.

Andræ, Carl Göran. *Revolt eller reform: Sverige inför revolutionerna i Europa 1917–1918*. Stockholm: Carlssons, 1998.

Björnhagen, Elisabet. *Pedagogiskt nytänkande: Per Sundberg och Viggbyholmsskolan*. Stockholm: Mandatus bokproduktion, 2008.

Bojer, Johan. *The Great Hunger* (1916). Translated by W.J. Alexander Worster and C. Archer (2006), available from Project Gutenberg, http://www.gutenberg.org/files/2943/2943-h/2943-h.htm

Bok, Sissela. Alva Myrdal. In *Encounters*, ed. Kai T. Erikson, 35–42. New Haven, CT: Yale University Press, 1989.

Bok, Sissela. *Alva Myrdal: A Daughter's Memoir*. Reading, MA: Addison-Wesley, 1991.

De Angelis, Ronald William. Ellen Key: A Biography of the Swedish Social Reformer. PhD diss., University of Connecticut, 1978.

Hirdman, Yvonne. *Magfrågan: Mat som mål och medel i Stockholm, 1870–1920*. Stockholm: Raben & Sjögren, 1983.

Lundell, Torborg. Ellen Key and Swedish feminist views on motherhood. *Scandinavian Studies* 56, no. 4 (1984): 351–369.

Magnusson, Lars. *An Economic History of Sweden*. New York: Routledge, 2000.

Nordstrom, Byron J. *The History of Sweden*. Westport, CT: Greenwood Press, 2002.

Pauli, Ebba. Fredrik Natanæl Beskow. *Svenskt biografiskt lexikon*, vol. 4, 85–88. Stockholm: Bonniers, 1924.

Scott, Franklin D. *Sweden: The Nation's History*. Carbondale: Southern Illinois University Press, 1988.

Sjöholm, Öyvind. *Samvetets politik: Natanæl Beskow och hans omvärld intill 1921*. Uppsala: Almqvist & Wiksell, 1972.

Sundberg, Gunnar, ed. *Per Sundberg och Viggbyholms Skolan: En dokumentär skildring*. Stockholm: Författares Bokmaskin, 1998.

Thysell, Sam, ed. *Natanæl Beskow som Kristen-social banbrytare*. Stockholm: KFs bokförlag, 1958.

5 From Kalle Pettersson to Gunnar Myrdal

The man who became Gunnar Myrdal was descended from an upwardly mobile family that originated in Dalarna, a province in central Sweden whose egalitarian social structure and distinctive cultural traditions were often seen as exemplifying the country's past but were, in fact, sustained by its atypical patterns of property ownership and inheritance. This vast upland region was tied together by the mighty Dala River (Dalälven). Its inhabitants cultivated small farms, logged the forest and burned charcoal, and engaged in handicrafts as well as seasonal labor migration. The river enabled them to send their products to the mining district of Bergslagen, Stockholm, and beyond. But their villages remained relatively autonomous, sustaining Dalecarlians' commitment to collective decision making and their tendency to resist both internal and external forces that might erode local solidarity.

The village of Solvarbo, nestled between thickly forested mountains and the river, had been home to Gunnar's family for at least 200 years. Like most villages in Dalarna, it was a dense cluster of houses, barns, sheds, and workshops surrounded by open fields and rough grazing. Most families owned small plots of land scattered in the common fields and the right to use forest clearings. They cultivated grain, but the growing season was short. Their mainstay was animal husbandry, as women tended cows, goats, pigs, and sheep and made dairy products and textiles. Since farming was unable to support most households, other sources of income were essential. During the winter, both men and women produced handicrafts for sale outside the village. Many men earned money after the crop was harvested by traveling to other villages, sometimes far from home, repairing farm buildings and equipment or working in construction. Groups of strong young women rowed down the river to sell handicrafts and cultivate gardens in Stockholm and other towns. Despite Dalecarlians' resourcefulness, work ethic, and thrift, it was hard to eke out a living. In the late nineteenth century, sons and daughters sought work in Stockholm and in small factory towns, and many emigrated to the United States.[1]

Natives of Dalarna were especially proud of the role their province had played in the nation's history. In the sixteenth century Gustav Vasa, on the run from an invading Danish army, took refuge in Dalarna, raised his own army, drove the invaders from the land, and went on to become one of Sweden's greatest kings. The country never had a fully developed feudal system; although the nobility owned large estates, it never exercised political authority, and state power was centralized in the crown. Dalarna was distinguished by the absence of aristocratic landowners and the nearly universal distribution of property. While landholdings were not equal, no one remained landless through adulthood. Most important, daughters as well as sons inherited land from both their parents, and lineages exercised rights over inherited land for several generations. Many young people married within their village or chose spouses from neighboring villages, working the land they inherited and exchanging parcels with others in a flexible communal structure.

These small farmers cherished their collective as well as personal freedom and were known for their periodic rebellions against royal tax collectors. In the early nineteenth century, many villages in Dalarna refused to undergo the process of land reform that reshaped the rural landscape in the rest of central and southern Sweden, in which the many small strips of land owned by each family were consolidated into more compact farms and village clusters were dispersed. As more fertile regions of Sweden developed commercial agriculture, with large estates worked by tenants and wage laborers, Solvarbo remained a community of smallholders. Many decisions were made by the Gustafs parish government, in which most farmers participated. They could also appeal to the county government in Falun, which was dominated by wealthier men, many of whom owned mines, iron works, and grist mills.[2] By the end of the nineteenth century, Dalarna had a growing working class, and miners and foundry workers began to organize unions.

The picture of Dalarna that Gunnar carried with him was that of Solvarbo, a small farming village with a relatively egalitarian society. In 1917 he wrote an essay on Dalarna for his history class at gymnasium, in which he drew heavily on the idyllic image of the rural village fostered by the National Romantic movement at the turn of the century. He began with a proud account of how "the poor men of Dalarna" had come to Sweden's aid "whenever freedom's cause called for a defender against foreign attack or domestic tyranny." This fierce attachment to freedom arose in a society where "no castle stood overweening to raise its turrets to the sky." For a thousand years, the "democratic social structure" of the county had "shaped the farmers and timber-cutters, who said 'du' to everyone and who obeyed nobody except the law and the king, the latter only if his policies won approval and confidence."[3]

The Dalecarlian man's patriotism, Gunnar claimed (using the male gender deliberately), rested on his passionate love for his birthplace, "the blue mountains and Dalälven," as well as his devotion to the Swedish church, which was evident in the province's "magnificent" churches.

"His own cottage could be dark and cramped, his bread . . . mixed with bark, but the man of Dalarna would have a temple worthy of God." The 18-year-old essayist hailed the work ethic which the "barren land" engendered in farmers. "Experienced in hard work from his childhood, the old man keeps going until the end to increase the size of his estate. . . . 'I don't take my pants off until I go to bed,' he replies if somebody tells him to rest in his old age." Poverty also made the Dalecarlians "Sweden's most intelligent" people, with a keen eye for business dealings and a penchant for independent thinking.

This portrait idealized the countryside, but it gave Gunnar a sustaining myth that he would carry throughout his life.

Forebears

The social organization of Solvarbo was centered in three kin groups: Knuts, Matts, and Pers (also called Myres). Each had a distinct reputation, based on their conduct in the past but embroidered with myths that had been passed down over time, which shaped what was expected of individuals and explained their personalities. Gunnar's mother, Sofie Karlsson, was descended from the two most important lineages, Knuts and Matts. Knuts folk were said to be blond and "filled with fantasy." Gunnar's father, Carl Adolf Pettersson, was from the Pers lineage, a poorer family that lived on the Myres farm, close to the swamp valley (*myrdal*) near Dalälven. They were regarded as outsiders who had not been part of the original Swedish settlement. According to local folklore, this lineage produced clever smiths and had a reputation for being able to perform magic. Villagers said that there was something "dark and melancholic" about the Pers.[4]

The young Gunnar wove these legends into an imagined landscape of Dalarna, which grew all the more important to him when his family was living in Stockholm. Although he did not in live in Solvarbo year-round after the age of 2, he and his family visited relatives in the village every summer, and he added his own experiences to what he heard from his elders. The surviving historical records of his parents' families tell a more complex story of small landholdings inadequate to support growing families, of steady accumulation of assets by some families and bold risk-taking by others, and of tensions between village cooperation and the individual pursuit of wealth.

We know something of the Matssons because Sofie's grandfather and father kept a log of the family farm from 1851 to 1929. Like many farmers' diaries, the journal is a terse record of weather and expenditures. Income from the sale of agricultural goods or other sources is not listed; there is no balance sheet or record of profit and loss. When Sofie's father, Knuts Matts Matsson (1833–1884), began the journal, the Matssons were a respected farm family, but they were not wealthy. They bought only necessities, often at the local cooperative store. In the 1850s they employed a male farmhand and a female servant. Purchases of flour and other commodities increased over time, suggesting a rise in their income but also a decline in their ability to provision their own household.[5]

It was impossible for a Dalecarlian farm family to make a living through agriculture alone. Sometimes the ice did not loosen its grip until May, and farmers had only about three months to plant, grow, and harvest their grain. Although days were long, an unusually rainy or hot summer could damage the crop, which meant privation through the winter and spring. Knuts Matts Matsson and his wife, like most of their neighbors, relied on other activities to support themselves. Known as clever and hardworking, the couple ran an inn in a nearby mining village. During the 1860s Knuts was postmaster of Solvarbo. He was active in the town meeting, served as a churchwarden, and was often chosen to speak for the village before higher officials. In 1870 he was commissioned by the local government to build a stone bridge over the creek that ran through the village, on which he employed his brother, his son, and two stone masons. According to a local history, the sturdy bridge stood "as a monument to Knuts Matts Mattson's knowledge and powerful will." Since it brought more traffic into the community, the bridge benefitted the local grain mill, in which another Matsson owned a share.[6]

The farmers of Solvarbo had long maintained a small flour mill on the creek, which ground the grain they grew to feed their households and sold locally for cash or credit. But when the water level in the creek fell, the mill stood idle. In 1827 and again in 1841, local farmers, with support from pastors in the vicinity, petitioned the district government for permission to ditch nearby swamps to increase the flow of water into the creek. Their petitions were strongly opposed by prominent men in other communities who saw a threat to their interests: the owners of ironworks and mines, large estates, and other grist mills objected that it would affect the water supply downstream. But the district courts granted permission to enlarge the mill. In 1847 a share of the mill was bought at auction by Svens Matts Matsson, and members of the Matsson family owned a substantial proportion of the enterprise for 71 years.[7]

In 1877 Carl August Matsson was appointed miller. The family celebrated their taking control of the operation as a triumph of local people over outside investors and the wealthy neighbors who had tried to interfere with the village institution. Carl August, now known as "Miller Kalle," became one of the most prosperous men in Solvarbo. He and his wife had a good deal of business acumen. In the early fall, farmers brought in their grain to be ground. While Kalle and his apprentices hurried to get the work done, Kalle's wife, Anna-Lisa, known as the capable and intelligent "mother" of the mill, served coffee and made conversation with the customers. This was the milieu in which Sofie Karlsson grew up, the oldest of eleven children, nine of whom lived to maturity.

She saw both mother and father constantly at work. Sofie remembered that at meals her father fed the youngest child in his lap while she and her mother served the other children. Although Miller Kalle's assets steadily increased, he ploughed much of the profits back into capital improvements, which did not leave much cash to spend on the family's needs. Kalle kept careful records of his expenditures, and the children learned the value of frugality and hard work.[8]

Miller Kalle employed four young men as apprentices. To help with the cleaning and childcare, the family usually hired two young women. When Sofie left school at the age of 12, however, her parents decided that they no longer needed paid female help. Sofie was given much more responsibility for her six younger brothers and two younger sisters, as well as for farm work such as herding and milking goats. As many as fifteen people lived in the household at one time. The lines of authority in the mill and at home were clearly defined, but the young employees lived and ate with the family. The Matssons and other villagers saw their apprentices and domestic workers, all of whom had been born in the locality, not as members of a separate and inferior class but as youths whom they were helping to get a start in life. To the young employees, this sense of equality may have seemed a pretense that masked subordination. Room and board were a large part of their compensation, and their wages were very low. The young men were paid twice or three times as much as the young women. All of the employees were furnished with clothing, a small cash allowance, tobacco and alcohol on special occasions, and a gift of money when they married. When their terms of service ended, they had little or no savings to take with them.[9]

Matsson took a great stride toward modernizing the mill in 1882 when he bought three turbine engines. Grain elevators soon followed. He had the creek dredged, increasing the flow of water to Solvarbo. In making these improvements, he was advised by his cousin, Knuts Magnus Eriksson, an engineer who was remembered as the cleverest man in the village. When Carl August Matsson retired to his farm in 1903, he could look back on more than 25 years of increasing productivity. After dry summers in 1900 and 1901 and a cold, wet summer in 1902, 1903 turned out to be "a good year," and Kalle sold his father's farm for a profit and bought a better one. In 1918 the mill was sold to the local electrical company; another Matsson was one of the directors.[10]

In contrast, Gunnar's father's family had a hard time piecing together a living on the Myres farm. Their reputation as mysterious outsiders with magical powers may have stemmed from the fact that they were descended from Finns who had migrated to Dalarna in the early eighteenth century. The Swedish government had encouraged "forest Finns" to relocate to sparsely populated areas of north-central Sweden and clear land for cultivation. Gunnar remembered that his father's ancestors were said to have "come from the forest." Church records show that one of them lived in Östra Silvberg, where many Finns had settled. His son moved to Solvarbo as a newlywed and cleared the low-lying land that became the family farm. It was called Myres, and the name became associated with the family. The farm name was perpetuated through the generations by being used before the owner's personal name and patronymic. Gunnar's grandfather, Pers Peter Ersson (1833–1911), and his father, Carl Adolf Pettersson, were born on the Myres farm.[11]

This family, which farmed a small piece of land reclaimed from the swamp and forest and lived outside the village, is seldom visible in local records. They were too poor to be liable for taxes. Solvarbo's local history rarely mentions either the Pers or the Myres families. According to the pastor's annual census, Gunnar's great-grandfather, Myr Erik Ersson, was unable to read. Gunnar's grandfather was 9 when Sweden passed its first compulsory school attendance law in 1842. When the pastor took the church census during the years 1868–1877, he recorded that Pers Peter Ersson could not read or understand the Bible or catechism, but that his wife, Sara Greta Jansdotter, could. In addition to bearing nine children, six of whom lived to adulthood, Sara Greta did farm work, including ploughing, in all sorts of weather.[12]

The Pers' reputation for being able to perform magic did not make them unusual, or even targets of suspicion. The forests that covered much of Sweden through the early eighteenth century were seen as dark and primeval, full of pre-Christian powers or evil spirits that threatened farmers. These beliefs were widespread across central and eastern Europe. But Swedish forests were said to have something special: trolls, who were particularly menacing during the long, dark winter. Parents were warned to watch their babies closely lest a troll slip in, steal the infant, and substitute a troll baby or changeling. An adolescent girl herding sheep or goats in the hills was told to keep her dog close by, or a troll might carry her off and force her to marry him. With all these dangers, timber-cutters might well have thought it prudent to learn magic for their own protection before venturing into the woods. Perhaps the newcomers were thought to be reciting a magical incantation when they were overheard speaking Finnish. By the end of the nineteenth century, any memory of Finnish culture had vanished from Gunnar's family, as the other three lines of his ancestry stemmed from the older Swedish inhabitants of the area.[13] Gunnar always thought of himself as Swedish, but the isolation and poverty of the Pers family lingered in memory, as did their reputation for melancholy.

Carl Adolf Pettersson, Gunnar's father, managed to finish six years of elementary school and had a few months of training as a carpenter at a technical school in a nearby town. While doing his military service in 1897, he visited the great Stockholm Exhibition, which celebrated the Industrial Revolution. The young carpenter looked up at the wondrous edifices with large glass windows built by corporations to show off their latest technology.[14] He was enthralled by Stockholm, a populous city illuminated by gaslights, its nightlife throbbing with cabarets, theater, and dance halls. The capital was growing at a spectacular rate, with plenty of opportunities in construction. After his military service Carl Adolf returned to Solvarbo, ambitious to succeed in the building industry.

In the spring of 1898 the courtship of Carl Adolf Pettersson and Sofie Karlsson began at a temperance society dance in Solvarbo. In this small village, each had grown up knowing who the other was, but their families were not close. At the age of 21, Carl Adolf appealed to the 18-year-old daughter of the miller. Strong and handsome, a hard worker, ambitious, and an avowed teetotaler, he seemed a good prospect for a husband. After a short time Sofie became pregnant, and the two were wed on May 15, 1898. In contrast to an illegitimate birth, a premarital pregnancy was not shameful.

When Gunnar was born on December 6 of that year, Carl Adolf and Sofie were living in a cottage in a tiny hamlet in a remote area in northern Dalarna where his father was building housing for railroad workers. Many years later, Sofie remembered that she had never been away from home before and was so shy and inexperienced that she feared getting blood on the landlord's bed when she gave birth. She had her husband bring straw from the barn and put it on the floor, where their son was born. Her mother soon arrived and helped to care for the infant. A couple of weeks later, Carl Adolf brought his wife, mother-in-law, and infant son back to Solvarbo on a flatbed car of a freight train, exposed to the cold winter weather. Sofie feared that the smoke from the engine would suffocate the baby, but they made it home for Christmas.[15]

What's in a Name?

Karl Gunnar Pettersson, who later renamed himself Gunnar Myrdal, was given family names with mythic connotations. By this time, it had become common for Swedish parents to give their sons the same last name as the father, instead of taking the father's first name and adding "son" to form his last name. This boy was given his father's first name, Karl, which was also the name of his maternal grandfather and of several Swedish kings. The name Gunnar had been passed down in Sofie's family to one of her brothers, and her family had owned a farm called Gunnars since 1747.

Local folklore provides various stories of how the farm got its name, three of which signify misfortune. One account identifies the original Gunnar as a soldier in the Swedish army who was walking alone back to his home after the disastrous defeat in Norway in 1719. This Gunnar stopped in Solvarbo, where he died of cold, hunger, and exhaustion on the site of the farm that was later named after him. In another story, the Gunnar who farmed the place drowned in the mill pond on New Year's

Eve in 1820. In yet another version, the original Gunnar abandoned the farm when he moved away to get married. In this telling, the farm fell into ruin and was taken over by a pack of wolves, whose howling scared local children on their way to and from school. In a fourth version, perhaps designed to counteract the farm's fatal associations, one of Sofie's ancestors named Gunnar was a pious man who built a communal house of prayer on the property.[16]

Gunnar Myrdal himself offered a more heroic story of the name's origin in "My Name Is Gunnar," an autobiographical article that he wrote for a Stockholm newspaper in 1943. He claimed that his parents named him for an Old Norse hero celebrated in the poem "Snöfrid," written by the popular Romantic Nationalist Viktor Rydberg (1828–1895).[17] This Gunnar is a courageous youth who is summoned in the middle of a raging snowstorm by Snöfrid, the "loveliest wood-nymph," who takes him sailing through the gale toward the "Isle of Felicity." He must endure three tests. First he passes by a cliff where trolls have stored a treasure and promise to give him the gold in exchange for his soul. Next he is tempted by giants, who promise him power on the same terms. Finally, a beautiful nymph seeks to lure him to her cottage in the forest, promising her eternal devotion if he gives her his soul. She turns out to be a Norn, a Valkyrie-like being who wants to weave his fate at her loom, depriving him of masculine courage and independence. Snöfrid admonishes the youth that it is "better to die for the right, though scorned, than to live famous in selfish striving; better than peace is the clasp of danger. Choosest thou me, thou choosest the tempest." She enjoins Gunnar to "boldly offer thy blood for the weak, willingly suffer, all things forsake, fight a hopeless fight, and nameless die." Then Snöfrid disappears in the fog and young Gunnar is left alone to ponder the "hard path" that lies before him. He fears getting lost in the mist, a symbol of moral uncertainty, but a voice reassures him that, if he shields "those too weak to face the harsh world's wrath," he will come "near heaven." After the twilight of the gods Gunnar would find himself in Idvall with the wood nymph whom he adores as a reward for his selfless courage.[18]

The choice of Gunnar as their son's middle name might be explained by its history in Sofie's family and association with Gunnar's farm. But Rydberg's poetry was popular among Swedes, and the poem might have added an additional gilding to Carl Adolf and Sofie's hopes for their first-born son. "Snöfrid" appealed to Gunnar's imagination, and some of its themes recur in his correspondence: the image of the mist as an emblem of the moral wilderness through which the modern hero must find his way; the idea that the hero must fight—to the death if necessary—for those too weak to fight for themselves; and the image of an inspiring woman who offers challenge and courage, in contrast to a seductive feminine figure who lures the hero with easy comfort.

For the first 14 years of his life, the boy was called Karl or, more often, "Kalle." Using the name "Gunnar" was part of his deliberately refashioning himself as a gymnasium student who aspired to make a mark on history. He remembered summers spent wandering around Solvarbo talking with relatives, exploring the fields and woods, dropping by the cooperative store, visiting the Good Templars' hall, and dressing up in a black frock coat "preaching" to all who would listen. He especially enjoyed visiting his grandfather's mill, where he was fascinated by the whirring turbines. As the family moved to Falun, Stockholm, an estate in Västmanland, and then back to the capital, Gunnar returned to his memories of Solvarbo, reweaving the elements of fact and myth in his imagination.[19]

Father and Son

In November 1900, after the birth of a daughter, Elsa, Carl Adolf moved the family to Falun, Dalarna's largest city and the site of the country's largest copper mine. For four centuries, the smelter had wreaked human and ecological damage, belching smoke, sulfur, and ashes that created darkness at noon. Travelers who came to Falun in the seventeenth and eighteenth centuries thought they had taken a wrong turn and ended up in hell. When Linnaeus visited the town in 1734, he found that most plants had been suffocated by smoke and sulfurous vapors. But it was the human consequences that most appalled him. Linnaeus found over 1,200 miners and laborers, "like black devils, surrounded by soot and fumes on every side. . . . Cave-ins are constantly dreaded. . . . At the slightest crack, [they] could take everyone's life, without refuge for a single one of the damned." The mine had one beneficial byproduct: the pigment for red paint, which was inexpensive and widely available to farmers. As the fashion spread from Dalarna to the rest of the country, the red farmhouse with white trim became a symbol of Sweden's rural past. It appeared frequently in the paintings of Carl Larson at the height of National Romanticism in the 1890s, as Swedes looked nostalgically to the culture of the home village as a refuge from the nation's rapid industrialization and chaotic cities. By the beginning of the twentieth century, Falun had 10,000 inhabitants and was expanding rapidly, offering ample opportunities for a builder. During the previous century, new technology had reduced, but not eliminated, the smoke and sulfurous fumes. Kalle remembered that, as a 3- and 4-year-old boy, he had an "abnormal curiosity" and enjoyed going on walks with his mother, peering into the windows of houses and wondering about the people who lived there. "How do they earn their living? Why do people choose certain occupations? What are their families like? Why do they act as they do?"[20]

In January 1903, Carl Adolf Pettersson, Erik Landberg, and Carl Gustaf Jönsson incorporated Pettersson & Landberg, a construction company, in Falun. Both Pettersson and Landberg listed their occupation as builder, and Jönsson identified himself as a roofer. The firm began with a working capital of 10,600 kronor, a considerable sum for skilled craftsmen in the construction trades to raise. Pettersson and Landberg put in 5,000 kronor each, and Jönsson only 100 kronor. Sofie's father, Carl August Matsson, and a Landberg relative each bought shares worth 100 kronor, as did a bricklayer, a carpenter, and another worker. In addition to building houses in Falun, in 1903 the firm received a contract to build a Good Templars' hall in Carl Adolf's home parish, which would also be used for the local school and other civic and recreational activities. Although another contractor submitted a lower bid, the parish council awarded the commission to Pettersson & Landberg. One of the Matssons was on the village council that awarded the contract. The poor boy from Myres farm proudly showed off his edifice at the dedication. Every time they went to church, his parents could admire the meeting place as a monument to their son's skill. But Dalarna could no longer hold the ambitious young man. After completing the community hall, he moved his family to Stockholm and sought to expand his construction business in the capital, which was in the midst of a great boom. The firm specialized in building apartment houses. By June 1907 Carl Adolf owned more than half of the shares; by the end of the construction boom the firm had more than doubled its working capital.[21]

Carl Adolf gained considerable experience in home renovation during his first five years in Stockholm, but he did so at the expense of his growing family. From 1904 to 1909, he relocated the family four times. He would buy an old house, move the family in while he fixed up the place, then sell it at a profit and buy another old house. Sometimes he rented and renovated a house or apartment building under contract with the landlord. The Petterssons' first residence, in 1904–1905, was an apartment in Vasastan, a neighborhood northwest of the city's central business district. There Sofie gave birth to the family's fourth and last child, Robert, in 1905 (see Figure 5.1). The Petterssons employed a young woman from the country to help take care of the children; she lived with them from 1904 to 1909.

In 1906 Carl Adolf moved the household to Södermalm, which offered ample opportunities for the renovation of old and poorly maintained buildings as well as new construction. Alva's family had lived in the same neighborhood briefly in 1902. In 1903 the square near Maria Magdalena church had undergone a dramatic transformation, as new stone buildings replaced ramshackle wooden houses.

At the age of 6, Kalle began his education at Maria's elementary school, where his classmates included many children from working-class families. He earned good grades in conduct and diligence and passed reading, counting, Christian learning, gymnastics, and crafts, having trouble only with handwriting and singing. During the 1906–1907 academic year, the family lived in the more prosperous Östermalm section. Gunnar's grades

Figure 5.1 The Pettersson children: Karl Gunnar, Elsa, Mela, and Robert, Stockholm, circa 1910. Studio portrait by A. Florin, Stockholm. Courtesy of Alva and Gunnar Myrdal's Collection, Arbetarrörelsens Arkiv och Bibliotek, Stockholm, Sweden.

slipped to Bs, although he was well-behaved. The Petterssons moved back to their old neighborhood in Södermalm in October 1907. Sofie and the children stayed for four years, but Carl Adolf spent most of the last two away from home on business. Kalle finished his elementary education at Maria's school, where he continued to be a B student but earned As in conduct and diligence. He completed his studies there in the spring of 1909, three months before Alva Reimer began hers at the same school. Kalle then attended Södermalm's Higher Public Middle School for three years, where he remained a B student except for his execrable handwriting. During his final year there, his grade for diligence fell from A to B. His report cards suggest the impact of his father's frequent absences. The anxious patriarch had nearly always signed his son's report cards from 1906 to 1908, but his mother often did so from 1909 through 1911.[22]

Altogether, the family moved fourteen times between Kalle's birth and his completion of his undergraduate law degree in 1923—roughly once every one and a half years, not counting summers spent in Solvarbo or other rural retreats. The boy changed schools six times during his primary and secondary education. He later claimed that these dislocations and the constant necessity of making new friends explained his mediocre grades, but there were also problems at home. When Kalle's paternal grandparents visited the family shortly after their move to Stockholm, he overheard his grandfather complain that their son, Carl Adolf, was not "nice" to Sofie, though just what sort of conduct that meant remained mysterious.[23]

Construction was a rough and tumble business. Most small contractors and subcontractors had started their careers as skilled workers and expanded their knowledge of the building trades by working at various construction sites. They rarely had any education beyond elementary school and perhaps a year of trade school. Contractors were often burly men with strong muscles and calloused hands, capable of cajoling and bullying a crew of construction workers. In a rigidly class-bound society, construction offered one of the few avenues to wealth for men who started out poor and lacked formal education, but it was highly competitive and entailed a great deal of risk-taking in a cyclical economy. During the boom at the turn of the twentieth century, little capital was required to make a down payment on a parcel of land, and banks would extend loans to builders. Labor was cheap and abundant as rural migrants flooded into Stockholm. Contractors did not get paid until the job was finished and the building sold. Cash-flow crises were common as builders raced to complete a project in time to repay the loan. Their families learned to adjust their spending habits to these exigencies, sometimes living well and sometimes doing without, but always anxious about the future. Contractors and their families were not welcome in refined and educated circles, yet they desperately sought to distinguish themselves from the mass of working people.

Many contractors ran with a hard-drinking and fast-living crowd, and Carl Adolf, fresh from the countryside, was eager to be accepted and to hear the latest news about land, suppliers, banks, investors, building codes, and potential buyers. In Solvarbo he had taken an oath that no liquor would never pass his lips, but this was the first of many promises he broke in the city. He had trouble holding his liquor and quickly became an alcoholic. Carl Adolf also relished Stockholm's theaters and dance halls. For a successful man from an isolated village, the capital's nightlife offered an endless spectacle of new sensations and amusements. When they were flush with cash, builders entertained their friends in taverns, which "respectable" women like their wives did not enter. After the birth of his fourth child, Carl Adolf lost interest in Sofie and turned his attention to other women.

For female companionship, Carl Adolf and his raucous crowd were able to choose from a wide range of options. In 1904 Stockholm had 34 "girl-houses" and 34 "party hotels" with a total of 405 rooms. The physician J.E. Johansson found that 96 percent of the city's prostitutes worked in "an industry controlled by hotel owners, landlords, and tavern keepers." Their ranks included registered prostitutes who had been officially inspected for venereal diseases and listed in the police records. Unregistered prostitutes, often working-class women who sought to supplement their meager wages, risked arrest and a sentence of hard labor if they were caught. Some of these women sold cigars or fruit in the streets; others waited on tables in taverns. The lowest-paid workers in the building industry were women who hauled buckets of cement at construction sites. Since their wages were insufficient to support them, some entertained men in empty buildings. Finally, some poor working women did not think of themselves as prostitutes but were willing to become the mistress of a prosperous man who would take them out and help pay the rent. Despite the official inspection process, a significant proportion of prostitutes were infected with venereal disease. Some gentlemen kept a syringe and medicine in their drawer for use in case they contracted gonorrhea.[24]

As Kalle faced his strong-willed, ambitious, and utterly self-centered father, he confronted many contradictions. Carl Adolf took his son to church and taught him traditional moral values but often flouted them himself. He was defensive about his lack of education and rustic manners. He wanted Kalle to attend gymnasium and university and to bring honor on the family through a distinguished career, but he inevitably saw his oldest son as a competitor, and in self-defense the boy developed a sharp tongue that often landed him in trouble. Carl Adolf was alternately overbearing and absent, his moods shifting from hot flashes of temper to playful indulgence and then to drunken incapacitation.

Sofie was not ambitious for money or social distinction, but she tried to present the appearance of a respectable, bourgeois household. She usually had a servant to help with the child care and housework, but she could not keep servants for long, in part because of her husband's roving eye. Regretting her own lack of education beyond elementary school, Sofie strove for self-improvement, encouraged the children in their school work, and read to them after dinner. Although unhappy in her marriage, she did not consider divorce; she was concerned about how it would look to others and affect the children.

In addition to his wife and children, other family members counted on Carl Adolf for support. He wove a web of financial dependency involving most of Sofie's six younger brothers, who found jobs as apprentices working for Carl Adolf in the construction trades or on one of his estates after he turned to agriculture. Additionally, he provided financial assistance to a couple of Sofie's brothers so that they could attend technical school. Although Sofie's family had been more influential than Carl Adolf's family in Solvarbo, the careers of her brothers who left home depended, in part, on the patronage of this hard-driving upstart from the Pers lineage.[25]

Because of the family's frequent moves and upward mobility, Sofie had few friends. She was devoted to her children but filled with anxiety about her husband and her children's future. As the oldest of nine surviving siblings, she had played a significant role in raising her younger siblings and had become a strict disciplinarian. While corporal punishment was common in that generation of Swedes, it was most often administered to the sons by the father. But with Carl Adolf frequently away from home, it fell to Sofie to discipline the children, especially her rebellious elder son. She frequently ordered Elsa to fetch a birch branch so she could punish Kalle. This worked well enough in the country, but at Christmas 1906, when Gunnar was 8 and Elsa 6, they were living in Stockholm when Sofie sent Elsa out on such a mission. Unable to find a birch branch, she brought a holly branch instead. Kalle never let his sister forget the pain he had felt from the thorns on his bottom, which continued to hurt for several days after his mother administered the thrashing. Forty years later, on the eve of his 50th birthday, Sofie still felt so guilty about having been "violent" in punishing her son that she wrote to him to apologize, citing her inexperience as a young mother.[26]

Kalle's childhood was full of uncertainty and anguish. He felt emotionally driven to rebel against an overbearing and often absent father whom he neither loved nor respected, only to find that it was his mother who meted out the corporal punishment. Since his sister was compelled to participate in the ritual, Kalle could not be sure whom he could trust and wondered whether anyone really loved him.[27]

The Pettersson family had remained loyal to the Church of Sweden, rather than joining any of the free churches that proliferated in Dalarna. Religious observance provided some continuity for the children as they moved from one place to another. The Pettersson children all learned the Bible and Luther's shorter catechism, studied religion at public schools, and went through confirmation. As a boy, Kalle enjoyed singing in youth choirs. Later, he remembered entering Maria Magdalena Church in Södermalm with a school friend. They admired the magnificent rococo interior of this early eighteenth-century building, with its depiction of Jesus' mother on the gilded, intricately carved pulpit. At that point, aged 11 or 12, Gunnar thought that no one could know for sure whether God exists, but that since nothing bad could come from religious belief, it was better to believe for the sake of safety.[28]

The General Strike of 1909 polarized Söder even more than the rest of Stockholm. With Carl Adolf away, Sofie and the children felt embattled in the predominantly working-class neighborhood, and Kalle received his first impression of class conflict. He was amazed at the hatred that some of the working-class boys showed toward the rich, and he heard students from his middle school exchange insults with poor boys in the street.[29] At this time, the Petterssons lived only a few blocks from Alva's family, which then resided in Mosebacke. Although both fathers were in the building industry, their families did not know each other.

Pettersson & Landberg made good money building apartments in Stockholm from 1904 to 1908, but the protracted conflict between labor and capital in 1909 brought new construction to a standstill. By 1911 Landberg and all the other original investors had left, and in April 1912 the firm filed for bankruptcy. Carl Adolf had already taken some of his money out to buy Gärdslinge, an estate near Köping in Västmanland. Soon he focused on improving the manor house and making the estate more productive. Carl listed the estate as his official residence for tax purposes, thereby shielding his home and a good bit of his wealth from creditors, although Sofie and the children continued to live in Stockholm while he supervised work at Gärdslinge. He took his family there for vacations during the summers of 1909 and 1910, but Sofie and the four children did not become year-round residents until the spring of 1911.[30]

Gärdslinge was a fairly large estate. In 1909, 136 people lived there, including tenants, male and female farm workers, and domestic servants. These employees and their children were crammed into small houses, and several elderly people who had formerly worked on the farm continued to live in their old cottages. Carl Adolf appointed Klas Valfrid Karlsson, one of Sofie's younger brothers, as "inspector," and Klas and his wife moved down from Dalarna in April 1909. Five months later Klas was joined by Matias August Karlsson, another brother, who was given the more important title of farm manager even though he was 2 years younger than Klas. As he set about making improvements, Carl Adolf added a stable master, stable boy, carpenter, and gardener. By the time he sold the estate in 1913, about 150 people were living there.[31]

For Kalle and the other children, living at Gärdslinge was very different from anything they had experienced while visiting relatives in Solvarbo. In contrast to Dalarna, where landownership was nearly universal and smallholding predominated, Västmanland and the other counties in east-central Sweden surrounding Stockholm and Lake Mälaren had been dominated by large estates for over a century. Most of the work on these estates was done by tenant farmers and wage laborers, usually *statare*, and agriculture had become increasingly commercialized. Modernizing one of these estates required capital and knowledge of new farming technologies, and Carl Adolf applied his construction experience to the restoration and improvement of the manor house and outbuildings.

Gärdslinge lay a few kilometers southwest of the hamlet of Munktorp, where Albert Jansson had grown up as a tenant on the parsonage estate. Köping was the parish from which Pastor Ekblom had burst forth in his righteous mission to impose theological orthodoxy. A small industrial city with ironworks, shipbuilding, and factories, it was also the home of Alfred Stärner, the radical editor of *Bergslagsbladet*, whose crusade for universal suffrage and leadership role in the People's Parliament had inspired Frederick Jansson in 1892 and drawn his son Albert into radical movements. Now Stärner represented the city in the Riksdag's second chamber as a member of the Liberal Party. Köping was also the site of the commercial school that Albert Jansson had attended to learn bookkeeping so that he could take his first steps out of the dependency and vulnerability he had known as a teenaged farm worker.

In contrast, Carl Adolf sent 12-year-old Karl Gunnar to a public middle school that prepared young men for gymnasium. Since the Petterssons' estate was some distance from the school, Kalle boarded with a family in Köping in the fall of 1911. As the conflict between father and son had intensified, Kalle began to use his middle name more often. While the family continued to call him "Kalle," he signed his school papers "Gunnar Pettersson." The lonely new boy from Stockholm set out to impress his classmates with some of the pranks for which he was already known in the family. He quickly gained a reputation as a troublemaker. Kalle may have assumed that, as the eldest son of a successful businessman turned lord of the manor, he had it made regardless of how he behaved. In the late autumn of 1911, he broke his right hip in an accident. He missed celebrating his 13th birthday and Christmas at home that year and lay in hospital in Köping until January 1912. In addition, a doctor misdiagnosed him as suffering from tuberculosis, casting a shadow over his future. By the time he returned home, he had failed the fall term because he had not completed his coursework or taken exams. But what stood out in the eyes of his parents was his poor grades in conduct and diligence during the time he had attended. His father was very angry and feared that his eldest son, whom he regarded as gifted, might let the family down.[32]

Kalle missed the entire spring term of middle school just as he was reaching puberty. While his hip was healing, he had nine months at home to worry about his future. Carl Adolf was frequently away from Gärdslinge, winding up his construction firm's affairs. It was unclear whether Kalle would be able to resume his education. At the end of the academic year, he hid in the bushes in a park outside the middle school and felt "awfully depressed" as he watched his classmates emerge jubilantly. There was not much doubt about the young man's intellectual promise and competitive drive on the rare occasions when he decided to apply himself, however. When the local pastor visited the Pettersson household for the annual census in 1912, Kalle outshone his parents in knowledge of the Bible and Luther's Catechism, receiving an A while his mother got a B and father a C.[33]

The troubled teenager's defiance at home continued unabated, and the situation in the family reached a crisis in the summer of 1912. He was now able to scamper about with a slight limp, and his behavior at home was so bad that his beleaguered mother forced him to sign a contract that he would "be absolutely nice and obedient and . . . quickly fulfill all obligations that my father assigns to me. . . . I also promise never to answer mother or father disrespectfully."[34] The contract is signed by Kalle, Sofie, and Sofie's brother Klas Karlsson. Although Carl Adolf is mentioned as the head of the family who assigned his son's duties, he was not present when the contract was drawn up, and Sofie evidently thought it necessary to have another male signatory and enforcer to convince her 13-year-old son that harsh corporal punishment would follow if his insolence and troublemaking did not cease.

Finally an angry Carl Adolf called the boy into his home office, where he kept his account ledgers as well as a set of scales for weighing farm products. The heavy-set businessman remarked that he had had to leave school when he was about Kalle's age and reminded his son of how hard he had worked since then. The family's current prosperity had not come easily and, with business affairs uncertain, his son's future was by no means secure. Carl Adolf told him that he had been "investing" in Kalle's education so that the lad could go on to gymnasium and university. "If you keep getting bad grades," he warned, "you can be an ordinary farm worker and I'll invest in Robert," Kalle's younger brother.[35]

Karl Gunnar Pettersson pondered the stark alternatives: if he got serious about his studies and went on to gymnasium and university, he had a chance to become part of Sweden's upper class; otherwise he faced a free fall into the working class, from which Carl Adolf had managed to escape. He chose the first option when he reentered school in Köping in the fall of 1912 to repeat the grade he had failed the year before. His marks and conduct improved significantly, and he won a prize for academic excellence in the spring of 1913. He came under the influence of the headmaster, who taught courses on the Bible and on Swedish literature. Although the headmaster's outlook was generally conservative, he admired Strindberg and ranked him second only to the Romantic Nationalist Viktor Rydberg, the author of "Snöfrid." Kalle displayed a talent for math and an interest in science. His defiant temperament was still evident despite his greater capacity for self-discipline, however. One of his teachers remembered a certain "willfulness," and another thought that Kalle's "eminent capacity to transform black into white" in his arguments presaged a great career as a lawyer.[36]

Academic work became Kalle's shield against family problems. He could avoid or minimize his involvement in difficult family situations by claiming that "I'm always working." Preparing himself for higher education was now his primary duty. He seemed to realize that excellence in his studies was the quickest route to eventual liberation from his father's tyranny and that the intractable problems between his parents offered opportunities for him to increase his leverage in the family by winning each parent's approval. Gradually, Kalle negotiated a different kind of relationship with

Carl Adolf and Sofie. By the time he finished middle school, he already had more education than either of his parents, who began to rely on their son's mathematical ability to help with business matters. Carl Adolf often sent him on errands to the bank and included him in discussions of how the family should manage its finances. "I think that I was more on the same plane as my parents," Gunnar recalled many years later, "and that was very unusual" at the time. Sofie also came to depend on her eldest son, and Kalle assumed greater responsibility around the house, often reading to his younger sister, Mela, who was frequently ill and had epileptic seizures. Kalle's education was now considered so important that in October 1913 the family moved to a rented house in Köping so he could be closer to school, while Carl Adolf supervised the final improvements at his estate at Gärdslinge, which he sold two months later.[37]

Although Kalle succeeded in channeling much of his restless energy into his academic work, he also developed techniques for managing his anger and containing conflict. He became adroit at maneuvering within his family, where he knew that things were not as they seemed. All four of the Pettersson children learned to keep up the appearance of obedience at home and of respectability in the community, pretending not to notice their father's drinking and frequent absences or their mother's unhappiness. They did not discuss their father's tangled business affairs and growing debt. Silence enveloped all these problems. "The whole family was very secretive about things that didn't fit the picture they had of themselves," Mela's daughter, Ann-Mari Carlman, remarked after reading Mela's diary of her childhood and youth. All of the children would "go to any length to avoid a quarrel" in front of their parents. This "denial" of family problems was "a form of lying" at which the Petterssons developed a certain skill. Kalle learned to choose words carefully when speaking in front of his parents, making ironic comments that had a double meaning instead of confronting his parents directly. In this way he communicated his discontent to his siblings without being punished for being disrespectful. Increasingly adept at wordplay, Kalle learned to express his anger indirectly with veiled but devastating sarcasm. He teased his younger siblings mercilessly. He did not understand that words could hurt, and his sister Elsa was easily wounded. Robert grew up under the burden of being dominated by his overbearing, highly competitive older brother.[38] As adults, neither Gunnar nor Elsa found it easy to trust people. They had spent too many years pretending not to notice the underlying problems that plunged the family into gloom. Gunnar managed to repress his hatred of his father, but the denial engendered a certain submerged hatred of himself.

Kalle's relationships with the other boys at school offered some relief from the repression of emotions that was required at home and with his teachers. His friends at middle school in Köping included boys from various backgrounds, but none was from the upper class. While his hip injury kept him from excelling at soccer, the team found a use for him in their psychological warfare against the opposing side: the sharp-tongued adolescent would stand behind the lines and hurl verbal insults at the other team. In July 1914 he signed a humorous "agreement" with another teenager with whom he had apparently quarreled. "We bind ourselves not to express our friendship through curse words as before," the boys affirmed, adding that "we will not try on each others' clothes" or "argue about politics." If either boy broke these rules, he would be "punished by force" by the signed witnesses, who included the son of factory workers.[39]

On August 17, 1914, as war broke out in central Europe and Kalle prepared for confirmation in the Church of Sweden and matriculation at the gymnasium in Västerås, Carl Adolf Pettersson petitioned the Royal Ecclesiastical Department to change the last name of his four children to Myrdahl, the name of the small farm his father's family owned in Solvarbo. Gunnar later claimed that the initiative for the name change came from his parents in conjunction with his confirmation, but both his mother, Sofie, and his sister, Elsa, later insisted that it was Gunnar who had pressed his father to adopt the more distinctive name in place of the common name Pettersson.[40] A few years later Gunnar and his siblings dropped the "h," bringing the spelling into conformity with the spelling of the farm's name. Their new surname was hardly aristocratic. Ironically, the ambitious boy had appropriated the name of the bit of marshland his father's ancestors had drained and cultivated in the eighteenth century.

The youth had already begun using his middle name, Gunnar, instead of his first name, Karl. His parents and a few friends continued to call him Kalle, but he introduced himself at gymnasium as Gunnar. Perhaps Carl Adolf and Sofie hoped that the new name might help their son to form a more stable identity. He had moved so often, but now both his first and last names represented small farms that his family had owned in Dalarna. The authorities approved the change just as the family was about to return to Stockholm from Köping.[41] Gunnar spent only the fall term of 1914 at the gymnasium in Västerås. His new gymnasium in the capital was one of the very best in the country and brought him into competition, though not friendship, with boys from the Swedish elite.

Notes

Unless otherwise noted, all translations were done by the author.

1 For an account of women's work on small farms in Upper Dalarna, see Isacson, *Vardagens ekonomie.* On Dalarna's cultural landscape, see Veirulf, *Dalarna*; Nässtrom, *Mitt Dalarna*; Sporrong, Province of Dalecarlia (Dalarna); Ekman, Revival of cultural celebrations of regional Sweden.

2 On Dalarna's unusually egalitarian social structure, see Isacson, *Ekonomisk tillväxt och social differentiering 1680–1860*; Sporrong, Dalecarlia in central Sweden before 1800; Lindström, *Distribution and Differences.*

3 Gunnar Myrdal, Dalafolket, AGMA.
4 Sofie Karlsson Pettersson, Släktkroniken, AGMA.
5 Knuts Matts Matsson, Bondedagbok, AGMA; Sjöberg, *Vår by*.
6 Sundwallson, *Gustafs år 1850*; Sjöberg, *Vår by*, 88. Bridge contract in Knuts Matts Matsson, Bondedagbok.
7 Solvarbo kvarn hundra år; Sofie Karlsson Pettersson, Släktkroniken; Sjöberg, *Vår by*, 80–81.
8 Carl August Matsson, Bondedagbok, AGMA; Sjöberg, *Vår by*, 90, 199; Fölster, interview, May 16, 2012.
9 Carl August Matsson, Bondedagbok, 32–36; Sjöberg, *Vår by*.
10 Carl August Matsson, Bondedagbok, 127–128, 188; Sjöberg, *Vår by*, 82–83.
11 Gunnar Myrdals levnadshistoria, AGMA; GMs Släktkroniken (genealogy chart) for Carl Adolf Pettersson, AGMA.
12 Sjöberg, *Vår by*; Gustafs parish Husförhör, 1868–1877, 301, Landsarkivet i Uppsala; Fölster, interview.
13 Broberg, *Finsk invandring till mellersta Sverige*, 18–21, 157–159; Wedin, *Det skogfinska kulturarvet*, 165–175, 235–239; Gothe, *Från trolldomstro till kristendom*, 53.
14 Gunnar Myrdals levnadshistoria; Hasselgren, *Utställningen i Stockholm, 1897*.
15 Gunnar Myrdals levnadshistoria.
16 Sjöberg, *Vår by*, 130–131.
17 Gunnar Myrdal, Gunnar heter jag.
18 Rydberg, Snöfrid.
19 Gunnar Myrdals levnadshistoria.
20 Olsson, *Falun Minne*, 48, 57. Gunnar Myrdal, Gunnar heter jag.
21 Patent och Registreringsverket, Bolagsbyrån, Registershandl. till Aktiabolag, Upphörda 1897–1960, E 3 A: 646, Riksarkivet. For the firm's projects, see Band 50, Blad 259, Akt 4987, 1906, AN: 0 4987, DN 0, 1179, June 13, 1908; AN: 0 4987, DN 0 2596, July 17, 1908; DN 0 2442, July 1911; Band 261, Akt 4987.
22 Karl Petterssons Förhålnings-bok, Gunnar Petterssons Förhålnings-bok, AGMA.
23 Gunnar Myrdals levnadshistoria, 2.
24 Johansson, *Reglementeringen i Stockholm*.
25 Knutsgård, interview.
26 Carlman, interview; Sofie Karlsson to GM; Lundborg, interview; Knutsgård, interview.
27 Fölster, interview; Carlman, interview; Bok, interview.
28 Gunnar Myrdals levnadshistoria, 13.
29 Kaj Fölster to Stellan Andersson, July 16, 1989, quoted in Andersson, Gunnar Myrdal, 18. See Norstedts Rabén multimedia, Söder i våra hjärten.
30 Patent och Registreringsverket, Bolagsbyrån, Registershandl. till Aktiabolag, Upphörda 1897–1960, Band 50, Blad 261, Akt 4987, Riksarkivet. Karl Petterssons Förhålnings-bok; Gunnar Petterssons Förhålnings-bok, AGMA.
31 Församlingsbok för Himmeta Församling, 1911–1920, 42–65; Kungsörsfogderi mantalslängder for Himmeta, 1909–1914, 322–367, Landsarkivet i Uppsala.
32 Andersson, Gunnar Myrdal, 19.
33 Andersson, Gunnar Myrdal, 19. Församlingsbok för Himmeta, 1911–1920, 42, Landsarkivet i Uppsala.
34 Contract signed by Karl Gunnar Pettersson, Sofie Pettersson, and Klas Karlsson, AGMA.

35 Janken Myrdal, interview; Andersson, Gunnar Myrdal.
36 *Trelleborgs Allehanda*, 8 April 1947; Nya namn i höstens bokflod, *Aftonbladet*, 25 Nov. 1949; Andersson, Gunnar Myrdal, 18–20.
37 Carlman, interview; Andersson, Gunnar Myrdal, 13; Församlingsbok för Himmeta, 1911–1920, 42, Församlingsbok för Köpings Stad, 1909–1919, 150, Landsarkivet i Uppsala.
38 Carlman, interview. Mela's adult daughter read her mother's childhood diary shortly after Mela's death and then, following her mother's instructions, destroyed it.
39 Gösta Lundqvist and Gunnar Myrdal, Contract, AGMA.
40 Lundborg, interview.
41 Ernst Törnell, Kungliga Ecklesiastikdepartementet, to C.A. Pettersson, AGMA; Andersson, Gunnar Myrdal, 20; Lundborg, interview. See also Jan Myrdal, *Barndom*.

References

Alva and Gunnar Myrdal's Collection (AGMA). Arbetarrörelsens Arkiv och Bibliotek (Swedish Labour Movement's Archive and Library). Stockholm, Sweden.

Gunnar Myrdal's personal documents, 1.2

Karl Petterssons Förhålnings-bok (School records), Östermalms Förberedande Elementarskola, Fall 1906–Spring 1908; Gunnar Petterssons Förhålnings-bok (School records), Södermalms Högre Allmänna Läroverk, Fall 1908–Spring 1911.

Contract signed by Karl Gunnar Pettersson, Sofie Pettersson, and Klas Karlsson. Gärdslinge, June 1, 1912.

Sofie Karlsson to Gunnar Myrdal. Nov. 24, 1948.

Ernst Törnell, Kungliga Ecklesiastikdepartementet, to C.A. Pettersson, Dec. 5, 1914.

Gunnar Myrdal's professional activities, 4.2

Gösta Lundqvist and Gunnar Myrdal, Contract. July 5, 1914.

Gymnasium essays

Gunnar Myrdal, Dalafolket (The people of Dalarna). Norra Real, 1917.

Alva Myrdal's family and kin, 6.3

Gunnar Myrdal's Släktingar (Relatives)

Gunnar Mrydals Släktkroniken (Genealogy chart) for Carl Adolf Pettersson, compiled by Alva Myrdal.

Knuts Matts Matsson, Bondedagbok (Farmer's diary).

Carl August Matsson, Bondedagbok (Farmer-miller's diary).

Sofie Karlsson Pettersson. Släktkroniken (Family chronicle).

Manuscripts

Andersson, Stellan. Gunnar Myrdal: Barn och ungdom år (Childhood and youth). Arbetarrörelsens Arkiv och Bibliotek, Stockholm.

Solvarbo kvarn hundra år: Skvaltkvarnen som blev storkvarn tack vare fånggevaldiger. Matsson family document in possession of Walter Jackson.

Interviews

Bok, Sissela. Interview with Walter Jackson.
Carlman, Ann-Mari. Interview with Walter Jackson. Stockholm, July 7, 2006.
Fölster, Kaj. Interview with Walter Jackson. Stockholm, May 26, 2012.
Knutsgård, Per Erik. Interview with Walter Jackson.
Lundborg, Ulla. Interview with Walter Jackson. Enköping, June 26, 2008.
Myrdal, Gunnar. Gunnar Myrdals levnadshistoria: Från barndomen (Life history: From childhood). Interview by Stellan Andersson, June 28, 1989. Arbetarrörelsens Arkiv och Bibliotek, Stockholm.
Myrdal, Janken. Interview with Walter Jackson.

Gunnar Myrdal's Published Work

Myrdal, Gunnar. Gunnar heter jag. *Aftontidningen*, 16 Aug. 1943.

Published Sources

Broberg, Richard. *Finsk invandring till mellersta Sverige: en översikt från medeltiden till 1600-talet*. Uppsala: Dialekt och folkminnesarkivet, 1988.
Ekman, Ann-Kristin. The revival of cultural celebrations of regional Sweden: Aspects of tradition and transition. *Sociologia Ruralis* 39, no. 3 (1999): 289–293.
Gothe, Richard. *Från trolldomstro till kristendom: studier rörande det kulturella tillståndet bland skogsfinnarna i Sverige under 16- och 1700-talen*. Stockholm: Författarens förlag, 1943.
Hasselgren, Andreas. *Utställningen i Stockholm, 1897*. Stockholm: Froléen & Co., 1897.
Isacson, Maths. *Ekonomisk tillväxt och social differentiering 16801860: Bondeklassen i By socken, Kopparbergs län*. PhD diss., Economic History, Uppsala University, 1979.
Isacson, Maths. *Vardagens ekonomie: Arbete och försjörjning i en mellansvensk kommun under 1900-talet*. Stockholm: Gidlunds, 1994.
Johansson, Johan Erik. *Reglementeringen i Stockholm*. Stockholm, 1918.
Lindström, Jonas. *Distribution and Differences: Stratification and the System of Reproduction in a Swedish Peasant Community 1620–1820*. PhD diss., History, Uppsala University, 2008.
Myrdal, Jan. *Barndom*. Stockholm: Norstedts, 1982. *Childhood*, translated by Christine Swanson. Lake View Press, 1991.
Nässtrom, Nils Gustaf. *Mitt Dalarna*. Stockholm: Askild & Kärnekull, 1972.
Norstedts Rabén multimedia. Söder i våra hjärten: Människor och miljöer i Stockholm 1870–1930. 1998.
Olsson, Daniels Sven. *Falun Minne*. Falun: Stiftelse Store Kopparberget, 2010.
Rydberg, Viktor. Snöfrid. In *Anthology of Swedish Lyrics from 1750 to 1915*, trans. Charles Wharton Stork, 106–110. New York: American-Scandinavian Foundation and Oxford University Press, 1917; reprinted Great Neck, NY: Granger Book Co., 1979.
Sjöberg, Sven. *Vår by: Gammalt och nytt om Solvarbo*. Borlänge: Borlänge Bokhandel, 1957.

Sporrong, Ulf. Dalecarlia in central Sweden before 1800: A society of social stability and ecological resilience. In *Linking social and ecological systems*, ed. Fikret Berkes and Carl Folke, with Johan Colding, 67–94. Cambridge: Cambridge University Press, 1998.

Sporrong, Ulf. The province of Dalecarlia (Dalarna): Heartland or anomaly? In *Nordic landscapes: Region and belonging on the northern edge of Europe*, ed. Michael Jones and Kenneth R. Olwig, 192–219. Minneapolis: University of Minnesota Press, 2008.

Sundwallson, Fredrik I. *Gustafs år 1850*. Gävle: Dokument på Lantmäteriverket i Gävle, 1996.

Veirulf, Olle, ed. *Dalarna: ett vida berömt landskap*. Stockholm: AB Svensk Litteratur, 1951.

Wedin, Maud, ed. *Det skogfinska kulturarvet*. Falun: FINSAM, 2001.

6 Gunnar the Outsider

With his new identity uneasily in place, 16-year-old Gunnar Myrdahl began his studies at the prestigious Norra Real gymnasium in Stockholm in January 1915 (see Figure 6.1). The family settled into a new apartment on Kungsgatan in Norrmalm, near the central business district and not far from Gunnar's school. During the first decade of the century, city officials had authorized the demolition of a poor neighborhood that had previously stood there. Kungsgatan was transformed into an elegant thoroughfare, lined with apartment and office buildings, connecting two major commercial centers. The street was wide enough to accommodate streetcars, motor cars, bicycles, and numerous pedestrians.[1]

Gunnar observed that most of his new classmates were from the upper classes, boys from old families with a sprinkling of the sons of wealthy entrepreneurs. The faculty was excellent and included several men with doctoral degrees. Even though the school was preparing young men from the elite for leadership positions, the students knew that their place in society was contested. Within sight of Norra Real gymnasium lay Norra Bantorget, soon to be called "Red Square" because workers' marches culminated in front of the People's House, where Branting and other socialist leaders addressed large crowds.[2]

The desire to enroll Gunnar in one of the country's top secondary schools seems to have been a major factor in Carl Adolf's decision to move the family from Köping to Stockholm. There was no prospect of Carl Adolf earning money in real estate, as he had a decade earlier, because the city's housing market had collapsed at the beginning of the war. It is not clear how he made money before 1917. That spring Carl Adolf took advantage of the distressed real estate market to buy an estate north of Stockholm, and the next year he purchased a second estate on the tiny island of Lidingö just north of the capital. He, Sofie, and the younger children lived there until the fall of 1919. When the housing market showed signs of recovery, Carl Adolf moved the family back to central Stockholm, installing them in an apartment in a building he purchased; the commercial street was being widened, and he expected property values to rise.

Figure 6.1 Gunnar Pettersson/Myrdahl as a gymnasium student, 1915. Portrait by Westman Studio, Köping and Arboga. Courtesy of Alva and Gunnar Myrdal's Collection, Arbetarrörelsens Arkiv och Bibliotek, Stockholm, Sweden.

Gunnar stayed put in order to concentrate on his studies, renting a room from the parents of a school friend so he could be near Norra Real during his last year of gymnasium and moving to another rented room when he entered Stockholm University in the fall of 1918. In October 1919, he agreed to help his father manage the building he bought in exchange for living in a basement apartment by himself.

At Norra Real, Gunnar quickly discovered that he was regarded as an outsider by the most of the students, who came from elite backgrounds. So he found a small circle of friends from middle class, upwardly mobile, or modest families. Fritz Thorén, his closest friend, was the son of a factory manager in Stockholm and was considered the most gifted student in the class. An intellectually intense young man who exerted a quiet charisma, he was nicknamed "Franciscus" because of his supposed physical resemblance to St. Francis of Assisi. His passion was science, and he spent many hours in the school's laboratory. Gösta Lundborg, another friend, was the son of a carpenter. Their circle also included Sven Tissell, whose parents ran a boarding house for gymnasium students where Gunnar lived.[3]

Although he had little time for extracurricular activities, Gunnar participated in the student Christian organization during his years at Norra Real. While his academic compositions offer ample evidence that he was questioning Christian doctrine, he liked singing in the choir and enjoyed the fellowship with other young men. The youth movement had started in 1908 among university students in Uppsala who sought to revitalize the state church, which had lost ground among educated people because of the rise of science and secularism and among ordinary Swedes on account of the rapid growth of the free church movement and socialism. The religious awakening had spread quickly through the "crusade" of 1909–1910, when students went out into the countryside to evangelize under the motto "Sweden's people—a Godly people." One of their mentors was J.A. Eklund, bishop of Karlstad, known for his battles against the free churches and socialism.[4]

The movement supported the Conservative effort to build up Sweden's defenses against a possible attack from Russia. When Karl Staaff's Liberal government declined to increase the nation's military budget early in 1914, a bishop headed a campaign to raise the funds to buy the navy a modern battleship, contributing to the crisis that culminated in the fall of Staaff's government. In opposition to Christian pacifist and Social Democratic attacks on the military, as well as Liberal budget-cutting in the army and navy, the Young Church movement espoused a doctrine of the church militant, defending Sweden, the Lutheran "light in the North," against the threat of Russian "barbarism." During the war, Eklund was openly sympathetic to Germany.[5]

In later years, Gunnar remembered mainly his doubts about religion and claimed that he had challenged Eklund on the theory of evolution at a meeting of the Christian gymnasium movement, based on his reading of pro-Darwin polemics by the German naturalist Ernst Haeckel and the Swedish botanist, secularist, and socialist Bengt Lidforss. Although he liked to remember himself as an anti-religious dissenter, he earned As in Christian education class, and he seemed to reflect Eklund's influence in a school composition that portrays the Church of Sweden as a bulwark of social order against free church sects and socialism. The state church formed a cornerstone of the *Storsvensk* (Great Sweden) ideology that Gunnar espoused during his gymnasium years, which exalted Sweden's warrior kings, celebrated the nation's brief period as a great power in the seventeenth century, and saw Swedes as the bearers of a culture superior to those of their neighbors in the Baltic region.[6]

Gunnar Myrdal's years at gymnasium, 1914–1918, coincided with World War I, but the war seldom impinged on the lives of these privileged students during its first three years, and the boys were insulated from the hardships that affected many Swedes in 1917–1918. Initially most upper-class Swedes saw Imperial Russia as their most dangerous enemy, since Russia had been the last country to invade Sweden when it seized Finland and the Åland Islands in 1809. They favored a neutrality policy with strong trade links to Germany. The Church of Sweden also had close cultural ties to the German Lutheran church. The king's consort was a German princess and niece of Kaiser Wilhelm II, and much of the aristocracy sympathized with Germany. The Swedish elite expected that the war would end with a German victory or a negotiated settlement that enhanced Germany's power. Those who espoused *Storsvensk* ideology could praise Sweden's ancient institutions and independence, yet feel an affinity with Germany as a Lutheran bulwark against Russian power to the east.[7]

Geopolitical Realism

At Norra Real, Gunnar had an extraordinary teacher who became the first of several father figures to whom he attached himself. John Lindqvist (1871–1942) had taught history, geography, and Swedish at the gymnasium for a decade when, at age 45, he encountered the 17-year-old. Lindqvist was highly respected for his learning and made his greatest impact as a history teacher. The history that Gunnar had previously learned was a narrative about kings, heroes, and battles designed to inculcate nationalism, patriotism, and civic obedience in schoolchildren. Lindqvist, a student of the Enlightenment, emphasized rational statecraft and the rule of law and admired Montesquieu's theory of balanced government. What most impressed Gunnar was his teacher's realistic approach to history, the tough questions he asked about how states pursue their national interests, his ability to place Swedish history in the context of international geopolitics, and his dispassionate analysis of the strengths and weaknesses of Swedish kings and political leaders.

Despite his admiration for representative government, Lindqvist was no friend of socialism or universal suffrage. His political views fell comfortably within the range of the Swedish establishment, whose rule had been threatened by the Great Strike of 1909, the rise of the Social Democrats after the expansion of male suffrage in 1911, wartime demonstrations and hunger marches, and the Bolshevik Revolution in Russia and ensuing civil war in Finland. Gunnar believed that Lindqvist was skeptical of democracy and thought that popular majorities were often wrong. His teacher was known not only for his brilliance and breadth of knowledge but also for his charm, sense of humor, and remarkable ability to get the best out of students. Confident of the power of reason to correct political error, he firmly but patiently guided his pupils toward leadership positions in a political, economic, and cultural elite that was besieged from below.[8]

In his essays for Lindqvist's classes in Swedish history from the Imperial Age to the closing years of World War I, Gunnar developed historical realism, narrative skills, and an interest in questions of bias, objectivity, and perspective. This new scholarly viewpoint was in tension with the penchant for hero worship, the nostalgic view of Sweden's century as a great power, and the romanticized picture of Swedish culture that had been instilled in him. In a January 1917 essay on "The Enlightenment," Myrdal sketched out his vision of the historical era when the ideal of reason guiding state policy commanded attention in Europe.

He began with a sharp contrast between the uniformity of belief enforced by religion that made the early seventeenth century an age of "ignorance and superstition" and the scientific discoveries of Copernicus, Galileo, Harvey, and Newton, which emphasized the vital importance of observation and empirical research. The extension of inquiry to societal and political questions led to a profound shift away from philosophical idealism and a questioning of absolutist and ecclesiastical rule. Myrdal set up a debate among Montesquieu, whose concern for civic responsibility he admired; Voltaire, the exponent of reason and "enlightened despotism"; and Rousseau, who emphasized the power of the emotions.[9] The student's triumphal account of the Enlightenment's breakthroughs in political and social thought is notable for its omission of the philosophes' discussion of natural rights and the democratic strain of Enlightenment thought that accelerated during the French Revolution. The Enlightenment remained a touchstone in Gunnar's thinking, and his conception of its significance eventually came to include the questions of rights and equality raised by the American and French revolutions. For the young Myrdal, however, the lesson was clear: educated men should use reason to guide the political and social development of the masses, who were not ready to govern themselves.

An essay on "The People of Dalarna" reveals that his emerging historical realism and advocacy of rational statesmanship was in conflict with passions and sentiments that were deeply rooted in his family background and upbringing. At times sentimental, at times ironic and satirical, the essay reflects both Gunnar's pride in the Dalecarlian tradition of stubborn independence from authority and his desire to win Lindqvist's respect. The central question he addressed was how Dalarna, imagined as the "heart of Sweden" and known for its people's patriotism, became infected by popular movements, including religious nonconformity, temperance, and socialism. Dalecarlians' most prominent characteristic, he contended, was a love of freedom. He conceded that the desire for independence "sometimes can go to excess and degenerate into contempt for and hatred of discipline and authority." But the Dalecarlian peasant "is not meant to obey, . . . he is not meant to be a proletarian or cannon-fodder."[10]

Why had "poisonous" movements appeared among this virtuous and intelligent people? While Myrdal acknowledged that farmers had legitimate grievances, he blamed outside influences. Dalecarlians had previously been "rather untouched by the outer world and its culture." Then poverty had driven thousands of them to emigrate to the United States, and kinship ties virtually "built a bridge over the Atlantic." Advancing a highly dubious argument for the sake of maintaining his belief in the essential character of his people, he blamed letters from their American kin for exposing Dalecarlians to religious sects, the temperance movement, and socialism. Gunnar contended that the "folksoul" needed a "fixed point," a "power of higher origin." Radical newspapers had stirred the excitable Dalecarlians with facile slogans.

These popular movements had mobilized the same love of freedom that Gustav Vasa had awakened centuries before. Yet the farmers did not understand that "contempt for authority was the movements' innermost driving force." Both socialism and the temperance movement "go so far as to declare the wants of the masses as law," Myrdal warned. But "every step forward for these . . . popular movements means a decline of the inherited love of freedom, birthplace, and country." In a ringing peroration, he affirmed that "every patriot's wish must be that the subversive forces should not reach deeper than the surface, so that the folk soul's good powers should be able to awaken a reaction, a reversal which shall carry the old ideals and way of thinking to honor among the people of Dalarna." No doubt John Lindqvist smiled as he awarded an "A" to this passionate outpouring of youthful romanticism. It clearly did not meet his standards of scholarly objectivity, but the writing style was witty and engaging, and the young author showed promise.

Under Lindqvist's guidance, Myrdal developed a more critical understanding of the interplay of economic interests, domestic politics, strategic military thinking, geography, and diplomacy, as well as the actions of "great men," in shaping history. Moreover, his mentor required students to address historiographical issues and matters of bias in interpretation. Although admiration for Swedish kings seeps through in some of Myrdal's writings, his essays are notable for their disciplined analysis of the balance of power among European nations, the interplay of political and economic forces within a nation state, and the frequent incompatibility between a country's ambitions and its economic, natural, and human resources. In the introduction to one essay, Myrdal acknowledged that "no historical writing can be so objective that it is not at least partly colored by the viewpoint and sympathies of its author." Indeed, a historian's bias shapes the form and style of the narrative so completely that it often leads to false conclusions. In the worst case, a historian interprets a previous era through the assumptions of his own time.[11]

In an essay on the half-century of parliamentary ascendance in Swedish politics that is retrospectively called the "Age of Freedom," Myrdal traced the trajectory of popular opinion from disgust with royal absolutism and militarism to support for a complex four-chamber parliament to the realization that the country needed a strong executive balanced by a more coherent parliament and limited by the rule of law. Although Enlightenment ideas of the rights of man were publicly debated for the first time and a broader spectrum of the citizenry was represented in the farmers' chamber, the "unwieldy" governmental structure led to power being concentrated in the council and a Riksdag committee of 100, which met in secret. In Myrdal's opinion, the result was not the rule of law but corruption. Inevitably, power devolved from the Riksdag to the higher ranks of the bureaucracy. "Then, as always," he commented shrewdly, "it was difficult for them to tell the difference between their own interest and the state's." "The lack of political insight among the people" was part of the problem. But "the most significant cause" was "the undeniable incompetence of the kings, who should have asserted their power and thereby reached a sound political equilibrium" with the Riksdag. Not coincidentally, Myrdal ignored the fact that during the "Age of Freedom" Sweden's population and commerce had flourished.[12]

The Place of Small Nations in the World

By the fall of 1917, the effects of the European war were reverberating in Gunnar's daily life. In a letter to his maternal grandmother, he described how dark Stockholm was at night. Coping with midwinter darkness was hard enough, but the shortage of oil and gas meant that the city was able to light few streetlights. "The people, who wade around in the puddles without galoshes, are miserably thin." Gunnar reassured his grandmother that he and his brother Robert had enough food because their boarding house had bread and butter, pancakes, and meat they could stretch by putting it in soup. Gunnar knew that he was fortunate to be in school. His mother's youngest brother, Adolf, who was the same age, had been drafted.[13]

Leading a regimented life of study in the protected quarters of his school and boarding house, Gunnar had little time to read the newspapers, and in any case the Swedish papers gave a limited view of what was going on in Europe. Like most Swedes, Gunnar did not recognize the growth of nationalism in Central and Eastern Europe and did not grasp the significance of U.S. President Wilson's advocacy of the right of nations to self-determination. Instead, Gunnar assumed that the European great powers would survive with most of their current territory intact. He wondered what role Sweden might play after the war. As he tried to look at the matter objectively, with a critical eye to the balance of power among states, he experienced an inner conflict between his romantic Swedish nationalism and his newfound historical realism.

Searching for a new conceptual framework for understanding world politics, Gunnar was strongly influenced by his reading of Uppsala political scientist Rudolf Kjellen (1864–1922), who represented the Conservative Party in the Riksdag. Kjellen's 1905 masterpiece, *The Great Powers*, offered Swedish readers a view of global politics that was breathtaking in scope and analytically complex.[14] This magisterial study surveyed eight great powers on three continents, including their complex rivalries and interdependencies in the global economy, imperialism, and exploitation of natural resources. In contrast to classical liberals, Kjellen saw states as vast "organisms" that competed with each other. Each had "evolved" according to its own dynamic. He contended that one must comprehend "subjective factors, the peoples' understanding of themselves and their environment," before one could comprehend the struggle for economic, political, military, and cultural dominance. In addition, he sought to measure the great powers' relative strengths according to certain "objective" criteria: geographical position, economic resources, population growth, racial composition, social conditions, military capacity, and constitutional and legal structure. Kjellen eschewed determinism, whether economic, geographic, or racial, in favor of complex, multicausal explanations. In a constantly shifting, uncertain universe, he contended, the political scientist can analyze institutional patterns, economic tendencies, and political and social trends, but cannot predict their outcomes.

As a citizen of a small state that had not been "great" for 200 years, Kjellen considered how the great powers treated both the minorities within their borders and their smaller neighbors. He differed sharply from many of his contemporaries who viewed European "races" as fixed types. Aware that history had always produced blends of different peoples, he thought that new national "personalities" were being shaped in countries as different as Germany and the United States. Although he envisioned a possible end to European dominance and saw potential greatness in several Asian countries, he shared the assumption of most Europeans of his time that Black Americans would not be assimilated into the new personality that was rapidly consolidating the descendants of peoples of northern and western Europe in the United States. Kjellen admired strong leaders, such as Theodore Roosevelt and Kaiser Wilhelm II, who intervened confidently in world affairs and extended the influence of their nation states.[15] To read Kjellen in 1917 was to see in bold relief the instability of the world before the war. He portrayed the great powers as sometimes pursuing their self-interest but sometimes guided by impulses that had been shaped by their distinct cultures. The conservative theorist assumed that the strong would continue to dominate the weak, as they had throughout human history, and that conflict was inevitable.

Gunnar eventually moved beyond Kjellen's conservatism and his assumption that nationalism was a natural phenomenon, but Kjellen had a lasting influence on his thought. As long as he was performing for Lindqvist, Gunnar's geopolitical analysis was measured and disciplined. But he wrote with greater audacity in his university years, especially in his speeches to student debating clubs and organizations. Henceforth, the young Myrdal saw politics on a global stage and resonated to Kjellen's breadth of vision, multicausal analysis, and sense of contingency. He shared the assumptions that state regulation of the economy was most conducive to national progress and that strong men at a nation's helm could be decisive. It was getting the right mix of economics, politics, culture, technology, and military power that mattered. Although he came to advocate reforms from a position of expertise, Gunnar always approached reform movements with a certain skepticism. A strong, idealistic movement was not enough: a small state or subordinate group had to recognize its interests and align them with those of other states or groups to win power and bring about change.

In late 1917 and 1918, Gunnar was most concerned with the question of how Sweden, which had escaped damage through its neutrality policy, could assert itself diplomatically, economically, and culturally after the war.[16] In an essay on "Small Nations' Contributions to World History" written in November 1917, he suggested that the historical examples of the Greeks, Romans, and ancient Jews proved that well-organized, disciplined small states with clear goals could enjoy their independence and have a disproportionate influence in a world dominated by great powers. Echoing Kjellen's categories, Myrdal postulated that, for a nation to exert an influence beyond its numbers, it needs strong natural resources, a good geopolitical location, talented people, "good social attitudes," skill in trading, and, above all, agreement on the "national 'mission.'" It is necessary "to organize" society so that "the thousands of component forces" function together in the national interest. "First, it must be maintained that the state comes before the individual." Second, reform must not be allowed to "degenerate" into "experimentation." Finally, Myrdal asserted that "democracy" is justified if it means equality of opportunity, but if it is artificial it is damaging to the country and the free operation of the labor market. Sweden had the requisite strategic location, abundant natural resources, and "good folk material," but Swedish leaders lacked "historical and realistic perspectives" as well as the "positive goals" needed to achieve greatness.[17]

Gunnar's *realpolitik* informed a critique of a manifesto published in a Swedish political science journal in October 1917 calling for a "United States of Scandinavia." His reply demonstrates his devastating ability to take apart opposing arguments, expose hidden assumptions, and find inconsistencies in the use of key terms, skills he later used to powerful effect in intellectual and political debates. Gunnar made no effort to conceal his contempt for what he regarded as the authors' enormous capacity for "self-deception" as they glossed over real differences of interest among the states with empty rhetoric about Scandinavian unity. He began by raising the fundamental question of whether a "convergence of interest" existed among Norway, Sweden, and Denmark. While the Norwegian and Danish economies were highly dependent on exports, Sweden had a greater capacity for self-sufficiency. The nation would be best served by preserving its sovereignty and strict neutrality. He then demolished the manifesto's impractical constitutional proposal that the three nations' parliaments select a president from among the countries' kings for a five-year term. The president would have no cabinet or council, and laws would have to be passed by all three parliaments. Myrdal underlined the fact that Sweden, which had the largest population, land area, and natural resources, would be treated as an "equal" of Norway and Denmark under the plan. He rejected any measures that would reduce Sweden's influence and thought it only natural that it should dominate Finland, which, with its "Swedish culture and partly Swedish population, together with many interests of state in common with ours," would make a more suitable partner than "our neighbors to the west."[18]

A couple of months before his graduation, Myrdal considered "Sweden's Contributions to History" in a sweeping essay that argued for the international importance of Swedish culture. Lacking some of the restraint and balance of his previous essays for Lindqvist, he gave voice to a full-throated Swedish nationalism. With its wistful account of lost empire, braggadocio about Sweden's contributions to science and the arts, and broad assertions of the supremacy of Swedish culture to others in the Baltic region, this piece is the clearest expression of *Storsvensk* ideology that he produced.

Myrdal was careful not to make any explicit argument based on scientific racism, although such views were common at the time. He contented himself with an indirect claim: "It has been said that our people are of higher quality than others." Taking this nationalistic view for granted, he continued: "If one understands this, one should not be surprised that our forefathers reached a political influence which we dare not dream of." He then traced the process by which the Swedish kings pushed out from the original kernel of Svealand to conquer the Baltic coast of Finland, bringing it up to "the same level . . . as the motherland itself." During the late Middle Ages, Sweden had been attacked by the Danes, who sought to incorporate it into a Greater Denmark. Revisiting the heroic saga of Gustav Vasa, Gunnar offered a romanticized account of peasant rebellions, which "showed that the Swedish farmer culture of the North had not been completely undermined by feudalism and priestly rule." Sweden's participation in the Thirty Years' War should be seen not as a religious matter but rather as a defense of the Baltic provinces against the Holy Roman Emperor's ambitious plans of conquest. Sweden had become "a great power with its Baltic empire unchallenged." Alas, Sweden's time as a great power had lasted less than a century. While conceding that Sweden was too small and too weak to hold an empire, Myrdal suggested that a "collection of unfavorable circumstances" was also to blame. In the succeeding two centuries, the kingdom's contributions to science and the arts had exceeded its political importance. Although he did not advocate future military adventures, he contended that Sweden could have greater "influence" internationally if its leaders focused more shrewdly on advancing its interests. "In a word," he concluded, "we lack the realistic historical perspective of positive state goals in our politics."[19]

While Myrdal called for historical realism, in this essay he gave way to romantic ideas about Swedish kings and Dalecarlian farmers, lavished uncritical praise on Swedish imperialism, and advanced a tendentious account of the past. During a painful chapter in European history in which the slaughter had continued on the Western Front and Swedes had suffered from hunger during a severe winter, Gunnar took refuge in the Golden Age of Swedish history and offered a paean to Swedish cultural superiority as a compensation for the loss of great power status. Despite the essay's failure to address issues of biases in historical analysis, flaws in strategic thinking, and the human capacity for "self-deception" that his protégé had raised in earlier writings, Lindqvist awarded it an A.

On May 15, 1918, Gunnar Myrdal passed his final examinations for graduation from gymnasium, a goal that fewer than 5 percent of Swedes attained and that no one in his family had ever come close to reaching. He could now don the coveted white cap that signified membership in this tiny elite (see Figure 6.2). Most gymnasium graduates went on to become university students, then leaders of society.

The next day, the graduates gathered at a dinner to honor Dr. John Lindqvist at a restaurant on the island of Djursholm. Several students collaborated in writing a lengthy tribute in blank verse, and Gunnar, the principal author, stood and delivered it. In the poem, we get a glimpse of Gunnar's deep longing for the ideal father he never had. The devoted protégé praised not only Lindqvist's logical reasoning, realism, and patriotism, but also his sense of humor, which lightened the burden of living up to his exacting academic standards. The teacher had shown infinite patience in the face of manifold student transgressions, enduring their silly "plans/ Of bettering the world," advocacy of "Revolutions" and "Demonstrations," truancy, and neglected homework. He assured his mentor that "none of us shall ever forget" his kindness and faith in them. In times of adversity, when others thought ill of them, they would be able to draw on their memories of the teacher "who earlier held us in high estimation." "You are and shall be our lives' working capital."[20]

In lavishing adulation on his teacher, Gunnar brought his own career at Norra Real to a triumphal end. He had long dreamed of being an orator, and this was the most successful—and certainly the funniest—flight of

Figure 6.2 Gunnar Myrdal wearing a student's cap upon his graduation from Norra Real gymnasium, May 1918. Portrait by Vasa Studio, Stockholm. Courtesy of Alva and Gunnar Myrdal's Collection, Arbetarrörelsens Arkiv och Bibliotek, Stockholm, Sweden.

oratory he had ever produced. Only three and a half years earlier, he had entered the prestigious gymnasium as a lonely boy from the provinces with a new name, in search of his teachers' and fellow students' respect. That summer, it was Gunnar's turn to be toasted by Carl Adolf at the villa he was repairing north of Stockholm, and the father had a chance to show off his son in the white cap on a visit to their relatives in Solvarbo.

Social Evolution

For Gunnar, the first year of university brought wrenching change. He found the law school curriculum narrow, highly technical, and inhospitable to the free-ranging intellectual inquiry he had tasted at Norra Real. It left little room for the imagination, speculation, or bold assertions; its only value was in providing a route to future security and a chance for a leadership position in government. He also felt cut off from the sense of community gymnasium had offered. Now he lived alone in a small room in central Stockholm. Stockholm University was housed in buildings scattered throughout the central part of the city, not on a campus where he could meet students who were pursuing other subjects. Gunnar found many of his fellow law students superficial, lacking any concern for larger questions.[21]

To mitigate his sense of isolation, Gunnar fell back on his small circle of friends from gymnasium: Gösta Lundborg, Sven Tissell, and Fritz Thorén. Fritz, now studying chemistry, was by far the closest. The two spent many hours talking about science and how scientific thinking might be extended to social analysis. Later in life, when Gunnar pondered why he had lacked a stable political viewpoint during his undergraduate years, he concluded that "I was under the dominance of Franciscus, who was not interested in these questions."[22]

Fritz started an informal debating club in 1918 that often met in the back room of a cheap Stockholm restaurant. One of the young men would give a talk and the others, well lubricated with beer, would then try to tear it apart. The club offered Gunnar one of the few paths open for broader intellectual discussion during the first year of university, and he came to be considered its cleverest debater. That fall Gunnar spoke on the revolutionary implications of Darwin's theory of natural selection for contemporary society. He had come to Darwin a couple years earlier through reading the German biologist Ernst Haeckel, whose books shaped had the public understanding of evolution in continental Europe at the turn of the twentieth century.[23] In his oration before the student club, Gunnar spoke of sweeping away the "metaphysical cobwebs," a phrase he repeated ten years later in critiquing the science of economics.

Haeckel had been one of the earliest champions of Darwin's theory of natural selection in Europe during the 1860s. Like Thomas Henry Huxley in Britain, he explored the implications of Darwin's theory of natural selection for human evolution even before Darwin himself. In the late nineteenth century, Haeckel produced volume after volume placing humans' descent from apes in the broad context of the evolution of the entire range of species. Some of his most important work was in embryology, and he was best known for the idea that the various stages of embryonic development repeat the stages of the species' evolution from earlier life forms. His most popular book, *The Riddle of the Universe at the Close of the Nineteenth Century*, asserted that science had provided "answers" to most of the questions that had perplexed philosophers for centuries. The universe was composed of "congregations of atomic elements swimming in a sea of ether" governed by the laws of the conservation of matter and energy. Ruling out any notion of a soul or mind independent of matter, he considered psychology a branch of physiology and contended that empirical research offered scientific explanations of psychic states and behaviors previously thought to belong to a "spiritual" realm. Both the German word for soul, *die Seele*, and its Swedish cognate, *själen*, had a broad range of meanings—mind, spirit, psyche, personality—to denote the inner emotional life and unique feelings of each individual and were often used in a nonreligious context.[24]

Haeckel saw peoples as constantly evolving, although in different stages and at different speeds. Like most of his contemporaries, he assumed that a hierarchy of races was part of the order of nature. He opposed "anthropocentrism," the idea that humans were unique. The human brain allowed people to develop faculties that differed in degree, but not in kind, from the apes. Yet "the difference between the reason of a Goethe, a Kant, a Lamarck, or a Darwin, and that of the lowest savage, a Veddah, an Akka, a native Australian, or a Patagonian, is much greater than the graduated difference between the reason of the latter and that of the most 'rational' mammals, the anthropoid apes, or even . . . the dog, or the elephant," he concluded. Monistic materialism taught the unity of nature, which demanded that the scientist specify "psychic gradations" from ape to savage to genius. Weighing in on the age-old question of whether or not humans have free will, he concluded that "the human will has no more freedom than that of the higher animals." While he disparaged religion as a foundation for morality, Haeckel rejected Nietzsche's conclusion that there must be a new morality to replace Christian ethics. Instead, he thought that science substantiated much of traditional morality and that natural selection not only fostered self-preservation but encouraged cooperation to promote the welfare of the group.[25]

Gunnar Myrdal, like many of his generation, resonated with Haeckel's blunt attacks on religious dogma and anthropocentric theories of nature. But what did this mean for the future of humanity? Haeckel's all-embracing theory of monism and celebration of the advance of science implied a certain optimism about the ability of humans to use reason to understand the world and improve themselves and society. Gunnar was less sure about that. When he took up the question of human evolution in 1918, he accepted Haeckel's idea that humans are subject to drives and instincts that have frequently been overlooked by "civilized" people, but he did not assume that these characteristics would lead to continuous progress. Teasing out the various mechanisms of natural selection, Gunnar noted that in the struggle for existence it is not always the strongest or the most clever that win: it is sometimes a case of one "out-eating" or out-breeding the other.[26] Myrdal was closer to Darwin than Haeckel in regarding evolution as an indeterminate process of adaptation rather than purposeful development toward perfection.

Gunnar's remarks on Darwin signal his growing interest in ethical uncertainty and his conviction that the universe has no inherent purpose or goal. He had come some distance from his celebration of the Enlightenment philosophes' advocacy of rational statecraft as a Newtonian science. But he was sparing in his discussion of humans, even in the context of a free-wheeling debating club. In his first paper for Lindqvist two years earlier, Gunnar had lauded the scientific revolution for stimulating a century of enormous progress in political and social science. Darwin and Haeckel made into him a materialist who saw humans as animals rather than spiritual beings, but he was much more cautious in assessing the implications of Darwinism for the social sciences.

Gunnar, Fritz, and their generation were fascinated by Friedrich Nietzsche's nihilism, contempt for traditional religion and morality, and concept of the superman who is "beyond good and evil." Nietzsche's writings had created a sensation in Scandinavia. August Strindberg was one of the first Swedish intellectuals to be attracted to Nietzsche, and his Promethean heroes were shaped by the Nietzschean superman. Nietzsche freed the hero from the necessity of fighting on behalf of humanity and the cause of justice, dismissing the myths of national heroes and the imperatives of Lutheran morality that Gunnar had been fed in school. Although Strindberg had rejected Nietzsche by the end of the 1890s, Nietzsche's writings continued to appeal to Swedish university students in the aftermath of World War I.[27]

Gunnar, a troublemaker who had learned to conceal his anger and rebelliousness beneath the façade of a dutiful, patriotic, and studious youth, resonated powerfully to Nietzsche's idea that guilt and "bad conscience" were man's instincts turned against himself. He had always wanted to be some sort of hero, and Nietzsche offered the tantalizing prospect that a superman did not have to subordinate his ego to a noble cause. Yet the Uppsala philosopher Axel Hägerström, a legal realist who rejected notions of natural law and based legal concepts on experience, observation, and experimentation and also explored problems of ethical relativism, had a far greater impact on Gunnar.[28]

By the middle of his first year at university, Gunnar was not sure that he believed in anything. As a schoolboy he had learned to play the dutiful son, spout the patriotic nostrums expected by most of his teachers, and learn his Catechism. Lindqvist had taught him realism in the application of the scientific method to the social sciences, but the gymnasium teacher's Enlightenment-based concept of reason was not a blunt sword to be used to hack away at all institutions and traditions. He assumed that his students would defend the family wealth they would inherit and the institutions they might be selected to lead, but they were supposed to do this in a far-sighted and "responsible" way that considered the needs of the entire community. Self-advancement would be held in check by a sense of stewardship, often formulated in patriotic language. But Lindqvist had not really addressed one of the most basic issues of political economy, especially what contemporary upper- and middle-class Swedish writers paternalistically called "the social problem": how are the great mass of poorly educated people to be made capable of earning a living in the market economy, and how are they to be made "responsible" citizens? Darwin had complicated the issue by bringing in the drives and instincts embedded in humans by natural selection. Kjellen had seen nations as organisms growing in unpredictable ways that might or might not be brought under control by wise statecraft. Nietzsche had exalted the irrational in humans and questioned whether any order at all could be imposed on nature or the social world. Hägerström had suggested that humans must collaborate in constructing all moral values and social institutions, none of which were natural.

Depression

During the winter of his first year of legal studies, Gunnar was overcome by anxiety and severe depression. "I felt as if I were experiencing the breakup and dissolution of my personality," he recalled in a letter to Alva six months later. His head had continued to throb throughout the spring:

> An overcast sky can bring me right down. For no special reason and often as a result of rainy weather, I used to feel very anxious and uneasy, a terrible sense of emptiness, remorse without cause, a senseless despair. It was like a pressure against my temples and made my fingers twitch nervously. I was scared of mirrors. In them I came across a pair of unknown, restless, staring eyes whose anxiety just made me even more anxious. I was pathetically frightened of people, often took circuitous routes to avoid running into acquaintances. I could not sit still, had to keep walking, walking—wandering aimlessly through narrow, dark streets where I would be less likely to meet anyone and where the risk of "malevolent eyes" on the back of my neck was therefore less. (G to A, Aug 9. 1919)

The idea of "malevolent eyes" was an old one in Swedish folklore. "Evil eyes" were thought to give one person magical power over another and had even been attributed to the dark and melancholy woodsmen of the Pers clan in Solvarbo, from whom Gunnar's father was descended. In this case, however, Gunnar saw "malevolent eyes" in his own reflection in a mirror, a visage that appeared strange, unfamiliar, and frightening. But he also feared that the "malevolent eyes" of others had the power to pierce through the back of his neck. Retrospectively, Gunnar would label these feelings a "clear case of persecution complex!" At the time, however, they were terrifying. He "sometimes felt tears choking [me], melancholy squeezing [my] heart."

Gunnar invoked a familiar metaphor when he complained about "the assault of the depression 'trolls.'" These fabled creatures in Nordic mythology represent the dark side of human nature, the evil instincts and desires that can take over a person and rule him, keeping him from understanding his true self and isolating him from the rest of humanity. Trolls were often portrayed as tiny but powerful beings that lived deep in the forests or in mountain caves. For Gunnar, who had heard many such stories as a child in Dalarna, the trolls served as a powerful symbol of depression because they have the capacity to make humans see only ugliness where there is beauty.[29] In Ibsen's *Peer Gynt*, a troll princess explains to Peer that in the world of the trolls "black seems white and ugly seems fair." In the spring of 1919, Gunnar Myrdal, like Peer Gynt, dwelled in a world that had suddenly been inverted: darkness replaced light, fear squeezed out trust, and terror extinguished hope.

Gunnar poured out his fears and anxieties to Franciscus, who had been his closest friend for four years. Fritz, he later said, had an "extraordinary nature." Gunnar looked up to Fritz as a scientist who was searching fearlessly for the truth, not a hired advocate twisting the facts to suit the interest of his client. Looking back on their friendship in his 80s, Gunnar made an extraordinary confession: "Neither before nor after have I come to be so submissive to the dominance of another person."[30]

We gain insight into this time in Gunnar Myrdal's life from Fritz Thorén's first novel, *En Son*, which was published under the pseudonym Fredrik Thomas, a pen name bearing the same initials as the author and whose protagonist, Gerhard Melcher, has the same initials as Gunnar Myrdal. Next to Gunnar's correspondence with Alva, Fritz's novel offers the most detailed picture we have of the milieu in which Fritz and Gunnar moved at Norra Real, Stockholm University, and the cold, indifferent city around them. The novel's protagonist bears a striking psychological resemblance to the young Gunnar. Fritz, who earned a PhD in chemistry and taught the subject in gymnasium for many years, did not publish *En Son* until 1936, but the novel vividly recreates the world of a lonely student during and shortly after the Great War. Gerhard Melcher, Fritz's protagonist, does not resemble Gunnar physically, and his family background differs. Despite his brilliance, he lacks the drive that ultimately made Gunnar successful academically. Like Fritz, he is a scientist whose worth is not fully appreciated by those in power because he lacks the guile requisite for success in university politics and in the world of corporate-sponsored research. But Fritz's protagonist, like Gunnar Myrdal, is compulsively introspective and subject to cycles of anxiety and depression.[31]

Fritz's "G.M." is most like Gunnar in his relentless self-monitoring, his obsessive self-preoccupation, and his earnest efforts to view himself with a studied scientific detachment. Gerhard Melcher is a divided self, so fond of analyzing his psychological states that his frenzied periods of self-scrutiny are often followed by dejection, indifference to those around him, and an inability to act. Like Goethe's young Werther, this character is too sensitive to live in the world. He understands too much and feels emotion too intensely to persist in such a hostile universe, and this *bildungsroman*, like Goethe's, ends with the protagonist's suicide.

The title *En Son* suggests that this novel is about the "sins of the father"—and, in Gerhard's case, the mother as well—being visited on a precocious and hypersensitive son. Fritz's "G.M." grows up in Stockholm. His father, Albert, is a charming salesman in the city's most elegant fabric store and a seducer who can quickly turn his rapt attention from one customer or mistress to another. A man of humble origins and limited education, Albert has a certain energy and craftiness as well as an appreciation for the city's nightlife, especially the large music halls where strangers meet. Gerhard's mother, Kristina, is an innocent country girl and daughter of a district judge and rich farmer. She visits Stockholm during a summer vacation, meets Albert at a boarding house, and embarks on a romance. When Kristina returns to her parents' home in the country at the end of the summer, she discovers that she is pregnant. She has an illegal abortion, which she considers to be murder, then returns to Stockholm to confront Albert, who has forgotten about her. Kristina proposes marriage and, although Albert is reluctant, he sees the advantage of getting financial support from her father. Albert starts his own store with help from her family, and Kristina gets pregnant again and has Gerhard, who was conceived to atone for her sin. Although he keeps up a brave appearance, the dapper Albert never succeeds in business and is frequently away from the family on business trips. He has affairs with various women, but his wife stays with him, taking refuge in a private religious cult of suffering. Kristina tries to find in her relationship with her talented son the bond that is missing in her marriage and gives birth to a second son while Albert is away. The guilt-wracked mother frightens both of her sons and never caresses them because she wants them to "respect" her. Albert, for his part, convinces himself that his wife has ruined his life by forcing herself on him, buying him, then turning cold and driving him to other women. He finds it convenient to believe that Kristina has taken all his energy, preventing him from achieving anything.

Gerhard feels like a "stranger" in his parents' house and hides under a pillow at night when he hears them arguing. One night he ventures out of his room amidst an argument and sees his father strike his mother with his elegant cane. Albert takes his son to a hotel for a night and then gives him five kronor, a handsome gift for a boy, when they return home the next day. Gerhard learns to keep silent and withdraw into his own world. He now fears opening the door to his room and seeing an unnamed Other Person. As he grows older, the boy develops techniques for avoiding intimacy and dependence on his parents. Withdrawing further into himself, he evades responsibility and refuses to face problems. Like Gunnar, Gerhard finds a temporary escape by rushing out of his parents' apartment into the streets of Stockholm and walking aimlessly for hours. Young Gerhard believes his father is strong and feels that "the son of a strong man must himself become strong." The narrator tells us that a "secret understanding developed between the two, and Gerhard attached himself to his father with a devotion filled with shame." On the son's first day at an elite Stockholm gymnasium modeled on Norra Real, his father walks him to school with great pride, thinking of how his own mother had taken him along to a "poor little elementary school." Now he is taking his son to gymnasium, the first step toward a distinguished career! "Mr. Melcher felt a moment of jealousy toward his own son, but he immediately thought: 'May I just live long enough to be his support'" (46–47).

In gymnasium, Gerhard develops a new academic persona that he feels is disconnected from his own unworthy self. He trembles at his first oral exam, and when he begins answering the teachers it is as if someone else were talking. "How strange it was to be called simply 'Melcher.' It was as if they were not talking to him but to a person who certainly was not a little boy but something much more important. A person whom Gerhard did not know, but for whom he must take responsibility." Gerhard remains a "stranger" to the other boys at school. When he shows little interest in student clubs and parties, he is derisively "classified" as "one of those study-machines of proletarian origin." He throws himself into scientific courses, finds a second home in the gymnasium's laboratory, and dreams of becoming a scientist, engineer, and inventor. Gerhard attends Stockholm's Technical University and, though still alone, begins work on what he calls an "accumulator," a machine for storing data and calculating sums, an invention he hopes will bring him fame and wealth.

Gerhard loses first his father, then his mother, and falls into depression, failing an exam for the first time. He throws all his time, money, and energy into manic work on his accumulator. In the city, he walks the back streets and hides in alleys to avoid running into people. When he goes home, he feels like a stranger in his attic apartment, which holds some of his parents' furniture. An insomniac, he takes sleeping pills and drinks. "All the time, a voice spoke within him: 'calculate, my little boy. Just amuse yourself. You know, in any case, that you will . . . never take your exams and never be able to create your accumulator.'" A second voice says, as his mother often had: "You are beginning to get a certain look in your eyes. . . . Come and lie down." Gerhard, who had tried to keep both of his parents at arms' length when they were alive, now feels their spirits remorselessly pressing in on him. He sees their lives as "two completely dreadful stories." Would his life be worthless too? How does he "create something valuable out of his existence" when he does not feel "capable" of doing anything? (182)

Gerhard is neither Gunnar nor Fritz, but Fritz drew on both of their life experiences in creating his character. Gerhard's persona as an obsessive but unsuccessful inventor draws on Fritz's own experiences, but Gerhard's emotional life is much closer to Gunnar's. We leave Gerhard here, a depressed, uncertain, and lonely 19-year-old with great ambitions but equally strong fears that he is not emotionally capable of realizing his aspirations. We shall return to Gerhard later, but now we resume our story of 20-year-old Gunnar battling his own demons as he completed his first year at university.

Student Politics

Gunnar prepared a rousing speech to deliver on the Swedish version of Walpurgis Nacht. On the evening of April 30, young people build bonfires to celebrate the coming of spring and fortify themselves with liquor in the hope of driving away any evil spirits lurking in the darkness. Gunnar drafted his speech for presentation at the Valborg celebration held by Stockholm University students in front of an enormous bonfire on a hilltop on Djursholm, the forested island where he had made his oratorical debut. The city was illuminated by a dozen conflagrations to celebrate the ebbing of winter's darkness, the rebirth of spring, and the awakening of youthful spirits.

Gunnar's address belongs to the genre of speeches that Swedish university students gave to their clubs, a tradition going back to the 1840s. In these orations, the student is presented as a Romantic hero, taking over from a faltering generation to carry civilization to new heights. Since university students were a minuscule group, these speeches were not a call for democracy, but the hero was supposed to speak for the people and rise above petty self-interest. For Gunnar, this genre carried associations with Goethe's *Faust*, Rydberg's "Snöfrid," and other Christianized versions of ancient Nordic myths, and recalled Prometheus, who was punished by Zeus for bringing fire to the earth. Six months after the end of the Great War, however, it was not easy to convince a cynical generation that the nation and the world awaited their heroism. The customary metaphors are there: youth, renewal, creativity, and heroic individual action on behalf of the public good; but so is worry that the effort will not be enough. The post-Darwinian view of humans as animals driven by emotions and instincts, more of a herd than a collection of individuals, fostered anxieties that humanity was not evolving to a higher level and that people were impervious to rational arguments. Gunnar's own depression merged with the cultural pessimism of the time to cast doubt on whether students could lead the renaissance he tried to summon. His ponderous and overblown style undercut his message.

The would-be orator depicted contemporary Sweden as a decaying civilization dragged down by mediocrity and the empty rhetoric of equality. University students offer the only hope, but even they are tainted by their nation's decline. "It is said that we are the sons of an aging generation," Gunnar's speech commenced. Most young Swedes lack the capacity to experience intense feelings and "to think freely and widely" like the bards and sages of old. Youth's "eternal fires of joy and rapture burn ever more faintly" in this generation. Some would say that "the intoxication, which this evening fills our souls with a feeling of joy, of freedom, of pride, truth and strength, might just be a matter of wine and spring fever." But the spirit of Valborg is not mere intoxication, he proclaimed with a hint of demagoguery. The "freedom" of the student "gives him his pride, the courage to think his own thoughts, . . . to hold nothing sacred except truth and beauty." "The student mind is mine and yours," and "in our stronger moments, we dream of making it the mind of the many."[32]

Yet no sooner had Myrdal invoked the populace than he recoiled. Freedom makes the student "impudent—bold enough to view his age with historical irony—daring to consider its modern prejudices and holy phrases as empty and ephemeral as those of the past, although shielded by the hoarse and heady 'yes' shouted by the masses." The student rejects the merely utilitarian and embraces more complex and profound truths. Scoffing at those who have "the soul and heart of the shopkeeper," Gunnar grandiosely declared war on mediocrity. Lamenting that "our present time hates everything great, everything . . . that breaks away from equality and grayness," he boasted that "I want to talk even more arrogantly." "We shall never forget that it is our duty to shape our surroundings according to us and not the other way around." "We don't need the world, but the world needs us." A year after his triumphal toast to Lindqvist, Gunnar penned these final words: "I raise my glass to the students—I do this in the firm intention of never myself betraying my proud words."

Yet these "proud words" were never uttered. We know them only because the manuscript survived in the papers of his younger brother, Robert. Did Gunnar lose his nerve at the last moment? In the text of this speech, he anxiously expressed his hope that those gathered before him would "not contemptuously scorn me." Was he paralyzed by fear, or was he shoved aside by the rowdy students and prevented from speaking? We shall never know. The Valborg address, exposing some of Gunnar's hidden insecurities and anxieties, contrasts sharply with the confident tone of his essays. The text of the speech he did not deliver gives us a glimpse of how powerfully Gunnar had to struggle to chase away his demons and nurture the voice of willed optimism that became so important to his mature writings.

Three months later Gunnar recalled his rebound from depression: "The whole month of May my head was full of student politics and I had no time to be sad." (G to A, Aug. 29, 1919) He attended meetings of the largest student organization, but the upper-class young men who dominated the group had no use for him, and he concluded that student politics "smacks of social climbing." (G to A, March 19, 1920) Then, with Fritz's encouragement, he submitted a less frothy but equally audacious version of his proud challenge to youth in a letter to the conservative newspaper, *Svenska Dagbladet*. In response to pessimistic comments by the chairman of the Stockholm University student organization about the students' "lack of idealism" and "profiteer ethic" engendered by the war, Gunnar claimed that student "philistinism" was of long standing and now made the student "a beautiful bastard of old-fashioned tradition and current intellectual emptiness and moral baseness." In addition to the general trend toward pursuit of material self-interest, he blamed the university curriculum, which failed to stimulate "broader, more fundamental" thinking. In his critical examination of student culture, Gunnar found two disturbing developments: the members of the army reserve officer corps "too often represented the polished and stand-offish spiritual poverty" of the age; and the students' "entertainment is beginning to be stamped by a culture which, if it is culture, . . . is the emptiest and most intellectually barren that can be conceived." Vulgar mass entertainment contributed to a "uniformity and leveling" process through which students had lost "the intellectual atmosphere which is the students' proper air." Gunnar nevertheless proclaimed it the "glorious duty of youth and students to hope for and believe in the new and in the future," signing off as "G.M., Student 1918."[33]

According to plan, a letter from Fritz appeared in the same newspaper the next day, in which he thanked the anonymous "G.M." for his perceptive criticism of student decadence. While not as flamboyant in his writing style, Franciscus echoed Gunnar in attributing the low level of student culture to excessive specialization of the curriculum. He touted his little discussion circle that gave lonely students an opportunity for "hearty friendship that knits them together for life" and promised to "be the embryo for . . . a real student renaissance." An unidentified "G.A." wrote in the following day to say that the situation was even worse than "G.M." had stated. The problem, according to this writer, lay in the dominant role that law students played in the student organization. They were more materialistic than other students, and their hegemony marginalized students from both humanistic and scientific disciplines.[34]

The letter-writing campaign concluded a week later with a manifesto on "Raising Student Culture," initialed by Gunnar, Fritz, Sven, and three other friends. The letter's fervent tone, conservative rhetoric, and unabashed advocacy of meritocratic elitism suggest that Gunnar was the primary author. It agreed that there was indeed a crisis in student culture caused by "democratic leveling" and the excessive specialization of the curriculum, but predicted that a new wave of thinking would be transformative. "The age of democracy breaks down ancient barriers of lineage, sex, and class, sometimes to the advantage of the whole society, sometimes not." Standards must be maintained "if the national culture is not to be put at risk." The process of equalization "does not extend to knowledge, capability, or talent," and leadership by men of merit is urgently required. If today's student is to assume the responsibility of civic leadership, he must attain not only "knowledge of a certain subject area calculated to earn his bread" but also a broader education and enhanced concern for the public interest. Students must bring about a "cultural renewal" if they are to achieve "victory over the times' turbulent desire for leveling." Since many questions now at issue in the public debate among all classes were previously "decided by authority," students have a "duty" to shape public opinion.[35]

As Gunnar emerged from a searing experience of anxiety and depression in the spring of 1919, this letter-writing campaign was an act of calculated optimism. He had failed to establish himself as a presence in student politics, but his letters had been published in one of the country's two leading newspapers. Gunnar gave notice to conservative readers that he was ready to lead a cultural and intellectual awakening among students that would reclaim their heritage from philistinism, cynicism, and seduction by cheap entertainments. His generation, which had entered the university during the last two years of the war, emerged with a more "far-sighted," "comprehensive," and socially responsible vision that was needed to lead Sweden through the dangerous era of universal suffrage.

In this last letter, Gunnar rehearsed a rhetorical strategy that he used throughout his career. He warned conservatives of impending disaster if educated men of vision did not take command and act in the public interest. But Gunnar was a self-appointed leader without a following. Only a handful of his friends were willing to endorse this project. Recognizing that his foray into student politics had led nowhere, he remarked that "I was never intended to be one of the student association bigwigs, anyway." Still, Gunnar had managed to strike back at the student leaders who had spurned him and taken up the role of social critic. If he could not be a knight or Viking hero leading a band of warriors, he could at least be more "far-sighted" than his contemporaries, exposing the shallow materialism of the day. The young orator felt called to something higher, if only he could summon the courage to reach for it.

Inside his family the web of interdependency grew ever tighter, as Gunnar agreed to manage an apartment building owned by his father in the fall. He would have an apartment to himself on the ground floor, and the rest of the family would live in an apartment on the second floor. This arrangement would provide some distance from Carl Adolf, but not enough. His parents had no idea of the psychological torture he had experienced that spring. He had to resume his balancing act of holding in his anger at his father and playing the role of the dutiful son in order to finance his education.

At the end of this tumultuous year, Gunnar and two of his friends from gymnasium, Gösta Lundborg and Sven Tissell, set off on a bicycle trip through Södermanland. This much-needed vacation from their studies and escape from their parents took them through the beautiful countryside near Lake Mälaren at Midsummer—the longest day of the year, when Swedes celebrated at least twenty hours of sunlight.

Notes

All translations were done by the author.

1 Erseus, *Kungsgatan*, 40–85. On this prestigious gymnasium, see Svedelius, *Norra Real.*
2 Andersson, Gunnar Myrdal. Hellbom and Gullers, *Stockholm*, 92.
3 Andersson, Gunnar Myrdal.
4 *Svenskt biografiskt lexikon*, available on line from Riksarkivet.
5 Frängsmyr, *Svensk idéhistoria*, vol. 2, 254. Skoglund, *Vita mössor under röda fanor*, sees the Young Church movement as part of a reactionary wave during this period.
6 Beyer, *Bengt Lidforss.* Andersson, Gunnar Myrdal, 13–15; Gunnar Myrdal, Dalafolket, AGMA; Gunnar Myrdal, Sveriges insats till historien, 191, AGMA; Program, Högre Realläroverket på Norrmalm, Reformationsfesten, AGMA.
7 On *Storsvensk* ideology, see Zander, *Fornstoradager, niodernå tider.*
8 See biographies of John Mauritz Lindqvist (1871–1942) in *Svenska män och kvinnor* and in *Svenskt Biografiskt Lexikon*, vol. 23, 529–530. Gunnar Myrdal et al., Tal för Doktor John Lindqvist, AGMA.
9 Gunnar Myrdal, Den s.k. Upplysning, AGMA.
10 Gunnar Myrdal, Dalafolket. See Näsström, *Mitt Dalarna.*
11 Gunnar Myrdal, Karl XIIs ryska politik, AGMA.
12 Gunnar Myrdal, Grunddragen av Frihetstidens statsskick, AGMA. See Lagerroth, *Frihetstidens författning*; Roberts, *Age of Liberty.*
13 Gunnar Myrdal to Anna-Lisa Matsson, Dec. 7, 1917, quoted in Andersson, Gunnar Myrdal, 18.
14 Kjellen, *Stormakterna.*
15 Kjellen, *Stormakterna*, vol. 1, 21–27; vol. 2, 87–100.
16 Andersson, Gunnar Myrdal. See Elvander, *Skandinavisk arbetar rörelsen.*
17 Gunnar Myrdal, Small nations' contributions to world history, AGMA.
18 Gunnar Myrdal, critique of article, Utkast till föreningslag för Skandinaviens Förenta Stater, AGMA.
19 Gunnar Myrdal, Sveriges insats i historien.
20 Gunnar Myrdal, Tal för Doktor John Lindqvist.

21 G to A, Nov. 30, 1919, AGMA.
22 Andersson, Gunnar Myrdal.
23 Richards, *Tragic Sense of Life*, xvii–xix, 217–276.
24 Haeckel, *Riddle of the Universe*, 90.
25 Haeckel, *Riddle of the Universe*, 124–127, 130–131; Richards, *Tragic Sense of Life*, 267–276, 401–402.
26 Gunnar Myrdal, Historisk, AGMA.
27 Lagercrantz, *August Strindberg*; Borland, *Nietzsche's influence on Swedish literature*, 17–43, 150.
28 Axel Hägerström, in *Filosofiskt lexikon*; Mindus, *A Real Mind.*
29 For a psychological analysis of trolls in Scandinavian mythology and their role in Peer Gynt, see May, *Cry of Myth*, 175–188.
30 Andersson, Gunnar Myrdal, 25.
31 Fredrik Thomas (pseudonym of Fritz Thorén), *En Son*. The page numbers in parentheses that follow direct quotations refer to this novel.
32 Tal av Gunnar Myrdal sista april 1919 på Skansen [Hölls dock aldrig], AGMA.
33 G.M., student 1918, Modern studentkultur: Stockholms studenter och de ideala intressena, *Svenska Dagbladet*, 6 May 1919.
34 F.T., student 1918, Studentkulturens dekadans, *Svenska Dagbladet*, 7 May 1919; G.A., *Svenska Dagbladet*, 8 May 1919.
35 G.M., F.T., B.L., J.A., B.K., S.T. (students admitted to the university in 1918 and 1917), Studentkulturens höjande: En kollektiv meningsyttring från de yngre, *Svenska Dagbladet*, 17 May 1919. Gunnar later identified the other authors as Fritz Thorén, Bertil Löfström, Josef Almqvist, B. Karth, and Sven Tissell.

References

Alva and Gunnar Myrdal's Collection (AGMA). Arbetarrörelsens Arkiv och Bibliotek (Swedish Labour Movement's Archive and Library). Stockholm, Sweden.

Correspondence between Alva and Gunnar Myrdal, 3.3

[cited as: G to A or A to G, date]

Gunnar Myrdal's professional activities, 4.2

Gymnasium essays

Gunnar Myrdal, Dalafolket (The people of Dalarna). Norra Real, 1917.

Gunnar Myrdal, Den s.k. Upplysning (The so-called Enlightenment). Norra Real, Jan. 13, 1917.

Gunnar Myrdal. Karl XIIs ryska politik (Karl XII's Russian policy). Norra Real, Nov. 15, 1916.

Gunnar Myrdal. Grunddragen av Frihetstidens statsskick (The main features of government during the Age of Freedom). Norra Real, May 2, 1917.

Gunnar Myrdal. Critique of article, Utkast till föreningslag för Skandinaviens Förenta Stater, *Statsvetenskaplig Tidskrift*, Oct. 1917, written Nov. 1917.

Gunnar Myrdal. Small nations' contributions to world history. Norra Real, Nov. 21, 1917.

Gunnar Myrdal, Historisk (on Darwin). 1918.

Gunnar Myrdal, Sveriges insats till historien (Sweden's contributions to history). Norra Real, Mar. 1, 1918.
Speeches
Program, Högre Realläroverket på Norrmalm, Reformationsfesten. Oct. 31, 1917.
Gunnar Myrdal et al., Tal för Doktor John Lindqvist. Norra Reals studenters högtidsfest på Hasselbacken den 16 maj 1918, uppläst av. G.M.
Robert Myrdals Arkiv, 4.6
Tal av Gunnar Myrdal sista april 1919 på Skansen. [Hölls dock aldrig].

Manuscript

Andersson, Stellan. Gunnar Myrdal: Barn och ungdom år (Childhood and youth). Arbetarrörelsens Arkiv och Bibliotek, Stockholm.

Published Sources

Ahlberg, Alfred, ed. *Filosofiskt lexikon*, 3rd ed. Stockholm: Natur och Kultur, 1951.
Beyer, Nils. *Bengt Lidforss, en levnadsteckning*. Stockholm: Norstedts, 1968.
Borland, Harold H. *Nietzsche's influence on Swedish literature*. Göteborg: Elanders, 1956.
"Eklund, Jonas Alred." *Svenskt biografiskt lexikon*. Available on line from Riksarkivet.
Elvander, Nils. *Skandinavisk arbetar rörelsen*. Stockholm: Liber förlag, 1980.
Erseus, Johan. *Kungsgatan: Ett sekel på Stockholms paradgata*. Stockholm: Max Ström, 2011.
Frängsmyr, Tore. *Svensk idéhistoria*, vol. 2. Stockholm: Natur och Kultur, 2000.
Haeckel, Ernst. *The Riddle of the Universe* (1901), trans. Joseph McCabe. Buffalo, NY: Prometheus Books, 1992.
Hellbom, Thorleif, and Peter Gullers. *Stockholm: Om livet på torgen*. Uppsala: Gullers Bild, 1996.
Kjellen, Rudolf. *Stormakterna*, 2 vols. Stockholm: Hugo Gebers Förlag, 1905.
Lagercrantz, Olof. G.H. *August Strindberg* (1979), trans. Anslem Hollo. New York: Farrer, Straus & Giroux, 1984.
Lagerroth, L. Fredrik B. *Frihetstidens författning*. Stockholm, 1915.
May, Rollo. *The Cry of Myth*. New York: Norton, 1991.
Mindus, Patricia. *A Real Mind: The Life and Work of Axel Hägerström*. London: Springer, 2009.
Näsström, Nils Gustaf. *Mitt Dalarna*. Stockholm: Askild & Kärnekull, 1972.
Richards, Robert. *The Tragic Sense of Life: Ernst Haeckel and the Struggle over Evolutionary Thought*. Chicago, IL: University of Chicago Press, 2008.
Roberts, Michael. *The Age of Liberty: Sweden 1719–1772*. Cambridge: Cambridge University Press, 2003.
Skoglund, Crister. *Vita mössor under röda fanor: Kulturradikalism och bildningsideal i Sverige, 1880–1940*. Stockholm: Acta Universitatis Stockholmiensis, 1991.
Svedelius, Carl. *Norra Real, 1876–1926*. Stockholm: Norstedts, 1927.

Svenska män och kvinnor, ed. Nids Bohman and Torsten Dahl. Stockholm: Bonniers, 1949.

Thomas, Fredrik (pseudonym of Fritz Thorén). *En Son*. Stockholm: Norstedt, 1936.

Zander, Ulf. *Fornstoradager, niodernå tider*. Lund: Nordic Akademisk Press, 2001.

Part II

Alva and Gunnar

7 "Faith is that which the heart trusts"

Gunnar was in good spirits as he and his companions set out on bicycles from the Pettersson family's villa to Södermanland. He had recovered from the depression that had stalked him in March and April and was escaping from the isolating grind of legal studies. Since Fritz did not come along, Gunnar was the group's dominant personality. The young men stayed at farms, usually sleeping in barns, and Gunnar wrote to his parents that he found the people friendly. They were given coffee, soup, and meat in exchange for entertaining people. Gösta painted portraits of farm women and walked on his hands to amuse the children. Gunnar played his lute and sang like a troubadour, recited poetry, and made funny faces for the children. He was able to relax, and seemed better able to reach out to others.[1]

The youths' white caps identified them as university students. Although the disheveled travelers looked like hoboes, Gunnar assured his parents that they felt like a prince, a field marshal, and an archangel! In Strängnäs, they ran into two tramps, and Gunnar was "glad that I had my revolver in my pocket"—the only record there is of his possessing a firearm. Their progress was slowed to a crawl by three days of constant rain that filled the deeply rutted roads with mud; they were soaked and quite discouraged when a churchwarden let them take refuge in a parish church. But the trio cycled on toward Eskilstuna, pausing occasionally to look at factories and old churches. Since it was raining again, Gunnar reported that they were hoping to find "some farm around here and settle down for the night sleeping on corn husks in a barn."

The farm they found was Slagsta. Early the next morning, Albert Reimer woke up his children with the news that three university students had stayed in the barn and asked Alva and Rut to take them coffee and rolls. Gunnar was instantly drawn to Alva, then 17, a slender, blonde young woman with engaging blue eyes. He found her self-confident and happy, with a mischievous sense of humor and a keen intelligence. Alva was struck by this lanky university student with dark blond hair and playful blue eyes. She had never met anyone quite like him: brilliant, wide-ranging in his interests, but funny.[2] A photograph taken that morning (Figure 7.1) shows Gunnar, Alva, Sven, Alva's sister Rut, and Gösta

Figure 7.1 From right to left: Gunnar, Alva, Sven Tisell, Rut Reimer, and Gösta Lundborg, Slagsta Farm, June 1919. Courtesy of Alva and Gunnar Myrdal's Collection, Arbetarrörelsens Arkiv och Bibliotek, Stockholm, Sweden.

leaning against a wooden fence at Slagsta farm. Gunnar is next to Alva and has eyes only for her. In another photograph taken that day or the next (Figure 7.2), Gunnar, Alva, and his friends are sitting on a straw stack in the farmyard.

Alva had to go to work that day at the Eskilstuna Town Hall, but she arranged to meet the students for lunch. Eating pastries, Alva and Gunnar talked about books, and she caught him in a lie when he claimed to have read a book that he had not. Later that day, she cycled with them to a town ten kilometers away, after asking Rut to tell their father she was going to visit a friend. It was a daring step for Alva to deceive her father, but conveniently Lowa was away, and nothing was said. The following morning Alva cycled home, excited over her adventure. Writing to his parents, Gunnar remarked cryptically that he had a "very nice" time in Eskilstuna and would write more later.

Before the young men continued on, Gunnar wrote to Alva and asked for something that seemed impossible. Addressing "our sister Alva" and writing "under the supervision of my friend Gösta," he sent their thanks. Sven Tissell had left them, having had enough rainy weather and perhaps lacking the necessary temperament to "take each day as it comes." The

Figure 7.2 From top to bottom: Gunnar, Alva, Sven Tisell, and Gösta Lundborg, Slagsta Farm, June 1919. Courtesy of Alva and Gunnar Myrdal's Collection, Arbetarrörelsens Arkiv och Bibliotek, Stockholm, Sweden.

lovestruck Gunnar had been singing to Gösta about "*das ewig Weibliche*," the Eternal Feminine, a reference to the final scene of Goethe's *Faust* in which the penitent sinner is forgiven and taken up to heaven amid a celestial chorus. The two students invited Alva to join them on their tour, suggesting that she take her bicycle on the train to the station at Dala-Floda, from which the three of them would cycle through Dalarna. (G to A, June 19, 1919) Alva may have been pleased to be associated with Goethe's paean to the everlasting virtue and sympathy of women, as well as keen on an adventure, for she accepted the invitation. Due to a "remarkable stroke of good fortune," Lowa was still away at a rest home, Albert had been persuaded that Alva was going to visit two female friends, and the town clerk's office gave her two weeks of vacation. Before she left, Alva wrote Andreas Arnesen, her Norwegian pen-pal who had planned to visit her in Eskilstuna, and asked him to call off his trip.[3]

Alva, Gunnar, and Gösta bicycled through Gunnar's native province, staying in barns or empty summer cottages and eagerly discussing books and ideas. Alva loved the beautiful and sparsely settled landscape, with forested mountains and valleys next to the wild river. One day Gösta left the two of them alone to pick up something he had left behind. Alva and Gunnar stayed up the whole night talking under the canopy of stars and felt themselves drawing closer. On Gösta's return, Gunnar proposed that they visit Solvarbo, where his parents were spending the summer. They sent their bicycles ahead by train, and Gunnar and Gösta constructed a raft on which the three of them floated down the Dalälven. It was the kind of adventure that Alva had dreamed of since her father had read her *Huckleberry Finn.*

Gunnar's parents, Carl Adolf and Sofie, were delighted with Alva and introduced her to their many relatives in the village. The Peterssons and the Reimers were similar in their rural background, customs, and work ethic, and Alva felt welcome as they stopped for coffee in various homes and visited the mill that Sofie's father had managed. Alone, Gunnar and Alva talked for hours about their dreams for the future. The long summer days were the perfect setting for an explosion of emotions that neither had felt before. The anxieties of fall, winter, and spring seemed to vanish with the darkness as Gunnar and Alva felt that they were creating a world of their own, marking this moment as the beginning of a new epoch in their lives and sealing them off from other concerns. Alva referred to it as their "enchanted" summer, with a magic they later struggled to keep alive.

Only after Gunnar had introduced Alva to his family did he dare to touch her. They were outside on a beautiful evening. With some hesitation, he laid his head on her lap, looking up to the heavens, and she stroked his hair. The following day, Gunnar recalled, "I felt very unhappy for some reason, but I did not know why. But the next night I impulsively went into the room where Alva slept and kissed her. At that moment, the ice was broken, and we lived in a happy world of love."[4] When a smith gossiped in the village that he had seen the couple sunbathing nude on the bank of the Dalälven, Gunnar's maternal grandmother went straight to the man, shamed him, and told him that he should not speak ill of Gunnar and Alva. The couple did not have sexual intercourse that summer, but Alva later wrote that she felt that she had "given" herself to Gunnar in Dalarna.

Their bliss was rudely interrupted when Gunnar received a telegram from Albert Reimer demanding to know where Alva was and insisting that she return home immediately. Lowa had come home and made quite a fuss. She was worried sick about her daughter's safety and horrified by how Alva's absence might look to their neighbors and relatives. The next day, Alva took the train back to Eskilstuna. Albert met her at the station, and the two walked home along the country road without much conversation. Albert had not known what to say, but Lowa did.[5] It was three months before Gunnar and Alva were able to meet again.

Gunnar and Alva began an extraordinary correspondence that allowed each of them to explore the self, discover the other, and strengthen the relationship through long separations. Taking joy in crafting romantic apostrophes to Alva's beauty, moral virtue, and uniqueness, he labored like a "miner" in search of a rich vein of words to explore "the emotional life's subterranean world." (G to A, Aug. 1, 1919) Alva, sharing a room with Rut in the new house that Albert had built at Slagsta, managed to find the privacy she needed to plumb the depths of this love, share her feelings with Gunnar, and respond to his graphic and sometimes jarring descriptions of the fear and depression that burdened him. They struck a multitude of poses, revealed different sides of their personalities, and experimented with a variety of writing styles as they sought to express their shifting emotions and respond to the other's revelations.

Their correspondence is characterized by an intense focus on their own emotions and feelings about each other to the exclusion of the larger world. Alva and Andreas Arnesen had written about politics and world affairs, often feeling like spectators unable to act effectively on their youthful idealism. Alva's letters to Gunnar rarely mentioned politics, on which they had quite different perspectives. They took no notice of the difficult economic conditions or the widespread class conflict in postwar Sweden. Instead, the letters nurtured the love that had blossomed that summer. Gunnar had never written to a young woman before, and initially he imitated the language of the Romantic man of feeling.

Autumn Rains and Psychological Honesty

"With every fiber of my being and every nerve in my heart, I long for you," Gunnar assured Alva in his first letter after they parted. Admitting that it was hard for him to express his deep love for Alva in writing, he claimed that his brain was accustomed to organizing his thoughts into logical systems built on abstractions. Gunnar contrasted his longing for Alva with the depression that had immobilized him the previous winter: "My hollow-eyed anxiety last winter pulled me out of balance so far from the normal." Depression had brought thoughts of suicide, "but thank God, my new mental illness is so filled with desire that I, for all the world, do not want to be 'healthy' again." He spent a good part of each day sitting on a stone in the Dalälven at a spot that he and Alva had visited, gazing at the river rushing over a waterfall, reading, and singing folksongs. His lovesickness made him seem remote to his family, and his sister Mela told him that he was acting pretty "crazy." His great consolation was the "certainty that you also long for me." Gunnar expressed his gratitude to Alva for "five hot nights and five sunny days." Now "every day's final goal . . . is to be one step closer to the time when I get to see you again, hold you in my arms, and kiss you." (G to A, July 12, 1919)

"What have you done to me?" Alva wondered in her reply. "I am no longer the main character in the drama of my life—at least I see you much more clearly than I see myself." She marveled at the intensity of their love. Alva clung to the memory of their time together, trying to keep "everyday trivialities" at a distance. Her longing and the pain of their separation only made her love more pure, she attested. Phrasing her romantic declaration in stilted, somewhat archaic language, she promised that in the

> moment when we shall again taste the bliss in the expression of our love for one another, then I shall look into your eyes and see what I hold most dear, then I shall be caught up in the power of your embrace, then I shall find solace in your kisses; in that moment you may perhaps perceive how dear you are to me. Until then, we can but yearn and remember. I have only one great thought, you; one great yearning, you; one great memory, you. (A to G, July 18, 1919)

Gunnar continued to press her to visit him, and in mid-August Alva apologized that, owing to parental vigilance, she could not yet make any definite plans. He would have to wait a little longer. She touched on some of the psychological issues they had discussed during their summer vacation. Alva's intense craving for self-revelation had tested the boundaries of her epistolary friendship with Per Sundberg, but with Gunnar there seemed to be no limits on what could be discussed. Everything could be put on the table to be analyzed—or so she thought. Alva did not hesitate to take the initiative.

"You once said that I should not consider religion as something to base a whole life on," Alva reminded Gunnar, "and I certainly do not any longer." Several years before meeting him, "I did think that religion could be seen as the most reliable basis for my life," but psychology had replaced it as her greatest interest. Alva confessed an awkward feeling of "pleasure" at analyzing her friends' problems. Training her analytical powers on Gunnar, she playfully remarked that "when we talked about charlatans . . . , I really thought . . . that you were talking about yourself. It seemed so natural that I didn't even think to mention it." "You certainly have a lot of the charlatan in you, Gunnar," she teased. "Born to deceive—conquer—rule the world, aren't you? Born to laugh at the whole of humanity despotically ruled by you. And this despot—how dear he is to me!" Alva asked him to imagine how it felt for her "to glimpse the vulnerability of the despot himself. . . . Do you wonder if I in my half measures lose myself when confronted with you?" Alva hinted that she had found new purpose as the protector and nurturer of her vulnerable ruler. (A to G, Aug. 15–19, 1919)

Returning to Stockholm, Gunnar answered Alva's letter on a rainy day a week later as he struggled with loneliness. He confessed that depression sporadically seized him, blocking out brighter moments when he fashioned himself as a man of destiny. "You call me strong," but "an overcast sky can bring me right down." Looking back on the previous winter and spring, he recounted in excruciating detail the anxiety and fear that had paralyzed him. Gunnar could not pinpoint any specific cause, but he had suffered from terrible headaches and nervous tension. His mind had felt disconnected from his body. A restless energy had propelled him through dark alleys and strange neighborhoods as he tried to lose himself. Filled with dread, guilt, and despair, he had been terrified that his self was dissolving. Then, pulling himself back from this vivid depiction of his prior mental state, Gunnar sought to reassure Alva—and, perhaps, himself—that "all that was a long time ago." Looking back on how he had weathered the emotional gales of April to emerge euphoric in mid-summer, he recalled Viktor Rydberg's poem "Snöfrid," in which the Norse goddess had steered the stalwart young Gunnar's boat through a snowstorm, helping the lad resist various temptations until he arrived at the "Isle of Felicity." Had he not met her that summer, he asserted, "I would have been pathetically anxious during these three days of rain. But how can I be unhappy, now that I possess your love? I held it up like a crucifix against the assault of the depression 'trolls'—and it helped." (G to A, Aug. 26, 1919)

Gunnar had done a fair amount of bragging to impress Alva during their summer vacation, but as the relationship deepened he began to reveal his insecurities and fears. Alva sought to improve his shaky self-confidence by admiring his exceptional intellectual gifts, reassuring him that he was destined for greatness, and insisting that, despite his fears, he was not "too sensitive" to be effective in politics. Still, Gunnar felt compelled to tell her that he was not entirely sure that he appreciated her humorous characterization of him as a "despot." Indeed, "your wild fantasies regarding my domination of the world frighten me." Gunnar objected that he was too honest to practice the deceptions necessary to gain power. Due to his "overbearing temperament," he often felt "friction" in socializing with other people and so avoided them, diminishing his "possibility of influencing anyone." Gunnar conceded that

> in my moments of arrogance, especially before when I was more ambitious, I have nursed proud plans to change the world. But since then I have discovered that, on the one hand, my thinking is too abstractly negative, and on the other hand, my nerves are not strong enough to stand up to my ideas.

So, like Schopenhauer, he had tried to comfort himself by

> viewing my time and my world *sub specie aeternitatis*. And seen through these remarkable glasses, it appears of very little consequence whether I should ever turn the axis of the earth by a few degrees before I go to my grave, or if I should end up a drunken small town lawyer somewhere, using my talents to help farmers raise their children or resolve their fights.

But those melancholy feelings of resignation had arisen before Alva changed his life. "You have now replaced eternity and I view life *sub Alvae*." Her love for him and their shared dream of creating a new world together had given him a sense of balance and helped him to avoid the extremes of grandiose fantasy and fatalistic passivity.

Although embarrassed that he was writing "the world's worst love letter," Gunnar explained his unsuccessful efforts to view himself objectively. Without Alva's balancing presence, his powers of self-criticism, so important in achieving intellectual rigor, could overwhelm his sense of self-worth. His feeling of being divided between subject and object was a familiar theme in German and Swedish Romanticism. He explained:

> There is something too deliberate about putting pen to paper to write a letter. This deliberateness always has the effect of objectifying me, i.e., I am split in two: one who writes, the object, and another who watches the writer, the subject. Immediately following the split, I, the subject, lose all sense of being able to write. With much anguish, the writing object nevertheless writes word after word, line after line, while the subject, scornfully grinning and uttering the most exquisite insults, informs the object of the emptiness and confusion of what he is writing. Finally, the object loses his temper, throws down his pen and grabs the subject by the roots of his hair, while the subject calmly retaliates by seizing the object by the scruff of his neck and reproaching him for his undisciplined behavior. After a short, vigorous argument, the object realizes his duty, picks up his pen and continues writing still under the same recurring justified scorn.

This humorous reflection led Gunnar to say that "reading your letters makes me shiver with happiness and I treasure them like relics." "But when I pick up the pen, I feel all the more frightened."

Gunnar's outpouring was more than a therapeutic release of repressed emotion. He cleverly crafted this painful confession to lead Alva toward an inescapable conclusion: he urgently needed her: "You talked about how before words never had to mean anything more than words. I discover to my horror that I can never ever give my words sufficient weight and power to mean something else. No, I want to talk to you, kiss you. . . ."

Since he could not find words to express his surging emotions, the only solution was for Alva to visit him as soon as possible. Mixing the practical with the romantic, Gunnar reassured Alva that she was more intelligent than she gave herself credit for and offered to tutor her to prepare for the university entrance exam. "Tell me: you are coming, aren't you? So far everything has worked out so smoothly, all circumstances have worked in our favor ever since that night when chance directed our tired feet to your father's hayloft. Why should that lucky chance [be lost] now?"

She would not be able to come to Stockholm for a while, Alva answered regretfully. Her father was keeping her close to home, and she could see the "common sense" of the decision. Momentarily striking a pose as a helpless girl, Alva claimed not to be a "very sensible person" herself and insisted that she would be crushed with grief if she did not have Gunnar's love. Struggling to understand the depression that Gunnar had described in his letter and examining her own experience, she turned to religious imagery, substituting love for faith as the power that enabled the pilgrim to continue his journey. The central metaphor of Johan Bojer's *The Great Hunger* gave a name to her aching for harmony and wholeness, and she tried to comprehend Gunnar's depression as a loss of illusions and a feeling of emptiness. "As one's strength gives way, despair takes the form of melancholy together with a yearning for an indefinable something: fullness, harmony, holiness perhaps. The soul trembles with the great hunger for the unattainable." Now that she loved Gunnar, she knew that "love gives so much more that even these moments of *Weltschmerz* bring forth a joy that completely outweighs the previous suffering. It is probably the contrast that intensifies the joy, replacing the earlier bitterness." "I chase away that great hunger by summoning forth the image of my soul which is filled with you." (A to G, Aug. 29, 1919) Although Alva recognized that maintaining an image of feminine attractiveness often required cultivating an aura of mystery, she could not resist the intoxicating self-disclosure and mutual discovery that the relationship with Gunnar offered.

Alva was elated when Albert and some other fathers agreed to pay for a private gymnasium course for girls at the Eskilstuna YWCA. More advanced learning was now within her reach, and she dived enthusiastically into her studies.[6] Sometimes, however, Alva yielded to the temptation to portray herself as the sort of woman she thought Gunnar wanted. Even as she steadily moved forward in her quest for a higher education, she thought it prudent to describe her ambition for achievement as a childish fantasy. Responding to Gunnar's demands that she develop her opinions and debate him on all subjects, Alva admitted that "I want to try to match your opinions" and that "my conscience is worrying me in case you overestimate me." She feared that Gunnar's expectations were "too demanding" and he would discover her limitations. "Do you remember that you once a long time ago said that your girl should probably have weaknesses but keep them hidden from you? Given that, every discovery now means a small chip off the ideal."

Alva tried to balance her expression of conventional middle-class femininity with her desires to strengthen Gunnar against depression and to develop her own talents. She confided to her lover the childhood ambitions that she had not dared to disclose to Per Sundberg. Now she cast Gunnar in the role of masculine hero, but drew on the tales and legends they had both heard from childhood to make the point that his strength would enable hers.

Gunnar felt confident enough to write a passionate love letter in response and hoped to prompt Alva to visit him in Stockholm right away. "I have known the happiness of having your being close to me, you, the thoughtful and loving girl of complete, warm and honest character." From the hostility he had experienced from his "enemies" in student politics, Gunnar knew what it felt like to be disrespected, and he assured Alva of his great "respect" for her. Blending his strong physical passion with a longing for her companionship, he affirmed his all-encompassing love:

> Alva, I have held you naked in my arms, I have felt your heart beat, I have kissed your lips and your neck and your shoulders, I have caressed your breasts until I felt your body shudder with voluptuous fear. With the strength of all my passion, the pathos of my idealism, I crave the fulfillment of your sweet promise: soon. . . . During the day I long most for your soul, but now, at night, I lust after your body. But why make that distinction when it is all the same structure? It's you I long for, you and nobody else.

"You are the only person in the world before whom I humble myself," Gunnar insisted. "I am not afraid of the devil or the trolls, but I dread making you unhappy. I have filled my world with a great Ego, which I inhabit like a God. . . ." (G to A, Sept. 4, 1919)

In response to Gunnar's final question, "How on earth will we manage another meeting?" Alva promised that she would come to Stockholm, where Gunnar was resuming his legal studies. She planned to tell her father that she needed to do some shopping in the city. But she felt guilty about lying and struggled with the moral burden it entailed. Resuming their discussion about the psychological processes by which people make ethical decisions, she sought to develop her own standard of ethics instead of blindly accepting her parents' rules. "As soon as I start thinking about morality, I reach such strange conclusions," she mused. "Actions hardly ever matter to me, and the only way I can know the emotions behind them is if they are my own. That is why I apply no general rule to my judgment of the actions of others." These new views, which were strikingly in accord with Gunnar's but quite different from her father's, left

Alva with a "thorn" of pain, which she regarded as punishment for her own sins. Looking back on her spiritual struggle two years earlier, Alva revealed that she used to be preoccupied by the state of her soul and the flaws in her character, but after studying psychology she had given that up. In retrospect it all seemed faintly ridiculous, although she had been in dead earnest at the time. Now she pulled down the walls of rules and regulations that had constrained here. Her only rule was: take the most direct route. Gunnar had filled her great hunger. Alva's introspection and harsh judgment of herself by the standards of external authority gave way to an honest self-revelation to a man who she believed loved her for her uniqueness. Yet she worried that Gunnar had created an impossibly ideal image of her: "Don't do it; it just makes me unhappy, beloved." Closing on a note of reassurance, Alva affirmed that she longed for Gunnar with both "body and soul." (A to G, Sept. 12, 1919)

Through September and October, the couple conspired to meet. Gunnar assured Alva that even if the king invited him to the castle, he would turn down the invitation so he could greet her at the train station. (G to A, Sept. 25, 1919) Alva wished they were on a desert island where they could work both individually and together with nobody else around. She explained that she was trying to make her writing style more simple and direct than the formal style she had learned at school, with its circumlocutions and lack of spontaneity. Alva now saw herself as a more serious young woman and complained that two of her friends had become interested in frivolous things, like romantic movies. Most people lacked balance, she concluded. The exceptions, the only wise ones, were the "harmonious" ones. (A to G, Sept. 21, 1919) Struggling with how to achieve this harmony in a discordant modern world, Alva wondered how two people in love could balance all their needs and desires.

Intimacy and Depression

After more than three months of separation, Gunnar wrote to Alva in late October from his basement apartment in central Stockholm. The rest of his family—Carl Adolf, Sofie, Elsa, Mela, and Robert—lived in a much nicer apartment upstairs. Although his feet felt "like blocks of ice and the temperature is dropping in both my brain and my fingers," his separate dwelling afforded him much-needed privacy (see Figure 7.3). He told Alva that he was writing a speech for a student organization on the psychology of mass politics that characterized the people as deeply irrational and argued for rule by a "party of the intelligent," which he assumed he would lead.

Confronting Alva's comment about the need to achieve a "harmonious" balance, he disagreed with her idea that "the exceptions, i.e., the psychologically healthy, are the harmonious ones." Gunnar then pointed to a major difference in thinking between them regarding the individual's

Figure 7.3 Gunnar as a student at Stockholm University. Courtesy of Alva and Gunnar Myrdal's Collection, Arbetarrörelsens Arkiv och Bibliotek, Stockholm, Sweden.

relationship to society. Alva hoped that individuals could cooperate for the common good. Gunnar, influenced by Darwin and Nietzsche, thought that an "exceptional" person like himself had to create his own inner balance in a world that was inherently full of conflict and disorder. "Harmony in a disharmonious world is impossible [and is] conceivable only in . . . the imaginary and unreal case of you and me finding a desert island," he lectured. One could only struggle to make his own inner life coherent and to bring it into balance with that of the beloved. As for the rest of humankind, Gunnar mocked their delusions and superficiality. (G to A, Oct. 27, 1919)

Referring to Alva's insecurity about her ability to stand up to him in an argument, Gunnar repeated his request that she challenge his opinions with her own. "It was only at the beginning of our journey that I feared that none of the windows of your soul faced me, but later I feared the opposite: that you had kept them open so carelessly that everything inside had blown away." Like many Swedes of his day, he used the word "soul" (*själlen*) not in a religious sense but as a more general term for an individual's unique emotional life. For the agnostic university student, Alva's "soul" was something she had achieved through self-cultivation and independent thought, and he admonished her to be careful not to lose it by absorbing too easily all the influences around her, including his own. "That you with your clear intelligence and wide learning possessed a soul I knew, of course, but imagine my pain when I thought I had discovered that you had suspended your judgment and critical faculty in reference to me. This had to be unnatural since, given the differences in our development, we had to view things differently." Yet, while urging Alva to develop her own opinions, Gunnar could not escape his egocentric tendency to appropriate everything around him. He declared that he prized Alva's capacity for sympathetic understanding and wanted to "make it mine." Ignoring the illogicality involved, he continued in the same vein: "You must nevertheless not lose your 'own possessions,' and if you don't want to do this for your own sake, do it for mine."

Like Alva, Gunnar believed that their intense relationship had so transformed his life that he no longer felt such a close bond with his friends. "I have discovered that I exist in a world sealed off seven-fold from almost everyone, terra incognita. At first it made me deeply melancholy, but now I find a reckless joy in it." Isolated from others, he lived in a "restless" world of books, ideas, and romantic longing. Nothing enabled him to feel that he was actively striving in the world. "Thinking plays quite a different role for me compared to you, because my masculine need for action at present has no other focus. As a result, I walk around constructing, pottering and tidying up my intellectual world day in and day out." Gunnar knew that Alva had read the philosophical idealists and had struggled to bring her own thoughts and emotions into a "harmonious" relationship with an absolute. Now he inverted the process, casting himself as the masculine subject. He flattered his sweetheart that "you have been given a place in this system: Yes, you are the top, the center, the red line, *quinta essentia* . . . you are the absolute, the axiom, the non-derived concept on the basis of and in relation to which the whole of the phenomenal world is arranged." Having so abstrusely pronounced Alva the quintessence of perfection, Gunnar explained why he strove so earnestly to systematize his thoughts and to transform his jagged emotions into a coherent whole. "My lust for power demands that I control and monitor my thoughts." Since he could not live in harmony with society, at least he could "derive an aesthetic pleasure from harmonious, well-adapted and firm processes of thought." In effect, Gunnar was telling Alva that he would epitomize a heroic, masculine subjectivity, constructing a system in which she, the embodiment of the eternal feminine, served as the absolute. While his prerogative as an exceptional man allowed him to claim this Faustian power to think logically and build his own order, what intellectual space was left for Alva?

Gunnar hastened to reassure his beloved that his systematic thought did not prevent him from "enjoying your lovely disorder." "Logic is masculine, while the artistic disorder—which in actual fact is not disorder but an order based on submerged and unconscious principles—is feminine."

> I praise the gods that my Alva does not think systematically. The feminine way of thinking is superior in that it does not get caught in barren fictions . . . as the masculine does, as well as in its ability to find the shortcuts; while the masculine often gets lost among conditions and conclusions, major and minor premises, and . . . takes longer to reach its goal.

Gunnar believed that men and women had different ways of thinking but could learn from each other. "Intuition" was "the property of women," but "the female intelligence" could also proceed by masculine "logic" when necessary. He concluded consolingly, but rather condescendingly: "Therefore, dear girl, do not grieve because you lack a system, because a system is not a goal"; her native intuition would guide her "like a compass."

At this point, Gunnar outlined the difficult balancing act that their relationship would entail for Alva. He wanted her to sharpen her logical capacity while retaining her feminine empathy. He needed her as a debating partner with a fully developed mind so she could engage in dialogue with him. What was at stake was more serious than what most people regarded as mere opinion. "What is an opinion? A thought with an arrow attached! A thought with direction, a thought which includes an aspiration. . . . I am born with an urge to act, with a desire to mold the world around me in my own image, according to my pattern, my ideals." Gunnar insisted that "opinions are always revolutionary, a symptom of dissatisfaction regarding its object. And since I am dissatisfied with everything in the world except you, I therefore have opinions about everything except you." By the same token, "You are also dissatisfied with everything and everybody—except me I hope—and therefore have many opinions." Gunnar urged Alva to develop her opinions as a way of overcoming the power of convention to stifle her personal growth. His own desire to think through and hone his opinions stemmed from "my lust for power: a well-argued point always represents power in our thoughtless world." Opinions are not "dry" abstractions; they "put me at the center of the world and give me the illusion of power to reform." Gunnar thought it would be difficult, even for an "exceptional" woman like Alva, to develop her opinions because they were not joined to the masculine drive for action and power. But he admonished her to try, if only for the sake of self-cultivation.

Gunnar followed this candid disclosure of the inner forces that drove him with a declaration that he no longer found the world so "dreary" now he had fallen in love with Alva. "Your love does not hold me back, does not weaken me, but develops and strengthens me," he affirmed. "I am now so much happier and calmer than before, in spite of your being so far away and of my restless longing." The "pain and sorrow" of her absence were surpassed by his feelings of "joy, joy that you exist and that you exist for my sake."

The patterns established during the first three months of their relationship proved to be both enduring and troubling. Gunnar disclosed his self-doubt, anxiety, and depression, but his love for Alva gave him hope, and his confessional letters to her were a powerful outlet when he was depressed. Alva reassured him of his potential for greatness and urged him to be "strong" when he lacked self-confidence. He tried to encourage her as well: he valued feminine intuition, but urged her to develop her own ideas. Most tellingly, what gave him the deepest joy was "that you exist for my sake." For Alva, that declaration had a particularly problematic legacy.

The Procrustean Bed of Gender Difference

As Alva and Gunnar resumed their correspondence after a joyous meeting in Stockholm in late October, their letters explored the contrast between Alva's intuition and Gunnar's empirical scientific approach, which reflected what Gunnar assumed were fundamental differences between men and women. At the same time, they discussed philosophical questions of knowledge and how morality is constructed in different societies and eras. Alva struggled with the contradiction between her faith in humanity and Gunnar's more pessimistic view of human nature. Through it all, she proved a sympathetic listener to Gunnar's problems with depression and psychosomatic illness and a source of reassurance for him, while Gunnar continued to write passionate love letters.

Nurtured by an idealistic father with a Rousseauian vision and surrounded by friends interested in spirituality and psychology, Alva found it difficult to accept the mechanistic materialism of the scientific worldview. Whenever she started thinking abstractly, she told Gunnar, she found herself plodding around in circles getting nowhere. Her temperament demanded a sense of unity in diversity, an all-inclusive force which is the basis of everything. (A to G, Nov, 1, 1919)

Moreover, Alva bluntly told Gunnar that he misinterpreted her sympathetic attention to his opinions as a sign of agreement when, in fact, she was listening and formulating her own opinions, which were often different from his. "Do you understand this, Gunnar? To me it seems a bit mad." In her correspondence with Per Sundberg, Alva had shown how unsparing she could be in her earnest effort to get beyond lies and uncover truth. But now she muted some of her opinions. She found herself wanting to "attack some of your points," but usually "said very little," especially if other people were present. Irritated at Gunnar's contentious style and perhaps a little confused about the person she was becoming, Alva insisted that "I was never in the least bit anxious to be considered intelligent by you and am not now either, because I fear that the dignity of [an] intelligent girl would grow too heavy in the long run." With a touch of irony, she reported that she had discovered that "my intuition is strong but my logic produces nothing at all."

Planning their next meeting in Strängnäs, a town on the railway line between Eskilstuna and Stockholm, Alva was troubled by having to lie to her parents. She announced with feigned bravado that "I have accordingly followed your advice and learned to tell lies." If necessary, she would do without moral principles. "Following one's heart is the only right" course of action. "If you have to think before acting morally, there is not much to your goodness." Still, Alva knew of no principle that said it is right to lie about love, so concealing her meetings with Gunnar must be wrong. But she resolved to put up with this mental conflict for his sake.

Gunnar was troubled by Alva's letter. Reversing roles for a change, he asserted that he was "by nature an optimist" and told her that they must have faith in their lucky star. He had been suffering from a "bad conscience" since reading that he had taught her to lie and offered to cancel their meeting if the deception was too burdensome for her. He asked her to forgive him for having been such a bad influence; he had forgotten that his own ethics were of a cruder caliber than hers. Gunnar was no stranger to prevarication: he had learned to maneuver around his parents' crises, conceal his father's alcoholism, and negotiate between the worlds of Solvarbo and the Stockholm bourgeoisie. "I lie out of long established habit," he acknowledged.

> The lie is an indispensable means of reducing friction and toning down human whining . . . of avoiding making people unhappy. . . . It has therefore never occurred to me to include lying in my ethics any more than I would cursing, for instance. Both seem to me equally unimportant and—from a moral point of view—interesting only as historical curiosities. (G to A, Nov. 6, 1919)

"Not until now have I understood what significance you place on truthfulness," he continued. Gunnar promised to be more careful in the future. "I may have noticed that you pondered ethical riddles, but when you talked about questions of truth, I always assumed that you didn't mean it so seriously." "I was quite blind to the possibility of such love of truth." After a discourse on various types of lies, such as how to distinguish a "positive, constructive lie" from a destructive falsehood, Gunnar advised her: "Don't worry yourself too much about ethical principles. It is not very good for you. It requires an instrument of greater strength and cruder structure than the brain of a girl—however quick and trained." While Gunnar lauded Alva as "simply not capable of acting immorally," he offered her a little advice on how to feel better about having to lie.

> Posit: that which I do is right, and then do what you want. When you have got used to this way of thinking, you can soon turn it around: the right is that which I do. In other words, once you are sufficiently arrogant you can do nothing but that which is right. . . . Arrogance is the mother of all virtues.

"Is this sophism? How stupid of me to think that you, dear sweet little thing, could be as morally crooked and opportunistic as I am." In mock shamefulness, Gunnar said that he did not deserve to see her but still hoped for another meeting soon.

When she received Gunnar's letter, Alva went straight to her mother and told her that she was going to Strängnäs to meet Gunnar. She decided to take responsibility for her actions even if it meant more trouble at home. In a letter to Gunnar, Alva parroted his teachings that "social conventions" and morality were not necessarily the same thing. It seemed to her that, in reality, individuals rarely make choices based on firm ethical principles. "Principles, which cause most of the trouble, are nothing but labels to make it easier to morally evaluate our actions. They are never an influence on our firm decisions." (A to G, Nov. 8, 1919)

After their brief meeting in Strängnäs in mid-November, the lovers each wrote of aching loneliness and tried to fill the void with a dialogue of ideas. Alva reported on her gymnasium studies. Gunnar wrote that he was "reading a good book about dreams by a psychologist from Vienna"—his first direct reference to Freud. He was also reading a book by a German doctor on neurasthenia, a nervous debility caused by overwork or mental strain and characterized by psychosomatic illness.[7] While immersing himself in this clinical literature, Gunnar developed an obsessive fear that a big stuffed bird he kept on the mantelpiece might contain arsenic. (G to A, Nov. 24, 1919) As he felt what he thought were symptoms of arsenic poisoning, he seemed oblivious to possibility that the book he was reading might have led him to experience these symptoms.

As Gunnar fell ill in late November 1919, he remembered their first, tentative physical encounter in Solvarbo and wished that Alva would "take my head between your hands and put it in your lap and laugh at me and call me a baby and caress me to sleep." Although she had tried to reassure him that he was "strong," he saw Alva as the source of all strength, calm, and peace. As his headache and depression had knocked him off the perch from which he usually surveyed human folly and stupidity, the staunch materialist toyed with the possibility that Alva might sense telepathically that he was ill, even though she was 100 kilometers away. Grasping for a scientific explanation of a possible connection between them, he noted that Fritz Thorén, who was studying chemistry at the university, had told him that it was now possible to identify matter and energy and explain the world in terms of interconnected systems. So, Gunnar reasoned, if he was one system which through lines of energy is connected to all other systems "from the inkwell to [the constellation of] Vega," then there must be many lines of energy connecting him to his "dearest, little Alva!" Thus did the materialist male, in a moment of suffering, try to bridge the gap between him and the intuitive, spiritual, "feminine" way of thinking he attributed to his beloved. (G to A, Nov. 26, 1919) He remembered a resonant line from Luther's catechism: "Faith is that which the heart trusts." (G to A, Nov. 6, 1919)

Alva's "Troll Circle"

Alva was also feeling terribly alone. She wrote bravely of learning to enjoy solitude, of creating a "magic troll circle" of self-containment. Claiming that she had never labored under any illusions regarding the narrowness of most people's minds, she was now determined to break out of the confines of her family and small town and open herself to a richer world. She thought it important to express her sense of vulnerability and told Gunnar that her "self" was not firmly fixed. Through careful introspection, Alva discovered that "everything is a strange conglomeration of passing fancies, intuitions, feelings, impressions." Gunnar had urged her to find a sense of "self-purpose," but she had not found it yet. While her beloved alternated between frantic anxiety and depression, Alva turned to music to ease her sorrow. As a 14-year-old, she had identified with Hamlet, not Ophelia. Now she sang "Ophelia's Lament," which became a kind of evening hymn as she acted out the Romantic ideal of the tragic, sensitive, suffering woman. (A to G, Nov. 27, 1919)

Alva saw withdrawal into her "magic circle" as a way to preserve her memory of her beloved and to contemplate their "special" world together. Gunnar took quite a different view: he saw Alva as casting a "spell" to sequester herself and deny him access to her inner thoughts. He even went so far as to suggest that for Alva to be so introverted was "masochism." He reproached her for not opening up more to him, not letting him into her heart, and wished that she would ask more of him and about him. (G to A, Nov. 30, 1919)

As for his admonition that Alva should find a "life purpose," Gunnar conceded that he was far from finding one himself. She should understand that he had written that letter when he was ill. "It is no minor matter when my brain starts acting up," he complained. He had been trying to write a letter to his dearest, but had suffered from a "thumping headache," and his eyes had been "feverishly shiny from anxiety." He had been doing his best not to show that he was not as mentally healthy as usual; he knew that "just a glance or small gesture" from Alva would have "chased away both the headache and the anxiety." Now that he was well again, Gunnar realized that he had not suffered from arsenic poisoning, yet he hesitated to apply a medical diagnosis to his malady. "I am always anxious to some extent," he acknowledged. But, he suggested, his recent illness was due to a lack of structure in his daily life. Neglecting his studies, he wasted his time reading twenty newspapers a day, thinking about a thousand things, arguing with fellow students, and inventing clever invective against the philistines. Soon he had to take an oral exam in constitutional law. Gunnar's only hope was to pull the wool over the eyes of his examiner and "do magic with my mouth." Despite his efforts to leaven his mood with humor, "I start wondering if this is a worthwhile use of my powers. So I try again, shut myself off to read, fail, develop a bad conscience, start to doubt my future. And there I go again!" Gunnar tried to comfort Alva and himself by resolving that "I am quite certain that I won't have that headache for a long time—if it was a real headache and I didn't just imagine the whole horror show." (G to A, Nov. 30, 1919)

Alva responded that she had sensed Gunnar's illness and had longed to be there to help him get through his "heavy days." She felt a conflict between her youthful optimism and desire to help people and Gunnar's more conservative, often cynical view of the masses. She wanted to develop a more realistic understanding of politics and society without losing faith in the possibility of human amelioration. Since her correspondence with Per Sundberg, Alva had believed that the condition of the world had been "obscured by cultural and social falsehoods" and striven to acquire the knowledge that would allow her to see beyond the lies of daily life. Although Gunnar might think her a "fool," Alva affirmed her belief in the potential of much-maligned humanity. She did not contend "that future humanity will turn out to be more angelic than we are, but that human beings, now and always, are fundamentally good." Alva tried to reconcile these contradictions by investing her hope in Gunnar as a hero who would do great things and by trying to bring out his more idealistic side. She had always intended to fall in love with a great man, and "in this case, I stuck to my intentions." In her faith in his goodness, "I have placed my whole longing for a person who outstrips ideals, who in his truth and strength becomes the savior of the world, the heavenly father of my religion." Alva referred to "the human longing for harmony and completion, the great hunger, which in a religious context would be called a need for a god, a yearning for eternity." "All that, as strongly as I felt it—I found in you. I need no God now that I have you. Crazy as this may seem, it is no exaggeration. It is my faith." Alva preferred that others should not "share" her "faith," "since that would mean I would inevitably lose you." Confident that Gunnar would become a great man, she proclaimed that "if humanity wants any part of you at all, they will have to make do with the historical person." (A to G, Dec. 2, 1919)

As Alva refashioned her thoughts and feelings around her idealization of Gunnar, her political opinions were being challenged as well. She grappled with what she was reading and engaged Gunnar in debate, rephrasing political questions in his elitist vocabulary and, for a time, moving away from her father's social democratic beliefs, at least in her letters to Gunnar. The rebellious 17-year-old rejected society's insistence that the rules of the group should override the desires and needs of the individual. Condemning what passed for "democratization," she declared: "I can't stand other people's wish to reduce all to one level, and I oppose the desire or perhaps rather the tendency to disregard human differences."

Gunnar rejoiced at getting a letter from his beloved as a blessed relief from early December's "suicide weather." But he was startled by her description of himself. It made him anxious "when you talk about [me as] the savior of the world and the greatest and want me to be a despot." "I want to try honestly [to be those things] in your little world—the outside world is of far less interest." "But when you, the best and most beautiful I know, believe in me as in someone who has outstripped the ideals that you see yourself, then I feel deeply crushed." He had always been central to his own vision of the world, but now, he insisted, he had shrunk to the edge of it and placed her at the center. Gunnar protested that she was his only ideal, and if he is in any way "better than bad," it is thanks to her. If Alva she believes in him, he has no choice but to believe in himself. "How would I dare to be weak if you think I am strong—how would I dare to be afraid if you think I am courageous?" (G to A, Dec. 5, 1919)

Turning to political philosophy, Gunnar remarked that he regarded Alva's claim that "man is fundamentally good" as "pure metaphysics." The concepts "man" and "man's fundamental nature" are nothing but empty abstractions. Unwilling to meet her halfway, Gunnar sought to root out what he saw as the vestiges of naïve socialist idealism and vague spiritual optimism in Alva's political outlook. "It is inconsistent to talk about . . . man's general goodness while at the same time objecting to demands for equality and to equalizing trends," he sneered. "Goodness is a cultural product dependent on the development of selfishness as well as aesthetic sensibilities, while the criminal tendency is innate and appears atavistically in everyone, even if only in sleep or on other occasions less controlled by conscious thought."

Picking up his pen on his 21st birthday. he wondered: "What will become of this child?" Looking back on his life, Gunnar claimed that he no longer felt as ambitious as he once had. Changing the world used to mean everything to him. "Now I love to look at the battle from the sidelines and feel hardly any desire to throw my sword on the scales where peoples and classes fight each other." He relished the sheer pleasure of thinking and presenting his conclusions to Alva. Gunnar thanked Alva for helping him in the "struggle for my ideas." (G to A, Dec. 5, 1919)

A week later, Gunnar responded to a letter from his beloved in which she anguished over the difficulties of sexual love.[8] Although he clearly wanted to take their relationship to a deeper physical level, he was careful to show respect for Alva's feelings and reassured her that he did not really "suffer" from their restraint. Gunnar thought that the expression of sexual love was healthy and rejected society's "superstitious" rules against it, but he understood the importance of mutual love and was conscious of the need for "caution" regarding pregnancy.

> A long time ago I kissed the confession from your lips that your love was stronger than your belief in chastity. To be loved so completely and strongly by the only girl in the world fills me with pride and joy which overcomes any suffering.

Gunnar asked Alva not to think about "caution" when she was with him. She could trust him to respect her limits; he was "stronger" and could handle it.

> It was not just "caution"—ouch, what an ugly sound—which stopped me from having you. Even if you no longer watch out for your chastity, I still do. I didn't have the courage—then. But I did have the courage to wait. That is also courage. Why? Superstition? No, but what I don't know.

Gunnar explained that he dared to tell Alva of his longing for greater intimacy because he tells her everything. He promised that next time he would write about political science so she would not find herself in the position of having to write another "difficult" letter back. Gunnar dares not disturb her with his "despotic possessiveness." Sometimes he would like to be her slave, but he knows that he wants and needs to be her "lord and master." (G to A, Dec. 11, 1919)

Gunnar, accompanied by his sister Elsa, spent the Christmas holiday visiting the Reimer family at Slagsta farm. The young couple found it difficult to relax under the constant surveillance of her family. In looking back on the visit three months later when he could afford to be more frank, Gunnar remembered "what a terrible pressure and what a strange mood there was during my visit." It hurt them both "to put our love into a space of such inhospitable heaviness and sorrow." Alva's parents "looked on everything with very distrustful eyes." Gunnar winced under this burden. The agnostic student feared that Alva's mother would find him impious, and he was so afraid of saying the wrong thing that "I nearly got lockjaw from terror several times a day." Gunnar remembered the scene at the dinner table: "your sister's confining and sarcastic seriousness; Elsa, herself terrified, yet with composure; you, clearly a victim of conflicting emotions, expressed yourself in a quiet monotonous giggle"; "your mother watching with a mild wondering gaze." (G to A, Mar. 26, 1920) The lovers managed to find a few moments alone, and their relationship survived this trial. It had been six months since they had met, and both Gunnar and Alva were eager to be together. Their separation continued to vex them for the next year, and the conflicting pressures that Alva felt from Gunnar and from her family tested her optimistic temperament and resilient personality.

Notes

All parenthetical citations in the text are to manuscripts written by Alva or Gunnar or Myrdal. All translations were done by the author. These passages may differ from the English-language versions quoted in other publications. Many of Alva's and Gunnar's personal communications are difficult to decipher because they were written rapidly in longhand, abbreviate common words, and often use dashes instead of more precise punctuation. Transcribing and translating them necessarily involves matters of interpretation.

1 Gunnar Myrdal to Carl Adolf and Sofie Pettersson, June 5, 1919, AGMA; Gunnar Myrdal, Minnesanteckningar, chapterl.
2 Bok, *Alva Myrdal*, 50–51; Hirdman, *Alva Myrdal*, 30–31; Lindskog, *Alva Myrdal*, 15–16.
3 Andersson, Gunnar Myrdal; Bok, *Alva Myrdal*, 51–52; Hirdman, *Alva Myrdal*, 31–34.
4 Quoted in Andersson, Gunnar Myrdal.
5 Bok, *Alva Myrdal*, 60.
6 Bok, *Alva Myrdal*, 46–47.
7 While neurasthenia was most frequently diagnosed in women, physicians assumed that it also might plague highly educated men who had no outlet for action.
8 Alva's letter has not survived.

References

Alva and Gunnar Myrdal's Collection (AGMA). Arbetarrörelsens Arkiv och Bibliotek (Swedish Labour Movement's Archive and Library). Stockholm, Sweden.

Correspondence between Alva and Gunnar Myrdal, 3.3
[cited as: G to A or A to G, date]
Alva Myrdal's family and kin, 6.3
Gunnar Myrdal's family and kin
GM to Carl Adolf and Sofie Pettersson. Eskilstuna, June 5, 1919.

Manuscripts

Andersson, Stellan. Gunnar Myrdal: Barn och ungdom år (Childhood and youth). Arbetarrörelsens Arkiv och Bibliotek, Stockholm.

Myrdal, Gunnar. Minnesanteckningar. Oral history memoir, early 1980s. In the possession of Sissela Bok.

Interview

Lindskog, Lars G. *Alva Myrdal: "Förnuftet måste segra!" Lars G. Lindskog samtalar med Alva Myrdal om skilda epoker i hennes liv.* Stockholm: Sveriges Radios förlag, 1981.

Published Sources

Bok, Sissela. *Alva Myrdal: A Daughter's Memoir.* Reading, MA: Addison-Wesley, 1991.

Hirdman, Yvonne. *Det tänkande hjärtat: Boken om Alva Myrdal.* Stockholm: Ordfront, 2006. *Alva Myrdal: The Passionate Mind*, trans. Linda Schenck. Bloomington: Indiana University Press, 2006.

8 "Souls as great as ours"

While Gunnar and Alva were together during the Christmas holidays, they talked about the possibility of becoming engaged and considered their future together. Back in his Stockholm apartment, Gunnar recalled that while they were kissing he had felt a sudden urge to be the father of her children. "It was not the desire to caress, even less the desire for pleasure which made me want to open your quivering virgin's womb and pour into it the hot juice of life—it was the urge to create." He acknowledged his self-centeredness and said he was "baffled" by his sudden desire for fatherhood. Gunnar was acutely aware of the practical obstacles. "Since we are talking about the general principle, have I, do you think, the right to get engaged, I who have only obscure, uncertain prospects and especially seem entirely to lack the knack for making money?" Even thinking about planning a conventional wedding with their families seemed dismal to both of them. (G to A, Jan. 4, 1920)

Gunnar urged Alva to agree that they would make as few concessions to society as possible. Responding to a question from Alva about the degree to which one should live one's life with "consideration" for the feelings of others, he exploded:

> Do you imagine that I would be here studying law if it were not for "consideration" of others and its crucial role in life? Consideration of mother who wants me to be a "good and proper person" and of father, who has more personal ambition than I do—not for himself but for me—and wants to see my name written in lights before he goes to his grave. My intelligence is father's great pride and joy. Were it not for these considerations, I would be . . . in Africa, in Algeria, or in Siberia.

Gunnar recalled that he had barely suppressed his erotic desires the previous summer and wondered about Alva's ideal of chastity. He accused her of insincerity because she had written that she wished she were more accustomed to "erotic sensations." "It is heartlessly unkind—no, thoughtlessly unkind—no, just thoughtless. Or did you perhaps have the tiniest impulse to say something hurtful? No, No!" With some exasperation,

Gunnar claimed that he was better at lectures and kisses than at writing letters and told Alva to lie in order to get away for a night. He also asked for her help with an essay he was writing on "The Main Issues of Educational Policy," asserting that he was very good at picking titles and organizing thoughts but not at getting everything down on paper. He then returned to an emotional appeal: "You simply must come. Can't you tell how much I long for you?" (G to A, Jan. 4–5, 1920)

Alva answered that she longed for Gunnar as well. Steering clear of explicit discussion of sexuality, she portrayed herself as having developed a stronger sense of independence. She expressed horror that Gunnar had enclosed a 10 crown bill in a recent letter, presumably to pay for her train fare to Stockholm. Alva was "appalled" at the thought of even talking to him about money. Gunnar's thoughtlessness in sending money in the same letter in which he had written of his intense desire for greater sexual intimacy deeply disturbed her. (A to G, Jan. 7, 1929)

That same night, Gunnar had a bad dream and suddenly was struck by terror that Alva had died. "I am afraid of death and jealous and anxious in all sorts of unreasonable ways," he admitted. Acknowledging a twinge of guilt over his persistent demands that she to come to Stockholm, he was less aware of his tendency to portray himself as a helpless victim in order to gain her sympathy. "Fate takes its revenge," he announced portentously. "I started all full of myself, sure that you would come, when instead I should have been satisfied and happy that you exist and love me—then came this rebuke: you could catch diphtheria at any moment and be taken from me." "What would I do with myself then?" Gunnar jumped from this anxiety to his guilt over having postponed their marriage until after he completed his university studies and the consequent risk that she might look elsewhere for a fiancé. "Right now I feel so anxious about you being exposed to the power of blind chance so far away from me that I dare not think of leaving you for months and years. And yet this is not just a possibility but a necessity." (G to A, Jan. 7, 1920)

Troubling Intimacy

The next day, Alva reassured her lover as much as she could and promised to be with him soon. (A to G, Jan. 8, 1920) Inventing another cover story for her parents, she took the train to Stockholm on Saturday January 10 and returned home the following evening. In that whirlwind visit, she comforted Gunnar and they discussed their hopes and ideas for the future. Now, seven months after they had met and a few days before her eighteenth birthday, Alva and Gunnar had sexual intercourse for the first time. Gunnar was anxious and depressed, so the experience was not as romantic as either had hoped. Had Alva taken pity on him or somehow felt that denying him sex was causing his melancholy? Gunnar and Alva had written each other frequently since they parted the previous summer, desperately striving to keep alive the passion that had united them and exploring each other's thoughts and feelings. Both had pushed away family and friends as they sought to create and nurture a special new world. It was almost inevitable that a brief interlude of lovemaking after so much separation would leave both of them feeling alone and troubled, as they had little time to communicate their emotions.

Returning home, Alva steeled herself to act as if nothing had happened and conceal everything from her family. Perhaps, given the brevity of this encounter, she was unable to assimilate the powerful feelings it aroused. Back at Slagsta at 11 o'clock on Sunday night, feeling numb but wide awake, she sat down to write Gunnar before she went to bed. Reflexively putting his feelings before hers, Alva began with the salutation: "My poor dear abandoned Gunnar!" She, too, was suffering from the sudden rupture. "Today I was with you. Then I left you. And now—I am incapable of writing anything about my grief, my loss, my love, or my happiness." Alva explained that "when I am utterly exhausted . . . my thoughts are clearer and sharper than usual. But all emotions vanish." She tried to reassure Gunnar, but was unable to speak spontaneously and joyfully about their love. The honest psychological self-examination that she had learned from books, tried playfully with Märta, practiced with Per Sundberg, and perfected in her dialogues and letters with Gunnar yielded a different result. "It hurts me that you are ill and upset," but "I am happy to be your beloved. This is true, I'm sure, but tonight my heart fails to beat faster at that thought; tonight my love must not be alive in me although I can feel it is there." She asked Gunnar to "forgive me if you feel that what I write now is hard." "But why should I suffer this alone? You need to know. I am too exhausted to be filled with jubilation, or hurt by any searing pain—my love is like a dull joy and my longing a faint echo." Writing in the tone of dispassionate self-observation that Gunnar had encouraged, she added, "The fact that I am able to write about it should tell you that my brain is functioning in an unpleasantly mechanical manner, yet also carefully like a good machine." (A to G, Jan. 11, 1920)

The next morning her longing for Gunnar returned, but she expressed herself guardedly, aware that she would not see him for some time. Alva invoked the familiar metaphor of the woman freely giving herself over to love, but their situation did not fit the trope. Gunnar was far away. Rather than a conquering hero or valiant knight, he was a student suffering from depression, demanding her succor, then expecting her to act the part of the enthralled Romantic heroine. In addition to performing these contradictory roles in her letters, Alva had to bear up under her mother's scrutiny, avoid giving away too many secrets to Rut, attend to her schoolwork, and do her chores in the house and on the farm. She faced these challenges with her usual irony:

> Now there is nothing to prevent my longing from rising up strong and powerful. Now I am no longer free from its domination. And I am a happy and contented slave who prefers death to freedom. To be a slave, to wish to serve—and then have her lord so far away that he can make no demands—it makes one so melancholy, almost bitter. (A to G, Jan. 12, 1920)

She yearned to submit to love, but their encounter had been so brief and ended so abruptly that she found herself withdrawing into her magic circle of solitude and puzzling over what had happened.

Turning to her decision to lose her virginity, Alva reassured Gunnar that she had cast aside the image of herself that she had cultivated as a girl and had embraced his idea that theirs was an "exceptional" relationship.

> Why should I be ashamed, dearest? As a well brought up girl, ought I to consider my behavior shameful, ugly, and inexcusable? Yes, perhaps, but I have given up being modest and well brought up and cannot judge my conduct toward you according to the same norm as one I would use when judging everyone else.

In sarcastic defiance of her mother's teachings about proper behavior, Alva asked,

> Why should I be shy? Because of my nakedness? Yes, since a modest girl must fear men's glances more than the devil's worst revenge. Because of my yearning? Yes, since a modest girl needs to learn the blessedness of being given everything while being cold and hard and giving nothing in return. And eventually the modest girls become modest wives, who in witty conversation express their horror at the shamelessness of their neighbor. No thank you.

Declaring that the principles of her mother's code of sexual morality "are stone dead," she affirmed that "I do not need well established, unwavering principles guiding my conduct . . . as I am in full possession of my spiritual faculties." What mattered was a person's moral intentions. "If I lose the will to goodness, no principles could save me; only fear would stop me." Alva concluded this seemingly bold defense of her conduct with a plea for reassurance: "Tell me, Gunnar, that I need not be ashamed of it all."

Gunnar also sat down to pour out his feelings about their passionate encounter, and his letter crossed Alva's in the mail. Absorbed in telling her how he felt at the moment, he failed utterly to offer the reassurance that she needed. While Alva's initial reaction had been emotional numbness and an attempt at detached psychological self-analysis, Gunnar confessed that their intimacy followed by abrupt separation had unleashed demons of fear and anxiety that had pushed him deeper into depression:

> Love, which should make us healthy makes us sick, pours into the nerves and blood a fever that overtakes us, drives us down to the abyss of despair and then up to the highest strength that passion can bring; takes from us sleep, hunger, joy of work. Tears apart instead of making whole. Our love becomes just as abnormal as our meetings: few and short. Love is no medicine to take with a teaspoon once a month.

Instead, Gunnar longed for "love as an everyday reality that shines over the little things of life." Rather than reassurance, he offered a cry of despair. (G to A, Jan. 12, 1920)

"It was good that you wrote as you did," Alva replied the day she received his letter. His shocking descriptions of pain had enabled her "to really feel" what he was experiencing at that moment. She had also been full of sorrow "very far down." But "my despair has not been like yours, as dark as night and deep as an abyss." She assured him that she did not regret their sexual intimacy: "It was good that you awakened me. It is undeniably better to live and suffer deeply than to be half dead and only feel emptiness." She had "longed so boundlessly" for their sexual union but, when the moment finally came, "the emotion required a space which I did not have." "In my terrible knowledge that soon after I would have to leave you, I wanted to be able to stretch my emotional capacity for life itself—and I did—to the outermost limits." Attempting to remember the moment romantically, she tried not to think about "the shabby circumstances which served to diminish and limit my most beautiful and most meaningful experience." Finally, after mulling all this over, Alva admitted that she had not been capable of feeling the full "emotional richness" of the experience because of the "brevity of the moment." (A to G, Jan. 13, 1920)

She then declared: "It cannot be true that love should give pain when it ought to be our greatest consolation. It cannot be true that it tears apart instead of uniting. It cannot be allowed, cannot." She resolved that "we shall overcome the despair of these days," but recognized that there were limits to what she could do from a distance. "How happy I would be if I possessed the means to console you, if I could change the sorrow of my beloved into happiness just once." Despite her desire to rescue Gunnar from his melancholy, it "has never happened." She signed off as "Your poor Alva."

Three days after Alva had left Stockholm, Gunnar moaned that his separation from her was a "nightmare" that was "unendurable for me down in my solitary room." "Longing is one thing and sick despair another. Longing brings light, because one has hope, but despair . . . is hopeless." Anticipating more love-making with Alva, he sought to reassure her: "You do not need to fear that every time I shall be as immeasurably depressed as last time, because I was sick then." He half apologized for having written obsessively about his problems in his earlier letter and admitted that perhaps he should have remained silent "out of consideration for you." But he quickly took that back, arguing that "one ought not to put one's emotions on the shelf" because "love is not a game." Gunnar reminded Alva of the pact into which they had entered. "When you, with a kiss, declared your love for me, you also took on the duty to bear anything that I have to bear." In his mind, the value of honesty trumped all other considerations. "I do not have the right to withhold the truth from you even one time. Who should have the right and the duty to hear it if not you?" (G to A, Jan. 14, 1920)

In this letter written during the darkest month, Gunnar revealed that "the fear or the danger of the intellect being plundered by sickness lies like a shadow over my consciousness." He was comforted by the fact that he had never "felt this cold shadow in you. I am accustomed to this hollow-eyed spirit; when I dream, I usually see him life-like." Shifting from literary metaphors to the medical vocabulary of psychiatry, he described his condition: "Every now and then, I have periods which I cannot explain except as sickness, and which are characterized by the most manic depression, anxiety and unhappiness." "Just now, I have gone through one of the worst I have ever experienced. . . . I was afraid I might have closed the fireplace damper one evening if I had not had you." He still struggled with thoughts of suicide. Gunnar promised that he would go to see a psychiatrist and feared that his sister Mela's epilepsy might indicate a hereditary cause of his illness. Gunnar sought to take refuge in his image of himself as a Romantic hero who was destined to experience higher peaks and lower depths of feeling than other people, but he could not banish the recurring idea from his religious upbringing that every blessing came at the cost of suffering: "Perhaps I have to reach these new states of anxiety as a payment for my exceptional capacity to experience rapture."

Alva responded immediately to this cry for help with an almost Biblical statement of commitment. "Your sorrow is mine," she pledged, echoing Ruth from the Old Testament. "What you bear of the day's heaviness and passion has fallen my lot to share. I accept the lot cheerfully and make a willing sacrifice from my heart." Imagining Gunnar "sitting alone and sick and unhappy and tormented," Alva affirmed that "I want to . . . be with you and find a means to dispel the gloom." (A to G, Jan. 15, 1920)

A week after their fleeting experience of intimacy, Gunnar was still blending professions of eternal love with anxieties about the effect of their separation on his mental health. Their love was almost too intense for him to bear. He considered the possibility that his recent illness was psychosomatic; he had not gone to a doctor because he had recovered but would do so if it happened again. Then, in a typically rapid shift, he tried to convince Alva and himself that his anxiety and depression could be explained by physiological factors and that he could bring his emotions under control. Gunnar insisted that men do not have to be ruled by Fate, as the Greek dramatists believed, or have their lives measured out by the Norns, the female figures of Old Norse mythology. With a "courageous heart," the hero could "point the tip of his sword at the Norns' breast and say, 'you must yield.'" But, he admitted, life was not that simple. (G to A, Jan. 18, 1920)

Gunnar was pleased that Alva had told him that she had not been "ashamed and shy" during their recent lovemaking. He declared that logic was "an ugly concept" in this context and she must trust her emotions. Her coolly analytical discussion of her reaction to their intimacy bothered him. He thought that Alva had been too self-conscious and self-controlled when they made love; it did not fit with his ideal of spontaneity and loss of control that a woman should feel in the grip of passion. Gunnar insisted that she affirm that "you lack the capacity to think when you are with me." Alva could exercise this ability in his presence, "but in my arms, you must never think." He pleaded with Alva not to call herself "unchaste" because that would mean judging him too harshly. Looking behind her words for motive, he inquired: "That was the answer you wanted, wasn't it?" (G to A Jan. 18, 1920)

As he thought back to their first meeting the previous summer, Gunnar recalled that he was so moved by passion that he had not thought very much about his feelings. Had he done so, he would have feared for his sanity, even though the beautiful weather had made him more "mentally stable" than he now felt. Gunnar suggested that Alva's emotional life was more complex and nuanced than his. Hers resembled an old Dutch painting with millions of variegated details, while his was more like a large nineteenth-century battle scene with large blocks of a single color. After stating all these contradictory things, Gunnar scrambled to fit their complex personalities into a Procrustean bed of traditional gender relations. He assumed that it was his "nature" to act, perform great deeds and function as "nature's instrument," while she was "nature's purpose."

Gunnar's quest for understanding the moral ambiguities of his relationship with Alva was reflected in his reading of Uppsala philosopher Axel Hägerström's book, *The Truth behind Moral Ideas*, to which he referred in this letter. Gunnar was struggling with Hägerström's concept that moral conventions are learned habits to which clusters of emotions have become attached. Gunnar wanted to be a detached, scientific thinker on questions of psychology and morality, but he tried to make his feelings for Alva conform to a nineteenth-century model of the male Romantic lover. He wondered how he could manage to shift abruptly from skeptical scientific observer to man of action in politics and then to spontaneous lover with Alva. He knew how he *should* feel in each role, but he did not always experience the right emotion at the right time. Instead, he often went into cycles of anxiety and depression in which he could not fulfill any of his cherished conceptions of himself.

Romantic Suffering

Alva steered away from the subject of Gunnar's depression and sought to assuage his fears that she had been too coldly analytical and insufficiently spontaneous during and immediately after their recent sexual encounter. Alarmed that Gunnar's extraordinary emotional demands on himself and on her were leading to disastrous consequences for them both, she tried gently to communicate her feeling that she wanted to find a harmonious and balanced life with him and did not demand that he become a great man in order to deserve her devotion. Backing away from her earlier stance of realizing herself through the great achievements of her heroic husband-to-be, she retreated to more attainable goals that seemed appropriate for a woman seeking to strengthen a man who experienced such anxieties and mood swings. Alva reassured him that achieving great things was "quite unnecessary" and that she was neither ambitious for him nor concerned about others' view of him. She suggested that there was something "suspicious" about ambition and asked, "What is it a cover for?" Revealing the influence of her father's socialist beliefs as well as the residue of the Christian virtue of humility, Alva declared that "ambition is an empty, rattling sensation." It was perhaps allowable if used to "do good," but not if it only served "self-interest." Alva assured Gunnar that her love for him was more powerful than any wish that he become famous. (A to G, Jan. 17, 1920)

Ambition might seem "empty and rattling" to her, Gunnar shot back, but he is ambitious. Does she not know how much he "relishes . . . applause"? Over time, he had learned to focus on the substance of his thinking rather than on receiving wide acclaim. "But the day I seriously have to give up my intellectual ambitions would be a bitter one for me." Yet his arrogance had taken a beating when he had fallen in love with her the previous summer. Alva had mentioned noticing the first day that he seemed displeased. His experience of a sudden infatuation had initially "irritated" him because it had undermined his hard-won habits of self-control. Gunnar had felt "defeated and dejected—but by what?" He had experienced love as a challenge to his management of his emotions. "You may not understand my strange vanity regarding freedom." Now, he bravely asserted, he could manage his powerful feelings of love for Alva, his fear of losing control over his life, and his dread of having to give up his intellectual ambition to support a family. In short, Gunnar sought to convince himself and her that he could be spontaneous and give in to his emotions when he was with Alva and still pursue his disciplined quest for intellectual greatness. (G to A, Jan. 19, 1920)

The next day, Gunnar returned to the topic of how to manage the powerful emotional crosscurrents sweeping over him. Alva had become such an "all-pervasive presence" in his life that he had "almost lost my individuality in time and space." If this were not love, he declared, it would be an illness. Gunnar's longing for his beloved was like a "force of nature." Comparing the repression of his desire to caging a lion or damming a river, he pronounced it a "crime against nature." Gunnar felt as hungry as a wild animal and wanted to tear her apart or play with her as a cat plays with a mouse that cannot escape him. Alva's letters could not assuage this great hunger, he asserted. Not all wild animals are prepared to lap milk from a bowl when they have no prey. He was "irritated" that she was not coming to visit him soon. (G to A, Jan. 20, 1920)

Alva responded that if Gunnar felt that his love for her had undermined his strength, he should remember that he still ruled over her. "When I gave myself to you with my whole soul, once and for all, and thereby felt that I gave up myself, then I experienced your strength—overpoweringly." When she had met him, Alva recalled, Gunnar had possessed an almost god-like pride in his intellect. It had seemed as if he were sitting alone atop a mountain with his thoughts shooting forth over the whole earth. Then suddenly his love for her had come, "which you were not yet lord over. This was something that lay buried deep down in the soul's innermost chamber." She compared Gunnar's experience of falling in love to "a hidden spring, which sprang up one day—and in it the whole of your strong intelligence drowned." Yet Alva assured him that love "is the common source of artists' desire to create." His physical passion for her did not "reach the depths of my love." One can only "reach the depth of everything with feeling." (A to G, Jan. 22, 1920)

Sinking back into introspection, Gunnar feared that he was not worthy of Alva's love and mused about the "appetite of the flesh" and the "incurable loneliness of the soul." If he thought that Alva had been too analytical and detached in describing their love-making, he worried much more about a certain emotional coldness that accompanied his loneliness. Striking the pose of the Romantic man of genius, Gunnar brooded that "it is hard to be different from everyone else, sometimes considered a madman, sometimes a genius, always a non-human." It was his own fault, he knew; he should do more to fit in with the ordinary people around him. He could hide his contempt, his lack of minor interests, his other quirks—if he wanted to. His few friends had gained his friendship by letting him have his way. But Gunnar was getting tired of himself. "That is real loneliness. Tell me, my girl, have you never felt the icy cold surrounding me? Cold and heat, both producing the same burning wound." Yet "I seem to lack that emotional register . . . which dominates the lives of most people." "Some notions are completely meaningless to me—[being] 'nice' for instance. But it is precisely in this middle register that life must be lived to be called happy, don't you think? I wonder if you can lead me there." (G to A, Jan. 23, 1920)

Despite his absorption in his own thoughts, Gunnar tried to understand the cost to Alva of loving a demanding genius with such a volatile temperament.

> When I think of you and me and the future, it often seems clear to me that it would be a stroke of fortune for you if I could just magically disappear from your life—then you would always have the memory of having belonged to an extraordinary man, of having been loved and desired more strongly than [most] women, but without paying for the relationship with your young life.

"You will deny this," he recognized; "otherwise you would not be the woman I love—you will say that self-sacrifice constitutes your happiness." Still assuming the persona of a Romantic poet, Gunnar continued: "But if you had a merciful God, would he not perhaps let me die—ideally in a slow manner, of tuberculosis, which would give you the lovely and heartbreaking memory of having loved without the hope of a happy life?" Gunnar wondered whether Alva had been fully aware of the tension between his two poles: "the positive and the negative, the strong and the weak, the ecstasy and the despair, the energy and the exhaustion, the heat and the frost." Leading her deeper into his interior world, he likened his inner self to an electric power station. Inside, she would see the huge generator at work, with blades going round and round, with tiny sparks from the metal brushes the only visible sign of the mysterious current. Alva's gaze would be fastened on the shiny poles between which 100,000 volts are passing, enough to burn her to a crisp within a fraction of a second. "As you stand there, breathing ozone fumes, listening to the muffled sound, you feel a demonic impulse to touch those gleaming brass rods. But once you return to the sunshine outside, you shake it all off and can no longer imagine what came over you just a few moments ago." "This "fear of power and danger" is "not a very beautiful image of love," he added dryly. Shifting to an image of himself as a heartless vampire, Gunnar painted a bleak picture of their future together. Instead of wasting away with tuberculosis,

> I shall probably live, and suck all your warmth and happiness out of you, uselessly trying to fill the empty abyss, the hollow vacuum that is my heart. You will sacrifice everything without my becoming any richer, then wander towards your grave, as empty as I, with or without me. This is hell on earth, Alva.

"Oh dear, how I exaggerate," he added blushingly a few minutes later. "Write that it is not true. I don't believe it myself except when my soul is really black." Recovering some balance, Gunnar declared that he hoped to be able to accept Alva's happiness without giving her his unhappiness in return. Picking up his pen again two days later, he felt guilty about having burdened her with all these dark thoughts. His moods are like the sun, the moon, and the stars, he explained. As an "extraordinary" man, Gunnar denied himself the comfort that most people find in "dogma and prejudices." (G to A, Jan. 25, 1920) His efforts to transcend pain led, not to a sense of harmony with the universe, but to loneliness and disorientation.

Addressing Gunnar as "My frail, faithful beloved," Alva sought to communicate the strength of her devotion and commitment. "I could not for long be contented to live egoistically for myself without wanting to live for you and your happiness." Alva asked rhetorically why he did not believe in her redemptive love. "Have you held me in your arms and still do not know that I love you, Gunnar! If I do not believe in you, whom shall I believe in? If I did not live for your sake—whom should I live for?" (A to G, Jan. 26, 1920) In reply, the agnostic Gunnar put aside his scientific method and affirmed that "I shall become superstitious and believe that a delicate little girl's love is as holy as Destiny." (G to A, Jan. 28, 1920) Three days later Alva again tried to offer him comfort. "If my thoughts, my love, and my self can fill the emptiness you create in your inner self, then I can surrender myself gladly, happy that I have given the most." She calmly assured Gunnar that "your happiness is more powerful than your coldness, that it isn't necessary for me to fear freezing in the cold that surrounds you." (A to G, Jan. 29–30, 1920)

As he started a letter on January 31, Gunnar suddenly remembered that it was Alva's eighteenth birthday. To feel her presence he got out all of "the loveliest souvenirs" that he kept to remind him of her: "one pile of letters, one photo, three hair pins and a belt—and am still not satisfied." Remarking that he had been reading psychology in conjunction with his study of criminal law, Gunnar noted the paradox of studying the health of the inner man by probing the motives of the criminally insane. Still a materialist in his view of psychology, he wondered if longing could be turned into brain energy. Then, realizing that what Alva had said was true and yet attempting to deny it, he acknowledged that Alva considered him "selfish." "You ask me if I don't have room for the thought that you are sad too." "Frankly—no! Is that selfish? Maybe." But he considered his admiration of her emotional strength and capacity for joy "more reverent." "I can't imagine you sad—I remember you as you were—yearning perhaps but in a lighter, more joyful way than mine." (G to A, Jan. 31, 1920) Gunnar's emotional need for Alva to be the cheerful one was so great that it seemed to crowd other thoughts out of his mind.

"Only kisses and caresses can ever bridge our personalities"

Two weeks later, on February 15, 1920, Alva made up another story about visiting a friend so she could spend two days with her beloved in

Stockholm. After she had returned home, her sister Rut guessed where she had been and could not resist the temptation to tease her older sister by making a sneering remark about Alva's loss of "virtue." Rut's comment punctured the magic circle in which Alva had tried to protect her secret world of love from the intrusion of her family. Thinking about how others would view her relationship with Gunnar, her romantic longings were tinged with guilt and anxiety. Part of her guilt stemmed from the continual string of lies that she had told her parents in order to get away. Truthfulness had always been fundamental to her sense of ethics, and she felt devoid of goodness as a result of all this lying. Her guilt went deeper than that, however, and she grew anxious concerning the consequences of their sexual intimacy and the future of their relationship. When they had been together, Gunnar had noticed her "silence," and Alva admitted that she had difficulty talking about herself. She was trying to express her feelings by writing to him in a less "stiff," more "natural," "conversational form." She pleaded for time to adjust to the intermittent nature of their relationship, insisted that things would be better in the summer when they would be together, and asked Gunnar to be more patient with her. "Over our few and short meetings lies an indefinite something that sometimes makes us feel hurried." (A to G, Feb. 16, 1920)

Gunnar came away from their February encounter glowing with love. When he heard of Rut's irritating behavior, he expressed his indignation as well as incredulity that Alva would believe "something as untrue as that there is nothing left of your virtue." Gunnar insisted that she was so good that nothing could really corrupt her. Of greater concern to him was his feeling, since their last meeting, that he was not capable of "understanding" her. Gunnar had felt Alva was like a sphinx, and her "inscrutability" frightened him. Because her distance chilled his heart, he had kissed her so desperately, so wildly until he felt that in her eyes he could see a hint of her soul trying to hide from him. "That indefinite something which hovers over our meetings is precisely the fact that only kisses and caresses can ever bridge our personalities." (G to A, Feb. 22, 1920)

"It is obvious that I shall never desire you as much as you desire me," Alva retorted in exasperation over his accusations about her coldness and withdrawal. To convince Gunnar of her love, she appropriated a language associated with male conquest and attempted a role reversal: "Tell me what I must do to win you, and I shall not leave anything untried. Of course, I know that you will answer that I should talk, but I wonder if that is enough." Although Alva had written frankly about her feelings of guilt, she insisted that Gunnar should not think "that I, with a bitter smile, watch [my] disappearing virtue or judge myself worse than 'honorable' people." "Even with the best intentions," people "distort" stories about others, and one cannot worry about gossip. Then Alva wondered if she had the "right to be so egoistic" in talking so much about herself. Her family had taught her to place the needs of others before her own, and she felt awkward about laying bare her soul in a letter. Resuming a more conventionally feminine posture, Alva implored Gunnar to "Forgive your poor, little girl who does not have a better way to show how much she loves you!" (A to G, Feb. 18, 1920)

Gunnar continued to worry that Alva's letters seemed more cold and distant, and he despaired that he just could not understand her. Considering himself "something of a psychologist," he used his newly acquired tools to pick apart Alva's various poses. She often said she did not want to trouble anyone, which he interpreted as "a little girl's conceitedness." Gunnar acknowledged that he seemed to turn spiteful when he wrote to her. Alva had always seemed mysterious and inaccessible. Now he felt angry that his love had failed to break the spell that she had cast to protect her inner self. Both jealous of her greater capacity for self-control and committed to the idea that their correspondence should be as intimate as possible, Gunnar perceived this spell as blocking her tenderness for him. He realized that he might be at fault and grumbled that he was not good enough to intuitively understand such "a complex little creature." But, he admitted, had she been less complicated, he would never have fallen in love with her in the first place. (G to A, Feb, 22, 1920)

"Girls are stupid little creatures," he opined, falling into the sharp-edged teasing he had perfected in banter with his sister Elsa. Girls are "emotionally most like an imaginary bastard mix between a pussycat and a St. Bernard dog." Gunnar quickly added that Alva was no ordinary girl but an intelligent and refined woman who, through reading and self-cultivation, had achieved something that most women lack: a soul. "It is known since the beginning of time that there is a rare flower: a woman with a soul. . . . I have dreamt of her for many years. I found her in you and loved you from the first moment." Before he had met Alva, "I dreamed of how much I should have in common with her; I thought that she alone and only she really could come close to me. For her, I wanted to open every secret cabinet, wanted truly to let her see what I could offer, what I wanted and what I thought." This ideal woman would be so special that Gunnar even "dreamed of the possibility of leading the beloved into the world of abstractions that I built for myself." Was this madness? Maybe, but he had also dreamed of sharing her world and hoped that she would let him in. Surely she thought so too? Now they were both sad, and Gunnar asked why. He had hoped that she would teach him to view things from her point of view, but in this she had failed. He did not think she had ever tried.

"Alva, my darling girl, don't give up," he beseeched her. "Don't forget at two people, who both possess souls as great as ours, can never be held together by erotic love alone." Seeking to get inside her mind and emotions, he declared that "if I've yearned more for your body it's been because I've possessed less of your soul." Gunnar was upset to read in her letter that, "with a bitter smile," you watch your "disappearing virtue." "Alva," he protested, "is that really how it seems to you? You gave yourself in a moment when not a trace of ugly or cowardly thought could have existed in either of us. How could that lead to the loss of any part of your virtue?" "If you really mean what you say, I'll never forgive myself—nor you either." "More than anything, I hope that you don't."

"White Negroes"

Stepping back and trying to view their situation in a broader perspective, Gunnar grasped for a metaphor that would contrast their intense pain and suffering with others' emotional placidity. In his discussions of Swedish politics, he had often disparaged "ordinary" people as unable to think the great thoughts of "exceptional men" like himself. Gunnar's self-conception as a tormented Romantic genius gave him a way of accepting his oscillation between self-confidence and utter dejection, since brilliant insights come from intense suffering.

Now he made a startling analogy: "If we always felt good, we'd be like white Negroes, and rather than that I'll be heartless enough to want my dear girl not to be spared occasional unhappiness." (G to A, Feb. 22, 1920) At the time, Myrdal had probably never met any Black people; the racist stereotype that Negroes always lived near the surface of life and were incapable of experiencing deep suffering was a rationale for enslavement and subordination that permeated mass culture.

Twenty years later, a wiser Gunnar Myrdal wrote a powerful critique of such racist thinking:

> In this magical sphere of the white man's mind, the Negro is inferior, totally independent of rational proofs or disproofs. . . . So the Negro becomes a "contrast conception." He is "the opposite race"—an inner enemy, "antithesis of character and properties of the white man."[1]

Writing Gunnar that same day, Alva reached for poetic inspiration and a sense of reconciliation. She contrasted their approaches to gaining knowledge: while he experienced life as a tension between polarities, she felt a deep need to try to reconcile opposing views and feel at one with humanity. "It oppresses me that you must always read through your wise glasses, which mercilessly betray every little loophole in thought." His rigorously analytical mind treated information as something to "use, to weigh, and sort." Alva claimed that her approach was more intuitive, even mystical. She had been reading Rabindranath Tagore, the Indian writer who had won the Nobel Prize for literature in 1913, whom she regarded as full of universal love and forgiveness for human frailty. Tagore's work stood in clear contrast to the "wretched literature of decadence" of contemporary Europe. From the perspective of the Indian philosopher, it was not so easy to draw a line between science and religion, the analytical and the intuitive. Seeking to escape an ethnocentric mindset, Alva tried to imagine how she would have felt about European civilization if she were encountering it for the first time from a different cultural or racial perspective. As a European, she had "effortlessly received a part of our thousand-year-old culture." But if she had encountered western civilization as a member of "a lower race," she imagined that "I should also have experienced it as a religion." Employing the language of her confessions to Per Sundberg, she observed that it was in her own stirring emotions that she found "rich enlightenment." Gunnar seemed to understand this part of her personality. "But," she asked, "can you not see how great my need is to have humanity at my side?" (A to G, Feb. 22, 1920) Tagore helped to rekindle her belief in the oneness of humanity, her desire to feel a sense of wholeness with the universe, her longing for forgiveness and reconciliation, and her experience of the divine in her interactions with other people.

Alva strained to play the roles of passionate lover, soul mate, nurse, counsellor, and debating partner for Gunnar. She had taken his demands as a challenge and welcomed the opportunity to grow out of the naïvely optimistic views she had previously held. A proud, independent girl before she fell in love with Gunnar, she had initially believed that she should strive to be the intuitive other half of a great man, strengthening him with her love. But Alva had moved ahead with her gymnasium education and involved Gunnar in discussions of books she had read. He insisted that she should also put aside her "feminine intuition" to think logically and "scientifically"—like a man—and offer him criticism and opposing viewpoints. Under the pressure of Gunnar's emotional crises, she would fall back on her skill as a nurturer. But this supportive role could easily slide into a more detached, clear-sighted clinical mode that undermined her romantic appeal in Gunnar's eyes, leading him to accuse her of emotional insensitivity. At times, under the harsh scrutiny of her parents and neighbors, the contradictions of these multiple roles became unbearable, and she would shut down emotionally or withdraw into what Gunnar derided as her "magic circle," repeating a survival strategy she had learned in her "Strindbergesque" family. As Alva became more adept at the dance steps required to keep up with his shifting moods and intricate demands, Gunnar—in spite of his great love for her—felt a dark compulsion to try to knock her off balance to see what she would do. Alva often referred to him as her "young god" and expressed her love in the language of religious faith. Gunnar, however, knew that he had a "devilish" side as well.

Ringing the Leper's Bell

In February 1920, Gunnar Myrdal felt that he ought to be happy. He had finally reached a level of intimacy with Alva he had hoped for, but the moment had passed swiftly. He had been unable to shake his depression, and Alva had seemed a bit distant. Instead of feeling united, Gunnar and Alva each felt encased in their own personalities. Now they were living 100 kilometers apart in environments from which each had become estranged. Neither communicated much with their closest friends; they depended wholly on one another. Yet that did not suffice. Gunnar wondered if he had done something wrong or somehow been inadequate, and he was puzzled by Alva's withdrawal into what he called her "troll circle." Instead of being swept away by passion, she had seemed cold, rational, and analytical as only a man was supposed to be. He felt afraid, helpless, and despondent.

Gunnar could not climb out of his depression, and he pressed Alva to write more often. "However well you understand me when I am healthy and mentally normal, you do not when I am tired and depressed." (G to A, Feb. 27, 1920) Alva replied that she recognized that this was a time of sickness for him and affirmed that she shared his sorrow. "Do you understand the comfort that is felt when another person cries for your sake?" She reassured him that "your little girl is near you in her thoughts every moment," and "when you are sad and depressed and care-worn, it hurts me." (A to G, Feb. 29, 1920)

Alva could only sustain such devotion at the price of inner turmoil. Three days later she wrote that she had been awakened by a frightening dream. Alva saw herself walking on a slippery path with deep abysses on either side. She began to slip and called out Gunnar's name. "You stood before me. You were tired. . . . I forgot the abysses and my fear." Her "one thought" was that "I must give you some rest." But Gunnar's presence was not enough to prevent her from falling.

> Then, can you believe, something wonderful happened. . . . You kissed me. You were the first thing I saw when I could open my eyes.—I saw how you fell alongside me and I believed that now my dearest was dead. With great efforts, you moved a little, laid your head on my lap, and happiness returned to me again. "He needs to sleep at least 3000 years," I thought. Of course I should keep a vigil during your rest.—I had forgotten to ask the gods if I could have such a long life that I would be able to behold your awakening.

Having indicated that they needed to care for each other and that her one-sided concern for Gunnar's mental health was imposing a heavy burden on her, Alva ended the letter. (A to G, March 1, 1920)

Gunnar got the message that Alva was feeling overwhelmed by his graphic descriptions of psychological pain, yet he could not keep from writing more. "I have just come through the darkest week I can ever remember having experienced," he declared. When such moods overwhelmed him, he was driven by compulsive thoughts, but was reluctant to put them on paper because he did not want Alva to regard them as a permanent part of his mental outlook. In a recent dream, someone had told him that he should ring a leper's bell to warn away all the happy people whom he might infect with his gloom. "He who has a rotting soul in this sinful world, he who is constitutionally unhappy and depressed," has a duty to keep these oblivious people out of his life. He especially wished to spare Alva. (G to A, March 5, 1920) Gunnar realized that he would have to get through this crisis by himself.

A couple of days later, Gunnar reported that he had spent a week in his "cellar hole" reading histories of the Roman emperors but had given it up because he had found it unhealthy to see his paranoia projected onto book after book. "I gained an emotional sympathy for Emperor Nero and came to liken myself to him, knowing that I also would have taken an exclusively aesthetic and dramatic view of my life." No one would have understood "the rhetorical beauty that I observed in the soul's splitting apart as Nero looked on Rome's ruins, standing on the balcony in a string-player's outfit and singing a poem about Ilium's fall." Gunnar was able to joke a little about his habit of portraying himself as a mad genius. "I have looked at myself in the mirror and seen that my eyes are empty and wild. Or let us say 'nervous' instead. It doesn't sound as romantic." (G to A, March 7, 1920)

In his next letter Gunnar asked if Alva was also sad and afraid. "I am so completely, happily egoistic, which makes me mad and tragic, and it doesn't occur to me that you also could be sad." "Inwardly I now want to trust you, but I do not know how." Gunnar worried that Alva did not long for him anymore. Telling her that he was now crying uncontrollably, he asked: "I wonder if you can cry, Alva?" Gunnar intensely desired to be with her but, feeling himself a moral leper, vowed that "I shall not touch you again." Alluding to her recent dream, he concluded: "Don't be sad any longer, little Alva. Sleep and dream of me, not on a slippery path and falling, but rather on a meadow of flowers and with angels' wings." (G to A, March 9, 1920)

In response to Gunnar's descriptions of mad, tragic solitude and retreat into a state of aesthetic contemplation, Alva counseled her beloved that the alternation of happiness and sorrow was inevitable. Although she had adopted his habit of referring to herself as "your poor little Alva" in her efforts to comfort him and make him feel like her "hero," Alva now chided Gunnar for his condescension, vowing that "If you dare to call me 'poor' again, I shall—yes, I haven't decided if I shall laugh out loud at you or be seriously angry." She acknowledged that they had been through a period in which both feared writing about their deepest feelings and found it difficult to trust each other. Alva reassured him that she still longed for his letters and rejoiced that "you, who are the sum of all the best things I know, are still in love with me." (A to G, March 11, 1920)

Having given this reassurance, Alva wrote again the next day to challenge Gunnar to accept the powerful love that she offered him. Before meeting Gunnar, she "had wandered so long in the forest of loneliness." "I thought of love as an intoxicating game, . . . nothing more." The men she had met before were "always missing something essential." But at last, Alva's "prince" had come along, and "all the barriers of artificial wisdom I had built up collapsed." Falling into the very rhetorical pattern she had advised Gunnar to avoid, Alva resorted again to self-deprecation: "I was not any kind of princess but just me—wretched, poor, boring, and starved." Recently, in a feverish dream, she had seen a ghost and had feared that Gunnar had turned away from her. Alva begged her sweetheart not to "awaken the soul's terrible fear, that ghastly demon from earlier times, the terror that perhaps nothing is there." Piling up all the metaphors she could think of, she declared:

> You are my home and my country; you are the wages of my labor and my riches; you are my faith's repose and my hunger's lovely meal; you are my nest to which I shall devote all my mercy; you are my young god, to whom all my affectionate devotion is given; you are my treasure of great value and my greatest thought; you are the whole world and more than the world; you are a man and you are mine. (A to G, March 12, 1920)

Alva followed this affirmation with an admonition: "If you seek to love me, you must also understand me." They had been through a time of testing that had made their love "stronger and more powerful." "Does this make you afraid? Am I violent? . . . If you want to have me tame and nice and sweet when it suits you, then you will not be such a powerful man. . . . Because you cannot extinguish it, not ever." Alva asked rhetorically whether Gunnar was prepared to "tell me . . . that I must be my mamma's nice girl, who curtsies and says 'yes, thank you,' if it pleases you to talk about love." If he did not want that kind of passive lover, then he should not "think that I am possessed because I dare to write things that no mamma in the world would permit, instead of closing them up inside myself."

"I should be afraid of your violence? Ha-ha!" Gunnar retorted. He was defensive about her suggestion that, if he did not accept her powerful love, he would be a less powerful man. "If you can feel things so much more strongly than I," then you must know that "your love has to battle in my mind with thousands of emotions and other ideas that course through my sensations with nervous and inexorable force." Denying that he had ever wanted her to be sweet and subservient, he inquired sarcastically, "How do you think that a nice and—alas—'passive feminine' girl would . . . have the capacity to rule and control my unquiet heart?" Incensed that Alva would accuse him of wanting a "conventional" woman, he scoffed that "I am sardonic and do not have the least 'respect for convention.'"

Guessing that Alva's self-assertion was driven by anxiety over her loss of virginity, Gunnar sought to reassure her of her moral worth: "You soft, warm girl—your purity, your innocence and virtue are something completely apart from and therefore more important than your hymen." (G to A, March 14, 1920)

"I—I—I!!" Gunnar exclaimed in a striking moment of self-awareness. "It is certainly the word that I most frequently write? It plagues me." Attempting to rise to Alva's challenge, he yearned to "leave behind these constant reminders of my overvaluation of self" and reminded her that she knows "how humble I am just toward you alone." Seeming to recognize that he had overstepped the bounds of romance by writing so obsessively about his symptoms of depression, he observed that "love, like life itself, is an art and among the fields of art most like the dramatic!" Gunnar hoped that, by transforming his suffering into art, he would make it seem more beautiful and tragic, or at least less weak and pitiful.

After five days' silence, Alva wrote that she had been ill and confined to her bed. It took all of her strength just to write a short note to her beloved in secret. (A to G, March 17, 1920) Gunnar worried that Alva's illness was due to pregnancy, and he engaged in a "thought experiment" to test the full range of emotions that prospective fatherhood evoked in his fevered imagination. His first reaction was "Perhaps Alva's sickness just means that she will give me a child. Then we have to shoot ourselves!?" After a moment's reflection, he ventured that, while they were both too young for parenthood, he could quit his legal studies and become a teacher "way up in Dalarna in a forest." They would live in a beautiful cottage. He would not concern himself with politics but devote himself to reading philosophy. "I wonder how you would be as a housewife?" he teased. Despite proclaiming himself "proud as an emperor" at the prospect of fatherhood, Gunnar clearly was anxious about having to give up his dreams. (G to A, March 19, 1920)

Although Alva was not pregnant, she was anxious about Gunnar's Easter visit to Slagsta farm. They would not have much privacy. She worried about Gunnar containing his volcanic temper and maintaining polite manners in front of her family, whom he found "stifling." She had to respond to Gunnar passionately and intellectually in a manner befitting an "exceptional" couple like themselves, but she also had to be careful not to betray to her observant parents the degree of intimacy that she and Gunnar had reached. Alva wondered what her parents thought about their relationship. Had they guessed that she had been lying about her trips to visit a female friend? She complained about the jealousy and intrusiveness of her sister Rut, who did not understand her "ideals" and whose thoughts were "purely conventional." Alva appealed to her "hero" to be strong and expressed confidence that he was "not afraid if ten thousand Ruts laugh a little." (A to G, March 27, 1920)

Gunnar tried to maintain his balance, offering solace and support to Alva during this stressful time but acknowledging that he had needed her strength during his many periods of depression. He considered it a compliment to say that Alva was the embodiment of his abstract conception of the perfect woman that he had longed for all his life. His paeans verged on the solipsistic: "You are nothing else than my own happy longing." "I have created you myself [out of] all my ideals and borrowed fantasies, a living expression of my own life's impulses." "If you do not know your genesis, then you must know that it is just a great miracle that your and my longing became [a reality] and [we] are one." (G to A, March 26, 1920)

While Gunnar could liken himself to a god-like artist who had created the perfect woman out of his imagination, he did not forget his profound helplessness and need when he was in despair. No longer did he think of ringing a bell to warn Alva away. "When I am unhappy and depressed, then I have in my love a secret bell to ring in my distress, but it is the only hopeful thing that I possess in those moments."

Note

All parenthetical citations in the text are to manuscripts written by Gunnar or Alva Myrdal. All translations were done by the author. These passages may differ from the English-language versions quoted in other publications. Many of Alva's and Gunnar's personal communications are difficult to decipher because they were written rapidly in longhand, abbreviate common words, and often use dashes instead of more precise punctuation. Transcribing and translating them necessarily involves matters of interpretation.

1 Myrdal, *American Dilemma*, 100. The phrases in quotation marks are from Copeland, The Negro as contrast conception.

References

Alva and Gunnar Myrdal's Collection (AGMA). Arbetarrörelsens Arkiv och Bibliotek (Swedish Labour Movement's Archive and Library). Stockholm, Sweden;
Correspondence between Alva and Gunnar Myrdal, 3.3
[cited as G to A or A to G, date]

Published Sources

Copeland, Lewis C. The Negro as contrast conception. In *Race Relations and the Race Problem*, ed. Edgar T. Thompson, 152–179. Durham, NC: Duke University Press, 1939.

Myrdal, Gunnar, with the assistance of Richard Sterner and Arnold Rose. *An American Dilemma: The Negro Problem and Modern Democracy*. New York: Harper & Bros., 1944.

9 "How to operate on the heart"

During the first week of April 1920, Gunnar visited Alva's family at Slagsta farm. It had been six weeks since the two lovers had shared a moment of intimacy. Although they had written each other nearly every day, they had seldom been in the same mood at the same time, and it was difficult for them to maintain their feeling of closeness. Alva's initial calm and self-control contrasted with Gunnar's abject depression, which he had expressed in graphic detail in his letters. Her carefully wrought love letters and efforts to reassure him could not stop his free-fall into the depths of despair, provoking complaints about her coldness as Gunnar sought to break the spell he believed she had cast around herself and gain access to the inner world of her thoughts and emotions. Finally she dared him to accept the powerful love that she was offering and to focus on their shared happiness as an antidote to his image of himself as an isolated, mad genius doomed to damnation. Her subsequent illness brought a partial reversal of roles as Gunnar sought to take the part of the stronger partner, but the challenge of building intimacy with Alva by letter tested the limits of his ability to get outside his own consciousness.

We have only a retrospective record of what happened at Slagsta farm during Gunnar's visit. It is clear that unresolved issues had been piling up. But the situation exploded when Gunnar confronted Alva with the revelation that he had had a sexual encounter with one of the thousands of prostitutes who walked the streets of Stockholm. The incident had occurred at the end of February, about two weeks after Alva's visit, after which there had been a striking lapse of correspondence on his part. Sensing that something was wrong, Alva had the harrowing dream she then described to him. (A to G, March 1, 1920) In turn, Gunnar had alluded to the "darkest week I can ever remember" and offered an arresting description of his "rotting soul." His wish for a leper's bell to warn people away was, perhaps, a metaphor for his fear of venereal disease as well as a symbol of his continued psychological distress that threatened to "infect" Alva, who had endured much as his counselor. (A to G, March 1, 1920) Although he had tried to shield Alva from the worst of his torment, Gunnar had still hoped that she would be able to heal him. In the aftermath of his sexual encounter, Gunnar had written so many descriptions of his acute depression that the normally healthy Alva had taken to her bed for a few days in mid-March, suffering from a fever that was probably worsened by the burden of his dark and self-lacerating mood.

During his time at Slagsta, Gunnar apologized profusely for his sexual transgression, claimed that the experience had been "meaningless," swore that he was still in love with Alva, and promised that his temporary lapse posed no threat to their relationship. There was no falling-out in front of the ever-watchful Reimer family. Both Alva and Gunnar struggled to carry on as if nothing had happened, and Alva agreed to continue the relationship. When he returned home, however, Gunnar was not sure that the issues had been settled. In his first letter, he revealed that at the end of the visit, "I had a strong desire to ask you if you still hold me dear, but I dared not tempt God." Then he expressed his feeling that "never have we loved each other as we do now. At least I haven't!" (G to A, April 9, 1920)

Alva took upon herself the responsibility for moving the couple beyond the crisis that Gunnar's act had precipitated. She began by reassuring him that he had made her "happier than anything" and she felt "ripe for greater and greater happiness." But then she moved swiftly to the point, writing in the carefully composed, formal style that she had learned from her reading. "When you were here I discovered some dark thoughts. Perhaps I believed that in the future I would suffer from these threatening thoughts." On reflection, however, she had concluded that "my prince is not completely dead and has not become just an [ordinary] man of the people," sparing Gunnar an indignity that would have struck at his cherished conception of himself. Since he had tried to flatter her by calling Alva the embodiment of his feminine ideal of perfection, Alva measured Gunnar against her own ideal: "I must do everything to satisfy my old demand that you must be a true copy of my poetic hero." Since he had emphasized the psychological value of speaking one's mind, he would understand that "it is necessary that I not nurture any disappointment that displeases me; therefore I ask that you . . . listen to me talk about that which I have been enjoined to forget." (A to G, April 10, 1920)

"I do not wish that my happiness should be knocked down by a lie"

In the wake of the Easter revelation, Alva revisited her memories of those turbulent six weeks when she had earnestly striven to understand Gunnar's depression and self-hatred, worried about his silences, and then fallen sick herself. Her beloved, who had taught her to lie to her parents, had now lied to her, shattering the pact they had made to share everything with each other. Then he had asked for her compassion for his guilt-driven depression, metaphorically putting his head on her lap as he had actually done during their first romantic encounter in Solvarbo the previous summer. In her own mind, Alva debated how much more information she needed before she could bring herself to forgive him. "My love may well die some day of my own feebleness, at least if I live long enough—but of nothing else." Yet she had the strength to endure: "You cannot easily crush my happiness." Indeed, given the intensity of her love, she worried that "I am almost too willing to forgive you." Alva saw honesty and emotional openness as the core values of their relationship and pressed Gunnar for total disclosure. "I do not wish . . . that my happiness, if dangerously ramshackle, should be knocked down by a lie or distortion." She entreated Gunnar: "Help me then, dear, to be able to hold onto my trust in you!" "Without it, without my full respect for you, I would come to feel mean and petty." During the past few days she had struggled "so much with this thing which, to be sure, is the greatest sorrow of my new life." "I do not want to conceal anything from you and, for that reason, I must feel able to write that which I scarcely wish to speak." (A to G, April 10, 1920)

In her response to Gunnar's confession of unfaithfulness, Alva used one of his favorite techniques and focused more on his intentions than the morality of the action. "I shall never be able to forgive you if you took the girl with the same emotions and thoughts which I am accustomed to receiving or with a certain resemblance." "I forgive—no, I do not even need to forgive—if you had her in spite of an ideal of virtue which you understood." Alva could imagine the emotions that "stirred within you" and forgive "the most ruthless sensual pleasure" if it resulted from Gunnar's having yielded to temptation through weakness and done something that he knew to be contrary to his principles. But she could "never forgive the ordinary, often masculine view" that justified a man using a certain type of woman for pleasure because the encounter was "meaningless." With some understatement, Alva pointed out that "you like to give in to a strange bravado" of defying convention.

Rejecting martyrdom, Alva refused to accept any blame for having neglected Gunnar during this time. She emphasized that she did not forgive him "out of ideal goodness" or "to put the best face on everything," but "in order to be content with myself." She then asked: would he "help me to preserve the peace of mind that is returning in my soul?" Having disclaimed any aspirations to sainthood and justified her forgiveness in terms of her own psychological well-being, Alva returned to their Romantic dreams: "I feel, as ever, that you are, of course, the incarnation of everything great, and I intend to believe it as long as I believe in anything in the world, otherwise I would sink hopelessly to the bottom in despair [and] wither in hopelessness." After getting her thoughts on this difficult subject on the page, Alva experienced a catharsis and exclaimed: "I am happy. I love you. I do not forget that I have made an eternal pact with your blood."

Despite this powerful declaration of love, Alva may have had second thoughts about the kind of pact into which she had entered. She enclosed with her letter a book about a character with the strongest of passions who had surrendered his soul to someone else: Goethe's *Faust*. Did Alva identify with Faust and feel that her soul was now under Gunnar's control? Or did she intend the more conventional meaning that, just as Faust had learned to temper his limitless desires and had been redeemed by Gretchen's forgiving love, so Gunnar would gain maturity and balance through Alva's devotion?

The next day, Alva took up the theme that she and Gunnar must understand each other's psychological motives and communicate about their intentions if they were to have a strong relationship. In response to his claim that she retreated into her "magic circle," she explained defensively that "I often conceal my intentions, without knowing and meaning to, because of my inferiority when it comes to communication." Looking at the marital problems of her own parents and of other couples she knew, she suggested that psychological understanding, tolerance, and openness would improve the quality of intimate relationships. "How can it happen that a human couple, who have pledged their faith in one another, do not understand that they will be happiest if they do their best for each other?" Assuming the harmony of the universe, Alva took for granted that "if two people were alone in the world, they should certainly love each other." Why do they not "understand that they, together and individually, are alone?" If they don't hold fast to each other, then "the outsiders who want to trespass can trample on [the couple] with impunity." Total unity was impossible; differences between husbands and wives that seem "ordinary" are "a thousand-fold mystery of life." "I sometimes get really angry when I see a person sigh under her hard fate and I know that she, with just some friendly words, ought to be able—maybe—to open another person's soul with the desire to understand, help, share, and support." This daughter of a taciturn father and an alternately controlling and absent mother became "angry" when she saw "people turn silent and uncomprehending, . . . when it lies within their own power to knock down the walls of difference and find forces that . . . work for their good." Nudging Gunnar to appreciate the crucial importance of honesty, she asked, "Don't you believe that I'm right when I see so many marriages as completely tragic?" (A to G, April 11, 1920)

By apologizing during the Easter vacation for his encounter with the other woman, Gunnar had indulged his love of confession, self-exposure, and self-analysis. Blurting out his disgust with himself, he had achieved a catharsis. Whether or not it was intended as such, his revelation had also been a test of Alva's capacity for detached psychological analysis, for putting her analytical abilities ahead of her spontaneous emotional reaction. Although Gunnar professed not to believe in traditional ideas of sin and forgiveness, he felt confident that Alva had already granted him absolution and that their relationship would continue. When he received her letter at his apartment in Stockholm, however, he felt that he had apologized enough. Refusing to accept the terms of her forgiveness, he seems to have seen the letter as posing an intellectual rather than a moral challenge. But Gunnar's response expresses more than his penchant for contrarianism, competitiveness, and playing the dominant male role. He genuinely could not accept Alva's carefully wrought formulation of the situation as the case of a "virtuous" man who had briefly yielded to animal instinct and now sought forgiveness. He had read too much Darwin, Nietzsche, and Freud to embrace what he saw as a false conception of human psychology.

The Experiment

With tongue in cheek and moral compass tossed aside, Gunnar claimed that he was accepting at face value her demand for an honest exploration of the intentions behind his sexual encounter with the girl in Stockholm. He proceeded to answer her questions in the language of a legal scholar performing an exegesis of a document and affected the cold detachment of a psychologist scientifically interrogating himself about motives, emotions, and behavior. In doing so, he drew upon techniques of Nietzsche and Hägerström in dissecting the language of moral statements and viewing them as bundles of sentiment with no logic or force behind them.

He began, "You request an analysis and you will get it." Claiming that he had "the capacity to instantly become cold and abstract and to analyze myself and others, I have therefore a sense of how to operate on the heart with a knife, scissors, and tweezers." Gunnar expressed the hope that Alva would not regret having asked him to be honest. She had wanted to know, "Why did I take the girl?" "I was depressed. You, my eternal dearest, had disappeared and gone away." In examining his motives, he concurred with Alva that his desire to defy authority and convention was paramount:

> First, you have the masculine, completely constitutional hunger for a woman, which you were no longer there to satisfy. Then curiosity and the intellectual interest in experimenting with [another] person. Moreover, it undeniably flattered my vanity and self-esteem to be able to subdue a little creature's will to the point of absolutely annihilating it, to pick her up on the street, and without ceremony, talk, or hypocrisy, to command her. My unhappiness and my defiance were incomparably the strongest incitements, followed next by . . . the flattery to my self-esteem, then the sexual instinct and last, the psychological interest.

Then, responding more directly to Alva's letter, he continued: "When you ask if I did it 'with a certain indifference,' I really must say that I did. I was so depressed that I did not puzzle over anything. But I do not think that was what you meant." (G to A, April 12, 1920)

Gunnar then addressed Alva's question of whether he had justified the action to himself on the grounds that it had no meaning. "I could not really, truthfully call" the sexual encounter "meaningless, except that it made me even more unhappy." Keeping up the calculated tone of scientific and jurisprudential detachment, Gunnar declared that "my intention was to write and report. Not in order to beg for *forgiveness.* I know not what forgiveness is. A brick in the construction of a religious dogma? Part of a contractual settlement agreement about restitution?" If so, "then it would be a logical falsehood, without reality. What is written is written and what is done is done."

Returning to his close examination of Alva's letter, Gunnar noticed that she had said that "you cannot love me without my being a prince!" Although Alva had intended this statement to prod him to behave better in order to deserve her approbation, he insisted on reading it as a fair estimate of his worth. "I understand that so well, otherwise I should not be able to live if I did not believe myself to be higher than all people." Returning to his preoccupation with the link between greatness and madness, he ventured: "When I am unhappy and unquiet in my thoughts, I always write a lot on account of mental illness."

Gunnar reiterated his claim that he had no "ideal of virtue" against which Alva might measure him. He had ideals about statecraft, rhetoric, and music, but virtue "does not exist for me as a universally applicable concept." While "virtue" had no meaning in law, politics, economics, and social behavior, Gunnar thought it possible for certain exceptional women to be virtuous, although it should not be associated narrowly with chastity. Feminine virtue was a kind of essential goodness that men could only admire. "'Virtue' is either fearful timidity, inexperience *or* love, not purity or goodness except to a pure and good woman." As for himself, Gunnar advised Alva that any "virtue" he had "exists merely in relation to you, my dream-girl." Therefore, "if it were not for you, my virtue would not exist."

Although he was undoubtedly proud of this "defiant" exercise in textual analysis, legal legerdemain, and self-exculpation, Gunnar wondered how Alva would react to it since it was hardly what she had expected when she had requested a full explanation of his motives. "Why do you ask for cold analysis if you cannot bear it?" Regarding his "experiment" with another woman, Gunnar declared: "Why have I not said: 'This is what I have done, this is what I am like. Try to forget.' Because it would be nothing but an empty, hypocritical gesture to say so, since I did after all notice that you still love me." After dropping this bombshell, Gunnar was eager to hear Alva's response. But he admonished her not to write in "conventional phrases" because he was "suspicious of kind-hearted and pious deception."

That same day, Alva penned a letter, which crossed Gunnar's missive in the mail, emphasizing how "indispensable" he was to her life. What she had once felt to be a desire for spiritual experience had now become a yearning for earthly love. "It is wonderful that a demand for love such as mine, a hunger and aspiration for the extraordinarily great, really gets to have its fill. I feel—sometimes—the dizzying greatness that I, who ask so unreasonably much, should get so unusually much." Once again she substituted Gunnar for God, paraphrasing the Lutheran communion to profess that "it is through you and for you that I teach myself to understand that which I am happy to experience." (A to G, April 12, 1920)

Thinking that the crisis was behind them, Gunnar wrote the next day thanking Alva effusively for the copy of *Faust* and regretting that she had not inscribed it to him. Turning to Anatole France's novel, *Queen Gåsfot*, he offered mock sympathy for Alva as a "refined and honest little woman" having to read a novel in which women are portrayed as "petty, grasping, little pussycats." He regarded the author as "very contemptuous of man in general but of women particularly," and added that "within the context of his time, this could be seen as [an] exaggerated protest against the prevailing insane worship of women largely thanks to your Ibsen, whom you in quite natural gratitude admire in return." But Gunnar demurred that Alva was "too intelligent to be overly influenced by this." (G to A, April 13, 1920)

Gunnar could not resist the impulse to take a poke at his beloved in the hope of getting a reaction. As a boy he had teased his sister Elsa mercilessly, ridiculing girls and their opinions, and sometimes he used this adolescent badinage with Alva. Now he professed to wonder why Anatole France's novel was so popular with the female reading public, though "one has to bear in mind such creatures' somewhat perverse desire for beatings in between caresses." Then he immediately interjected: "I cannot understand why I am always rude to women." He mockingly implored Alva to reprimand him for it; he expected a "thrashing." Then Gunnar ventured an astonishing but inadvertently insightful answer to his question about why he was rude to women: "It couldn't be because I am myself a little like a woman, could it?" If so, he quickly reassured Alva—and himself—that only with her had he let down his guard and relied on his emotions.

Quickly retreating from his startling moment of self-questioning, Gunnar fell back into analyzing his and Alva's mental differences in more conventional terms. She wanted to view everyone "passionately," subjectively, and "from the inside," while he wanted to view everyone from the outside, ironically, and objectively as a scientist. "You view people from the point of view of their own assumptions and independent purposes. I view them on the basis of my own assumptions and . . . for my own purposes." Gunnar confessed that he had "always had an irresistible desire to laugh at people. I have to laugh . . . to deal with people as instruments, as statistics. Abstraction is the alpha and omega to political science, sentimentality its worst enemy." As a lawyer, he should not become deeply involved in the lives of the people he worked with. As a woman, Alva was by nature willing and able to penetrate the souls of others. He was relieved that she lacked those special characteristics that enabled him to appreciate Anatole France; if she did not, she would be a "scary monster." Gunnar nervously concluded his letter by suggesting that, despite the different ways in which he and she saw things, they both had a passion for the truth.

"Ban the Troll"

When she read Gunnar's extraordinary, "objective" account of his emotions while having sex with another woman, Alva felt stunned. She had dreamed of him, she told Gunnar, and "sorrow pressed on my heart like a load of lead." In composing a response, "I have great difficulty in expressing myself." Alva had once hoped that their intimacy might allow her and Gunnar to understand each other intuitively as well as analytically. Now she was confronted with the fact that she did not know him well and that part of his personality was cold and calculating—and not just with respect to his "scientific" studies. Alva regretted that she could not talk to Gunnar face to face; she found the act of writing "a sad surrogate for life." (A to G, April 13, 1920)

The following day, Alva resolved to take Gunnar's blunt letter as an inducement to attend more to her own inner needs. Addressing him as "You clever, dumb, and most beloved one," she did not confront his assertions directly but observed that "my soul has been out of balance for more than half a year. If it continues, the damage will be irreparable." Alva explained that "a certain part [of the soul] needs time to be brought up to the same level as the others." She thought that her soul had grown "unevenly" in childhood, as "fantasies gained the upper hand," but that more recently the reasoning part of the soul had replaced the imaginative side. "Now I wonder if it is not time to set things right." In saying that the emotional and intellectual parts of her soul were not in equilibrium, Alva implied that Gunnar's personality was far more unbalanced and needed much more significant repair. She affirmed that "I have enough power in my soul both to love with full intensity and to live another part of my life in full measure." Alva resolved to attend to all the parts of herself "not directly connected to you." In an ironic riposte to Gunnar's "cold," supposedly clinical analysis of his sexual behavior, she declared: "I am so tired that I am not able to warm [your] massive psychological coldness with a single little word of love." Signing off without the usual endearments, she demanded a long letter from him in response. (A to G, April 14, 1920)

Gunnar professed to agree with her, albeit in a condescending manner. It was "unhealthy for a young girl" to concentrate so strongly on her relationship with her beloved that she neglects all of her old interests, he opined. After a few more expressions of concern about Alva's feelings, he mentioned gingerly that he had not yet heard her opinion of "the analysis you required from me." Gunnar wondered anxiously "if I should be worthy of your 'full respect,' and if you should be able to be a little in love with me without feeling demeaned?"

> Perhaps you wanted that report in the . . . hope that I should have enough tact to lie a little to preserve your peace of mind. But you ought to know well that, in such a thing I never lie, not even for the best purpose. It would violate my scientific conscience. (G to A, April 15, 1920)

Alva responded satirically, addressing her next letter "to a great man, interpreter, king and philosopher; a fool, knight of the realm and messenger of the lord in heaven, to him whose mighty love's power has overwhelmed me." After reading Gunnar's letter, she had felt overcome not by love but by depression, which she represented as a troll. Alva recalled a folktale about a person walking in the mist who was hit in the back of the head by a troll. But when the sun broke through the mist, the troll, who could only flourish in darkness, evaporated, leaving only the crackling sound as he disintegrated. Improvising a poem on this theme, she wrote:

> And I drank in the sunshine and much happiness,
> Everything crackling with the troll's dry skin.
> For me an expensive, costly pleasure:
> I am pleased in my happiness to ban the troll.

Alva drove home the point by observing that "I am experiencing just that feeling of support having been taken away by a foul sort of cunning." No doubt, she noted dryly, "he who has sinned much has the prospect of winning the most grace," but she was still reeling from the blow to her head from the troll's stick and was in no mood to minister to his need for forgiveness. (A to G, April 16, 1920)

Three months later, after Alva and Gunnar had a chance to discuss these issues in person while on vacation in Dalarna, she was more willing to speak frankly about the searing pain she had felt in the immediate aftermath of Gunnar's "experiment." At the time, she had suppressed these emotions and tried to strike a dignified tone, replying forcefully, rationally, and with some wit to Gunnar's outrageous self-report. Alva hated the role of victim and detested whining. Playing the martyr and sobbing about one's pain was for weak people like her mother. Alva had also thought it prudent to take into account Gunnar's susceptibility to anxiety and depression. She was intimately acquainted with the fearful, guilt-ridden boy behind the mask of the masculine superman. At 18, Alva knew that she loved Gunnar and thought him brilliant and full of dazzling potential, but she drew a certain strength from his stunningly candid confessions of his fears, weaknesses, and failures. She was quickly moving beyond the motherly role to that of counselor and companion. While Gunnar crudely boasted of his "cold," "calculating," "rational," and "scientific" mind, Alva knew that she was more capable of containing her emotions. In her mind, banning the troll—a deformed, misshapen, angry creature that was less than human—and attending to herself was a more effective response than trying to make him feel her anguish. Moreover, this approach enhanced her power in the relationship. Focusing on her own needs for a while and reading more deeply in psychology would enable her to craft a stronger self to debate, analyze, counsel, and love this extraordinary but vulnerable man who had briefly been able to entertain the possibility that his derision of women might stem from his being "a little like a woman myself." Ultimately she would help him to construct a stronger and more effective masculine role in the larger world while demanding from him more consideration for her needs and aspirations. At the time, Alva thought of it as helping him "grow up" and "become a man." But could she find the strength both to love him and to reserve part of herself for independent cultivation and growth?

While Gunnar tried to pretend otherwise, there were serious consequences of his breaking Alva's trust and his claim that the damage was repaired by his unflinching self-analysis. Both of them skirted around the problem in their letters during the second half of April, trying to bridge the difficult time apart with word games and jokes. While Alva turned inward and shared little of her feelings, Gunnar spent more time with Fritz, speculating about all manner of ideas and theories, and found in his friend reinforcement for some of his opinions about women.

The Virgin and the Whore

Gunnar's psychological reaction to his encounter with the prostitute shares some compelling similarities to the experiences of Fritz Thorén's fictional character Gerhard Melcher in his novel *En Son*.[1] As Fritz and Gunnar emerged from adolescence in the all-male world of gymnasium and university, these lonely youths were unsure about how to attain adult masculinity. They did not want to be like their fathers, and they were ignored by the young men from the upper class who dominated student life. They were rarely invited to social events where they could meet "refined" young women from "good" families, and many of those girls lacked education and imagination. To Fritz and Gunnar, marriage seemed to be mainly about money. Wives' demands for material goods spoiled scientists' or scholars' dreams to make a contribution to knowledge. Neither young man would be able to support a wife for some time.

Fritz and Gunnar saw women as potential obstacles to their intellectual ambitions. Literary realists, especially Strindberg, had demystified the idealized lady of romantic poetry and sentimental fiction, stripping away layers of pretense and defenses to get at the real woman, and what they saw was not so pleasing. In late nineteenth and early twentieth century novels, the bourgeois woman is often portrayed as a sexually frustrated creature striving for control in her marriage. Blocked from a career of her own and excluded from public and political life, this stereotypical character emasculates her husband, projects her ambitions onto his career, and stifles the emotional growth of their children. Ellen Key pointed to alternative possibilities for women, but was derided by Strindberg. In their small rooms and coffee shops, Fritz and Gunnar mostly talked *about* women, not *to* them. Love and sex were mysteries they were eager to explore, but they fretted about being ensnared by a woman who would drain them of their creative energy, divert them from their careers, and force them into an endless round of boring family and social events.

Like many young men at that time, Fritz and Gunnar felt a dichotomy between their vision of idealized romantic love and their sheer sexual "hunger." Gunnar, despite his professed wish to toughen himself, had secretly yearned for a refined woman who embodied Goethe's "eternal feminine," an exceptional woman who would give him the support he needed as well as the freedom to pursue his great work. He liked to imagine Alva as the embodiment of this feminine ideal, although he also encouraged her to become his debating partner. Meanwhile, she lived 100 kilometers away, and Gunnar felt intense sexual hunger every day.

The notion that they were Nietzschean supermen who could have both love and sex was a fantasy that nicely suited Fritz and Gunnar. It was easy for them to believe that men were "naturally polygamous," gripped by a "constitutional need" for sex that had to be satisfied. The superman had to be "ice-cold," with nerves of steel. Yet Gunnar also imagined himself as Romantic hero, irresistible to women and able to feel the emotions of love more fully than other men. In the novel, Fritz's Gerhard Melcher finds it impossible to reconcile romantic love and sexual desire. This character, who encompassed qualities of both Gunnar and Fritz, found his emotional development arrested on the cusp of his transition to manhood.

When we left Gerhard he was 19, living in a garret in Stockholm, too depressed to concentrate on his scientific studies or to work on his great invention and convinced he was a failure. "Day followed day, week followed week, empty, tired, meaningless." One rainy night G.M. takes a walk in the city, trying to get away from his obsessive fears and haunting memories of his parents. "The circles in which his thoughts coursed grew ever more narrow." Suddenly, the despondent young man hears the clump-clump of high heels on the sidewalk, and "near the darkness of the cellar, a red gown shone like a piece of newly cut meat." Gazing through the mist, Gerhard wonders if the figure in the red dress walking toward him is an apparition. As she stops and raises her face to his, he thinks she resembles a clown with a "white mask, red lips, and dark, sunken eyes." The melancholy scientist speculates that she is "just a condensation of the wet darkness" until she laughs and says "good evening" in a hoarse voice. "Do you want to go home to your place?" she asks. Gerhard considers her silently, feeling a touch of pity for a fellow creature "suffering" in her wet clothes in the rain. "Are we not akin?" he muses to himself. "And we walk on the same sidewalk of life. Outside the facades, outside and in hell." His sympathy suddenly turns to longing and a feeling of "rapaciousness," and he seizes the opportunity to experience what he calls "the great mystery," inviting her to his apartment for a drink. When they arrive, "Emmy," as she styles herself, reclines on his elegant sofa, downs some gin, and promptly asks for ten crowns. She explains that she would like to do it for free but that her "boyfriend" will not permit it. The innocent but eager Gerhard obliges, and Emmy "mischievously lifted her dress, put the ten crowns in her stocking, and smiled amorously." "'It is like putting a coin in a machine,' Gerhard thought with great coldness during this excitement, which did not reach higher than his waist." (184–189) Emmy took off her blouse, and they set about their business on the sofa that Gerhard had kept after his parents' death. As a novelist, Fritz dwells more on the tawdry than the titillating and offers no more details on the night's events.

When Gerhard awakens the next morning, he feels a "deadly disgust." "'Go now, if you please,' he said with his face turned away" from Emmy. Touching her body gave him a feeling of shame mixed with "a deep hostility" (186). Trying to start a conversation, Emmy comments that the sofa must be expensive, spurring Gerhard to blurt out that she can have it. He then throws open the windows to let in some fresh air and runs down the stairs into the street. He walks furiously to nowhere in particular. Suddenly he darts into a store, buys a cheap revolver and some ammunition, then heads back into the street with the pistol in his pocket.

Gunnar's *doppelgänger* feels a sharp pain but also an "ice-cold coolness" as he stops to sit on a park bench, thinking that his "shadow life," a mere "molecular combination," must now come to an end. "Must it happen now?" he asks himself, his hand tensing as he grips the revolver. He suddenly falls asleep on the bench, and when he awakes he is "gripped by shame and loathing." "Are you sick?" someone asks. Gerhard decides not to pull the trigger. His tortured life must continue a little longer. When he staggers home to his apartment, he sees two dodgy-looking characters lurking in the shadows. They have come for the sofa. "It's for my girlfriend," one of them explains (190). Gerhard watches them carry the heavy sofa down several flights of stairs, glad to part with the last tangible reminder of his childhood.

In the novel, Gerhard slowly develops a friendship with Berit, a "proper" girl who comes from a wealthy family. It is the young scientist's first serious relationship, but he does not allow himself to be swept away by passion. He brings to the relationship with Berit some of the techniques for avoiding intimacy and dependence that he had developed as the son of two difficult parents. In Berit's arms, Gerhard is temporarily freed from "voices, reservations, watchfulness, protests, curiosity, scorn, calculations, incitement, sorrow." He respects her chastity for a long time, and when they finally have intercourse he needs to convince himself that he had remained tough and warded off any feelings of dependency, that he had "played ruthless and become so." Yet Gerhard soon experiences a return of depression and becomes painfully aware of "his half-heartedness, his fears and his incapacity to be genuinely happy." (311–316)

When Berit is out of town, Gerhard misses her at first, but after a week he is able to work on his invention and realizes that he feels no "guilt" over the fact that he is not entirely dependent on her. He writes her some stereotypical love letters, but his body aches for sex. "For many years Gerhard had been able to discipline his sexuality," the narrator tells us, but now he felt lust that "exceeded all boundaries." So he "picked up a girl from the street." He had a bit of "luck" because the girl was not "stingy" with her favors.

> Gerhard had prepared himself for a difficult struggle with his conscience, but remarkably enough . . . it had not been so bad. Actually he had never felt so satisfied. . . . In many ways, it had been more natural, more honest, and more free of reservations. It felt right. It had been like a man quenching his thirst from a sturdy wooden bucket, instead of sipping carefully from a fragile glass.

Gerhard experienced "a feeling of manly, raw power" and thought: "'Is this really so simple? Can one never bridge the two sides of love, as I honestly had tried to do?'" (323–324)

Berit is still deeply in love with him, and Gerhard resumes the relationship with her when she returns to Stockholm. Although they use birth control, which for him adds more coldness and distance to the sex, Berit gets pregnant and wants to marry him. But Gerhard fears the entanglement that marriage would bring and the loss of time and energy for his work. Haunted by the memory of his own childhood, he is horrified at the thought of becoming a father and angrily demands that Berit have an abortion. "I don't want to have children!" he explodes. "Not with you, not with any other woman . . . . I forbid you to have a child by me. Do you hear? . . . Surely a man is allowed to decide such a thing himself?" (333) Deaf to Berit's pleas, he cruelly rejects her. Putting all his efforts into his invention, Gerhard works with a company that he hopes will bring it to fruition, but other scientists steal his ideas. He sees no future. Having thrown his revolver away, Gerhard finds his childhood chemistry set and poisons himself.

Although Berit is a simpler soul than Alva, Gerhard's emotional reaction to the relationship recalls some of Gunnar's struggles with his feelings about Alva. The law student was more passionately drawn to the object of his desire than the fictional character was to her counterpart, but Gunnar did try to put some brakes on his emotions. He feared a loss of control of his feelings and dependence on a woman whose needs might hold him back from the lonely greatness to which he aspired, and he anxiously probed his behavior for any signs of weakness. A divided self like Gerhard, Gunnar was constantly observing himself "scientifically," studying his reactions closely, and feeling disengaged from the active self that he was monitoring. To achieve greatness, he sought to toughen himself and to remain cool, which led him to devise experiments to test his ability to control his emotions. As he reached for a mature male identity, Gunnar, like Gerhard, feared a repetition of childhood trauma, a recurrence of his dependency on unreliable parents, and an inability to control what was happening to him.

Crime without Punishment

Unable to be with Alva who, in his view, had withdrawn into her "troll circle," Gunnar reflexively fell back on his hyper-masculine literary persona in his letters in late April. To be sure, there were elements of self-parody in these letters, but since they also contained "honest" expressions of his emotional distress Alva had to tread carefully, learning when to laugh and when not to. Neither of them wanted to reopen fresh wounds by resuming their analysis of the relationship in the mail; both thought it best to wait until their next meeting. So Alva wrote less often, seeking to conjure up some of her own magic against the marauding troll that she knew only too well. After the epic battle at Slagsta during the Easter holiday, each of them seemed content with skirmishing, at least for a time.

Alva had sought to hold Gunnar accountable for his behavior by reminding him that he was her "prince" and that he needed to act like one in order to live up to her masculine ideal. In reply, he tried to provoke her by suggesting that "you are not completely in love with me. You love a fantasy-creation, which you call a . . . prince, a g6d, and a hero." Gunnar was scornful of the "honor" that such a hero was supposed to exhibit and suggested that he could not be the strong knight on whom she wanted to rely in her feigned feminine weakness. He characterized Alva's ideal as the "Platonic form" of a lover, which is "just a little different from his earthly likeness." Her prince was "great and strong," free of "tiredness, boredom, surliness, weakness." The only problem was that he bore little resemblance to the real Gunnar. He has one advantage, though: "he is real." Is it so ridiculous, he asked, that the "dumb likeness" should want to be loved as he really is, not as his beloved imagines him to be? He hoped for more understanding from a "foolish little girl longing for a kiss." (G to A, April 17, 1920)

Gunnar was still trying to explain himself, hoping to soften the blow of the troll's club. The ethical relativist faulted himself for brooding too much over "morality . . . my honor, your respect, and other boring subjects." Perhaps thinking of Alva's identification with Peer Gynt's search for the self, he nervously proclaimed that "I stand by the axiomatic sentence . . . 'I am what I am' and feel content." Gunnar ended the letter by reassuring Alva that he felt "much, much in love with my little, precious, young and beautiful toy." (G to A, April 19, 1920)

The law student continued reading books on criminal psychology. Pondering the emotional impact of a crime on the perpetrator, he wondered what it would feel like to steal a book. Gunnar professed to have no moral objection to doing so for experimental purposes, but was curious about whether he would experience a tormented conscience afterward. So the faux scientist set out for the book section in a large Stockholm department store. Once inside, he suppressed any sense of fear and "mechanically" stuffed a book into his briefcase. Gunnar wrote Alva that he was "proud" to have carried out this experiment without experiencing even a twinge of guilt. But, like Dostoevsky's Raskolnikov, he was unable to convince himself that his crime deserved no punishment. Gunnar immediately went to see Fritz, who commended him on handling the business with a mind free of morality. "One can believe in everything, both evil and good," Fritz declared in a burst of Nietzschean enthusiasm. (G to A, April 22, 1920)

Later that evening, the two young men discussed the experiment at some length. "Are we what the legal psychiatrists call 'moral idiots' or something else?" Fritz and Gunnar wondered. Not surprisingly, the members of this mutual admiration society decided that they were "different." In describing the experiment to Alva, Gunnar made a Nietzschean argument that most people feel a conflict between envy and servility. He and Fritz, however, had what most people lack: a passion for truth, which served as the "only egotistical instinct." The account is laced with humor, but Gunnar was committed to the idea that an "exceptional man may breach ordinary barriers in pursuit of scientific truth." He wanted to believe that he, like Faust, could commit transgressions and be redeemed by the eternal feminine. Alva was not like most women, he constantly assured her; she belonged to a "special sex."

While Fritz greeted the book-stealing experiment with approbation, Alva did not deign to respond. She knew that deep insecurities lay beneath Gunnar's show of bravado. Which of his ambitions were dreams she should nurture and which were illusions she should question? In her own letters, which images of herself were literary constructs used to make a point and which represented her "real" self? It was not always easy for her to tell.

A few days earlier, Gunnar had surprised Alva by suggesting that he might be "a little like a woman" himself. Now he signaled that he would not be so easily soothed by her conventional efforts to reassure him by comparing him to a storybook hero or allow her to use an unrealistic model of masculinity to prod him into behaving as she wished. As usual, however, Gunnar backed off this line of pointed questioning and closed the letter with an expression of his gratitude. He was aware that his demands required much self-control on her part, and he worried that he was asking her to make "too great a concession." "Alva, it is not good for you. Reflection is painful. . . . Least of all would I wish you to be reflective. You must think small, beautiful, and sweet thoughts, but heaven forbid that you should think difficult, heavy and solid [thoughts] like I do." (G to A. April 24, 1920) Although Gunnar was teasing her, he wanted Alva to fulfill all his contradictory expectations.

In reply to Gunnar's reference to her as his "little toy," Alva retorted that "there is a vast difference between your and my ideas of how to play. You need a toy to amuse you; I play best with large imaginary toys while in conversation with someone, in whatever role suits me for the occasion." With regard to his many "thought experiments" and the intellectual puzzles that filled his letters, she complained that "you gave me one dumb moral question after another." He should realize that "when a person meets you, she sees a large placard, saying: 'Think before you speak!'" Sometimes she would like to be free of that "duty," but she knew he could not grant her such freedom. (A to G, April 27, 1920)

Gunnar feared that Alva's epistolary small talk could be a sign of her "indifference" to him and warned that if she stayed within her "forbidden magic circle" and allowed him no more than a glimpse of her inner feelings, he might "unintentionally wound" her. Although he enjoyed spirited debate, any letter from Alva that did not include expressions of total honesty and a spontaneous outpouring of emotion was unacceptable. "I cannot figure out what is now making you sad," he confessed, acknowledging that he was "big and dumb and clumsy" in his relations with her. In the aftermath of his disastrous experiment, Gunnar believed that he had been completely honest with Alva, that this was the only relationship in his life based on candor, and that he had exposed all his failings to her. "When it concerns other people, I think, on the contrary, that I am a matchlessly clever manipulator."

After stripping away the self-mockery, braggadocio, and deliberate condescension from Gunnar's letters, Alva did not lose sight of the moments of astonishing candor that remained—a level of self-criticism of which most men, including Fritz, were incapable. Ultimately, this capacity for self-awareness and growth in spite of great egotism and profound insecurities made Gunnar a very different man from the fictional Gerhard. Both obsessively monitored their own thoughts and feelings, but Gerhard kept it to himself, intensifying his self-absorption until he became totally disconnected from reality, while Gunnar reached out for a dialogue with Alva. Of course, he flattered himself by anointing Alva as an exception, a "woman with a soul." But, in contrast to Gerhard, Gunnar's need for companionship and escape from his depression led him to take different sorts of risks, to explore uncharted territory of the self, and to see an honest dialogue with Alva as offering the best hope for his life. To Alva, emotional honesty and the willingness to engage in complex psychological analysis seemed to make up for Gunnar's shortcomings.

When the year began, Alva had already perfected the nurturing role and was working on becoming a worthy companion to an exceptional man, as well as improving her talents as a debater. After the crisis of February and March 1920, she began to try out the therapist's role as well. Her long-anticipated embrace of sexual intimacy had not gone well. Her prince had been dejected, not charming. Instead of sweeping her off her feet, he had laid his head on her lap in search of reassurance. She had to leave their bed abruptly and looked back on the experience with doubt and confusion. Forcing herself to write to him, she found herself accused of being cold and rational. Alva had thought that their second try in mid-February had gone better. But only two weeks later her beloved, unbeknownst to her, had tried an "experiment" with a prostitute, momentarily steeling his nerves in a pose of scientific detachment, after which he had collapsed into the most severe depression she had ever encountered. Alva had to improvise techniques for handling her lover's mood swings and conflicting demands. Eventually she became adept at negotiating these hairpin turns in her letters, shifting among her portfolio of roles. It gave her a sense of self-confidence and power. But Alva had only begun to calculate the cost.

Note

All translations of the letters written by Alva and Gunnar Myrdal and of the novel written by Fritz Thorén were done by the author. The passages from Alva and Gunnar's letters may differ from the English-language versions quoted in other publications. What they wrote in longhand is often difficult to decipher, with abbreviations for common words and dashes instead of more precise punctuation. Transcribing and translating these manuscripts necessarily involves matters of interpretation.

1 Thomas, Fredrik (pseudonym of Fritz Thorén), *En son*. Page numbers in parentheses refer to this Swedish-language novel.

References

Alva and Gunnar Myrdal's Collection (AGMA). Arbetarrörelsens Arkiv och Bibliotek (Swedish Labour Movement's Archive and Library). Stockholm, Sweden.

Correspondence between Alva and Gunnar Myrdal, 3.3
[cited as: G to A or A to G, date]

Published Source

Thomas, Fredrik (pseudonym of Fritz Thorén). *En son*. Stockholm: Norstedts, 1936.

10 "I was surprised that you understood me so well"

Toward the end of April 1920, Gunnar reminded Alva that it would soon be Walpurgis Night. He polished his speech on "The Masses and Intelligence," drafted the previous fall and presented to his and Fritz's little debating society, to deliver to the festive gathering of university students. In May 1919 the Riksdag had established universal suffrage for men and women, without restrictions based on property ownership or marital status, and the political consequences of this step toward equality were still controversial. On the morning of April 30, Gunnar and Fritz went to Djurgården, where Stockholm University students assembled at a popular restaurant with a large garden. He had written a speech the previous year, but his nerves had been too shaky for him to deliver it. This year would be different, Gunnar resolved.

Gunnar and his best friend hoped that his oratory would "convert" the students to the idea of a "Party of the Intelligent." Gunnar would "talk until I had their minds completely under my power," he bragged to Alva. When the moment came, Gunnar climbed up on a chair and launched into his speech, but the students had already had too much to drink. "It was the same ordinary cackle of the crowd, one just like the other, empty, nasty yelling after the first glass." (G to A, April 30, 1920) Gunnar's appeal for an elite to guide the masses under universal suffrage was shouted down, as the students behaved far worse than newly enfranchised voters from the underclass.

"Everything fell apart," Gunnar wrote Alva the next day. "It was unthinkable that I should speak in front of those people—one ought to have some respect for his own ideas even if they are ineffective." After he stopped speaking, he noticed that he was crying. The two "intellectual aristocrats" tried to find some consolation in their sense of "distinguished superiority to all the world's rabble." But Fritz "drank alcohol like water" until he "was ripe enough to take off his coat and challenge their leader to a boxing match on the platform." To escape from the humiliation, Gunnar hastened to a nearby dance hall. A visiting band of Black musicians was playing, and he was unfamiliar with their style of music. "I tried to feast my eyes on the rose-scented Negroes," he sneered, "but found that I had to drink still more to understand the brilliant Negro rhythms." "I drank more until I lost consciousness sometime today on my sofa." Awakening with a headache, he remained defiant. "With every disillusionment I become more arrogant." He claimed to feel "a kind of *Schadenfreude* in my conscious diabolism" when his thoughts turned to the mob. His ambition in shambles, Gunnar observed that, while Alva had the ability to "play with a fantasy, . . . I live my game with the bloodiest seriousness." Sending her a copy of his speech, he wrote teasingly, "It is my mistake to have longed for a girl with whom I can talk." (G to A, May 1, 1920) When she read this, Alva underlined the sentence and scribbled a sarcastic "thank you" in the margin of his letter.

Two days later, between 10,000 and 15,000 men and women assembled for the Social Democratic Party's annual Mayday celebration. Hjalmer Branting, Gustav Möller, and Rikard Sandler spoke in the morning, hailing the achievement of universal suffrage and advocating the socialization of the economy to alleviate poverty. Then the trade unions—typographers, bookbinders, factory workers, electrical workers, store clerks—and other organizations, especially women's clubs and temperance groups, marched in an enormous parade. On the thirtieth anniversary of the party's founding, the Social Democrats were poised to mobilize the newly enfranchised working class.[1]

Meanwhile, Gunnar was in his basement apartment nursing his bruised ego, while Alva remained in Eskilstuna. In the wake of this fiasco, Alva refrained from raising any controversial issues of her own and made every effort to offer sympathy to her dejected hero. Ignoring the obvious contradiction between the elitism of Gunnar's speech and her own quest for harmonious social relations, she declared that "I feel really proud that you were [so] courageous." (A to G, May 5, 1920) Three days later, she felt "inexplicable angst," sadness, and fear because Gunnar had not gotten better. She had been reading another self-absorbed, depressive young intellectual, Sören Kierkegård, whose beloved was unable to reach him when he was in a state of despair. "She could not break my melancholy silence," Kierkegård had lamented. Troubled by Gunnar's inability to pull himself out of depression despite his endless psychological self-examination, she was reminded of the nineteenth-century Swiss philosopher Henri Frederic Amiel's observation: "Self-analysis has annihilated me." (A to G, May 8, 1920)

In the pit of depression as he prepared for his law school exams, Gunnar was acutely aware that he was not living up to either his own or Alva's masculine ideal, and this sense of inadequacy drove him to some unconventional ideas about their relationship. "I do not have the right to hold you dear when I am so listless and sad, because a guy ought to be a guy and not whine like a hysterical old woman." Sensing the toll that his continued revelations were taking on Alva, he commented: "I want to be your lord, but only when I am healthy and happy. But I suggest that we exchange roles when I become exhausted." With unusual perspicacity, he acknowledged that "if I must be the ruler then, I become a cruel and sorrowful oriental despot." While recognizing that his depression sometimes left him incapacitated and dependent on his beloved, Gunnar believed that a man should do what he could to "bear one's sorrows oneself." (G to A, May 9, 1920) Two days later, Gunnar gushed gratefully to his "little comforter": "I have received so many letters in so few days that it is impossible for me not to feel consoled. . . . Anything else would be a grave discourtesy to my gracious ruling princess." (G to A, May 11, 1920) Now he looked forward to being with Alva again. On May 16, after more than a month apart, they met in the town of Västerås, where (although Alva did not yet know it) her grandfather had once done time in jail for wife-beating.

"Pretend that I am your Valkyrie"

After the joy of their brief meeting, Alva and Gunnar resumed their analysis of the relationship. She was happy to have played the role of supportive, intuitive woman in helping Gunnar through his dark period, but she wanted to be more of a comrade. Seeking to share his life, she imagined herself as one of the strong young maidens with divinely given powers who fought alongside male heroes in Old Norse mythology. "Can we not pretend that I am your Valkyrie? Perhaps it is silly to play at being serious in order to be serious, but . . . tell me where the day's battle is, and I shall be there at your side! At least let me try." (A to G, May 17, 1920)

Gunnar, thrilled that his short meeting with Alva had brought a renewal of the happiness that had eluded him for much of the winter and early spring, admitted that he was sensitive to Alva's laughing at him. She had developed this response as defense against his overbearing personality, relentless irony, and cruel sarcasm. As a boy he had winced when his father made fun of him, and he was still recovering from his humiliating experience on Walpurgis Night. But he resolved not to let it get on his nerves. Gunnar tried to recover his dignity by taking up his pose as Alva's teacher, remarking on "how much younger" than he she was and regretting that their living apart prevented him from having "a more active influence over your development." He hoped that she would "always be silly and charming and little and dear." (G to A, May 18, 1920)

"Do you expect me to be irritated at your surly expressions?" Alva fired back, refusing to be baited by his "mischief" into a discussion of her intellectual capacity. Shifting to more advantageous ground, she refocused the discussion on Gunnar's emotional "oscillations," which she experienced "as if you were a stranger to me." But she saw no reason to suppose that he would always remain this way, referring obliquely to the "knowledge" that he had gained from his experiment two and a half months earlier. If Alva was to be the Valkyrie to his "warrior," she thought it best that she "should speak freely and honestly from the heart" about his "changeable moods." "I cannot deny that I see in you a man in great pain," "born under an unlucky star," who feels inner discord. (A to G, May 22, 1920)

Alva then turned back on Gunnar the very critique he had made of her six months earlier: that her desire for a "harmonious" society was a fantasy in the modern world. Perhaps he would have been happier if he had been born in another time as "a chief ruling over a great tribe, preferably with superhuman standing." In this fairy-tale world, he would have been free to "experiment" in governing, untroubled by "the questions" that "torment and lacerate" modern men. But such a harmonious paradise was not to be his. Gunnar seemed condemned to live "with the soul perpetually swinging like a pendulum between enthusiasm and depression." Alva found it "so inexplicable" that he never knew when a change of mood would begin and fretted that he would "waste away because of this." Expressing genuine sympathy for her tormented lover, she underlined what she saw as her role in his life. He would feel better, she ventured, "if you let me take part of the obsessions and all the suffering" from which he was unable to free himself. She worried that he would "lose balance in this whirling dance" and feared for him "every time you take a step further down into the valley of the shadow."

Ignoring Gunnar's condescending comments but affirming that she enjoyed the challenge of his letters, Alva replied directly to his advice about her intellectual development. It is good, she agreed, that he "expects too much rather than too little" of her. "I am always spurred and strengthened by confidence and demands." She would be of even more value to him "because I am not afraid of my own Life."

"I was surprised that you understood me so well," Gunnar marveled the next day. "Thus I am not crazy. Or else you are too. And I would rather be crazy with you than clever and alone." While Gunnar affirmed their mutual interdependence, he did not realize that she was claiming more space for her own development, which she thought would make her a stronger and more valuable companion. He still assumed a dichotomy between an intellectual debating partner and a sweet, supportive, intuitive complement to his aggressive male personality. Gunnar did not understand that Alva gained more satisfaction and power in the relationship from being his therapist than from playing the role of intellectual adversary. If she felt that he had knocked her down, why did she not avenge herself? "Have you become like the pious, leaving vengeance to God?" While Gunnar was grateful that Alva was willing to follow him down into "the valley of the shadow," he insisted that she must never go there. (G to A, May 24, 1920)

Gunnar ignored Alva's offer to become a Valkyrie fighting at his side and returned to his own needs, considering his old fear that being in love with a woman would drain his energy and weaken his determination to achieve great things. That might happen to most men in his situation, but he was convinced that Alva's love and devotion would strengthen him. He preferred a pure and loving maiden who would inspire her knight to go forth in battle to a Valkyrie, armed and dangerous, riding alongside him toward an uncertain fate.

During his elevated moods, Gunnar imagined himself as a great political leader, bringing his knowledge of the social sciences and law to bear on national problems. He hoped to combine the Nietzschean superman's "will to power" with the scientist's detachment from ordinary sympathies and prejudices to become an intellectual giant who stood above the usual petty concerns of politics. Empowered by the social sciences, he could achieve this kind of world-historical role and, indeed, become a "prince of tomorrow." But Gunnar knew that his "earthly likeness" was quite different from his own ideal, much less the ideal he imputed to Alva's imagination. He could be rude, surly, self-obsessed, and insensitive to others. During his frequent periods of depression, he felt helpless, terrified, self-hating, and even longed for death. As he reminded Alva, he was like a small boy lost in the woods looking for his mother. At such points, Gunnar's greatest desire was to put his head on Alva's lap and feel protected by her nurturing love. He craved Alva's calm temperament, good judgment, and almost clinical skill in talking him out of those states.

When Gunnar was neither on a peak nor in a valley but felt that he had achieved a difficult "middle" ground, he thrived in his relationship with Alva. When he looked at her through the eyes of nineteenth-century romanticism, he believed that he was superior in the realm of logic and in the public sphere, while she had remarkable powers of intuition, sympathetic understanding of other people, and a greater capacity for love. Their physical attraction to each other and delight in companionship was usually enough to allow Gunnar to ignore the obvious contradiction between his desire for a morally earnest, true, supportive, and sometimes fanciful and playful woman and his powerful need to refashion her into a more rational, scientific thinker, intellectual companion, and debating partner.

Self-Analysis

After ten months of seeing each other only on brief visits, the two lovers managed to get away on a "secret" vacation for three weeks in June 1920. Again they wandered through the mountains and woods of Dalarna, ending in a visit to Gunnar's family in Solvarbo at Midsummer. It was a glorious celebration of their year together. The young couple, who had struggled so hard to keep their love alive by letter, lay side by side at night staring into the starry sky and talking about their lives. At the end of their holiday, Gunnar began his summer job substituting for a judge in the town of Norrtälje and Alva returned home to Eskilstuna, and they settled into a month of analyzing themselves and each other following their passionate time together.

After resolving to attend to her own soul in response to the crisis of February and March, Alva had been reading psychology. Now she resumed her self-directed study. She was still considering a career in medicine, which her father had encouraged (G to A July 12 and July 18, 1920), and specializing in psychiatry appealed to her. In addition to following her own curiosity, Alva was trying to stake out a greater degree of independence in the relationship. Since Gunnar was fascinated by psychology but had not read so deeply in the subject, she would be able to continue her dialogue with him from a solid base. Alva floated the idea that her pursuing an independent career or path of intellectual development would strengthen, rather than threaten, their relationship.

Alva felt able to write more "honestly" and freely to Gunnar after their trip. Before, she had been holding in her anger and afraid to upset him by talking too much about her feelings. Now she suggested that "perhaps our love's great riddle was just a practical problem": they had not been able to spend enough time together. Alva conceded that there was something to Gunnar's claim that she sometimes retreated into a "magic circle" of silence.

> While my reticence deprives us of the constant feeling of enchantment, it is inevitable. But don't you really think that, with a few words, we come unexpectedly close to each other? And don't you think that the affinity—not only physical—that we feel in kissing and embracing has a meaning other than a momentary one?

Separation inevitably produces a degree of mistrust, and "to expect that a miracle should lead us to the same place would be almost insane." The transition from the spontaneity of being together to more deliberate communication by letter was difficult, but essential. "It is not enjoyable to make our love . . . into an object of thought." Shifting from a romantic to a "scientific" perspective, Alva found it "almost astounding to think what cold hearts we must have to be able to reason about this." (A to G, July 2, 1920)

The distance that Alva had traveled in a year is indicated by her comment that her complex but challenging conversations with Gunnar had displaced her previous yearning for absolute goodness and a mystical sense of unity with humankind. She suggested that he had made her feel valuable in her own right and their love freed her to be the strong woman she wanted to be, rather than a passive victim of society. (A to G, July 3, 1920)

She sat alone at Slagsta on a "quiet and light summer evening that ought to conjure up my most beautiful emotions and let me melt away in good will toward humanity." But her thoughts were "imprisoned and turn around an axle, around you."

> Sometimes I believe that I possess an intrinsic value, not just as a luxury article, designed to be possessed and, in the happiest case, to be enjoyed by someone. Earlier, I considered it an unfortunate destiny to be born of the female sex. I could never really reconcile myself to it, because a creative devil in my soul denied a premonition that I should . . . be confined to life as an intellectual parasite.

Now she believed that she had overcome the "self-pity" she had felt at puberty when she came to the bitter realization that she would not be able to fulfill her dreams of striving to achieve great things in the world. (A to G, July 8, 1920)

Alva sketched out her ideal picture of a creative, emotionally strong woman who finds balance in marriage to a great man and as the mother of their children.

> I understand the beauty and richness in coming close to another being, with [his] own body and own soul. And I also have my share of creative power and creative will and creative joy. These new viewpoints have led me to give up my earlier pitiful way of looking at my unhappy condition.

The new conception emphasized her desire for an independent self or soul, retaining creativity and strength as she chose to enter a union with a great man and raise children.

In her customary fashion, Alva then retreated a couple of steps and reassured her beloved that she wanted to "participate in everything that you want to do." She understood and fully supported his ambitions. As evidence of her devotion, she reminded Gunnar that when he had, five months earlier, proposed to quit his legal studies and become a school teacher in Dalarna, she had said no. "I value your life much more highly than mine (naturally)." She spurned the idea that, "like an ordinary fellow," he should "take a secure position" so they could marry. Alva did not mention the fear that she was pregnant that had led Gunnar to make this extraordinary suggestion, nor did she allude to the fact that he had threatened to commit suicide in the same letter. "I consider your life too valuable to be dragged down to just running a business," she protested. She wanted him to be happy in his work and longed to share his "rapture."

Gunnar, meanwhile, was enjoying his short stint as a judge in Norrtälje. Ensconced in the judge's chambers in the city hall, he heard minor criminal cases and delighted in handing down verdicts and sentencing offenders. This position of authority restored his self-confidence after his public debacle on Walpurgis Night. He recommended clemency with conditions for a man whose crime was "alcohol addiction."[2] He took pleasure in having lunch with the mayor, the civil engineer, and lawyers from the district court, all of whom were well-read and relished discussions with a university student. Gunnar was reading a book on "the biology of inheritance" and confided that "I dream of using the penal law for race improvement purposes." When he was not working, he enjoyed nature hikes as well as swimming in the Baltic. Yet his evenings were lonely without Alva. "I love you in a different way than before," Gunnar confessed. He no longer felt the "secret uncertainty" that had contributed to his "suffering this past winter." (G to A, July 9, 1920) Now he assured Alva that he loved her more than he loved himself. He fondly remembered how he had put his head on her lap and stared at "the heavens" in Solvarbo the previous summer. Gunnar expressed his deep gratitude for her support of his aspirations: "You must hope that I am the great exception, just as I do—but you shall also hope that you are the great exception, just as I do." (G to A, July 18, 1920)

That summer, Alva encountered Freud's work through a 1916 book by Uppsala University professor John Landquist, which introduced Swedish readers to psychoanalysis. She then read Freud's *Interpretation of Dreams*. An analysis of mental illness by Bror Edvard Gadelius (1862–1938), professor of psychiatry, seemed to have some bearing on Gunnar's condition. Alva opened a new window on her troubled teenage years when she read and annotated Edvard Lehman's recent book on the psychology of adolescence.

Alva's adroit juggling of the roles of innocent sweetheart and venturesome analyst extended to her interpretation of her own dreams. Freud's theory of sexuality was still regarded as scandalous by many Swedes in 1920, and while she wished to present herself to Gunnar as intellectually fearless, she hesitated to probe too far in seeking latent sexual content in her dreams. "As far back as I can remember, the strongest emotion in [my] dreams has been terror," which she suggested was rooted in her "great uncertainty about everything." "But I don't know if I can find causes closer to home," she added, retreating into self-censorship.

> I also feel—and with undeniable happiness—that I have discovered that my dream life is relatively free from points of connection to the sexual. . . . I do not think it can be proven that my fantasy is preoccupied with sexual life. Our embraces are happy and beautiful memories, and I can and will long for you as a suitor who embraces me, but if the fantasy went further, I should find it unhealthy and ugly.

She asked Gunnar to "let me know if I am allowing some prejudices and fears to hinder me from thinking clearly!" (A to G, July 6, 1920)

"Your attempt to interpret dreams is excessively optimistic," Gunnar retorted. "Among all merely neutral stirrings of the soul, few are so connected with sex life as emotions of anxiety." He fumbled as he sought to reconcile his image of Alva as a pure young woman with his readings about the sexual content of dreams. "I know that you are the purest and finest young girl in existence, but this by no means requires that your inner life should be free from influences from the sexual sphere." Underestimating her guile, Gunnar observed that "your innocence shows up in the unformulated and unconscious way you express yourself when your fantasy works without conscious steering."

> You must not be sad if, after reconsidering this, you reach a different conclusion regarding the sex life's influencing the emotional life. The great school among psychologists that is named after Freud comes close to saying that every little negotiation in life has a sexual meaning. (G to A, July 12, 1920)

Psychology or psychiatry might just provide the leverage that she needed, Alva surmised. She had already begun her practice on her beloved. When Gunnar had fallen into the abyss, she had become his "doctor of the soul," offering analysis and advice when he was utterly dejected. Alva knew that her troubled lover needed her to ask provocative questions and offer judicious analysis as well as the healing balm of love. So she dispensed remedies or pointed to the warning signals when he became anxious. She was particularly worried about the possible consequences of his being alone in Norrtälje. In late July Alva asked him to let her know about every change in his mood: "I am so dreadfully afraid of every sign of depression and can seldom be truly calm about you." (A to G, July 26, 1920)

Yet it was with mixed motives that Alva tested him by suggesting that his love for her might be "mostly a habit," employing the term from Hägerström that Gunnar had used to explain how people develop ideas of morality: "Perhaps the whole of your love is nothing more than a construction with a building up of defenses that you created when you once desired to kiss a girl who lay next to you." So she proposed that he "should think about whether you should try to see how you feel about being free of me!" "If I were not afraid of worsening your loneliness, I almost think I would give you permission [to have an affair]—one time." But permission was not granted because she had been "thinking about your bad business" earlier in the year when he had conducted just such a sexual experiment. (A to G, July 5, 1920) The next day, Alva disingenuously backtracked: "Forgive me for having looked for an expedient way to help you." (July 6, 1920)

"And now you want to give me freedom," Gunnar scoffed. "Do you not... remember that I was free for a week" four and a half months earlier? (G to A, July 9, 1920) In a subsequent letter he declared that "I believe it is very healthy that you make such great efforts to understand your soul's mechanism."

> I am also happy that you can also think clearly and coldly about your love—I don't find it as weird as you do. My experience, which is only three years older but perhaps also richer in the stirring of the soul than yours, tells me that nothing is more important for spiritual health than always having a clear and unfalsified conception of the soul's content. (G to A, July 18, 1920)

"You know well that I do not wish to 'be untrue,'" Alva replied, heartened by Gunnar's reaffirmation of unsparing honesty as central to their relationship. (A to G, July 27, 1920) She spoke of having been "erotically unawakened" before she met him, what it had been like to fall in love with him, and the shock she had felt when he had told her that he knew how to "operate on the heart." (A to G, July 26, 1920)

Alva's testing of Gunnar did not always proceed on such a putatively clinical basis. Throughout the month, she dropped hints that other men were interested in her. At the beginning of their time apart, she told him that her mother had invited families with sons to visit them at Slagsta. Alva was "prepared to talk about the right to vote" and joked about dressing as a "bluestocking" to scare away conventional young men. (A to G, July 1, 1920) Three days later, Alva professed to offer Gunnar reassurance that she was holding herself aloof from the social whirl in Eskilstuna, yet hinted at its temptations. Since she had other suitors, he should realize that "it means something" for the development of her "self" that she has "chosen" him. (A to G, July 3, 1920) Echoing Gunnar, she declared that "I just call this loneliness freedom. I can study people without being their friend." (A to G, July 4, 1920)

For most of July Gunnar managed not to take the bait. Then Alva reported on a visit to her paternal grandmother, Anna Sofia Jansson, who was staying in the neighborhood with her daughter, Mimmi. Anna Sofia's life in Munktorp had not changed much, but Mimmi had come up in the world. After leaving home at the age of 12, she had spent more than 20 years as a servant in well-to-do households, including that a noble family. At the age of 35 she had married Arvid, a widower who owned the farm at Slagsta adjoining Albert and Lowa's. Mimmi had stepped confidently into the role of stepmother to Arvid's three sons, determined to whip the household into shape with her formidable knowledge of etiquette and well-honed housekeeping skills. She and Arvid had one child together, a boy named Gunnar, on whom she doted. Mimmi was obsessed with outward appearances, refined manners, and bourgeois respectability, which did not endear her to her niece.[3]

Testing Gunnar's limits, Alva reported that, while staying with her grandmother, she had attended a neighborhood dance with a farmhand who had walked her home at 3 a.m. She admitted that she had found the lad physically attractive. While she insisted that she had remained true to Gunnar, she speculated that if she had met him a year earlier she would have been tempted. At this point, Alva believed that science had shown that men were, in fact, naturally polygamous. But she wanted to signal to Gunnar that women felt physical attraction as well, and conveyed what it felt like for her to be confronted with sexual temptation as she recreated the scene of her late-night walk home: "In the evening—a moonlit, magic summer's night . . . when he talks about everything that has been going on inside him, how he has longed and cursed—while I myself longed so desperately for a little romance. . . . He is passionate—I am cold." She made it clear that her loyalty to Gunnar came at the price of forsaking a chance for immediate pleasure. "I know that right now his blood is singing a wild song about me." Her coldly analytical self was at war with her passionate self, and "I almost feel like cursing myself for being so monogamous." Alva teased Gunnar that she hoped that he, in "blind jealousy," would not "taunt" her as he had about her friendship with her Norwegian pen-pal. (A to G, July 36, 1920) The circumstances of Alva's brief dalliance were far more innocent than Gunnar's "experiment" with the prostitute. But in her reconstruction of the event in a letter, her aim was no less deadly than Gunnar's had been in his calculating description of what he had done.

This time, Gunnar exploded in fury. Although he had gently suggested that his pure and refined girl analyze her dreams for latent sexual content, those dreams were supposed to be about him. He knew that Alva would not be interested in a serious relationship with an uneducated farmhand; both his own and Alva's father had struggled mightily to escape from life as a poor farm worker. But something about the image of a strong, healthy young man triggered pent-up rage in the heart of this socially awkward student, who was self-conscious about his old hip injury, his propensity to take vertiginous plunges into depression, and the suspicion of mental illness in his family occasioned by his sister's epilepsy. Gunnar knew that his was not a "healthy" temperament, but his love for Alva had offered hope of healing and he had entrusted the most vulnerable side of his personality to her care. The image of her flirting with a farmhand snatched away the promise of this happier life just at the moment when he had finally decided that he really deserved it, wanted it, and could have it.

Although Alva could not have known it then, her late-night walk home with the farmhand had stirred painful memories in her father's family of the events in Västerås 25 years earlier. When her Aunt Mimmi had warned her earlier in the summer that her relationship with Gunnar would ruin her reputation, Alva had shrugged it off as the jealousy of a middle-aged busybody, unaware that Mimmi and Albert had both been traumatized as children when they witnessed their parents fighting on the front porch of their home after Fredrik had publicly accused Anna Sofia of adultery. Now Anna Sofia herself seemed to overreact when Alva came home late from a dance accompanied by a farmhand. Word quickly reached Albert and, throughout the fall, Alva was under even greater scrutiny from her parents as she resumed her sequestered life at Slagsta while preparing for the fall term of gymnasium studies.

In response to her asking how he felt about her "scruples" or moral principles, Gunnar replied that he was not opposed to them, even though

> I have lived the greater part of my life on a different plan than ordinary people's lives. At least the intellectual life for me always takes so much of my interest and my attention that not much has been left for the soul's aspirations for nobility and freedom from reproach. If I am good, I am so because of nature or must have been led thereto by my environment—if I am wicked likewise. (G to A, July 11, 1920)

To this, Alva responded:

> When I have ransacked myself, it has not been from the viewpoint of making myself better, except on how I must develop the capacity for more of this or that appearance, or how I might be able to distance myself from this or that cause of unhappiness and doubt. There is also the cold, theoretical hunger for knowledge. (A to G July 16, 1920)

"I believe it is very healthy that you make such great efforts to understand your soul's mechanism," Gunnar reflected. "I am also happy that you can also think clearly and coldly about your love—I don't find it as weird as you do." Gunnar suggested that they could put much unhappiness behind them by analyzing the causes.

"Fetus of the Devil"

During the autumn of 1920, Gunnar and Alva sought to reassess their relationship as they resumed their old pattern of living apart with only occasional short visits. The summer had its ups and downs, but they were able to see each other in June and August. As Gunnar settled back into his basement apartment and began his third year of legal studies, he was in much better shape psychologically than he had been in the winter and spring, but he girded himself for another year of law school, eight months of bad weather, and the prospect of having to soldier on without his beloved near him. Alva strained to keep alive within her the secret world that she and Gunnar had nurtured as she tried to guard herself from her intrusive and critical family, who worried that he would not marry her. Outwardly confident, she too feared that Gunnar might turn away. Both used their letters to test boundaries, probe feelings, and seek reassurance.

As he picked up his pen, Gunnar thought carefully about how to position himself. Although he could still write beautiful passages about love, too much had happened for him to recover the fresh tone of the romantic prose that had given his early letters such a lyrical quality. Gunnar desperately needed to confide in Alva whenever he struggled against anxiety and depression, but he knew that reading his descriptions of torment took a toll on her. "It really is quite a risky business being in love with you," she had told him bluntly in July. "One ought never to attempt it unless one already has both heaven and hell within one's power." (A to G, July 1920) So Gunnar wrote with some care when he described his efforts to control his tendencies to anxiety and depression. Affirmations of how Alva's love restored him to good health generally followed passages about his struggles with what Strindberg had called "the dark powers."

At the beginning of September, Gunnar complained that the weight above his eyes was heavier than usual and that his nervous anxiety was spiraling out of control. "This mental illness irritates me." "I can't stand knowing that I am 'ill' since I hate that notion." When he thought about it in an unbiased way, he found that if it were not for "this intense irritation that I feel at most exterior impressions" and the subsequent "anxious exhaustion," he would consider himself fundamentally sound. (G to A, Sept. 4, 1920) Gunnar insisted that his inner self was healthy, but that the friction of his personality with the outside world made him sensitive and vulnerable. For the first time, he referred to the "armor" that he tried to develop to protect himself. His "male instincts" pushed him to assert himself in spite of his environment, but his "armor" took a beating. This defense of the self required a lot of energy and could make him "selfish," and Gunnar often worried that he might "infect" Alva, whom he saw as perfectly healthy. The thought occurred to him that he, who is ill, is inferior to her and deserves her compassion. But he did not want to be in the position of a beggar. Gunnar wrote that, as far as he could tell, Alva had never felt disgust at his ailments. Or had she, but kept it hidden out of compassion? He yearned to be the hero Alva dreamed of. Surely this hero was not a mental invalid? In framing his letters, he felt the need to show himself as he actually was—no worse, no better. The most important thing was that she had given him back his life, rescuing him from his tendency toward abstraction and detachment. (G to A, Sept. 2, 1920)

Gunnar admitted that it used to bother him that Alva seemed so "shy and afraid." If only she could understand that what she sees as intimidating is just the surface defensiveness of a poor human soul who loves, hopes, and believes but also hates, fears, and suffers anguish. Now he was relieved that she has learned to laugh and talk and live for the moment. "From the very beginning you have been as if you were bewitched. How can I be anything but happy that the magic circle is beginning to disintegrate?" Gunnar reassured Alva that she must not be afraid that he will ever see her as just a cute little girl. The more lonely he is, the more he is troubled by fears, the more he is forced to find everything in her: friendship, advice, comfort, understanding, security, rest, courage. Gunnar reminded Alva that they had agreed to be uncompromising, to tell each other when one of them disappointed the other. (G to A, Sept. 2 and 3, 1920)

Under increasing scrutiny from her parents at home, Alva focused on her gymnasium studies, counting the days until she could take her examination and enroll in the university in Stockholm. During a chemistry lesson, she managed to write Gunnar a note intended to help him out of his cycle of anxiety and depression. Reminding him that he needed to tell her all of his weaknesses, Alva worried that Gunnar's "obsessive thinking" could "paralyze" him, turn his fears into reality, and ruin his nerves. Explaining that she and Märta had recently had a good conversation about nervous disorders, she claimed that Märta had once succumbed to this pattern. Alva insisted that Gunnar did not need to worry that these problems were a sign of "mental decay"; she was confident that his free and healthy mind could resist these pressures. (A to G, Sept. 2, 1920)

Now Alva switched her voice from that of psychologist to that of the worshipful devotee and conjured up a lavishly Orientalist setting for one of her most outrageous declarations of devotion. Confident of Gunnar's love and dependence upon her, she compared herself to a figure that, in the European imagination, represented the most lowly creature in the world. Whimsically envisioning Gunnar as a sultan, Alva declared that "I would not want to be a courtesan . . . who, with all her charms, still does not remain for long in her lover's mind, perhaps not even for the duration of the love feast. I would prefer to be the female slave—maybe nothing more than an old shriveled Negro crone who, out of pity for her slavery, is allowed to gaze at the radiant splendor" of her sultan. Even if she were allotted no place in his heart and mind, she would nevertheless have the joy of secretly seeing and serving him, and she need never be forced by a cruel god to consider the possibility of his infidelity. (A to G., Sept. 4, 1920)

That Alva intended this comparison to be ironic is affirmed by the self-assurance with which she immediately switched back to her more academic voice modeled on Gunnar's own. Comparing Gunnar's self-absorption to Strindberg's obsessive thinking about himself, which had led the writer into the overwhelming depression chronicled in his *Inferno*, Alva dismissed Strindberg's writing as a psychological curiosity without much literary merit. While Alva might have pressed Gunnar to reveal his innermost weaknesses to her, that was only in the unique and secret world they had made together. Strindberg's "shameless way of turning the innermost sanctity of the soul out into the banal has made me blush," particularly after reading *Legends* and *Inferno*, which portrayed an especially dark period in the author's life after his marriage had collapsed. "Nobody with a great and sensitive soul, struggling against the gods, would think of sending his observations" to a publisher, Alva protested. "The way the man craves an audience is frightening." Strindberg's ragged, demon-filled soul and his compulsion to reveal it both fascinated and repelled her, much as Gunnar's similar qualities did.

Gunnar continued to worry about exactly what role he wanted Alva to play as the catalyst of his regeneration, and he twisted himself into knots trying to fit his emotional needs and her manifold gifts into the categories of male and female as he understood them. Gunnar desperately needed Alva as a counselor and intellectual companion and was willing to grant her a measure of independence within the relationship, yet he had to be the man, absorbing the blows of the outer world to protect her from harm. She had given him a belief in himself and made him feel manly. Her letters send a current of health and joy through his body and give him comfort and courage. Gunnar was touched by Alva's offer to move to Stockholm to be at his side, even though it meant that she would have to give up school and take a "soul-destroying" job, but he would never allow it. It was he who should quit his studies to support her, he reasoned. Gunnar had looked into the careworn faces of his paternal grandmother and other farm women in Dalarna and seen the ravages of factory labor in the bodies of poor urban women. His beloved could be a student but not a drudge. It would be a crime to expose his fragile dream girl to life's "nasty reality," Gunnar insisted. She must continue to view life through the eyes of books and master it through him—not in any other way.

> Alva, my dearest beloved, you are not made to rebel and fight. Don't try to shoulder my burden—it would be too hard for you. You cannot live a man's life and take his place—if you could, you would not be equipped for life as a woman in love. (G to A, Sept. 4, 1920)

"It is no easier to live as a woman than as a man," Alva replied sensibly.

> We may not have to come to terms with the conflict between what we want and what we can achieve. Instead we have the paralyzing, bitter thought that we are not even creatures with the right to want to achieve.

She wondered if she would ever be mature enough to put her own life aside in favor of teaching her children how to live. Whatever strength she has is dedicated to him. The prospect of living her own life, attending to his needs, and nurturing children seemed daunting indeed. But Alva forced herself to pull back from this line of thinking and professed excitement over setting aside her old goals and becoming his wife and the mother of his children. It would be "selfish" to put her career first. (A to G., Sept. 26, 1920)

Gunnar was grateful that Alva was an "anchor" in his life. Without her, he thought, he would be lost in a world of dreams, fears, shadows, and pain. "It is reality that is my enemy," he confessed. Gunnar attributed his fear of losing his intellectual power to the fact that he spent so much of his time theorizing about restructuring institutions and society without ever having the means to implement his ideas. He would begin to doubt the reality of his thinking and the need for the changes he was working out, and finally question his own ability. This left him with a "paralyzing sense of nothingness, aimlessness, and meaninglessness." The most difficult thing about intellectual work without subsequent action was the lack of "reality criteria," he observed. (G to A, Sept. 7, 1920)

Having identified the dominant tendencies behind his "obsessions," Gunnar described himself as a young man fighting a tough battle against the feeling that he is fumbling around among "unrealities" in his work. He therefore needed to feel certain of Alva's commitment to him. Gunnar was well aware of Alva's skill in arranging the world around him, accommodating herself to his needs in order to dampen his anxieties. But he did not want her to nourish his health by falsifying reality. He insisted that she must never lie to him or pretend interest in order to please him. After laying out all of the things he wanted her to do for him while admonishing her to be feminine and to let him defend her from the world, Gunnar underlined his insistence that Alva must always be "honest" with him. He needed to believe that she was the one source of honesty in a world of doubt, illusion, and menacing "dark forces." He understood that there was a risk that he would ask too much, but he could not help it. Otherwise, his love might turn into "madness" or "despair." (G to A, Sept. 7 and 9, 1920)

"Why can't I manage to control the dark spirits that are gripping you?" Alva wondered. Taking his problems as a practical challenge, she sought to turn his pain into "a desperate strength." Alva felt that she had the power in her hands but could not reach her beloved. Despite her eagerness to help him, she prudently disclaimed any wish to lead Gunnar into a "fat, inert contentment that would dull you and rob you of your strength." Thinking of the enervating demands that her mother had made on her father, Alva insisted that she did not want to deprive Gunnar of even the tiniest part of his power. (A to G, Sept. 12 and 10, 1920)

Alva knew that she had to tread carefully when she brought up the subject of children, but they always appeared when she envisioned the perfect world that she and Gunnar would create for each other. She tried to get him to think of himself as a paterfamilias surrounded by adoring offspring, and Gunnar tried to oblige her by evoking his happy dreams of her as a housewife, of his children, and of himself in an old dressing gown sitting at an enormous desk. But as he wrote this, he felt that every little thing in his room, including the light and the air, grinned at him in quiet but frightened scorn. Just writing the word "father" required a genuine effort. Living in his basement room under the apartment of his troubled family, he could see the specter of Carl Adolf mocking him as a boy who was not ready to be a man. "You cannot imagine how contradictory my feelings are on this subject," he gasped. "It is the power of the past over the present, but it is weakening." (G to A, Sept. 4, 1920)

The woman who longed to become a mother met this confession with her usual reassurances, but she alluded to some of her own fears, which she had been hiding to avoid hurting him. Psychological honesty required her to tell him about important feelings; otherwise, walls would rise between them. Alva worried about the psychic cost of concealing her feelings as she constantly shifted among the roles of adoring lover, mother figure, and counselor, but the metaphor she chose suggested failed motherhood as well as destructive, repressed anger. Her description of her dread of derision from others replicated Gunnar's own anxiety.

> If I hide, my soul may laugh sarcastically—at itself. Have I told you before, when I hear the self-mocking laugh, then I am in trouble. When I live with that laughter like the fetus of the devil inside me, I understand what it is to walk in the shadow of death. I have been close to that.

In an apparent reference to her reaction to Gunnar's Easter revelation, she added that "last spring I heard that screeching whine and I thought it was the tolling of the knell that was intended for me." (A to G, Sept. 26, 1920)

Gradually Alva and Gunnar began to agree on the terms on which they would continue their "exceptional" relationship and tentatively broached certain issues in anticipation of their eventual marriage. Although she, of necessity, was sometimes calculating, Alva did not try to make Gunnar feel guilty about the fact that they had intercourse before being married, or even engaged. She refused to play the role of victim or to ask for pity. Alva claimed that she had learned to live with the risk of unwanted pregnancy. If they were to break up, she said, she would eventually find another love. It would not be as strong as her love for Gunnar, but she would find a good man who did not mind the fact that she was no longer a virgin. (A to G, Sept. 9, 1920)

"Now you . . . owe me an equivalent confession," Alva demanded. "I know that men are in theory constitutionally polygamous, and I think I will cope with this in practice too." Alva believed that science, from Darwin to Freud, was clear about this fact. But what would it mean for an "exceptional" man like Gunnar? Despite her brave rhetoric in earlier letters about loving fearlessly and without concern for convention, Alva was anxious about whether Gunnar would stay loyal to her and whether she could adapt to a marriage in which he would have other lovers. She also felt strain from the elaborate deception and psychological compartmentalization that she had been forced to practice with her family. (A to G, Sept. 9 and 10, 1920)

Since Gunnar had been receiving reassuring letters from Alva in the wake of his fears, depression, and sense of being disconnected from reality, Alva's raising the issue of sexual fidelity came as a jolt. But he proceeded to offer a "clinical" self-examination, despite his being in the grip of "disharmonious" emotions. Men's strong sexual desire can be sublimated into intellectual creativity, he posited. While it was true that most "ordinary" women rob men of intellectual creativity, Alva was not like that. "You are part of the process," he avowed. He was sure that Alva did not really mean to say that she could adjust to a lover who was promiscuous, and he blamed her assertion on "superficially assimilated prejudice" from reading psychology books. (G to A, Sept. 12, 1920) Accustomed to alternating between treating Alva as an intellectual peer and wanting her to be a nurturing woman, Gunnar seemed to feel that she had gotten the signals wrong on which line she was supposed to take on this subject.

"I command you to insist on complete fidelity in every little thing," Gunnar declared unequivocally. He claimed to have sublimated his strong sexual desire into love for Alva and expected the same from her. If she were unfaithful, he swore that he would kill her and then himself. Six months earlier, the superman or Faust figure had arrogated to himself the right to try any intellectual or sexual experiment. Now, in response to Alva's clever prodding, Gunnar redefined fidelity as a sign of male strength. This was possible only because Alva was an "exceptional woman," lifting him up as the chorus of angels at the end of Goethe's Faust representing the "eternal feminine" had raised the penitent sinner to heaven. Conversely, he would find it "humiliating," Gunnar averred, to lower himself to the level of a woman who would not be his equal and with whom he would have a purely sexual relationship. He reassured Alva that she need not fear his living in a city with thousands of prostitutes; he would not succumb to temptation. Having told Alva what she was supposed to think and feel, Gunnar closed with a familiar, albeit contrary, admonition: "I command you to be honest always!"

Alva responded to this imperative with complete approbation and no doubt smiled in triumph. "I would never question your faithfulness now," she assured him. "I am happy in the knowledge that you are the exception to all horrible rules." Alva had gradually brought Gunnar into compliance with her wishes through devotion, admiration, and solicitude for his suffering, but also with shrewd psychological prodding and a large dollop of flattery. Now she could write that she "longs beyond all measure" for her "Master," knowing that she could hold him to the standard he had insisted on for them as an "exceptional" couple. (A to G, Sept. 13, 1920) Alva's broad vision of social improvement was not erased by her pact to forge a special relationship that demanded deep seclusion with this intellectually dazzling and emotionally needy man. But the dance with Gunnar, in which they each adapted to but challenged the other, remained at the center of Alva's life. As she wondered about combining motherhood with all the roles she had to play for Gunnar, Alva's focus was on developing her independent viewpoint and continuing her self-education rather than making plans for a professional career.[4]

That fall, they had reached a new level of candor, trust in each other, and confidence that their love would endure. Gunnar wanted to reassure her that, because of her love for him, his depression was not as bad and he did not need "fireworks" as much as before. Alva did not encourage in him a childish dependency on her; rather, she tried to forge the two of them into a strong couple moving toward a great destiny. She spoke to him frankly about building an outer shell that would free some of the talents locked inside him. Such a protective exterior would help him overcome his fears and become a great man instead of a brilliant student who fears derision when he stands up to speak in public. Gunnar asked more questions about her childhood and adolescence and seemed to be genuinely curious about her feelings. They moved away from the idea that they lived in a bubble cut off from the world to considering how they could support each other so that both could develop their talents and he could become a great man.

Notes

All parenthetical citations in the text are to letters written by Alva or Gunnar or Myrdal. All translations were done by the author. Some passages differ from the versions quoted by Yvonne Hirdman in her book about Alva Myrdal and in her edited version of their letters, *De blå kuverten.* Many of Alva's and Gunnar's personal communications are difficult to decipher because they were written rapidly in longhand, abbreviate common words, and often use dashes instead of more precise punctuation. Transcribing and translating them necessarily involves matters of interpretation.

1 Gustav Möller, who served as Minister of Social Affairs during the late 1930s, joined the Myrdals as architects of the welfare state. See Wilsford, *Political Leaders of Contemporary Western Europe*, 332–333. Rikard Sandler, who began in the workers' education movement, followed Branting as Prime Minister in 1925. Quotation in *Social Demokraten*, 4 May 1920.
2 Gunnar Myrdal to Rådstururätten i Norrtälje, June 28, 1920.
3 Persson, interview, May 30, 2011.
4 The author does not believe that Alva was a helpless victim of Gunnar's domination or that their relationship was sadomasochistic, as Yvonne Hirdman has suggested in *Alva Myrdal.* The author found no evidence in their letters from 1919 through 1924 of the physical abuse that Hirdman says Gunnar meted out to Alva, sometimes at her invitation. His occasional "chastisement" was purely verbal, and the "soreness" to which she alluded several times followed vigorous and prolonged sexual intercourse. The passages Hirdman cited as supporting this theory cannot be construed as documenting abusive or sadomasochistic behavior. This historian does not share Hirdman's abstract model of gender relations and her resulting interpretation. Most important, to Alva and Gunnar matters of gender, sexuality, and power were worthy of open discussion within their intimate relationship and in their

social and cultural context, and Alva saw them as amenable to societal amelioration. For a Swedish feminist's alternative to Hirdman's interpretation, see Vinterhed, *Kärlek i tjugonde seklet*, and Vinterhed, interview.

References

Alva and Gunnar Myrdal's Collection (AGMA). Arbetarrörelsens Arkiv och Bibliotek (Swedish Labour Movement's Archive and Library). Stockholm, Sweden.

Correspondence between Alva and Gunnar Myrdal, 3.3

[cited as: G to A or A to G, date]

Gunnar Myrdal's professional activities, 4.2

Gunnar Myrdal. Rådstururätten (the right to counsel) i Norrtälje. June 28, 1920.

Interview

Persson, Anne-Marie. Interview with Walter Jackson. Stockholm, May 30, 2011.

Vinterhed, Kerstin. Interview by Walter Jackson.

Published Sources

Hirdman, Yvonne. *Det tänkande hjärtat: Boken om Alva Myrdal*. Stockholm: Ordfront, 2006. *Alva Myrdal: The Passionate Mind*, trans. Linda Schenck. Bloomington: Indiana University Press, 2008.

Myrdal, Alva, and Gunnar Myrdal. *De blå kuverten: Kärleksbreven juli 1919–augusti 1920*, ed. Yvonne Hirdman. Hedemora: Gidlunds, 2003.

Vinterhed, Kerstin. *Kärlek i tjugonde seklet: En biografi över Alva och Gunnar Myrdal*. Stockholm: Atlas, 2003.

Wilsford, David, ed. *Political Leaders of Contemporary Western Europe: A Biographical Dictionary*. Westport, CT: Greenwood, 1995.

Part III

Gunnar in Crisis, 1941

11 The Dialectic of Love and Power

Alva and Gunnar Myrdal's relationship continued to be marked by the contradictions that appeared during these first years. The tensions that arose between them were complicated by each of their internal emotional conflicts, as their struggle to combine love and work met obstacles that came both from the constraints of gender and from the structures of feeling each had developed while growing up. Unsparing honesty, self-reflection, and psychological analysis did not shield them from the most troubling, even paralyzing dilemmas they confronted, sometimes together but often separately. This chapter traces their working and personal relationship as it developed from their third year together until 1941, when Gunnar was in the United States and Alva in Sweden.

In the early 1940s, the conjuncture of psychological and global events exacerbated the difficulties they had faced before. What Gunnar had come to call his "manic depression," which today would be termed bipolar disorder, was apparent to both of them. By this time he acknowledged that his extreme mood swings were a form of mental illness, but he had found few ways of coping with it. Gunnar was less aware of his utter self-centeredness. Although he sometimes regretted his childlike dependency on Alva, he often assumed that he deserved her exclusive attention. Alva struggled with serious dilemmas of her own as she tried to meet the conflicting demands made on her as a wife and a mother while pursuing her own work as a feminist reformer and Social Democratic activist. Ironically, their most serious crises arose when both were at the height of their powers, critiquing existing patterns of socioeconomic relations and proposing a coherent program of fundamental change. The troubles they encountered called the continuation of their marriage into question. Yet the love they had discovered in their youth and built upon in subsequent decades proved to be a wellspring to which Alva and Gunnar returned again and again to renew their relationship.

An Experiential Education

The lovers lived apart for two years following the "magical" summer of 1919, with Alva continuing to reside in her parents' farmhouse near

Eskilstuna while Gunnar plodded along in his undergraduate legal studies at Stockholm University. The time and expense of a half-day's train trip made visits infrequent. In their carefully crafted letters to each other, they strained to preserve a sense of living in an enchanted realm and tried to block out their families and quotidian routines in order to nurture their love. As a young girl, Alva had dreamed of becoming a leader and doing great things, but by the time she reached puberty she had grown more "realistic" about the possibilities open to her. She had found a refuge in the world of books, but was held back by feelings of inadequacy and wondered if she would ever find a man with whom she could share her interests. At the age of 17, meeting Gunnar had freed her from the worst of these anxieties. She experienced an exhilarating expansion of the self and felt that she was exploding with new intellectual and psychological insights. Gunnar's heartfelt praise of Alva's physical beauty, feminine intuition, and keen intellect enlarged her own understanding of herself. He worked to pull her out of her tendency to withdraw from controversy, insisting that she develop her own ideas and become his debating partner. As Alva imagined that she was beginning a new life, she burned all of the vestiges of the old: diaries, letters, and poems went up in flames.

Nine months into the relationship, when Gunnar fell into a period of depression marked by lacerating self-hatred, Alva realized that she would have to become his counselor. By the time she moved to Stockholm to begin her university studies, she had become a virtuoso at juggling the roles of romantic partner, intellectual interlocutor, and psychotherapist. Her childhood and adolescence had been so unhappy that Gunnar's moods seemed a manageable burden. In her early 20s, she was happy to have found a life partner and accepted the idea that she could be different in her "feminine" temperament, yet equal in her standing within the relationship. Alva increasingly recast her ambition into becoming the companion of a great man—albeit one whom she had to protect and strengthen so he could fulfill his destiny.

During the years that Alva and Gunnar were living separately in Stockholm, they considered and rejected many possibilities for the future. Alva decided not to become a physician, as the training was long and would have required her to depend on her father financially. In order to support herself and assist Gunnar, she could teach or work in an office, but those typical women's vocations seemed like dead ends instead of challenging and worthwhile careers. Gunnar was briefly tempted to practice law and to become a judge or civil servant, but the routine seemed deadly. He also flirted with becoming a writer. But he quickly settled down to complete a PhD in economics. At several points during this time, Alva half hoped, half feared that she was pregnant, which would have required them to be more practical. But in the absence of a child they could nurture other aspirations. At times Gunnar doubted his destiny, in part because of what he called his "tragic temperament"; at other times he was confident in his ability to subject the economy and society to scientific analysis.

In the fall of 1924, after Alva completed her undergraduate degree in Scandinavian literature and Gunnar was in his second year of graduate work, the couple married. Alva was then 22-years-old and still uncertain about her future. Gunnar's doctorate in economics was their highest priority. Alva taught adult education courses and typed successive versions of his dissertation. She deeply wished to have children, but her recurrent hopes that she was pregnant were perennially disappointed. In the summer of 1926, she had at least one miscarriage.

Earlier that year, Alva had begun a "Diary of Him and Her," which she intended as an experiment in recording the intimate thoughts and feelings of both husband and wife in the hope of building a closer relationship. But Gunnar, immersed in his academic work, had contributed only a few lines and neglected to read her entries. Alva increasingly expressed exasperation at her subordination and isolation:

> This is true loneliness: to live hour after hour with a man who has said he wants to live united with me but who lives his life among his books and lets me live mine or not live at all, whatever I like. Who communicates with me by screaming: Put the potatoes on to boil! By his habitual question: How are you? Occasionally by a conscience-stricken, "Dear heart"—and then—every now and then at night—but wordlessly.[1]

In a moment of calm clarity, she summarized her situation incisively: "I am not unhappily married in the bourgeois, banal sense of the term. But I am most definitely married to you, while you are not married to me—not a bit." (Feb. 17, 1927) In the late fall, she became so desperate that she contemplated throwing herself off St. Erik's bridge. (Nov. 16, 1926) Yet she also found strength in recognizing her existential aloneness. "This, in fact, is marriage. This urgent nothingness. And this, in fact, is death, that great empty threat. . . . This is the gift of vast loneliness: the feeling that at every moment I choose my life. It is never up to me to decide how, but always if." (Feb. 17, 1927)

When Alva finally felt a baby quicken, she was gratified by the fulfillment of her long-deferred dream. But then she considered what being the mother of a separate person might mean. Writing as if addressing Gunnar, but aware that he would never read it, she mused:

> Even this child—I will give it so much—but for what? For the pleasure of watching it grow, of course. . . . I receive nothing in addition, not as far as love is concerned, nor company except what I in my imagination can make myself take. Not even this beloved child will give me anything of its own free will, not even to this child will I ever

> dare to say anything about myself. We will, of course, treat each as other strangers, as you and I do. Since love has not helped us come closer together in one direction, why should it be able to do this in another? (Feb. 17, 1927)

In this case, Alva's fears proved well founded.

The situation improved the following spring and summer: Gunnar was awarded his doctorate with highest honors, and Alva gave birth to a son, Jan, in July 1927. After enduring postpartum depression, she plunged into graduate study in psychology, taking the train twice a week to attend classes at Uppsala University. The next two years were happy ones, as Alva and Gunnar enjoyed sharing their discoveries in their respective fields and regularly entertained a circle of young intellectuals who debated social problems and politics long into the night.

The couple faced a difficult decision in the spring of 1929 when both Alva and Gunnar were awarded Rockefeller fellowships for study in the United States. The fellowships required travel to universities in different cities and did not include any provision for children. At Gunnar's insistence, Alva reluctantly agreed to leave Jan with Gunnar's parents in the country. Placing a child in the care of relatives for an extended period was a common practice in rural Sweden, so what the Myrdals did was not remarkable. Indeed, the word for bringing up a child, *uppfostra*, refers to other adults as well as parents.[2] The Myrdals departed a month before their son's second birthday and returned home a month before his third. Alva was wracked with guilt for leaving him behind.

In the United States, Alva plunged into her study of child psychology and early childhood education with some of America's most distinguished professors and practitioners. She studied John Dewey, Boasian anthropology, and the progressive sociology of Robert and Helen Lynd. She met psychologists, educators, and social workers involved in child guidance and parent education and came in contact with many women active in education and reform. Alva began self-consciously to question prevailing ideas about differences between men and women. The old model of gender that posited distinct masculine and feminine temperaments rooted in biological differences came apart at the end of the 1920s as she studied psychology and puzzled over the conundrums inherent in juggling marriage, motherhood, and meaningful work.

After spending the next year in Geneva, Alva and Gunnar returned to Sweden in 1931, as the worldwide depression triggered mass unemployment and the parliamentary election of 1932 brought the Social Democrats to power. Both resolved to use interdisciplinary social scientific research to bring about dramatic policy changes. In the wake of his book, *The Political Element in the Development of Economic Theory* (1929), which offered a compelling critique of neoclassical economics, Gunnar was appointed to the only chair in economics in the country and became a leading advisor to the new government, a member of the upper house of the Riksdag, and a governor of the Bank of Sweden.[3] Alva initiated parent education programs, became the founding principal of a college for preschool teachers, and wrote books on play. Most importantly, she advocated reforms in housing that would allow families to have common dining and recreational areas and daycare in their apartment buildings to help employed couples balance work and family.

In order to put their conception of an egalitarian marital partnership into practice, the Myrdals realized, many of the activities that were now performed within private families had to be done cooperatively. The Stockholm Exhibition of 1930 had dazzled four million visitors with the wonders of modern architecture and urban planning. Young Swedish architects, including Sven Markelius, designed glass and steel buildings that were shorn of ornamentation in order to reduce the cost of construction. Apartment interiors were designed to be "functional," making optimal use of limited space. Furniture was spare, glass lamps hung from the ceiling, kitchenettes freed space for family rooms, and minuscule bathrooms replaced outdoor privies and eliminated the need for weekly visits to bath houses. These small but efficient apartments, planners hoped, could be produced at a cost low enough to relieve the critical housing shortage in Stockholm and other rapidly growing cities.

Functional architecture was in part a response to a rigid class-bound society, which had fostered habits that were now seen as wasteful and incompatible with modern urban life. The exhibition captured the imagination of young Swedish intellectuals and strengthened discussions already in progress about "rationalizing" other social arrangements. Alva worked closely with Sven Markelius to construct an apartment building where families could enjoy privacy but cooperate in basic housekeeping tasks and, most importantly, have their young children cared for in a large, professionally staffed "children's room." Not only did this provision fulfill Alva's vision of high-quality early childhood education that would enable mothers to pursue employment, but it also served as a prototype for the future, when socialized, subsidized daycare was implemented as a matter of public policy. The Social Democratic Party had already adopted the idea that the nation should become what Per Albin Hansson called "the people's home," and when it entered the government it combined the economic stimulus program that Gunnar Myrdal and others advocated with the vision of a modern society that met many of people's needs through collective arrangements.

Gender Equality and Family Policy

While focusing on changes in public policy that would improve family life, Alva considered the fundamental question of where notions of femininity come from in an article published in a women's journal in 1934.[4]

In it, she drew on social scientific research to argue that no "natural" differences between men and women have been proven and that individual personality is formed by environmental forces. Sociologists and anthropologists, she claimed, trace the rigid division of labor in society to notions of women's "impurity," such as the Christian idea of sin. Conventional concepts of femininity are rooted in women's economic dependency on men and kept alive in women's psyche by an "inferiority complex" inculcated in them.

Early in life, according to Alva, girls learn that they are less important than boys when they hear the expression, "just a girl." Their play is more restricted and their chores are centered on housekeeping, which they come to see as their "natural" task. The socialization of girls discourages ambition and independence, and adult women are "doomed to dependency, to a second-class life." Alva contended that socially constructed "gender consciousness," not biological difference, is the cause of women's inferior position. Turning to the recent idea that men must be the sole economic support of the family, she asked: "How is this working in the twentieth century?" In the uncertain modern economy, she reasoned, "the strong arm, which is supposed to support us," is not so strong. Marriage does not guarantee financial security, and it cannot be a woman's "final goal" (see Figure 11.1).

In this brief, provocative essay, the 32-year-old psychologist and political activist sketched out a few ideas about how the education and socialization of girls should be changed in order to overcome this "slave mentality." Girls should be allowed a full range of active play and sports, Alva argued. They should not be restricted to dolls or the "limited sphere" of the home and neighborhood. Girls should be freed from their isolation and enabled to become independent and self-confident. Above all, Alva stressed that the patterns children observe in the family "color much thinking in adult life." Traditionally, their father's occupation defined the family's social identity, and the mother's housework was devalued. It was time for children to see different patterns in family and society.

One year after Hitler's seizure of power in Germany, Alva imbued her argument with a sense of urgency by contrasting her concept of women's equality and individuality with the Nazi ideology that women are "only daughters, wives and sisters" whose tasks are confined to "children, kitchen, and church." She concluded that customary ideas about femininity are so "pervasive" that we do not know what the "feminine psyche" is. To find out, Alva asserted, we shall have to allow women "a freer development of the self." Many of these views had been expressed by feminists before, but there had never been such a direct, clear, and succinct statement of the environmentalist position on gender differences by a Swedish social scientist. Remarkably, Alva's essay anticipates much of the argument that Simone de Beauvoir would make in *The Second Sex* (1949), especially the assertion that "One is not born but becomes

Figure 11.1 Alva Reimer Myrdal, Stockholm, 1932. Portrait by Anna Riwkin. Courtesy of Alva and Gunnar Myrdal's Collection, Arbetarrörelsens Arkiv och Bibliotek, Stockholm, Sweden.

a woman." In a talk given that same year, Alva suggested that women did not really know themselves, and she challenged the members of her audience to reexamine their individual lives. "The woman as she really is does not exist," Alva boldly declared. "We shall have to discover her."[5]

These ideas formed a component of the broader social vision articulated in Alva and Gunnar's coauthored book, *Crisis in the Population Question*, published in November 1934.[6] They argued that modern urban, industrial society demands a new kind of human and that we must rethink the family, work, housing, education, public health, and other social institutions. While Social Democrats had long called for a reshaping of society to foster greater equality and to protect those who were most vulnerable, the Myrdals sketched out specific policy proposals, several of which would become law as the Swedish welfare state took shape from the mid-1930s through the postwar era. Alva and Gunnar wanted to use the social sciences as the foundation for a kind of "social engineering" to promote opportunity in a society in which the majority of people were poor and an elite few had more than enough. They were driven by a sense of urgency, not only because of high unemployment and a housing crisis, but also because they felt it imperative that Sweden achieve greater democracy and stability at home to diminish the appeal of the rival totalitarian ideologies of the two, much larger neighboring states, German fascism and Soviet communism.

Crisis in the Population Question gained widespread public attention because Alva and Gunnar presented their Social Democratic reforms as a solution to an anxiety that had gripped many Swedes: the fear that the declining birth rate meant that, in a couple of generations, Swedes would "die out" as a people. In fact, the birth rate had been declining for some time in most industrialized nations, and the depression accelerated its fall. Economic insecurity caused many young people to delay marriage and have fewer children. In Sweden, the "population issue" had been stalemated for at least 20 years. The Conservatives and their parliamentary allies had outlawed birth control in 1911 because they feared that continued population decline would weaken the national defense and lead to higher wages. Many also worried that easily available contraception would open the door to sexual immorality, encourage more women to enter the paid workforce, and hasten the "demise of the family." While Swedish Conservatives rarely invoked the openly racist theories that motivated Nazi pronatalist policies, their rhetoric linking the preservation of Swedish culture to the reproduction of the nation's old racial "stock" inevitably carried associations of Nordic racial superiority. Social Democrats, on the other hand, staunchly defended the right to birth control, which working-class and farming families needed so they could support the children they already had. They were suspicious of pronatalist policies, including subsidies to families with numerous children, as promoting low wages and reinforcing a notion that the country needed more "cannon fodder." There the matter stood in 1934, as the Riksdag debated policies to promote economic recovery, alleviate unemployment, and create more and better housing.[7]

Both Alva and Gunnar had considered the population issue during the preceding five years, and in the summer of 1934 they left Jan with Gunnar's parents, retreated to a cottage in the mountains of Norway, and directed their enormous energies into writing this book. *Crisis* proposed a variety of incentives to encourage poor couples who want children to have them, while guaranteeing birth control, which allowed couples to avoid unwanted pregnancies and plan their families. The book created a huge controversy, becoming an immediate bestseller in Sweden, and Alva and Gunnar addressed many public forums around the country.

In *Crisis*, the Myrdals argued for a new family policy as part of a larger reorganization of Swedish society along Social Democratic lines, which required national economic planning, full employment, and a redistribution of income sufficient to lift the lower class out of poverty. On the basis of this new economic foundation, the Myrdals recommended policies specifically designed to help families: allowances and tax deductions for families with children, government subsidies for housing, free health care for children, free school lunches and textbooks, and free public daycare centers. These radical changes were required, they contended, because the traditional patriarchal family in rural Sweden had broken down under the impact of industrialization and urbanization. Particularly distressing to the Myrdals was the way children were being raised in the small, nuclear family, which they regard as "almost pathological." "That a modern adult should stay at home and devote herself to taking care of one or two children is utterly absurd," they declared. Instead, parents need to "free children more from ourselves" by enrolling them in daycare centers where they have an opportunity to interact with other children.

Alva and Gunnar recommended major changes in the Swedish educational system as well. The current competitive approach promoted a "false individualism," they charged, and children should be taught the skills in cooperation that are useful in a democratic society. Reflecting the influence of John Dewey, they argued that children should not be taught to repress their emotions but be allowed to develop into more spontaneous persons. The Myrdals insisted that a Social Democratic population policy must not infringe on women's rights. Not only should birth control be easily available, but the state should also guarantee a woman's right to keep her job if she has children.

The part of *Crisis* that would be most controversial in the future was considered mainstream in the 1930s: eugenics, the idea of improving the population through careful social regulation of reproduction. The Myrdals rejected any eugenic policy founded on race, religion, or class, maintaining that all healthy Swedes are equally desirable as parents. When it comes to individuals, however, they argued that modern society demands better "human material" than rural, agricultural life had required. They proposed compulsory and voluntary eugenic policies to "root out all types of physical and mental inferiority within the population, both the mentally retarded and mentally ill, the genetically defective and persons of bad character." To prevent the birth of children suffering from hereditary defects, the state should impose sterilization on those who were unfit or incapable of making a rational decision. The Myrdals conceded that too little was known about the causes of schizophrenia to warrant compulsory sterilization, and they suggested that manic depression "does not . . . unequivocally make the person valueless." The implicit reference here was to Gunnar's own mental illness. Epilepsy, which afflicted his sister Elsa, was a similarly ambiguous condition, as it was physiological but not necessarily inherited. Nonetheless, they argued that there were thousands of persons with environmentally caused mental illnesses who would not make good parents and should be advised strongly by social workers and doctors to seek sterilization voluntarily, and the state should provide free contraception, abortion, and sterilization to them. The Myrdals saw these eugenic policies as an integral part of social medicine and public health, which would enable Sweden to produce the human capital that was needed for modern industrial work and full participation in a social democracy.

The consequences of their faith in the ability of experts to make these decisions became apparent seven years later, when Alva's younger sister Maj died from an abortion and sterilization operation approved by Sweden's Medical Board under the 1938 law passed in accordance with the Myrdals' recommendations. Maj's husband Olle, who suffered from depression and anxiety, had been in a mental hospital for several weeks in the spring of 1940. After his return home, Maj became pregnant. Concerned about both her husband's recent breakdown and her own weak back, she applied for a legal abortion. Initially it appeared that permission would only be granted on the grounds of her husband's mental illness and that she would have to agree to be sterilized as well. After investigating the case, the Medical Board suggested that Olle should be sterilized instead. When he refused, Maj volunteered to be sterilized in connection with an abortion. In March 1941 she died of postoperative complications at a clinic in Södermanland. No evidence has come to light suggesting that Alva was involved in advising her sister on the operation, and Maj signed four separate documents consenting to the procedures.[8] Nonetheless, this tragedy brought home the potential consequences of such a policy, particularly for women.

The Myrdals were among many reformers who advocated eugenics. As the population debate developed in the early twentieth century, Social Democrats had to answer Conservatives' arguments that increasing public spending on social welfare programs would produce a Malthusian nightmare, an explosion in the number of children born mentally retarded or mentally ill, which would overwhelm the resources of private charities and the government. According to this logic, in order for the vast majority of workers and farmers to have healthy children who could be educated to assume the responsibilities of citizenship and train for skilled jobs or professions, the state had the duty to "weed out" those few who were deemed incapable of producing healthy offspring. A total of 62,888 people were sterilized in Sweden between 1935 and 1975, 90 percent of them women. Eugenics was discredited only after World War II, when the Nazis' genocidal policies and horrific experiments on prisoners were revealed.[9]

At the time *Crisis in the Population Question* was published, Sweden was undergoing an acute economic crisis. The Myrdals presented their ambitious project of social engineering as an urgent necessity in a nation where thousands were unemployed, many families were crowded into tiny apartments, and many children were poorly cared for.

Neither Alva nor Gunnar was prepared for the furor that the book provoked. Three of Gunnar's colleagues reviewed it harshly in major Stockholm newspapers. While his mentor, economist Gustav Cassel, contented himself with a rigorous scholarly critique, political scientist Gösta Bagge and economist Eli Heckscher added some personal innuendo to their reviews and implied that Alva was unqualified to write on this subject. The book triggered an intense political debate across the country, most of it substantive, but the coauthors, especially Alva, drew some derisive comments for their advocacy of birth control and sex education. Gunnar was incensed by Bagge's and Heckscher's reviews and by the personal attacks on Alva. The "Myrdal couple" fought back in this supercharged atmosphere. They spoke at forums and used the new medium of radio to reach people all over the country, refusing to let the critical reviews in the Stockholm press define the debate. The Workers' Adult Education Association, for which Alva had taught, sponsored study circles in which men and women read pamphlets by Alva and Gunnar on the population question, listened to debates on the radio, and argued about the issues among themselves. Thus Alva was introduced to many Swedes as part of the firm of AGM, social engineers, and Gunnar and Alva's bond was strengthened by his vigorous public defense of her work (see Figure 11.2).

Prime Minister Per Albin Hansson and the Social Democratic Party leadership did not initially endorse the Myrdals' book, but chose to wait and see how it would be received. When the public response seemed to be favorable, Hansson appointed a Royal Commission on Population, headed by economist Nils Wohlin, who served in the Riksdag as a member of the Agrarian Party, with Gunnar Myrdal as vice-chair and director of research. Although population had been more Alva's issue than Gunnar's, she was not invited to serve on the commission, although she contributed a research memorandum on "The Sexual Question" toward the end of its work in 1938. During the three years of its existence, the Population Commission proposed many of the reforms that the Myrdals had advocated in *Crisis*, and Gunnar, who had been elected to the upper chamber of the Riksdag in 1936, carried on the fight for these reforms in parliament. With support from the Social Democratic leadership, the Riksdag approved legislation for constructing housing in urban areas and providing subsidies to pregnant women, loans to couples who could not otherwise afford to get married, aid to orphans and the children of widows and disabled men, and an increase in the tax deduction granted to families with children. In response to the report of a commission on the employment of married women on which Alva served with other feminists, parliament made it illegal for an employer to fire a woman or reduce her salary because of marriage, pregnancy, or childbirth. The significance of Sweden's prohibition of a "marriage bar" to

Figure 11.2 Alva and Gunnar Myrdal, 1938. Joint portrait by Wilmer Studios. Courtesy of Alva and Gunnar Myrdal's Collection, Arbetarrörelsens Arkiv och Bibliotek, Stockholm, Sweden.

women's employment at a time of high male unemployment reverberated in other countries, where feminists fought, often unsuccessfully, against proposals that allowed the state and private employers to discriminate in favor of married men.[10] But these reforms fell far short of achieving the radical redistribution of income or fundamental change in child-raising patterns that Alva and Gunnar had advocated. In the spring of 1938, Prime Minister Hansson declared a "reform pause" while Sweden built up its military defenses.

To America and Back

During this prewar lull in reform activity, Gunnar Myrdal received an extraordinary offer from the Carnegie Corporation of New York to spend two years in the United States writing a book on America's "Negro problem." This supposedly "unbiased" foreign observer would head an interdisciplinary team of American social scientists who would undertake collaborative research on race relations in the United States. A man whose ambitions centered on Swedish politics would not have been tempted by this assignment, but Gunnar saw himself as a social scientific problem-solver with an international perspective. When Alva agreed to the move, he resigned his seat in the Riksdag and his position as a governor of the Bank of Sweden and took a two-year leave of absence from his professorship at Stockholm University. Alva also took a leave from her job and interrupted her political activism, but she did not initially view the move to New York as a sacrifice. She had found herself professionally and intellectually during her year in the United States in 1929–1930, when she had formulated reform ideas that were central to her subsequent work in Sweden. Not only had she met many women reformers and intellectuals, but she also felt freer in America, which seemed less class-bound than Sweden. The Carnegie Corporation provided two years of support for Alva to write a book in English on the Swedish experiment in family policy.[11] By then, Gunnar and Alva had three children: Jan, age 11; Sissela, age 3½; and Kaj, age 2. The whole family moved to New York in September 1938.

In the spring of 1940, the couple interrupted their research to return to Sweden when the German invasion of Denmark and Norway raised the possibility that Sweden might soon face the same fate. Although they supported the nation's traditional neutrality, both were horrified by the silence of the Swedish press on the situation in Nazi Germany and the countries it occupied. In the face of a possible invasion, many journalists resorted to self-censorship, and the government confiscated issues of newspapers and magazines critical of Germany. In a jointly written book, *Contact with America* (1941), the Myrdals urged Swedes to strengthen their "psychological defenses" against totalitarianism by educating the public on the democratic principles that distinguished Sweden from its fascist and communist neighbors. Their book included critical chapters on American society and government, but the authors pointed to "the American Creed" as a model for Swedes who, in their view, needed to able to explain clearly what their country stood for.[12]

Notes

All parenthetical citations in the text refer to manuscripts by Alva or Gunnar Myrdal. All translations were done by the author. What Alva and Gunnar wrote in longhand is often difficult to decipher because they abbreviated common words and used dashes instead of more precise punctuation. Transcribing and translating them necessarily involves matters of interpretation.

1 Alva Myrdal, Dagbok Han och Hon, Nov. 16, 1926, AGMA. In this section, all dates in parentheses refer to this manuscript diary.

2 For insights into how dual-career couples coped with the often incompatible demands of work and family at that time, see Berg, Florin, and Wisselgren, *Par i vetenskap och politik*, which includes Hirdman, Från firman till slagskepp, on Alva and Gunnar Myrdal, and Östlund, Växelverkan, bildning, sak och person, on Ebba and Eli Heckscher.
3 See *The Essential Gunnar Myrdal*. On his intellectual history, sees Appelqvist, *Political Economy of Gunnar Myrdal*; Barber, *Gunnar Myrdal*. For recent reevaluations, see Carlson, Gunnar Myrdal reconsidered; Cherrier, Gunnar Myrdal and the scientific way to social democracy.
4 Alva Myrdal, Uppfostrad till "akta kvinnlighet," AGMA.
5 Alva Myrdal, Moderna kvinnoproblem, AGMA; de Beauvoir, *La Deuxième Sexe*.
6 Alva Myrdal and Gunnar Myrdal, *Kris i befolkningsfrågan*.
7 See Carlson, *Swedish Experiment in Family Politics*; Ohlander, *More Children of Better Quality?*; Ohlander, The invisible child?; Ekervald, Alva Myrdal; Herman, Children, feminism, and reform.
8 This account is based on Olle's and Maj's medical records as well as on family accounts, especially a letter about Maj's death from Annika Reimer to Walter Jackson, July 2012.
9 On eugenics in Sweden and its postwar reevaluation, see Broberg and Roll-Hansen, *Eugenics and the Welfare State*; Broberg and Tyden, *Önskade i folkhemmet*; Ekervald, The modernist manifesto of Alva and Gunnar Myrdal; Tyden, *Från politik till praktik*.
10 Frangeur, *Yrkeskvinna eller makens tjänarinna?* For a summary of the debate in comparative perspective, see Sommestad, *Agrarian Women*, 132–135.
11 Alva Myrdal, *Nation and Family*.
12 Alva Myrdal and Gunnar Myrdal, *Kontakt med Amerika*.

References

Alva and Gunnar Myrdal's Collection (AGMA). Arbetarrörelsens Arkiv och Bibliotek (Swedish Labour Movement's Archive and Library). Stockholm, Sweden.

Alva Myrdal's personal documents, 1.1

Alva Myrdal. Dagbok Han och Hon (Diary of him and her). Stockholm, 1926–1927.

Alva Myrdal's published works, 2.1

Alva Myrdal. Uppfostrad till "akta kvinnlighet" (Taught to protect "femininity"). *Idun*, no. 8 (1934). 2.1.2

Alva Myrdal's manuscripts, 2.3

Alva Myrdal, Moderna kvinnoproblem (Modern women's problems). Manuscript of lecture delivered to Social Democratic youth group, Jan. 13, 1935.

Interview

Reimer, Annika. Personal communications to Walter Jackson, July 2012.

Alva and Gunnar Myrdal's Published Works

Myrdal, Alva. *Nation and Family: The Swedish Experiment in Democratic Family and Population Policy*. New York: Harper & Bros., 1941.

Myrdal, Alva, and Gunnar Myrdal. *Kris i befolkningsfrågan (Crisis in the Population Question)*. Stockholm: Bonniers, 1934.

Myrdal, Alva, and Gunnar Myrdal. *Kontakt med Amerika (Contact with America)*. Stockholm: Bonniers, 1941.

Myrdal, Gunnar. *The Essential Gunnar Myrdal*, ed. Örjan Appelqvist and Stellan Andersson, trans. Richard Litell and Sonia Wichmann. New York: New Press, 2005.

Published Sources

Appelqvist, Örjan. *The Political Economy of Gunnar Myrdal*. London: Routledge, 2013.

Barber, William. *Gunnar Myrdal: An Intellectual Biography*. London: Palgrave Macmillan, 2007.

de Beauvoir, Simone. *La Deuxième Sexe*. Paris: Gallimard, 1949. *The Second Sex*, trans. Constance Borde and Sheila Mallovany-Chevalier. New York: Vintage, 2011.

Berg, Annika, Christina Florin, and Per Wisselgren, eds. *Par i vetenskap och politik: Intellektuella äktenskap i moderniteten*. Umeå: Boréa, 2011.

Broberg, Gunnar, and Nils Roll-Hansen, eds. *Eugenics and the Welfare State: Sterilization Policy in Denmark, Sweden, Norway and Finland*. East Lansing: Michigan State University Press, 2005.

Broberg, Gunnar, and Mattias Tyden, *Önskade i folkhemmet: Rashygien och sterilisering i Sverige*. Stockholm: Gidlunds, 1991.

Carlson, Allan. *The Swedish Experiment in Family Politics: The Myrdals and the Interwar Population Crisis*. New Brunswick, NJ: Transaction, 1990.

Carlson, Allan. Gunnar Myrdal reconsidered. *Society* 38, no. 5 (July/August 2001): 62–65.

Cherrier, Beatrice. Gunnar Myrdal and the scientific way to social democracy, 1914–1968. *Journal of the History of Economic Thought* 31, no. 1 (March 2009): 33–55.

Ekervald, Hedvig. Alva Myrdal: Making the private public. *Acta Sociologica* 43, no. 4 (2000): 343–352.

Ekervald, Hedvig. The modernist manifesto of Alva and Gunnar Myrdal: Modernization of Sweden in the thirties and the question of sterilization. *International Journal of Politics, Culture and Society* 14, no. 3 (Spring 2001): 539–561.

Frangeur, René. *Yrkeskvinna eller makens tjänarinna? Striden om yrkesrätten för gifta kvinnor i mellankrigstidens Sverige*. Lund: Arkiv, 1998.

Herman, Sondra. Children, feminism, and reform: Alva Myrdal and Swedish reform, 1929–1956. *Journal of Women's History* 4, no. 2 (Fall 1992): 82–112.

Hirdman, Yvonne. Från firman till slagskepp: Alva och Gunnar Myrdal's rörelse in världen. In *Par i vetenskap och politik: Intellektuella äktenskap i moderniteten*, ed. Annika Berg, Christina Florin, and Per Wisselgren, 303–336. Umeå: Boréa, 2011.

Ohlander, Ann-Sofie Kälvemark. *More Children of Better Quality? Aspects of Swedish Population Policy in the 1930s*. Uppsala: Acta Universitatis Upsaliensis, 1980.

Ohlander, Anne-Sofie. The invisible child? The struggle over social democratic family policy. In *Creating Social Democracy*, ed. Klaus Misgeld, Karl Molin, and Klas Åmark. 213–236. University Park: Pennsylvania State University Press, 1992.

Östlund, David. Växelverkan, bildning, sak och person: Ebba och Eli Heckscher. In *Par i vetenskap och politik: Intellektuella äktenskap i moderniteten*, ed. Annika Berg, Christina Florin, and Per Wisselgren, 206–251. Umeå: Boréa, 2011.

Sommestad, Lena. *Agrarian Women, the Gender of Dairy Work, and the Two-Breadwinner Model in the Swedish Welfare State*, trans. and ed. Grey Osterud. New York and London: Routledge, 2019.

Tyden, Mattias. *Från politik till praktik: De svenska steriliseringslagarna, 1935–1975*. Stockholm: Statens offentliga utredning no. 22, 2000.

12 Collapse and Catharsis

In the early spring of 1941, Gunnar returned to the United States alone. Alva and the children were to join him when Alva had arranged a leave from the early childhood education college she was directing. But the worsening course of the war meant that their departure was repeatedly deferred. This Gunnar proved unable to accept.

That spring and summer, Gunnar's letters to the absent Alva oscillated between professions of his ardent love and urgent need for her presence, on the one hand, and repeated threats that if she did not join him immediately he would commit suicide or divorce her, on the other. His missives are littered with expressions of self-pity, but then they suddenly turn lacerating, even cruel: "I think a clear majority of women would consider you perversely cold." (G to A, April or May, 1941) Gunnar framed their involuntary separation as a matter of her choice. Since it was too dangerous for the children to cross the Atlantic during the war, she must come by herself.

> Don't worry about leaving the children. They will under no circumstances come to any harm. . . . Think about poor me instead. I had to leave both you and the children under circumstances at least as uncertain. You will just be traveling from one part of your family to the other—albeit the most important.

He stated what he saw as the only real question bluntly: "Is your choice me, or the children? And do you then choose to give the children five times as much of yourself as you give me? Is that fair to me or to you?" (G to A, April 10, 1941) "I think you misjudge yourself," he insisted. "Even as a professional woman, your more important work right now is here; as a wife you should of course be at my side." (G to A, April or May, 1941)

These importunate demands were familiar to Alva. What was different this time was her response to the situation. While Gunnar was barraging her with letters from America, she argued forcefully against his dismissal of her work. At the same time, the couple considered whether during their separation each of them should be allowed to have an affair.

Then, in a reversal of past patterns in which Alva remained faithful while Gunnar did not, she had sex with a married man they both knew. Alva felt in touch with her own sexuality in new ways, since until that time she had never been intimate with anyone else. In her letters, she endeavored to speak of this event lightly, focusing mostly on the issues she and Gunnar needed to address in their own relationship. But Gunnar found her honesty devastating and replied with revelations of his own. This chapter traces the arc of this crisis, probing the intersection between their individual psychological issues and their struggles to develop a more equal relationship that was not fatally undermined by societally defined patterns of asymmetrical gender relations.

The Agony of Separation

In March 1941, Gunnar Myrdal wrote Alva that during the two months since he had seen her, he had plunged into a "melancholy" state. "Dearest," he confided, "I have felt tired, sad, lonely, and pessimistic. It is an unprecedented strain to be as lonely as I am—so absolutely lonely. I can't remember anything like it." Again and again, Gunnar warned Alva that "If you don't come, there is no doubt that I'll be so wretched that I'll totally collapse." (G to A, April 7, 1941) His repeated expressions of his dependence on his wife were intended to prod her to put aside her work and political activities in Sweden, leave the children with relatives, and come to his rescue—despite wartime travel restrictions.

As their time apart wore on, Gunnar's letters became longer and more troubled, and the couple considered whether they should grant each other a "license" to have a "temporary idyll" with someone else. That would mean giving up monogamy—which Gunnar, ever the economist, called "monopoly"—at least for the duration. (G to A, April 19, 1941) They came to no definitive agreement, but they expended quite a lot of theoretical energy in discussing how such an experiment could be undertaken without "breaking up the family firm" or marital "partnership." In their eyes, the worst vices were lying and being "careless," acting without thought or intention, not considering the consequences for oneself and others. Honesty was the greatest virtue, in personal life as well as social-scientific work. These children of the Enlightenment believed that all problems should be discussed rationally, yet they also had a post-Freudian view that the repression of emotions could produce troublesome "complexes." Thus each could engage in no-holds barred psychological analysis of the other, but both were expected to write candidly about what they were thinking and feeling. Alva was not fond of the long, stream-of-consciousness letters that Gunnar favored. Accustomed to a caregiving and peace-making role in the family, she expressed her ideas diplomatically. This sometimes infuriated Gunnar, who thought that she was glossing things over, or even lying.

Escalating the rhetoric in his letters, phone calls, and telegrams, on April 22 Gunnar cabled Alva that if she stayed in Sweden until the fall, then he considered the "license granted." Alva replied, "no license wanted, only counting weeks." But Jan, then 14, was having problems in school, and Alva worried about leaving Sissela, 7, and Kaj, 4, when she might not be able to return until the war had ended. Nonetheless, aware of the importance of clearly voicing her intentions, she declared: "I meant it when I said that I certainly shall travel."[1]

Three weeks later, Gunnar sent Alva another desperate plea. He made it clear that the most serious matter was the relationship between husband and wife, not parents and children. "Don't take the risk of there being a lasting separation," he warned. In his mind, the threat of a rupture in their relationship far outweighed the danger of crossing the Atlantic in wartime. "Why can't you take the risk for me and for you, if you think the children are not ready to take it?" (G to A, May 14, 1941) Gunnar judged his wife guilty of dereliction of duty. Then, abruptly adopting the stance of victim, he wailed: "Dearest, forgive my loneliness." "How can you keep yourself away from me?" In a telegram, Alva replied succinctly to the accusation that she was ambivalent about joining her husband: "No hesitation, only love." (A to G, May 26, 1941)

In a marathon letter written over the course of two weeks in June,[2] Gunnar complained that he felt "sick in the stomach, sick in the nerves . . . crazy." The German invasion of the Soviet Union two days before Alva's scheduled departure via the Trans-Siberian railroad disrupted their plans. Writing about himself in the third person in a clumsy effort to mask his fury and present an "objective" account while projecting his own guilt onto her, Gunnar informed Alva that "he has adjusted to the fact that you are not coming. It was not so difficult: he had never really believed it." Like the lawyer he had once been, Gunnar methodically made the case that Alva had wronged his client: "He has not chosen this. He would have preferred that you had traveled with him in January." In an effort to appear empathic but make Alva feel guilty, he suggested that you "now really wish you had gone; you now realize how unimportant everything at home is compared to your separation." Gunnar-the-lawyer disingenuously claimed that Gunnar-the-husband did not want to "put the blame on you." (G to A, June 2–16, 1941, letter 1)

Gunnar switched back and forth between the third and first and persons and between blame and forgiveness, as if he could deflect responsibility for his own statements and actions. Describing his psychological self-observation in the third person, Gunnar asserted that "he is not going crazy. He holds himself together. He works: reads and reads. He no longer has the strength to wait and long for you, however." Resuming the letter two days later, Gunnar took back some of the blame-shifting that his lawyer persona had leveled at Alva: "I love you above everything, throughout this separation, however long it turns out to be, without reservation or reproaches." But he expressed this sentiment perversely: "You can rest assured that I have completely eradicated from my emotional life every memory of your guilt in this matter." Gunnar promised to "think and write thoughts that span the generations and humanity's central problems while the war rages around the world. My destiny is completely right, except that you should be with me." Seeking to reassure himself, he declared that "Now I am completely in harmony with you, because I know that you will come if you can." Before ending the letter with a romantic flourish, Gunnar suggested that Alva have an extramarital affair. "Especially if you are going to stay home several weeks, I think that you should have the courage to take your license." "I am not being at all affected here," he insisted, "just coldly serious." Concluding the thirteen-page letter he had taken two weeks to write, Gunnar entreated Alva to "come to me, my dearest, my own girl." (G to A, June 2–16, 1941, letter 1) His emotional instability is as visible in his tendency to careen between extreme but opposite statements as it is in his description of his psychological collapse.

The next day, facing the likelihood that he would have to endure the summer alone, he tried to reassure himself that he could manage and that their relationship would not be irreparably damaged. But he immediately shifted back into a discussion of his own needs: "Dearest, my heart is so broken, something seems to be screaming inside it. . . . My soul lies naked and cries. [The suffering] is boundless!" Surveying the immense task ahead of him, Gunnar claimed that he could not write the book on American race relations alone. "You must help me turn the Negro investigation into a great work—and you will be acknowledged accordingly." (G to A, June 17, 1941, letter 2) "I have a deadly fear about my work; I need to have your support and your personal inspiration; besides I simply need your help." (G to A, June 26, 1941, letter 4)

By the end of June it became clear to both of them that Alva would be unable to travel that summer: all sea, land, and air routes were closed indefinitely. As Gunnar tried to write his big book without Alva at his side, he argued that she, too, could undertake a major piece of writing in America that would be more valuable than anything she could do in Sweden. While he outlined the possibilities that lay before her, he played upon played on her insecurities about her intellectual abilities. Why not build on "some of your earlier writing about women?" he asked, proposing that she write "a historical and sociological yet forward-looking book about women and the women's movement in Sweden." He also reminded Alva that she had talked about drawing on the ideas of John Dewey as well as her practical experience to propose reforms that would democratize Sweden's class-based educational system. "You know that you are the person who could do it better than anyone else. With an international vision, along constructive lines." "I believe this is just what you ought to do," he urged. "You are making a mistake if you do not listen to my advice." Facing writer's block himself, Gunnar counseled Alva: "If you feel that you lack inspiration, pretend you are talking to me." (G to A, June 27, 1941, letter 5)

Pseudo-clinical descriptions of his suffering alternated with grandiose visions of the work they would do. Since he could not "talk to you about the Negroes and democracy," he vowed that "I shall live so that I feel the vibrations of the globe and the heartbeat of humanity. I shall emerge from this [ordeal] . . . stronger: freer, wiser, and more certain. I shall again be visionary. I shall never again fear anyone." But he wanted Alva to be a scholar of global importance as well: "You have to do the same kind of sublimation." (G to A, June 27, 1941, letter 5)

As Gunnar grew more frantic, his long, diary-like letters veered from begging to badgering Alva to do her "duty" and join him. Protesting Alva's suggestion that he wanted to "punish" her, he insisted that "We are both punished." "I have been here for four months now and have not accomplished anything." That evening, Gunnar said, "I will take out the car and go up in the mountains to drink coca-cola, get some fresh air and watch the sunset with my secretary girl." The Carnegie Corporation had hired a college graduate who could take dictation and type. "I have no evil intention but it is so hot today and it is beautiful with a little blond woman to look at and talk to." (G to A, June 29, 1941, letter 5)

Then Gunnar abruptly switched back to his imperative need for Alva. Mixing supplication and threat, he stammered: "My heart is confused. From a purely rational point of view I should put in for a divorce, but I cannot cope with it. What am I complaining about? My careless woman, perhaps you are not doing any better." With more than a hint of self-pity, Gunnar acknowledged that "I must not be as tough as I always thought I was." "I long for you so intimately." Blaming her for being the absent object of his longing, Gunnar implored, "Alva, Alva, why are you not here with me, why do you condemn me to be alone without leaving me alone?" (G to A, June 29, 1941, letter 6)

In the Throes of Manic Depression

In a long letter composed over four days, Gunnar assumed various postures: lonely and aggrieved husband; suffering child demanding his mother's attention; patient reporting to his psychoanalyst; and intellectual mentor admonishing his student to get on with her academic work. Late one night, after listening to the news and realizing that the war would not be over any time soon, he bluntly declared: "You should have chosen me and not the children." (G to A, July 6, 1941, letter 8) The following day, Gunnar sighed: "I am as lonesome as a hermit in the desert. There's nothing I can do about it. Suicide does not appeal to me, as it does not appeal to the Negroes." (G to A, July 7, 1941, letter 8) After receiving a long telegram from Alva which she intended to be reassuring, he protested, "the only thing I get annoyed at is when you appear so irrational that you promptly rearrange the whole story." (G to A, July 7, 1941, letter 8) He found it impossible to see himself through her eyes.

Gunnar again lectured Alva that she, too, should undertake a major intellectual project. Comparing them to Plato's elite, he assured her that this was not the time for the "guardians of culture" to act, but to "research, think and plan." "Western culture will survive in a few individuals who are superior to the nervous, short-sighted everyday people," he prophesied. Suggesting that an intellectual aristocracy could shape human destiny, Gunnar solemnly declared that "you and I and a few others . . . survive stupidity and wretchedness even when they triumph. We depend on almost nothing because we have the most inner strength. Therefore, we are not opportunistic like all the other small people who cannot afford to be free." He admonished his wife that they should not "waste our abilities needlessly" and recommended "isolating ourselves in the world of books and thought." To counter Alva's image of the intellectual as an engaged activist who worked closely with the people to solve practical problems, he contended that she should not be preoccupied with a nation as small and powerless as Sweden, but focus on a large-scale work of social science—jointly with him. (G to A, Aug. 30, 1941) He had been reading Ralph Waldo Emerson's essay on "The American Scholar," which emphasized the self-reliance of the solitary, original thinker in a democratic society. That was the "only . . . way for you to save your soul and preserve your intellectual fellowship with me, if that should interest you," he declared testily. Afraid that she would fritter away her time on political and organizational activities, he warned that "I shall keep account of how you use the time you have deprived us of." (G to A, July 6, 1941, letter 8)

While Gunnar was writing these massive letters filled with mixed messages, Alva was away on a bicycle trip with Jan. When she returned, she was incensed when she opened Gunnar's letter of June 29 in which he threatened her with divorce and teased her about taking his "little secretary girl" on a drive in the New Hampshire mountains. What most infuriated her was his accusation that she had deliberately delayed her departure from Sweden to hurt him. Firing off a telegram on July 8, she threw down the gauntlet: "Your accusations preposterous. Remember hindrance [to] leaving [and] risks. . . . Urging you dearest to find peace [in] work. Not minding anything. Create temporary idyll. Starting work. Not losing hope because not losing love." (A to G, telegram, July 8, 1941) That same day, Alva crafted a letter that would have a devastating impact on her husband when he received it eleven days later.

Before he received her letter, Gunnar observed that their separation had wrought a change in his personality and half-jokingly addressed her as "Damned Alva who is not here." He admitted that "I write egocentric letters," but explained it as the natural result of isolation. "This is not a letter; it is a monologue, an eternal monologue." (G to A, July 15, 1941, letter 9) Nonetheless, Gunnar could not restrain himself from tormenting his wife about the temptations of his "little secretary girl." "I have kissed her a few times, but it tasted like water."

> I am through with it now. I have actually not seduced her, although I easily could have: in my lonely arrogance, I imagine I could seduce the Virgin Mary. Virgins do not appeal to our calculating bachelor: they bleed, make a fuss, and turn everything into a tragedy; once is enough. And professors' wives here are as cold as beer.

Swinging from bottomless despair to a boundless exuberance that resembles mania, Gunnar continued:

> In some ways, I think that we are now actually separated: I think that we must begin almost from the beginning again. I do not feel that I possess you, and you certainly do not possess me. But I feel that I have an absolutely endless capacity to fall in love with you again: with the splendor and glow of youth and the experience of middle age. . . . You know that I am capable of metamorphoses: my eyes burn, so I do not actually dare to look at myself in the mirror. And life stretches out so endlessly before me. . . . I feel nothing is impossible if it just depends on me and my powers: I could easily write a novel, I could write poetry, I have the subjects for ten books in my head: I notice how I can charm the people that I meet by chance. Of course I am narcissistic, but I believe it is true as a judgment. And I think that it is a sin on your part that I do not get to enjoy myself here. I feel like I did when we were ablaze in England and I wrote my dissertation, except more full of Satan. (G to A, July 15, 1941, letter 9)

Gunnar had been afraid to look at himself in the mirror during a period of intense anxiety in the spring of 1919, just before he met Alva; now he had come full circle as he felt her support ebbing away from him. After confessing to narcissism, bragging about his youthful energy, and trying to induce guilt in Alva for not being with him, he warned her not to take everything he said too literally, closed his letter with the customary endearments, and set out for the post office on the morning of Saturday, July 19.

Rupture

Waiting for him there was a letter from Alva, which she had written on the same day as her telegram. Alva had not yet received Gunnar's marathon letter, but she had heard enough in his earlier letters and in their phone conversations. She let him know that she was fed up with his bullying her to abandon her children and professional responsibilities to join him in America and with his teasing her about the temptations offered by other women. She not only gave him permission to have affairs but revealed that she had done so, albeit briefly.[3] Ivar Högbom, a lecturer in Economic Geography at Stockholm University, was Alva's choice for the "temporary idyll" that Gunnar had often suggested. Högbom and his wife were part of the Myrdals' social circle in Stockholm, but they had not been close to either Gunnar or Alva. He was a safe choice because he would not want to compromise his own marriage by revealing his fling with Alva.

Although Gunnar had been unfaithful himself, this revelation was utterly devastating. Rushing to his typewriter, he began, "Damned Alva. I sit and brood and brood over your letter." Describing himself as "wildly jealous" and "more shattered than ever before," he said that "my system of beliefs and values is faltering." "I am so disoriented. . . . The whole pattern of my life has collapsed into an indecipherable riddle." Trying to step back and analyze the situation rationally, he acknowledged that "from an abstract and intellectual point of view, I think you are acting correctly and well," and observed that "you have certainly gained self-confidence." But "we human beings, and especially me, are so irrational." Indirectly admitting that he had been unfaithful to Alva, Gunnar acknowledged that "your 22-year monogamy has been a foundation in our marriage." Then came a stunning declaration that he had long regarded his wife as part of himself: "We are, once again, two different human beings." (G to A, July 19, 1941, letter 10)

"I cry like a child who has lost his mother in the woods," he wailed.

> What shall I do with my freedom? My immediate reaction is to say that I don't want it. . . . I don't even need it for my sense of self. Here I am, having constructed my little temple of self-protection and worked out a balance between a vast loneliness, . . . consistent work and an endless longing—and suddenly you blow it all down.
>
> As a friend, I can honestly understand your catharsis and congratulate you on it . . . but what will this mean for our lives—for my life to start with? I feel very deeply that something terribly decisive and fateful has happened, is happening and is yet to come. What? Where are we going, you, I, and "we"? What have we set in motion?

Contradicting his earlier opinions, Gunnar questioned the idea that a relationship outside the marriage could be kept within certain bounds. He implored her: "Promise me that you will write and tell me every time, otherwise I will go even more crazy, and, perhaps, don't do it more often than passion or a need for self-confidence demands." Gunnar feared the consequences of his wife's abandonment of monogamy.

> You probably don't know how much this sanction has meant to me. I hadn't realized it myself until today, when I suddenly no longer have it over me; the dynamic produces only chaos, nothingness, a sense of the ridiculous, fatal loneliness.
>
> It is sheer self-preservation instinct that now makes me almost want to pray to God that you will come to me. We would patch this up in no time—and then have time to calmly discuss the catharsis we really can afford and want.

Since the beginning of their relationship, Alva had helped Gunnar to construct a masculine persona as scholar and political leader that shielded the insecure boy she knew. Protecting the self against feelings of despair and possible suicide had been his greatest need, and she had known how to meet it. Now he felt that everything had been shattered.

Catharsis by Correspondence

The next day, Gunnar groped for words to explain his shock. He felt a sense of "nameless terror and desolation." "I am so disoriented . . . , so utterly lonely." Searching for a metaphor to express the idea of a man who had sought freedom only to experience uncertainty and confusion once it came, he ventured to say "I feel like my Negroes after emancipation." (G to A, July 20, 1941, letter 11) Gunnar's letters poured out a stream of consciousness, weaving a patchwork of details of daily life, self-deprecation, philosophical musings, Strindbergesque dreamscapes, and bits of Swedish and African American poetry and folklore. Based on their understanding of psychoanalysis, Gunnar and Alva both believed in the importance of purging one's emotions and the cleansing value of catharsis. To conduct this process by letter, rather than in therapy, was a dubious experiment, but Gunnar considered honesty the greatest virtue and thought that if he confessed everything he could begin to rebuild his life and marriage.

The terror of losing Alva tore away his mask of cynicism, intellectual superiority, and tough-mindedness. Filled with sentiments he normally would have been too proud to express directly, Gunnar's letters are saturated with raw emotional outbursts and childish self-pity. These cries of pain were, at some level, calculated to win sympathy from Alva, to make her feel guilty, and to convey his utter dependence upon her. But Gunnar also respected Alva as a strong, rational woman and believed there was a benefit to laying out these emotions, then stepping back to analyze himself. He expected Alva, whose actions had wounded him and whose words had exposed his deepest weaknesses, to offer an objective analysis of his own feelings as well as suggestions for how he might recover.

The day after receiving her letter, he felt "hit between the eyes" by Alva's revelations. Despite his advocacy of the Enlightenment belief in the power of human agency, he admitted that he felt like a puppet whose strings were being pulled by fate, the gods, or the devil. Gunnar mixed metaphors from classical thought and Christianity to express his sense of suffering and his penance for having claimed a superhuman immunity from ordinary ethics. His elaborately constructed masculine identity was collapsing around him. He considered it "something of a natural catastrophe when a strong fellow breaks down and just cries; it is not like when a little mademoiselle weeps over a sentimental movie. Damn it, there is a difference of the sexes here." He asked Alva to "consider the breaking down and rebuilding that characterizes such a violent emotional upheaval. It is as if years and decades were compressed into a climactic ending." He insisted that "I do not write it to torment you but to cleanse myself. I am lonely now, Alva. Catharsis." (G to A, July 20, 1941, letter 11)

In the immediate aftermath of receiving Alva's bombshell, Gunnar was unable to sustain a dialogue about how his psychological problems could be overcome and their marriage could be saved. During this period, he suffered acutely from bipolar disorder, oscillating between manic bursts of extreme self-confidence and creativity and depressive feelings of worthlessness and suicidal ideation. He recorded his frequent mood swings in his diary-like letters. In the 1950s, Gunnar would be treated by a Swiss psychiatrist, who prescribed lithium for the depression.[4] In 1941, however, he allowed himself only the option of self-analysis and catharsis by correspondence with his psychologist wife. Alva referred to her husband as "egocentric" and "narcissistic," and he pleaded guilty on both counts.

Gunnar had constructed a set of masks. In the 1920s, he imagined himself as a Nordic hero and a Nietzschean superman; in the 1930s, under Alva's influence, he presented himself as a social democratic intellectual supporting the cause of working people. As he worked on the study of American race relations, he continued to think of himself as destined to become a figure of world-historical importance. But now he felt his identity disintegrating. "I have completely lost my arrogance and that inner carelessness . . . constructed by a clever subconscious [as a] defense mechanism." (G to A, July 21, 1941, letter 12) Then Gunnar assumed the mindset of a man struggling to put his affairs in order before his death. Fearing moral and emotional "bankruptcy," he weighed the good deeds against the bad in his life as a business accountant adds up credits and subtracts debits. "I have included everything: the great deceptions, the small, personal acts of negligence, the professional obstructions, the pressure of my personality and everything else on the debit side; I must complete the credit side in order to make everything balance." "*We* are all square," he told Alva, "but I am not all square with myself." (G to A, July 22, 1941, letter 13)

Defining the task he faced, Gunnar wrote that in his isolation "there is nothing left except the debt to myself, to my innermost self, my infinite potential for good and evil, my great ruthless infinite passion for myself:

ME AND THE WORLD." Gunnar invited Alva to witness "the annihilation, the consuming hubris," and to watch his life "melt as in a crematorium and flow out in ethereal, gleaming bright ideas and gray ashes." Promising to finish the Negro study, Gunnar switched into English to sum up his accomplishments and failings.

> I have had a fine life, a great life in a way. I have never sold myself for money. I have been a lucky boy: what I touched turned to pure gold. I was a go-getter. I wanted to explain the whole world and reform the universe. I had the ambition to get a doctorate, and I got it. I wanted to be a professor, and I got the chair I wanted. I wrote books and they are now classics, and some of them changed society. . . . I was loved by Alva. I did wrong things, cruel egoistic things, I lied. . . . I was never brought under the order of ordinary human beings. (G to A, July 21, 1941, letter 12)

On the positive side of the balance sheet, Gunnar suggested that "there was something fundamentally honest and upright in me." His self-observation in a putatively clinical voice lapsed into the idiom of Romantic heroism:

> I had my history of frustration, I had my periods of depression, there were long periods when my eyes were not sparkling but anxious. My mind was sometimes darkened and I was impotent. But meanwhile I just overflowed. I was truly the darling of the gods. Probably I was one of the true geniuses springing up through Mendelian capacity from the peasant stock of this Scandinavian Peninsula. I must sometimes have been annoying as hell, but looked on in retrospect I was Nature's gift to myself and my surroundings.

Casting himself as a modern hero, he recalled that "I talked to the populace, and I always took the strong man's stand for the underdog: the youth, the women, and the broad masses." Then, swinging back to suicidal despair, the letter repeated: "I am tired and want to die. I want to dissolve the human accident I was into the great universe. I have never felt so before." (G to A, July 21, 1941, letter 12)

Obsessed by the idea of a moral "balance sheet," Gunnar hoped that his book on African Americans would tip the balance in his favor in whatever final reckoning came at the end of his life. His fixation on the idea of moral bankruptcy and his desperate balancing of his good deeds against his sins in life's ledger had deep roots in his religious and family background. As a child growing up in the Lutheran church, he would have heard sermons about sinners being called to account. The Swedish word for "guilt" also means "debt," a point Nietzsche had emphasized in *The Genealogy of Morals* when he had traced the linguistic evolution of the Christian concept of a "bad conscience" from the civil law relationship of creditor and debtor. Schopenhauer had given the metaphor a more secular, but quite harrowing meaning by comparing the "the vanity and suffering of this world" to a hell that surpassed Dante's. The metaphor of guilt as debt had another source closer to home, as his father had filed for bankruptcy once and had come close to bankruptcy several times. Gunnar, with his training in law and economics, had advised his father on how to conceal his debts from public view. Carl Adolf's close scrutiny of balance sheets was not limited to finances, however; growing more religious in his later years, he had brooded on the consequences of his adultery, alcoholism, and ambition. Gunnar, as a theorist of the Stockholm school of economics, had advocated deficit spending as part of Sweden's recovery program in the 1930s. When he contemplated his sins against Alva and his titanic struggle to write the Negro study as an offsetting accomplishment, Gunnar distilled anxieties rooted in religion, ethics, family, and profession into the metaphor of the balance sheet.[5]

In his next letter, he again sank into self-hatred and lashed out at his wife. In Gunnar's perfervid imagination, he cast himself as a modern Prometheus, whom Alva had condemned to a state of perpetual suffering. He spurned her advice about undergoing a catharsis, sneering that "you know very well what kind of a catharsis I need." Spurning Alva's claim that she had not known how her actions would affect him, he snarled: "Oh, you see it well enough now, even if neither I nor you saw it before." (G to A, July 22, 1941, letter 14)

Then, writing in the third person, Gunnar portrayed himself as a Romantic figure in a titanic emotional struggle, his strong feelings reflected in all of Nature in this drama of *Sturm und Drang*. He invoked his favorite metaphor of equilibrium, but now he cast himself as a victim, with the unbalanced scales as an emblem of a disordered personality in a chaotic universe. "He is poised atop the sharp point of a precarious balance that will never be in equilibrium again," he lamented. And "you advise him to be carefree," he added scornfully. "Just then, for a moment I felt like killing you. You are crazy." The next moment, he positioned himself as the victim: "I have acquired an enormously enhanced capacity for suffering . . . [but] I don't have you. It means that I shall die." Turning his rage on Alva, he asked sarcastically: "Why are you so much more clever: cheerful, cocky, strong? I don't give a shit about anything else. In order to live, I must attend to two things, just two: the Negro study and you. You are incomparably more important, but the Negro study binds me as well." Conceding that his recklessness had driven them to this point, Gunnar reversed the judgment he had made in a letter two months earlier, this time concluding ruefully that "*we* have played and *I* have lost." (G to A, July 22 1941, letter 14)

On the fifth day of his crisis, Gunnar poured out his thoughts in three letters. "I keep brooding without interruption," he testified. "Yes, Alva, I hate myself. . . . I have suffered from moral insanity, I have lived without character: swinish, indolent, slovenly, opportunistic, to and fro, [taking] shortcuts." Gunnar reflected that he had been given only two things, a good brain and a faithful wife, and he had abused both. In response to Alva's criticism that he had been "careless," he exploded: "I have never been more serious: I am as serious as a premeditated murderer, or—more accurately—a suicide." Facing his fear that his close bond with Alva was lost and realizing how much his whole identity had been bound up with hers, he repeated his observation that "now, we are two different people—a first for me." (G to A, July 23, 1941, letter 15)

Mixing psychology and spirituality, Gunnar declared that "I have seen death now. The experience is imprinted on all my cells, and it will never go away." But if Alva should come, "then I am completely sure that I won't fall apart." "I shall be tender," he pledged. "I shall lift you, I shall carry you. I shall make you rich. We shall be blessed. We shall never be separated again. We shall hold fast to each other. I shall be an open temple for you. You shall go freely in me as in paradise." But this confidence ebbed away at daybreak. Crying out, he exclaimed: "Dear God, let me not perish. I want to live. . . . I am frightened to death." Begging Alva to come, Gunnar transformed his image of his wife from vengeful Zeus to forgiving Madonna and vowed that "I would give five years of my life—if you bargain, more—so that I could lay my head in your lap just one more time. I ask nothing in return." Gunnar was awakened from this dark night of the soul by the hooting of an owl, symbol of Minerva, goddess of wisdom, who "sits and watches me." "Since the beginning," he reflected, "the symbols, sent by the gods, have played a role in the nameless tragedy." (G to A, July 23, 1941, letter 16) He had come late to wisdom, reaching it when he looked back on the wreckage of his life and realized the truth of Hegel's aphorism: "the owl of Minerva flies only at dusk."

Notes

All parenthetical citations in the text refer to manuscripts written by Gunnar or Alva Myrdal. All translations were done by the author. Many of their personal communications are difficult to decipher because they were written rapidly in longhand, abbreviate common words, and often use dashes instead of more precise punctuation. Transcribing and translating them necessarily involves matters of interpretation.

1 G to A (telegrams), April 22 and May 6, 1941; A to G, May 1941, AGMA. See also Bok, *Alva Myrdal*, 154–155.
2 Not only did some letters take Gunnar many days to finish, but he sometimes wrote several letters in a single day. Thus some letters are identified by number as well as date.
3 The text of this letter from Alva to Gunnar, July 8, 1941, has not survived, but each of the Myrdals refers to it in subsequent letters. Gunnar quotes from it in his letter to Alva, July 24, 1941. See also A to G, August 14, 1941, two letters written on the same day.

4 Dr. Georges Bickel to Gunnar Myrdal, June 20, 1956; G to A, June 25, 1956; Gunnar Myrdal to Mr. and Mrs. Derek C. Bok, June 25, 1956; Gunnar Myrdal to Walt W. Rostow, June 25, 1956; Gunnar Myrdal to Dr. Stig Bjorkman, October 29, 1956; G to A, Nov. 17, 1956. All of these letters are in Correspondence between Alva and Gunnar, 1955–56, 3:3:36, AGMA.
5 Bok, *Alva Myrdal*, 63–64; Jackson, *Gunnar Myrdal*, 36–59.

References

Alva and Gunnar Myrdal's Collection (AGMA). Arbetarrörelsens Arkiv och Bibliotek (Swedish Labour Movement's Archive and Library). Stockholm, Sweden.

Gunnar Myrdal's correspondence, 3.2

Dr. Georges Bickel to Gunnar Myrdal, June 20, 1956.

Gunnar Myrdal to Mr. and Mrs. Derek C. Bok, June 25, 1956.

Gunnar Myrdal to Walt W. Rostow, June 25, 1956.

Gunnar Myrdal to Dr. Stig Bjorkman, October 29, 1956.

Correspondence between Alva and Gunnar Myrdal, 3.3

[cited as: G to A or A to G, date and in, some cases, number]

Published Sources

Bok, Sissela. *Alva Myrdal: A Daughter's Memoir.* Reading, MA: Addison-Wesley, 1991.

Jackson, Walter A. *Gunnar Myrdal and America's Conscience: Social Engineering and Racial Liberalism, 1938–1987.* Chapel Hill: University of North Carolina Press, 1990.

13 Trolls, Strindberg, and Faust

Gunnar engaged in this intense process of emotional expression and reflection in the hope of reaching a catharsis. He drew on all his cultural and intellectual resources to comprehend and communicate his predicament: figures from Nordic and classical mythology; Enlightenment conceptions of human agency through reason; Romantic images of the solitary hero; and psychoanalytic notions of human irrationality, narcissism, even solipsism. None could keep his nightmare visions at bay, for all betrayed internal contradictions. But all fortified him to persist in the struggle for self-knowledge and enabled him continue writing to Alva through his darkest moods.

Visits of the Trolls

Gunnar imagined his anxiety and depression as a troll. "I catch a glimpse of the troll's hairy scalp," he wrote Alva in a nocturnal cry for help. As he tried not to "surrender to" despair, "a devilish troll peeks out and laughs wretchedly." (G to A, July 23, 1941, letter 17) For Gunnar, trolls symbolized the irrational elements of human nature. They served as a powerful metaphor for depression because they were supposed have the capacity to make humans see only ugliness and falsity where there is beauty and truth.[1]

Who was this sneering troll that haunted Gunnar's imagination? In Fritz Thorén's novel, *En Son*, Gerhard M, the protagonist, hears a recurring voice derisively judging him and undermining his self-confidence. Fritz's literary device was intended to represent the "sins of the father" preying upon the son's mind, an ever-present voice of doubt that pushed Gerhard into depression when he was trying to concentrate on his scientific work. When Alva had first suggested that they have children, Gunnar had responded that he could not envision himself becoming a good father because he was overcome with shame at the thought of his own father. For more than twenty years, Gunnar had assumed the pose of the dutiful son, outwardly showing respect for Carl Adolf while inwardly seething with anger. Covering up his father's drinking and adultery had made him a skillful liar and clever manipulator of others. The rage at his father that he had held in for so long inevitably spilled over into self-hatred. Despite his efforts to refashion himself, Gunnar knew that his personality had been profoundly shaped by his relationship to Carl Adolf. As he contemplated the wreckage of his marriage and felt pulled toward suicide in July 1941, Gunnar felt laughed at by a troll: a diminished, disfigured, emotionally stunted creature who nonetheless had the power to drag him into deep depression.

Alva, too, had used the image of the troll to hold a mirror up to Gunnar at his worst moments. In 1920, after her lover had written her the cynical letter in which he had offered a naturalistic description of his sexual encounter with the prostitute and falsely claimed that he had felt no emotion at the time, Alva had replied by saying that she felt as if a troll had hit her in the back of the head with a stick. Their relationship had survived that crisis, but was now in peril because his adultery had been concealed by lies, violating the most fundamental rule of their marriage contract. In the summer of 1941, Gunnar again struggled to free himself from the trolls' clutches.

A Strindbergesque Inferno

In his spectral imagination, "another devilish troll peeked out" and whispered to Gunnar: "It is of course a chimera that she is coming." Gunnar frantically parsed Alva's last telegram, worrying about "small imps between the words"—ambiguous phrases that concealed her intentions about coming to the United States. "My Alva," he lectured, "compose your telegrams meticulously: they will be read through by a person just as crazy as Strindberg in Paris. But do not tell any fibs. Write precisely what you think." (G to A, July 23, 1941, letter 17)

Alva had used the word "we" several times in her latest telegram, giving Gunnar hope that they still had a relationship that could be repaired. "I find my thoughts intertwined with yours like two lovers embracing (troll)," he wrote. "Spiritually, you and I can never be separated. You can find your thoughts throughout my sketch" of the Negro study; "we have thought so much together and I have absorbed your ideas and you mine." Trying to rebuild their relationship by focusing on their shared work, Gunnar continued, "I am your friend . . . for life; and you mine (no trolls peek out). The foundation cannot be shattered. I no longer say . . . that nothing can separate us, because I know better: I can imagine that we, on different sides of the ocean (and God help me: as far as I'm concerned, even on the same side) can absolutely sever our marriage. But my friendship and my comradeship will continue through all circumstances until death."

Gaining hope as he wrote, Gunnar said bravely, "To hell with the troll for a while." Reminding Alva of how profoundly she had shaped his life, he acknowledged that "you took . . . the awkward gymnasium student with the impudent, devious eyes, gave him all of youth's happiness, dragged him through military service and boring studies, educated him, breathed life into his mad ambition, made him feel born to succeed (he was not 'the lucky boy' before), fetched books from the Royal Library, directed his higher studies." Temporarily forgetting her writings on femininity as a social construct, he reached back to June 1919 when, after meeting Alva at Slagsta, he had cycled on with his friends while reciting the final lines of Goethe's *Faust*: "Woman, Eternal, shows us the way!" Gunnar invoked this essentialist concept of the feminine as he praised Alva: "You personally freed him from all ordinary standards, from all comparisons, by personifying an infinite, heavenly ideal."

Gunnar could not end his letter without returning to his deep sense of guilt and feelings of worthlessness. In addition to his own "balance sheet" of sins and accomplishments, he felt the need for a separate set of accounts of their relationship. "My own balance sheet with you . . . is the one that is driving me insane: I must get it into balance. We are alone with our consciences, you and I. You do not need to cry: let me tell you firmly and tenderly before I go further. It is I who am the problem. Toward you I have fantastic debts of lying, deception, neglect, and pure wickedness." Acknowledging Alva's desire for independence, Gunnar suggested that each person in the marriage had to establish his or her own personal equilibrium and then the two dynamic personalities had to be brought into balance. This account was not a static model of debts and credits but resembled his economic concept of "dynamic equilibrium" in a continually developing socioeconomic system. In this case, two individuals, each with a complex life in society, were constantly adjusting the terms that held them together. "Between two people there are two equilibriums, not just one," he explained. "I have never thought of it before now: . . . it is not like an economic transaction, where a plus sign for the one is a minus sign for the other and vice versa. This is very important, a great discovery. . . . It was never grasped by Strindberg, whom I have been thinking about since Saturday."

The reference to Strindberg's view of marriage is, at first glance, an odd choice in the context of Gunnar's expressing contrition and seeking to win back his wife. The great Swedish dramatist had been a critic of the feminists of his day, especially Ellen Key, whom he regarded as cold and asexual. Strindberg's public quarrels with his three wives and his bitter polemics on relations between men and women had earned him a reputation as a misogynist. In the late nineteenth century, however, Strindberg had electrified Swedish audiences with his unvarnished portrayals of the power dynamics in middle-class family life.[2]

When Gunnar said that he was "as crazy as Strindberg in Paris," he was referring to the playwright's portrait of himself in *Inferno*, which he had read and discussed with Alva in 1920. *Inferno* is a fictionalized account of the agonizing time in 1894–1896 after Strindberg's second wife, Frida, had left him. The 45-year-old dramatist had written Frida 22 diary-like letters in 19 days. *Inferno* offered the most compelling model in Swedish literature for an anguished husband pouring out grief and rage, mixing accusations and self-abasement in daily letters to an estranged wife. Creating a portrait of a living hell in which the narrator dwelled on his transgressions and argued with God about the consequences, the exiled author had imagined that God used a bookkeeping system of guilt and punishment. In 1896, convinced that a power beyond himself was guiding his destiny, Strindberg drifted close to madness, with hallucinations, fears of being persecuted by demons, deep depression, and thoughts of suicide.[3]

Gunnar Myrdal, like Strindberg, had been raised in a bourgeois family and rebelled against his Lutheran upbringing under the influence of modern science, yet constructed a view of himself as a Romantic hero. In confronting his marital crises, each man was overwhelmed by emotions of guilt and terror. Each conducted an internal dialogue in which the conscience critiqued the behavior of the self. In both cases the stringent self-criticism led to a counter-tendency to defend the self against charges of worthlessness, to achieve an integration of conscience and self, and to emerge from his ordeal purified and instructed by suffering.[4]

Strindberg wrote his *Inferno* in French in 1897, after he had emerged from the worst phase of his psychological crisis. Although the book is loosely based on Strindberg's diary, biographer Olof Lagercrantz has demonstrated that the author was able to reflect on this episode and render it as a work of art. Strindberg's Narrator is clearly stronger than the Victim character he depicts.[5] In Gunnar Myrdal's letters to Alva, the process is much more immediate, with Gunnar "purging" himself of his emotions at the hour of his greatest woe, then stepping back to analyze his divided self undergoing these torments. Yet Gunnar knew enough about the Christian tradition and the examples of Dante and Strindberg to believe that he had embarked upon a process of contrition, penance, and purification, and he hoped that eventually he would achieve a kind of personal salvation through his "intellectual honesty" and redemptive labor for human betterment. He wanted Alva to serve both as his intellectual guide, Dante's Vergil, and as his spiritual inspiration, Beatrice—two strikingly different, even incompatible roles.

Confession

Following his ruminations about Strindberg, Gunnar acknowledged with bitter irony that his "old theory of expediency" regarding extramarital relationships had come back to haunt him. He and Alva had both criticized the hypocrisy and lying that had been common in bourgeois families, and they had publicly advocated giving women a wider range of choices about reproduction, childrearing, family life, housing, healthcare, and employment. In their private dialogue with each other, Gunnar and Alva had discussed whether a modern marriage should include the right for each person to have sexual relationships with others. Gunnar had been inclined to argue, at least in theory, that exceptional men and women should not be bound by ordinary rules. In practice, he and Alva had seldom been apart for long periods of time, and his love for and dependence on her had never been called into question. Gunnar's hatred of lying and deception and his intense connection with Alva made it psychologically difficult for him to become involved in extramarital affairs behind her back while they were living together. He had never seriously considered leaving her for another woman. Now that Alva had acted on this advice and was quoting his theory back to him, it struck Gunnar as vulgar sophistry. The woman he had looked to as a moral guide or conscience was now claiming the same liberties and rights to self-fulfillment that he had claimed. That was a consequence he had never envisioned. (G to A, July 24, 1941, letter 18)

"I know now, and it is a bitter knowledge, what it is like to suffer from the other," Gunnar admitted. "To be completely honest here. . . . I have always known it but cleverly lied about it or tried to lie about it. The whole theory of expediency breaks down because of this." The measured tone of Alva's letter of July 8, with its disembodied, philosophical discussion of extramarital experiments, infuriated Gunnar. Dispensing "with epistolary courtesy" in what he regarded as "a matter of life and death," he charged: "You lie, you deceive yourself." "What particularly humiliates me to the depth of my soul is that the lack of intelligence and vulgarity show up precisely . . . where you are busy adjusting yourself to my old self." "I know it now and it stings my conscience." Unable to see beyond his egocentric conception that Alva was imitating him, he hurled Alva's accusation of "carelessness" back at her. Chastened by the unexpected consequences of his past teachings, Gunnar affirmed that "love and the soul should not have to coexist with lying."

Up to this point, Gunnar had described his faults in rather general terms. Five days after receiving Alva's letter, he detailed his previous transgressions, confessing his affairs in the belief that admitting his guilt was a necessary part of a catharsis that would be an essential precondition to restoring his relationship with Alva. He announced portentously, "Tonight I shall write a difficult and important chapter in the purging, clear and honest as in my scientific writings." (G to A, July 24, 1941, letter 19)

Gunnar informed his wife that he had slept with a young Swedish countess in New York in May—before Alva had slept with the young professor—and again in early July. He had met her husband when both were gymnasium students, and the count was now working for a large corporation in New York. Gunnar described the woman as rich and beautiful and attested that "she was the finest woman I have ever met, next to you." In a passage that must have been excruciating reading for Alva, he described his feelings about the countess by quoting the very words that Alva had used in her letter of July 8 to recount her affair with Ingvar Högbom in Stockholm. "Just like you, my pupil in sin, I said to myself that it was 'meaningless'—'an episode immediately forgotten'—'I am totally free'—'I regret nothing'—'quite literally a pleasantry.' You certainly cannot expect an old sinner to feel 'white as an angel.' But, like you, I [felt] 'a delirious pride of conquest.' . . . In saying to myself that it did not have any other meaning for me personally, I lied, as you did later. And, as you calculated, I wanted 'to avoid all that in a letter because you never know what mood the other is in when it arrives.' In my innermost thoughts . . . 'my wicked calculation was even worse: I did not want to say anything because I did not want to awaken . . . a desire for compensation on your part.'" Stepping back from his relentless sarcasm, Gunnar declared: "For this and for what follows I seek no forgiveness, nor do I grant myself any."

Ratcheting up the tension, Gunnar explained that the count and countess were expected to turn up that weekend. "Now I am free and must make up my mind. She belongs to the most subtle, hygienic and romantically attractive of Substitutes. I only have to flap my arms and flash my eyes at her and she would, of course, come running on any terms." But Gunnar assured his wife that the affair was over. The countess had been in "psychological trouble" when she had taken up with Gunnar. He promised to tell her that the relationship could not continue.

After this bitter outpouring of confession, savage irony, and braggadocio, Gunnar tried to convince Alva that he wanted to change not only his sexual behavior but his whole way of relating to other people. Repeating Alva's admonitions to him, he promised that "I shall not be a person who irritates, teases, hurts and provokes others, entangles them devilishly—and pilfers now and then. I shall be a good person, who makes others strong and not weak, who gives them trust and not doubt, so that they can depend on me and gradually even put their faith in me." Gunnar reminded Alva that their personal happiness had enabled them to support each other's professional ambitions and be honest with each other until their arrival in America in 1938. Then their many separations had put pressure on the marriage.

Gunnar revealed that he had also had a brief sexual encounter with a woman during a two-month trip in the U.S. South in the autumn of 1938. "I got lazy," he explained. "Was it the shadow of the war or the fear I felt over the Negro study?" Gunnar referred to it as "a case of pure carelessness" and gave no further details.

An affair with more serious consequences had occurred in Sweden the previous summer when Gunnar had become involved with Ingrid Gårdlund, the 24-year-old wife of his junior colleague, Torsten Gårdlund, who had been away when Alva was out of town. He claimed that Ingrid had seduced him when he stopped by the couple's house to drop off a manuscript and that her husband had not been attending to her sexual needs.

He had not told Alva because "I wanted to protect you." But when Alva had returned home, Gunnar had been impotent: "I went to pieces physiologically as you will recall." He attributed this "erotic neurosis" more to his anxiety about lying to Alva than to his feeling of guilt about committing adultery: "I was like an embezzler trying to be as honest as he can over a lie [but] forced into ever more monstrous ones."

"It is so difficult to be absolutely honest," Gunnar recognized; "even memory is . . . opportunistic." Reflecting on Strindberg, Gunnar wondered, "How do ordinary bourgeois people ever manage such situations; how do ordinary people even live their lives?" But perhaps an ordinary person would not have been "as careless and arrogant as I have been." Gunnar concluded this extraordinary letter by asking Alva: "What [do] you, on the whole, think of me?" He insisted that "I am much changed." He had taken the risk "that you will break away from me forever" after reading his confessions. It was not just a matter of settling the differences between the two of them; he was laying out these details as part of reckoning his "life's balance."

The next day Gunnar sought to convince his wife that he was working hard to heal himself. Alva had told him that she was tired of dealing with him as a "problem child," a term they usually applied to their son, and insisted that she could not be his therapist. Gunnar agreed that he did not want to be her "problem child and patient," and promised to "be my own doctor." "I have . . . had a great cleansing of the soul." (G to A, July 25, 1941, letter 20)

In the first eight days of his emotional crisis, Gunnar had turned from Nietzschean apostrophes to the "übermensch" to tropes expressing passivity, terror, and self-abasement. The dominant metaphor was the trolls, embodying darkness, pessimism, and repressed instinctual forces that returned to haunt him. In this state of gloom, Gunnar's brief allusions to African Americans had also been cast in tropes of passivity and powerlessness. He had fallen back on his religious upbringing, then thought of Strindberg in Paris as a model for the emotional purging he that believed was necessary so he could emerge from the crisis a stronger man.

In the next phase of his crisis, Gunnar considered a figure that embodied hubris, spectacular moral failings, and redemption through hard work and altruism with the help of feminine forgiveness. After his consideration of Faust, Gunnar's engagement with the American race question deepened, and he returned to the commitments that he had originally brought to the issue.

Faust and the Negro Study

Endeavoring to lift the discussion onto a philosophical plane, Gunnar remarked that he could find little help for their marital dilemma in Kant's moral philosophy because their experiences differed so markedly from those of ordinary people. "There are no patterns in books or other peoples' norms." "We have lived so differently from all others that we are forced to be original." Gunnar contended that "I have honestly worked on this with seriousness and originality, as in my professional life." Just as "I would not construct a book about the Negroes . . . on the basis of other people's experiences," he approached his problems as an empiricist, trying to subject his own experience to rigorous analysis. (G to A, July 26–27, 1941, letter 21)

He compared himself to the figure of Faust, invoking a complex web of symbolism surrounding the mythical German scholar whose desire for knowledge led him to make a pact with the devil. Gunnar and Alva had often discussed the Faust theme in the early years of their relationship. Children growing up in Sweden were exposed to the Lutheran morality tale in which Faust was carried off to hell for the sin of pride, having tried to extend the bounds of human knowledge into realms known only to God. During his gymnasium years Gunnar read Goethe's *Faust*, in which the sinning scholar was portrayed more sympathetically as seeking experiential knowledge. In his current, penitent state, Gunnar thought of himself as a man who had wanted everything: unbounded knowledge, political power and influence, adventures with a colorful mixture of people in different countries, a loving and intellectual wife as a soulmate, and affairs with other women. In this shattering personal crisis, Gunnar seems to have feared that he, like Faust, was being dragged off to his own personal hell where he would be cut off from Alva, plunged into a world of darkness, and unable to write. In Goethe's version of the story, Faust had redeemed himself through self-knowledge and altruism. Gunnar's letters to Alva expressed his sorrow and remorse, while he hoped that his work on the Negro study would enable him to overcome his selfishness.

Gunnar begged for Alva forgiveness. "Dear," he implored, "you must be like God, who does not cast away the wheat because of the chaff." As Gretchen had forgiven Faust, helping to ensure his salvation, so Alva would also embody the qualities of spirituality and redemptive love. But before Faust could be saved, Goethe's protagonist both strove for self-understanding and looked outward from his divided soul to work actively for human betterment. Only after Faust had turned his genius to altruistic work did he ascend to heaven. Gunnar acknowledged his own ethical responsibility and regarded the Negro study as the selfless act that would bring him redemption. "Whatever you do with me," he exclaimed to Alva, "I must save my own soul." (G to A, July 26–27, 1941, letter 21)

Gunnar made a remarkable statement about the connection between his book on African Americans and the problems in his marriage: "All that I wrote" in the first part of the manuscript "is just a fantastic symbolic expression of my own life's problem," although "it also could be objectively true." He observed with irony: "It must be funny in some way for you to read my sketch for the Negro book: from the first to the last page it is about just me and us." Vowing that "it shall be written with my blood," he alluded to Dante's *Inferno* in suggesting that "it shall be concerned with the sighing of creatures and the needs of humanity who were not saved." "It shall be the book on the Negroes with all the facts and data, with fine curves and inspiring methodological discussions for future research," but "the great pattern is my life's problems." Gunnar realized that he was undercutting his claim to objectivity by admitting that his own emotional conflicts were the source of his insight into the issue of race in America. Nonetheless, he had applied social scientific methods to the analysis of his data and "brought it up to this plane of generality." "Cleansed of my life's problems, and still standing is just humanity's elemental tragedy: that good people turn life into a pure hell when they live in social relations." (G to A, July 26–27, 1941, letter 21)

After pleading with Alva to understand his need to write the Negro study as a way of overcoming his sense of creative impotence, Gunnar said that "I have perhaps never loved you as deeply, admired you as much as I did" when they were writing *Contact with America* together. In the midst of intellectual exhilaration and creativity, "every day I noticed how beautiful and desirable you were." Later on, he explained, it was "not a turning away that made me impotent but the terror of the box of ashes in my past"—his recent affair with Ingrid Gårdlund—"which I had not the courage to open." Rebutting an accusation from Alva about how he and other men thought about women, Gunnar suggested, only half-jokingly, that while it was important to consider these issues scientifically, a man should not be neutered. "Now I certainly don't think that a man should think with his testicles, but neither should he think without them: or more correctly, he should not be inhibited by knowing as a biological and psychological foundation that he has them." In this respect, Gunnar insisted, "I am one of the healthy. . . . I need a wife, or more precisely: my wife, my friend, my companion in work."

Veering abruptly to the opposite image of himself, Gunnar said: "My wantonness and your cheerful adjustment have brought us to the gates of death and here I walk, pale as an open-eyed corpse." He concluded this extraordinary letter, in which he had ranged from sexual dysfunction to redemptive altruism, by saying what he thought Alva wanted to hear. "Come to me. I am no longer broken; I am consistent and clear; easy to live with. Certain and tested, humble beneath the pride. Not a patient. Serious. Tough. I can speak so well of myself because I have gone through all the pieces, bandaged, patched, . . . and mended [everything]. You will come to me not because I need you, but because, after all, you need me." "Beloved," Gunnar inquired anxiously, "Now we are on the same side (Are we not???)."

In his next letter, Gunnar analyzed the differences between their temperaments. In his view, Alva was able to keep everything compartmentalized, but he was not. He understood the intellectual appeal of the idea that both husband and wife should be able to have relationships outside their marriage, but jealousy was his "Achilles heel," a "physiological fact, the nails in my breast, blood in my eyes." Gunnar considered his jealousy "unfair, irrational, illogical, unreasonable, but there it is, filling all of space." He begged her to burn all of the clothes she had worn during her encounter with Ivar Högbom. Gunnar contrasted his own panic and irrationality with the unnerving calmness and detachment with which Alva analyzed the philosophy of open marriage, which made his blood run cold. Fearing a loss of objectivity about his situation, he admitted: "I work so hard just to hold onto a feeling of reality: I am paralyzed by doubts that perhaps I live in pure fantasy and phosphorescent words." (G to A, July 26–27, 1941, letter 22)

Referring to himself in the third person, Gunnar painted a picture of an isolated scholar not unlike Faust in his study, but added a more feminine image of spinning and weaving, reminiscent of the Norns of Nordic mythology or the three Fates of Greek mythology. Switching back and forth between English and Swedish, he sought to put into words "a tentative formulation of fundamental beliefs or life hypotheses." Figuring himself as a knight struggling against injustice, he began in English by affirming that

> G. is convinced as he always has been of his own value in a sense, that he is born to a destiny, that whatever is the fate of the world he will have a front to fight on, he believes that his courage is uncorruptible (*sic*) and his sword sharp and heavy; he believes he should have twenty or even thirty years to continue his struggle; he thinks he is just now reaching full maturity and the culmination of his strength; nonetheless, he knows how the worm turns and the possibility of frustration.

He affirmed that "G. loves Alva 100%; he believes he has a greater intensity—and on the contrary also a greater capacity for going crazy and falling in ruins."

Blending romanticism and the social sciences into pseudo-clinical observation, Gunnar declared that he and Alva were geniuses who had formed each other's identities. "He considers himself very much a creation of her; she has been the most important 'environment' shaping his 'nature', although she should not be held responsible for all the misfits." With this power, he advised Alva, comes duty: "she cannot shirk responsibility; he knows also that . . . she is his creation in a similar way and degree." Almost as an afterthought, he mentioned that he loves Jan, Sissela, and Kaj and wants to be in their life, although he had not thought very much about fatherhood before.

Gunnar resumed writing in the first person to make his final point about throwing himself into his work for human equality and social justice: "Personally I have no other desire for adventure left except to concentrate more powerfully than ever on my plan of work, ideas, ideologies and struggle." (G to A, July 27, 1941, letter 22) In reply to Alva's accusations that he was egocentric and inattentive to the needs of others, Gunnar added: "In this respect, I have definitely overcome the petit bourgeois attitude to life . . . within the past half year." The Negro study was more than a "cure for loneliness"; it would be a contribution of world-historical significance. Having renounced his class heritage, Gunnar betrayed himself a moment later when he employed the metaphor of the family firm to refer to their working relationship. "I believe in A.G.M. I believe that when we join forces in work we accomplish something better than either of us would individually; I believe that it would be detrimental to the world if the firm should go under."

A few days later Gunnar acknowledged that he and Alva were now both "free" to seek a separation or reconstruct their relationship, but insisted that "even if we should decide to go our separate ways, we must still reason it out with each other; and we must find a lasting contact" with each other. But he could not maintain this tone of equanimity, admitting that "I am explosive: full of love and, yes, hate. Come before I become completely crazy." (G to A, July 30, 1941, letter 24) Later that day, he elaborated. "I am finished with myself but not with you. I must tell you that I hate this Alva of July 1941. I hate myself in you: when I see my cunning, half-conscious calculations mirrored in you, my most beloved." "If you do not come, we are doomed to the grimmest suffering, perhaps doomed to cause each other suffering. But let us fundamentally examine our life's problem, let us think it through." Gunnar affirmed that "we need each other as old married friends. We must have a secure contact through all these intermittent letters. We believe in reason in everything, even in family life: we have expounded our views publicly and we ought to be ashamed not to stand fast by our principles. We are lonely, we suffer, life is difficult, but . . . we shall have each other intellectually, even though the contact may pull us apart." (G to A, July 30, 1941, letter 25)

As his suicidal impulses abated, Gunnar took courage from the statistics showing that African Americans, who had the heaviest reasons for despair, had a lower suicide rate than whites. "There is a joke in the South that things have so gone awry that whites steal hens and Negroes commit suicide." He continued seriously: "I tell myself that I have kept the ethos of my research inviolate, that it is objective, never written opportunistically." Admitting that he was "greedy" for praise, he asserted that "here in America I notice that I have a position that I have created without falseness." His career in public life, "on balance . . . has had the same character: no pretense." In analyzing the sources of his drive to champion the oppressed, he recognized that "I have striven for the underdog, partly perhaps because of still bleeding resentments of an underclass character but partly also truly, honestly driven by conviction and idealism." (G to A, August 2, 1941, letter 27) In this way, Gunnar articulated to Alva what he would never have disclosed to anyone else: behind his mask of an intellectual aristocrat, he believed that his own sense of having been born into a family with poor, rural origins underlay his commitment and insight into the struggles of African Americans and other oppressed groups.

On August 3 and 4, Gunnar received telegrams from Alva, in which she admonished him, "Don't lose courage dearest." She faced "certain delay," which was "involuntary of course," but pledged her love. Her "hope" was "undamaged," but she was "scared [about] your status." Alva signed the cable, "unfailingly lovingly only yours." On August 8, Alva cabled that the first part of her journey, from Stockholm to Britain, was "imminent." Though she could not be sure of gaining passage to America, it was "impossible staying here" and she was determined to go "halfway" with a British visa as a correspondent for a Swedish magazine. (A to G, Aug. 3, 4, and 8, 1941)

"I am a new person," Gunnar beamed in a letter the next day, "and you would know it if you met me." "I am not as rotten as you make me out to be. I must preserve an ounce of self-confidence because when the ounce is gone, I die." But he no longer threatened suicide; instead, he conjured up an image of self-purification through eighteen-hour days working on the Negro study to vanquish racism. "Regardless of what you do with me and our relationship, I must hold fast to the primary duty on me to complete my work; if you abandon me, I have just that duty left." Gunnar followed this promise with a declaration that "I do not permit you to come in order to save my life. Only come to me for your own sake." "Hell, I have some pride too," he added in English, declaring that he did not want her to come out of a sense of "nobility." (G to A, Aug. 9, 1941, letter 30)

Notes

All parenthetical citations in the text refer to manuscripts written by Gunnar or Alva Myrdal. All translations were done by the author. Many of their personal communications are difficult to decipher because they were written rapidly in longhand, abbreviate common words, and often use dashes instead of more precise punctuation. Transcribing and translating them necessarily involves matters of interpretation.

1 For a psychological analysis of trolls in Scandinavian mythology and Ibsen's *Peer Gynt*, see May, *Cry of Myth*, 175–188.
2 Bok, *Alva Myrdal*, 28; Meyer, *Strindberg*, 560–561; Meyer, *Sex and Power*, 504–516.
3 Strindberg, *Inferno and From an Occult Diary*; Meyer, *Strindberg*, 306–310, 327–329, 337.
4 Brandell, *Strindberg in Inferno*, 57–58, 128–132, 159.
5 Lagercrantz, *August Strindberg*, 282–284.

References

Alva and Gunnar Myrdal's Collection (AGMA). Arbetarrörelsens Arkiv och Bibliotek (Swedish Labour Movement's Archive and Library). Stockholm, Sweden. Correspondence between Alva and Gunnar Myrdal, 3.3
[cited as: G to A or A to G, date and, in some cases, letter number]

Published Sources

Bok, Sissela. *Alva Myrdal: A Daughter's Memoir.* Reading, MA: Addison-Wesley, 1991.
Brandell, Gunnar. *Strindberg in Inferno*, trans. Barry Jacobs. Cambridge, MA: Harvard University Press, 1974.
Lagercrantz, Olof G.H. *August Strindberg*, trans. Anselm Hollo. New York: Farrar, Straus, Giroux, 1984.
May, Rollo. *The Cry of Myth.* New York: Norton, 1991.
Meyer, Donald. *Sex and Power: The Rise of Women in America, Russia, Sweden, and Italy.* Middletown, CT: Wesleyan University Press, 1987.
Meyer, Michael. *Strindberg.* New York: Random House, 1985.

14 The Feminist Complex

At this point in their correspondence, Alva brought up the contradictions in her own life. She had aspired to be the perfect complement to her lover's outsized yet fragile ego, striving to live completely for him but finding herself in competition with him as she sought to be intellectually worthy of his companionship. She had learned to be his therapist, and her fascination with psychology had led to a deeper exploration of her own needs and desires. Before she could develop her own career, Alva had helped Gunnar to construct a thick, protective shell that would enable him to take criticism in public and develop a masculine persona suitable for his talents, only to find herself shut out by his self-preoccupation and his work. In her 30s, she had proclaimed herself a feminist and helped to provide solutions for employed women with children, but at the cost of becoming the junior partner in the firm of AGM. Although she had written most of *Crisis in the Population Question*, Gunnar had been appointed to the Population Commission. When she wanted to run for a seat in the Riksdag, she was blocked by the fact that her husband was already in parliament. Alva had worked hard to establish herself as a child psychologist, yet she found herself continually undermined by the childishness of her husband and the adolescent troubles of a son who needed more attention from his father.

While Gunnar compared himself to Faust, Alva did not intend to share the fate of the unfortunate Gretchen. Her practical, social democratic feminism ruled out her playing the role of the "eternal feminine" her husband envisioned. At the same time, Alva found their exchange full of "intoxicating honesty." In early August she wrote a flurry of letters replying to some of Gunnar's questions and setting forth her ideas about what had happened between them and how their marriage might be reconstructed on a new basis. Alva was able to be more candid now that she inferred, from telephone conversations and telegrams, that Gunnar had moved beyond the threats of suicide he had made in mid-July, but she underestimated his capacity for relapses.

Alva's Perspective on their Marriage

On August 3, Alva wrote that she was only then coming to terms with the fact that she had hurt him. "You must have noticed," she observed drily, "that I have not been especially overwhelmed by guilt before." After reviewing their apparent agreement to change the ground rules of their marriage during their involuntary separation and Gunnar's shocked reaction to her admission that she had taken his suggestion that she have a "temporary idyll" as consent, Alva objected that

> much of what you said during the first moments must be untrue. For example, the idea that the sanction I created was the foundation for "us." If this were true, it would mean that you were disappointed now because we are two human beings, and not only you. (A to G, Aug, 3, 1941, letter 22)

Throughout their marriage, Gunnar had been "the one who acts, the one for whom our lives are arranged, the one for whom permissions are given," while she had been "the one who suffers." After reassuring him that "of course I'm sufficiently in love with you to let you be the center," she warned him that the "concessions" she made in sacrificing her desire to be "just as much in the center myself" demanded recognition and even reciprocation. His one-sided demands posed a problem "for my theoretically feminist way of thinking." When she stepped back and looked at the pattern, she was troubled. "In everyday life" sacrificing equality for love is "almost always a source of joy." "But is it right? Is it a viable way of living?" She insisted that the pattern of her acquiescence to Gunnar's wishes must be changed. Now "both of us must give up something for the whole to be great."

Referring to Gunnar's history of having affairs but objecting mightily when she did the same, she declared forthrightly that the double sexual standard was unjust. They had endeavored to have an intimate emotional and intellectual relationship, and she had tried to tolerate his brief affairs when they were apart; but she had expected him to inform her about them without going into painful details. He had not kept this promise. "It was you who considered the matter too petty," she charged. "What we have lived on has been partly a love momentarily really happy and fulfilled, partly . . . my inability to be so crude and disloyal that I would mix in someone else when I had you." Beneath this unstable arrangement had been an uncertainty about whether "a long absence would make things different" and they "could live a more uncoupled life."

After laying out her version of how the marriage had evolved, Alva concluded that "you must not say that something fatal has occurred." Recent events "must not give direction for the future." She resolved that "we shall decide about our future when we meet again. That will not be done by letter, when one talks and talks oneself out only to be thrown into a sea of lava a month later." Alva reassured Gunnar that she was not seeking "petty justice." "Not even here, far away, have I wanted to hurt you." Underscoring the ambivalence of her position, she claimed that "now everything is so blurred that I don't want to bind you. That is also so petty."

Alva held out the hope of a complete reconciliation, but cautioned that it could not occur until they were able to talk things through face to face. She wanted him to use the next few weeks to think about whether he really wanted to resume the marriage on these new terms of equality.

Alva followed her measured reproach and calculated negotiation with a passage saturated with romance. Paraphrasing one of Gunnar's first letters to her in 1919, she wrote reassuringly:

> Through every fiber in the body and every movement in the soul, we know that we are made for each other, that we have each other and that we can love to the envy of the gods and shall so love—forever. This is so much beyond doubt, Gunnar—we cannot clear up anything on our own. But we can live trusting one another, can't we? Dearest, let the guardian temple stand! No moaning shall come from me over the Atlantic except over our separation. Therefore no great humility either. Only this grand faith that we belong to each other. Don't lose it, my beloved dearest man. We shall carry it high over our heads, above all the people around us.

Then Alva explained why she would not respond to Gunnar's request to define "monopoly." Since he often transferred terms from economics to intimate relationships, she understood him to mean "monogamy." Alva demurred, as she thought the topic "our most vulnerable" point. "Certain kinds of confidences hurt more than they serve. It is sane to keep some kinds of limits. I have extracted a couple of painful details from you—remember that I haven't forced you to give away a lot of them, agree with me on that, my only man—but it has hurt a hundred times afterwards. A thousand. Sometimes in the most inopportune moments." Gunnar had also requested a "meticulous" discussion of what he called "the wanton alternative" and the "consequences" of casual sex "for all parties involved." Alva brushed this aside, as she had in earlier letters, and affirmed that "now I refuse to go on drilling" for more muck beneath the surface. "It comes dangerously close to where we are now not supposed to go . . . and that around which we must now close a ring of silence." (A to G, undated, filed after Aug. 3, 1941)

Alva exulted that now "we are seeing things so alike that I might as well copy your letter and send it back." "I think we know so many of the same things," she affirmed. "If we then only choose the same way also, then I believe in us. But the same way it must be." Referring to the traditional European contrast between the virtuous, asexual woman and the scarlet woman, she rejected the feminine role in which Gunnar had cast her. "The saint and the fool is a fairy tale that is over. The red and the white girl also. . . Let us be many-colored, both of us!" They were separate people, to be sure, but "through the differences, what we know gets larger."

Gunnar's Response

Gunnar promptly countered Alva's assertion that she did not "have a life" because she had sacrificed so much for him. He accepted responsibility for the fact that Alva had made concessions in order to support his career and fulfill her duties as a wife and mother. But he insisted that she had accomplished a great deal and had a bright future before her, even without him. Gunnar was especially concerned that Alva's statements betrayed an "inferiority complex" regarding her professional work. "I have just one intensive need," he declared, construing her achievement as his necessity: "that you do not let . . . your decision be influenced by pressure and feelings of inferiority. You are free, strong and independent. You have possibilities for a life. I hate it when you have this crazy idea that without me your life would be over." He urged her not to let her decision about their marriage and possible divorce be influenced by the attitudes of other people in Sweden, many of whom would feel a kind of *Schadenfreude* over the troubles of this talented couple. Gunnar admitted that "I have deceived you devilishly," but his lies had made him "sick and hysterical," applying to himself a term that most psychiatrists of his day reserved for women. He expressed his belief that with a "little hygiene of the soul, it will never be repeated," although he recognized that Alva might see it differently. As he slipped back into self-pity camouflaged as critical detachment, Gunnar urged her to salvage what she wanted from the wreck he felt himself to be: "I invite you to come and look me over with whatever skepticism and whatever mental reservations you want: you can just as well have me as a lover as anyone else. If you can come to me you can have what's left of me until the end." (G to A, Aug. 9, 1941, letter 30)

A few days later, Gunnar returned to the theme of Alva's independence and professional accomplishments, but only after the customary purging of his own emotions required by his conception of "mental hygiene." The previous day he had received seven letters from Alva written from July 22 to 29, none of which have survived. He lamented that they were not really relevant because they were written "before the great clash." Likewise, he warned that some of his letters that she was now reading "are not suited to the occasion." "But what can one do when the mail is so slow?" He could only keep writing, even though "synchronization" was impossible and it often seemed as if they were writing past each other. (G to A, Aug. 12, 1941, letter 31)

Setting that problem aside temporarily, Gunnar returned to the issues Alva had raised about equality in the marriage. "I want to protest against your insistence that I always have a life, even if we separate, while you do not have anything." "You have the whole of our milieu left, while I am thrown out; and you have relatively the better conscience." He strenuously objected to "the perception that you have a false position in Sweden." Her standing was secure, while "I am away and soon I shall disappear without a trace." Gunnar added parenthetically:

> Do not totally lie about the effect of our marriage on this point: in certain important considerations it has limited you greatly, I know it, but the firm has also had its positive sides, and from me you have not only stress but also inspiration—I speak honestly in this settling of accounts.

"You stand in certain respects as the country's foremost woman," and "perhaps you would not have accomplished this without me also, although one cannot be sure." "Do not burden me with the claim that I closed you in and limited you, because, in sum, it is not true. You should not create for yourself an unnecessary inferiority complex in this crisis."

Attempting to come up with a formula for equality within the marriage while acknowledging that resources were distributed unequally, he declared:

> It ought to be clear between us that we both understand that as society is now constituted, I have a greater income than you and that this . . . means that I take the whole [financial] burden of the children, the house, taxes, etc. But the position of wife has been to you such a hindrance that I need to say to you that everything that we have or that I ever earn is also at your personal disposal.

"Do not plague us, therefore, with an economic inferiority complex," he concluded.

Having settled this question in his own mind, Gunnar addressed what he considered the psychological "complex" that was driving Alva to seek greater independence. Making a startling assertion in the midst of this crisis, he protested: "I see no reason why I should not still get to be your very best friend" in offering psychological advice. He pronounced the fact that "you feel that you want to experience your solitude, independence, and our separation" to be "another inferiority complex you must protect yourself against." Her sense of inadequacy was "completely irrational and ought to be eradicated through intellectual analysis."

The Problem of Being a Woman

Alva was reading Gunnar's sketch of the Negro book, which she called a "stroke of genius," as she composed these letters setting forth her views of their marriage. (A to G, Aug. 8, 1941) Although she did not comment directly on the outline, she kept the issue of women's equality before Gunnar while he was writing about the struggle for racial equality. Turning to her husband's painful confession of adultery, Alva spurned his explanation that it had been an impulsive act or a moment of temporary insanity. She suggested that it had been more calculated and stemmed from an inferiority complex of his own. "So is it so obviously banal, so complex-free?" she asked. "Or is it a more like a melodramatic attempt to impress me, as with the whole countess thing and all? The triumph of the proletarian faced with a wife all too knowing?" (A to G, Aug. 13, 1941, letter 41)

"Now there is one more thing," Alva continued. "And I think I had better bring it up now in this state of intoxicating honesty . . . . Quite simply [it is my] damned intellectualism. The feminist complex." They had felt free to analyze each other's "complexes," and Gunnar had interpreted her desire for independence as evidence of an "inferiority complex." For Alva, this would not do. Employing the metaphor of dancing, she wrote: "You always 'lead'—which I could do too. I think I could well dance solo! But not 'follow.' I am too inventive, too playful, too strong-minded, too unsubtle—call it what you like. But I don't think I have any great ability to follow." She did not want to go as far as her friend Eve Burns, "who leads even when women are not supposed to lead." But, Alva admonished her husband, "let us arrange this coolly and well. Otherwise some of your actions will look like sheer manifestations of puberty." She acknowledged that "after this summer, our problem is more complicated and I myself am even more complicated," but with this new honesty as a "point of departure," at least "life is clear."

Alva's mask of Apollonian reason slipped when she turned to answering Gunnar's questions about her views on an "alternative construction" of marriage. "Now I have a bad conscience about everything," she typed early the next morning. She explained in some detail why she did not like the idea that each could have affairs while they were apart. She began with "the terror of knowing that, in spite of all honesty, there must be certain limits." "Sometimes I fear that I shall not be able to keep them. Sometimes I also fear that holding feelings in will cause them to burst out." Her conflicting emotions were "so complicated: revenge, the wish to smooth everything over for you so that you would not have unpleasant associations, a real effort to be noble, to set you free." An open marriage carried the "risk that our integrity might be worn down. Once you have given yourself permission and done something, it will be easier the next time." It might be difficult to compartmentalize when having an affair, and one might be tempted to continue it even when the couple was living together. Another danger would be that "one would give more than one meant to." Referring to the "fear of not being able to stay within the limits" of an affair, she asked: "How long can one or should one control himself?" It was difficult to stifle one's emotions and to repress thoughts in order to prevent "loyalty to the outsider" from overwhelming the marriage. Worse still, "we would not be unfaithful at the same time." Alva could not accept the idea that they would "never know where the other was, never come home and know that one had the right to be close to the other." "No. Impossible," she declared. (A to G, Aug. 14, 1941, letter 41)

Finally, Alva raised concerns about hurting a "third party," the "trusting wife" or husband of a lover. "For heaven's sake, let the loving couples remain loving couples," she implored. Despite not holding herself to Kantian standards of morality, she "wanted to have a philosophy that was good also for others," which involved a rejection of Gunnar's longstanding claim that they were "different" from other people. "Now," she sighed, "I want to be liberated from this problem."

In a recent telegram, Gunnar had written about the importance of trust. Alva replied, "Beloved husband, what right have I to be certain about you?" In the abbreviated English of the telegram, he had promised "Absolute exclusive love" and written that he was "Demanding tenable solution," to which Alva responded that she did not need an "ultimatum" to love him. "Your love is a blessing more than a right. I know that it is fragile. I have to be careful with it. It is a miracle. Something incredible. A gift that I live to repay."

"These letters are driving me crazy," Alva complained as she sat down at the typewriter to begin a second letter on August 14. That day she had received three missives from Gunnar demanding explanations for her behavior. "I cannot begin on July 8," she insisted, referring to her affair. "I did not intend to settle any accounts. Believed that I was acting on an understanding of how we then were. Had no idea that you were suffering on account of me." "Beloved, forgive, forgive, forgive. I did not suspect that you were willing to have such a fundamental settling of accounts." Alva entreated Gunnar to "take me just as I am now. And understand that I want to get out of our dishonesty. But I always was afraid to demand too much. I think now that we are precisely 'on the same side,' that we 'think completely the same on all complicated issues.'" (A to G, Aug. 14, 1941, letter 42)

Alva assured Gunnar that "for me, everything is now answered," and she felt they were ready to affirm the basis of their love for the future. Her "Philosophy of love" was that "every love needs to be surrounded by peace to reach its peak." Alva also explained her "Philosophy of marriage: if there is to be happiness for both, there must be a partnership in work, children, and the home. The intimacy that gives one courage to talk about everything." She also emphasized "Belief in yourself. What you are now. What you shall become. What we shall do. How we shall experience the world in this terrible time, become better and stronger people. How we shall write books. Possibly even be involved more directly in the process of reconstruction" after the war. Alva reassured her anxious partner that "I believe in you as part of us."

"There is just one thing that has not been cleared up," she added: "trust in myself. The eternal problem of being a woman. . . . I know this is fraught with momentous consequences." Alva reminded Gunnar that her life was so packed with family, professional, and civic responsibilities that she rarely had time for herself. "I am aware that this summer could have been my opportunity, perhaps the only one I'll get, to think through this alone, to allow myself solitude, to break the continuity with you. If I am to divorce, I must do it now." Usually "I do not even care about myself, that is how much I care about you." This was not the time for her to think about "what you can get from me," but to consider "what I can get from you and our happiness in being together." Returning to the themes of forgiveness and reconciliation, Alva declared: "You can do what you want with me. I believe that it is more difficult for you to accept something soiled. I never believed for a minute that you should 'take me back' if I had lied to you as you did to me. Deceived." Looking back on their extraordinary correspondence, Alva observed that "I do not believe that you wanted, that either of us wanted to write this series of dramatic letters, so hateful to each other. Beloved—erase all the stupid stuff. There is quite enough of reality to work through as we grieve."

In her third letter written that day, Alva resumed her discussion of the practical difficulties of maintaining a sexual relationship outside the marriage. "As I warned you a thousand times, I am much less capable than you of having any kind of cynical double moral standard." Alva suggested that she would inevitably fall in love if she became involved with someone else, and consequently become unable to love her husband. At the same time she realized that she "would become eternally discontented when I know that no one can replace you." Under such circumstances, it would be difficult for a married couple to remain honest with each other because "honesty shatters the idyll." (A to G, Aug. 14, 1941, letter 43)

Alva initially declined Gunnar's invitation to a mathematical "settling of accounts" with him and expressed satisfaction that she had achieved a sense of "clarity" and catharsis after her affair. She was more interested in reckoning "my position in relation to my own self" and asked, "What should be the guideline for my life alone?" Allowing herself a rare flash of anger, she reminded Gunnar that she had consistently sacrificed herself to his career: "This is the outstanding balance in my settling of accounts." She claimed that, while Gunnar's career was firmly established, "my life's plan does not exist. Or it is you? . . . I give up becoming a member of Parliament because you have to be in America for the sake of continuing honorably in your work of global responsibility. And you say to me: 'if you had been an ordinary wife?' Ha!" Taking a leaf from Gunnar's book, Alva suggested that

> if I had met you as a mature adult with the plan of my life all set out and my feminist philosophy in place, . . . then at least I could have an achievement to set beside yours so that you would not have to whine and ask derisively 'what major contributions can you point to in order to justify your being away from me?'

Having disclaimed any intention of a mathematical balancing of the books, Alva now embraced it with relish. "See here, my beloved," she insisted,

> I have not finished my settling of accounts. If I knew how you or I might have handled things differently or planned differently, I would not be so unhappy. But I turn to you as my friend in my loneliness. And thus we can never forget the connection between my insecurity about you and my insecurity about myself. Between the problem of our love and the devilish problem of "the woman's place." Between my ability to imagine freedom, strength, [and being] "alone with my own self"—as well as my actual dependence [on you].

These tensions "drove me to become a feminist." Bristling at Gunnar's "totalitarian demands," she asserted that she had to include "civic and professional life" in this discussion of the relationship. Referring to their fame in Sweden as "the Myrdal couple," she remarked that "I am not even a name without it." Gunnar had repeatedly pushed her to analyze their relationship objectively, and Alva retorted: "Can you ask for more objectivity than that?"

In her fourth and final letter that day, Alva cautioned that "I don't understand why one should have a balance sheet for everything. . . . I don't understand why it must be divided between persons." Jokingly adopting the language of economics, she asked if one should put plus and minus signs on omissions as well as on active deeds. Moreover,

> I don't understand, on purely scientific grounds, how you can talk about balance when you do not say a word about the coefficients. How much money is equal to how many kisses? How many happy hours are counterbalanced by heartbreaking unhappiness? It is not a live issue for me. For me, really, the only thing is whether we shall live together.

Alva resisted Gunnar's continued demands for explanations and his insistence upon "intellectual clarity." "Don't ask me what I did and what it meant in toto for me. I DON'T KNOW," she shouted. In response to Gunnar's incessant demands for details, she replied that "I must . . . be sparing. All the bits I gave you have been subjectively true at the time I gave them. Even the silliness. Even—and this is the worst—what you call a suggestion of promiscuity." Defending herself against these accusations, she asserted that "I knew on July 8 that it was enough for me. Now I know what this was all about, felt freed from that particular complex and realized that I preferred loneliness as a substitute" for Gunnar. (A to G, Aug. 14, 1941, "Thursday evening")

Separation, or a More Equal Partnership?

The following morning, Alva admitted that she had been unable to sleep after reading three of Gunnar's letters in which he discussed the possibility of permanent separation, hinted at suicide, and blurted out "I hate this Alva of July 1941." She reassured him that, if wartime conditions continued to keep them apart, "you do not have to be afraid that I shall be 'unfaithful.' . . . I know . . . that it would be ruinous for us. I have suspected that neither you nor I chose this. And that has made me strong." As she struggled with "these enormous difficulties," her plan was "fidelity, trustworthiness," and "a violent sublimation, work." "I do not say that I can keep it up," she added: "the balancing of the soul is having a technical breakdown." (A to G, Aug. 15, 1941)

"When I first understood . . . that you had experienced a fundamental settling of accounts," she reflected, "I also understood what a serious thing I had done." "Do not repudiate me," she beseeched him, "because you see before your eyes a process that you yourself suffered through much more slowly and alone." Alva affirmed that "I long to be under the great sanction" of monogamy. "Which protects us, beloved. Protects against little things from each other. Against the mixing in" of another person. Alva now understood that her "salvation" had been in her "reservations" during the affair, holding herself back emotionally and regarding the liaison as a temporary flight from her marriage. "But at the same time, I found that I had to give up something and that it [was] (This is written . . . slowly, the typewriter cannot reveal how my heart trembles) OUR HELL WHERE I AM THROWN BECAUSE OF YOU." (A to G, Aug. 15, 1941)

Finally, Alva provided Gunnar with a few of the details he had demanded about her affair. "My poor unenlightened one," she commenced,

> I first made love "cold-bloodedly," in an illusion that the whole thing was meaningless, mechanical, then . . . in an hour [I felt] a piercing, momentary consciousness as if I were in a slaughterhouse. I experienced it as a horrible neurosis—and you understand that not a word came from my lips then—that this was a . . . dangerous Lie. It was a question of something else. Of reality. Of something that I had believed throughout my life was ours. (Gunnar, if you could hold my hand [while I write this], it would be better.) I made myself . . . fail a little. I didn't create a "fiasco," but I had to desert you for a few minutes.

"In the end," Alva concluded, my "reservations" were "my defense for us." Her love for Gunnar had made her hold back emotionally during her night with someone else. "And yet—you call me promiscuous?" she asked with calculated incredulity. "But I have chosen to save us, dearest."

"I know that there is no simultaneous" love of more than one person, Alva affirmed. "Every illusion about it is over. I knew that long ago. But just intuitively." She offered a threefold "explanation" for her actions. She had wanted to "lure" Gunnar into recognizing that his own affairs had disastrous consequences for their marriage, so that he would "quit" having them. She had tried "to convince myself that the little I gave up was not dangerous, since I was ready to let you give up more." And she had hoped "to free you in order to get the answer I had desired and begged for." But she had been shocked that "all this touched you on a deep level." Writing about it forced her to confront the unacknowledged feelings that had led her to take this step. "Now I can say it as a general truth which I always believed in when I warned about terrible broken-heartedness but which now lives fiercely [inside] me. IT IS EITHER US—or something completely different. There is no . . . compromise that we can live with."

Joking about her public image in Sweden as an expert on women and family life, Alva reminded Gunnar that "my letters are just a painful process" of working out thoughts.

> Not the Woman Leader's secure, instructive, illuminating solutions to all problems. We are not strong enough. But if it were true that now you also—for the first time in your life—treated our marriage commitment with great respect—What a blessing. Gunnar, then our life would be different.

A solution required an emotional accord, not just a resumption of cohabitation. "Tell me if we shall soon be Together again?"

The next day, Alva sat down to write a final letter before beginning her dangerous journey to the United States. Assuming that Gunnar would not receive it until after she was on her way, she wrote frankly of her pain, reiterated her criticisms of his behavior, and ended with an affirmation of her desire to be reunited with him. "Now the devils are with me again," she began. Gunnar's actions had hurt her, but she understood "that you never actually engaged in two parallel relationships. That you never maliciously intended to leave me." But Alva had awakened that morning knowing that she had to attend a social engagement with Gunnar's younger colleague, Torsten Gårdlund, and his wife Ingrid, whose affair with Gunnar a year earlier had resulted in such guilt and anxiety that Gunnar had become impotent. Alva had resolved to appear "simply radiant, translucent of understanding," and to offer Ingrid "really good professional advice" as she had done before. She had then gone to a desk drawer and pulled out Gunnar's letter, written on July 24, in which he had confessed to three affairs. As she reread the words, "which are, of course, unmentionable," she first attempted to reconstruct how he had behaved during his affair with Ingrid while Gunnar and Alva were writing *Contact with America* together. Whether he had the affair while she was in Stockholm or during her trips out of town, it meant that he had been making love to her and to another woman during the same period of time. (A to G, Aug. 16, 1941, letter 45)

Alva's next comment reveals much about her view that honest confession and emotional expression enable an individual to confront difficult issues and move on with life, but it also suggests a striking metaphor for what a person does with these feelings and new insights once she has analyzed them. "Yesterday I thought that . . . I should, after fighting through this, find rest ... [and] put aside the documents in the fundamental archive that builds my life. But now everything collapses again." These raw emotions, evoked in letter after letter, are not as easily set aside as a rational social scientist might wish. Gunnar's earnest confessions, although intended to clear the air, had unintended consequences. She was prepared to believe "that you, out of consideration, did not want to open what you had behind you," but Gunnar's "recurring calculations" of sins and virtues on his life's ledger kept reopening old wounds. She had lost the hope that she had felt the previous day. "Now, of course, it is . . . such crying, difficult crying, again today, at losing you." "And on this," she added, "I cannot get an answer."

Ever the psychologist, Alva assured Gunnar that her grief, anger, and tears would not prevent her from performing her professional and social duties. Referring to the engagement with the Gårdlunds, Alva sneered that "of course I shall be so happy when we meet today. But now I fight against it. Yesterday I was so happy that, at bottom, I felt nothing but friendliness." Alva reminded Gunnar that, over the years, she had developed a "process by which I identified with you: I am ashamed when you are ashamed. . . . I feel guilt when you feel guilt. I feel friendship when you feel friendship." But all this sympathy for his feelings and denial of her own needs had not stopped him from betraying her. With Gunnar's disclosure of his affairs, she hoped "that a little abscess had been lanced, so that it was left behind [and] we could be on the same side. Now—I shall cry so that I do not risk doing it later." Alva strove to maintain the appearance of self-control and critical detachment that she would need to get through the day's performance. "It was . . . a rather important thing that I learned yesterday: That I.G. took you over last fall. Now I conduct myself accordingly. With my objectivity. Against myself. And go" to the party.

For eight months, Gunnar had faulted his wife for not accompanying him to the United States and had made himself out to be a pathetic victim of Alva's supposed coldness. Now she turned the tables and asked: "Does this mean, as I protest again and again, that you left in order to get away from the ashes of what you call a meaningless relationship?" "In this you are not my husband," she declared, or "not the husband I know." Alva asked rhetorically whether Gunnar's affairs behind her back mean that "we should not stay together." "I could not bring myself to answer the letter," she explained. "Honesty drives me—but at the same time, I am so scared that too much would become fixed if it were put down on paper." Alva underlined the fact that she would return to Gunnar, but asserted that she had also changed. Struggling with her conflicting feelings, she insisted that "I anticipate such happiness with you, that the giving up of temptation becomes a poor sacrifice—it's the most natural thing of all." She conceded that "I have misunderstood you on many points." Then she threw in some self-criticism to balance the devastating accusations she had hurled at him. Referring to her affair, she claimed that "it was a mixing up of you (and opportunism) that made me try my experiment." But Alva did not want to keep "rehearsing" these points.

After speaking bluntly about their marital confrontation, Alva concluded with a romantic flourish: "And now I long for the healing, dizzying happiness of being with you. Much can touch us, beloved, but nothing can destroy us. We shall be together, dearest. We shall . . . entwine ourselves around each other so we can feel every little bit of our souls and our bodies." (A to G, Aug. 16, 1941, letter 45)

On the Verge of Reconciliation

Before receiving the last batch of Alva's letters, Gunnar had written: "I agree to end the purging letters." Quoting from her latest telegram, he noted hopefully that "you are 'agreeing only tenable philosophy exclusive absolute love.'" Aware of his precarious position and trying not to presume too much, Gunnar concluded: "I dare not call you anything other than Alva, and I am at the point of calling you Alva Reimer"—her maiden name. (G to A, Aug. 15, 1941)

Although Alva had repeatedly reassured Gunnar that she foresaw a bright future for them once they talked through their problems in person, he was still haunted by guilt. He had overcome much of the shock and depression of mid-July, but feared that another bolt from the blue might finish him off. In a letter written a month after receiving the letter from Alva that had unhinged him, he compared himself to a figure in a Greek drama whose hubris had led to an inevitable tragedy. Gunnar struggled to hold on to his conviction that humans could shape their own destiny, hoping that their drama "would not be a tragedy of fate." "I want to live. I want to have you," he exclaimed. "Alva, is it possible? But let us whisper quietly about this. Let us not irritate the gods. No arrogance. Who knows what [thunderbolts] shall strike down in the morning. . . . Now I am not playing." (G to A, Aug. 19, 1941, letter 35)

After midnight Gunnar returned to the typewriter. "I have been reading Du Bois now for a few days," he reported. "He is a poet." W.E.B. Du Bois had brought the German Romanticism of the divided soul to the psychology of African Americans in his discussion of "double consciousness" in *The Souls of Black Folk* (1903), and Gunnar had reached back into that tradition to describe his sense of inner conflict between his image of himself as a heroic scientist and the reality of his emotional dishonesty in his relationship with Alva. For Du Bois, "double consciousness" had given African Americans a unique perspective on American culture as well as enduring pain. For Gunnar, the "dark" side of his personality threatened to overwhelm the good. Finishing his work and making an "honorable" contribution to the Negro struggle was, in his view, a heroic mission he had to complete to attain moral redemption for his misdeeds.

The next day Gunnar trembled at the prospect of responding to his wife's letters. "Alva, I am so deathly afraid. Before I open them I just want to bless you and say that I love you eternally." Reading through Alva's letters, none of which have survived, he reported mood swings from "drowning in a storm of misery" to feeling more "happy and calm than I have been in a month." Gunnar replied to her accusations with clear, succinct admissions of guilt rather than bottomless wallowing in self-hatred. "I deny nothing that you say about my deception and my depraved desire." Yet "from my side it seems different: it is a little cowardice that makes me lonely and . . . hysterical." He admitted his dishonesty, but saw it less as calculated hypocrisy than as a clumsy, improvised attempt to cover up frenzied outbursts that he had been unable to control. "When I sought refuge in my scientific character in this crisis," he claimed, it was obvious "that I first needed to come to clarity with myself."

> You do not understand that the fundamental deception is committed against myself; what you simply condemn as intentional sexual depravity is for me a [state of] hazy confusion and insanity. There remains your question of whether dishonesty is not something fundamental in my character: if one can be honest in work and false in life? Yes, Alva, I am afraid that one can be so and that I have been such a man. Do you want a declaration? It is probably true that from childhood I have always taken work and ambition with deadly seriousness but have lived life recklessly and carelessly. (G to A, Aug. 19, 1941, letter 35)

Gunnar also responded to Alva's complaints that she had been required to subordinate her career to his and sought to banish her insecurities about her own professional work, which he had inflamed by his sarcastic comments in his letters. He reiterated that her "feeling of inferiority" about her work was "completely unwarranted." Finally, Gunnar agreed with his wife that "we should be prepared to make real sacrifices for each other."

Alva concluded the exchange of letters with her husband in September during her sojourn in Britain, reflecting on the intense psychological drama that had unfolded between them while Gunnar was trying to write his book on race relations in America. Her carefully composed letter combined a testimonial to Gunnar's resiliency—in which she referred to him in the third person—with an attempt to put the accusations and bitterness behind them. Although she tried to recover her voice of psychological authority and her well-honed skill at ethical analysis, her pain and anger cry out at several points. Alva professed awe at "how magnificent your settling of accounts was." "When I look back on it all, I must say that this man was worth loving, was exactly the way I want him—having waited for him for 22 years." She marveled at "this man, who all by himself manages to break through the dreadfully convenient 'haze'" of moral confusion. "Who on his own and, without my having demanded it, is ready to give up this loophole approach" to settling accounts. "Dearest, this is greatness," she exulted; "I hope that I shall be ready to match it when I come to you." "I have done just enough to bring myself to correct the step that I took outside my boundaries" and to face "that eternal insecurity about whether I am worth anything as I am." (A to G, Sept. 1941)

Shifting the focus back to Gunnar, Alva contended that "it is not me that we should be talking about. . . . I am not just thankful for but proud of your ruthlessness" in identifying and admitting mistakes. "If anything can save us, that is it. Discussing who is most or least at fault would be utterly ridiculous." The work they had done that summer in clarifying the terms of their relationship was "much more important." "However much I gasp in pain at some of the things that are happening to me or to us, that pain is not directed at you." Alva pronounced herself "almost sure" that "you do basically want to preserve us." "If you had decided to destroy us, you would not have stopped at this and would not have been so unhappy yourself." In an effort at conciliation, she stressed that "I am a good bit more prepared to see your point of view than all this sounds. And I am even more prepared to believe that you might have been unhappy. I suffer with you, beloved. Sometimes I move completely out of myself and enter into your troubles as my troubles." In closing. Alva praised her husband for having pulled through this crisis.

Note

All parenthetical citations in the text refer to the correspondence between Alva and Gunnar Myrdal. All translations were done by the author. Many of their personal communications are difficult to decipher because they were written rapidly in longhand, abbreviate common words, and often use dashes instead of more precise punctuation. Transcribing and translating them necessarily involves matters of interpretation.

References

Alva and Gunnar Myrdal's Collection (AGMA). Arbetarrörelsens Arkiv och Bibliotek (Swedish Labour Movement's Archive and Library). Stockholm, Sweden.

Correspondence between Alva and Gunnar Myrdal, 3.3

[cited as: G to A or A to G, date and, in some cases, letter number]

15 Dilemmas of Gender and Race

Through these months of emotional upheaval, both Gunnar and Alva mustered the energy to write important books that reframed public discussion on deeply contested social issues of race and gender. The persuasive power of their proposals for change rested not on any simplification of the problems at hand, but rather on their penetrating analyses of the fundamental contradictions within and between egalitarian ideologies and pervasive patterns of domination and subordination. Within this shared conceptual framework, Gunnar addressed the connections between race and gender in a society that remained deeply patriarchal, while Alva probed the conflicts that married women with children experienced as they struggled to combine breadwinning with caregiving.

Work and Family

While Gunnar tried to write *An American Dilemma*, Alva's English-language book on population policy, *Nation and Family*, was in press. Aimed at an international audience of scholars and policy makers, the book lacked much of the passion of *Crisis in the Population Question* but offered a comprehensive analysis of family issues and a rational, planned approach to all aspects of family life. Alva advocated sex education, contraceptive counseling, the right to abortion in limited cases, free prenatal care, government subsidies to families with children, public housing, guaranteed healthcare, and social security.[1]

Most of *Nation and Family* was written in a voice of social-scientific authority to lend the legitimacy that was accorded to expertise to these radical ideas in the eyes of a skeptical international audience. Alva presented her policy recommendations less as her own proposals than as the social democratic consensus in Sweden. But in the last chapter, provocatively entitled "One Sex a Social Problem," she struck a more personal note as she placed before her predominantly male readers some of the unresolved issues facing women in Sweden and other industrial democracies (398). Earlier in the text she had contended that "monogamous marriage is considered the ideal love relationship between man and woman. Marriages, and particularly marriages of young people, should be encouraged" as a vital step in increasing population (187). She argued for a transition from patriarchal to "partnership marriage," in which most married women as well as men were gainfully employed and husbands and wives made joint decisions in an egalitarian manner. Alva warned that the carefully planned reforms of family policy would not work if women remained "fundamentally dissatisfied." Blending irony with the language of contemporary American sociology, she declared that "the feminine sex is a social problem" and argued that there could be no modern family policy without full equality for women. "Whether a woman is young or old, whether she is married or not, whether a wife works or not, she is likely to be a problem." "This problem is largely economic in origin because marriage and family are as yet poorly adjusted to the new economic order" (418). The solution had to come on many levels. A new relationship between men and women would not automatically fall into place through industrialization, urbanization, and legislative reforms. Fundamental rethinking was necessary. Most importantly, the issue concerned men as well as women: "This is of vital importance to the individual and society as the family is the essential societal relationship" (425).

Alva focused especially on "the dilemma of the working mother," suggesting that she had not found a "satisfactory adjustment to the demands upon her time by husband and children" as well as her job. No doubt reflecting on her own situation, she addressed the "psychological dilemma" of the family, suggesting that it would take much time and effort to transform the attitudes and behavior of both men and women with regard to housework and child-rearing. She called for innovative terms to describe the roles of men and women in the family and for changes in the mass media's portrayal of those roles, as well as "a fundamental change in the teachings of home, school, and church about the natural superiority of men and their duty of being sole supporters" of their wives and children. "As it now is," she pointed out, "few [men] are educated or mentally prepared for the new mode of family living." After describing the tensions that married women felt between family and work, Alva acknowledged that many of her readers would think that she had "willfully exaggerated" them. But these problems "are already at work in the subconscious of wives and of all women." In private, women are "brooding over riddles, which are never solved and rarely even openly expressed."[2] Citing "a wealth of discussion in fiction, magazines, and books on the subject," she concluded that "mothers are in danger of becoming a mentally malcontent group," which could affect women's willingness to have children. Indeed, there was a risk that "the whole population program might fail because women are fundamentally dissatisfied with the status defined for them." Public officials in and beyond Sweden had "failed to tackle the very problems of marriage itself." And more than the birth rate was at stake. At a time when Europe and Asia were engulfed by war and American intellectuals worried about whether their depression-scarred society could stand up to Nazism,

Alva concluded with a warning that reinforced her argument that feminism was a preventive reform. "The risk is great that society will proceed so slowly in solving these problems of women's existence that new and even more desperate crises may invade the whole field of women, family, and population" (423–426).

Nation and Family did not attract much attention in the United States because it was published in December 1941, when the country's entry into the war overshadowed everything else. But over time it became a sociological classic.[3] Alva's points about the psychological pressures on working women with children were a major theme in her correspondence with Gunnar. In her letters, she often referred to her psychological dilemmas as a consequence of being forced to subordinate her career to a husband who made so many demands on her. Gunnar agreed with all of her public policy ideas on the status of women, but did not accept or act on her conclusion about the radical attitudinal and behavioral changes required of men as well as women by the new "partnership marriage." Indeed, he would often respond to Alva's points about her role in their marriage by discussing these issues as purely personal psychological problems divorced from the broad social context she had sketched out in her book. Still, Alva's arguments had made enough of an impression on him that devoted a section of *An American Dilemma* to comparing Negroes and women as oppressed groups, in which he drew on Alva's insights.

Parallels in the Positions of Blacks and Women

Gunnar Myrdal's magnum opus, *An American Dilemma* (1944), influenced the contemporary debate on civil rights and gave many whites a framework for understanding the Black struggle. The thesis that racial segregation and subjugation posed a moral dilemma for whites who were committed to the "American Creed" that, as the Declaration of Independence put it, "all men are created equal" and "endowed by their Creator with certain unalienable Rights," had emerged when Gunnar and Alava were writing *Contact with America*. But it derived its sharp focus and emotional intensity from Gunnar's personal conflicts and his guilt about his treatment of Alva, his desire to reaffirm the Enlightenment principles of equality and justice, and his conviction that people need honesty and consistency in their lives. He believed that white Americans felt guilty about their mistreatment of Blacks and that whites' divided minds provided leverage for African Americans who were asserting their civil rights. It would be another decade before social psychologists explored "cognitive dissonance" and the methods by which people hold conflicting attitudes at the same time. On the basis of his own experience, Gunnar Myrdal was certain that white Americans could not live with the tension between their creed and their deeds.[4]

Convinced that "resentments" from his "underclass" background enabled him to empathize with the black struggle, Myrdal portrayed

African American organizations as active and militant. Black Americans, he contended, were newly confident because they knew that they had the American Creed and a considerable body of world opinion on their side. Equally important, whites would be unable to resist their claims whole-heartedly because of their own moral dilemma. The daily drumbeat of egalitarian rhetoric from Alva had strengthened Gunnar's commitment to a vigorous defense of African Americans' rights within the context of American liberalism. Her interest in the psychology of women's oppression led Gunnar to examine the psychological effects of racism on Black Americans, but his position as a foreign observer of a rapidly changing wartime political environment precluded his making the kind of detailed policy proposals for bettering the lives of the disadvantaged that he and Alva had made in *Crisis in the Population Question*.

Gunnar believed that the problems of the Negro family and Negro culture were urgent issues that Black Americans should confront and overcome with the support of the rest of the nation. But he could not bear to give these matters his full attention. Claiming that the field was understudied, he assigned the writing of the chapters on "The Negro Community" to his assistant, Arnold Rose, a 23-year-old Jewish graduate student in sociology at the University of Chicago, who finished them late in 1942 after the Myrdals had returned to Sweden. With no prior background in the study of African Americans, Rose summarized the existing literature, which had been written mainly by Black sociologists trained at the University of Chicago.

The discussion of Black culture in Rose's chapters stands as an ironic commentary on Gunnar Myrdal's own troubles. Rose wrote: "In practically all its divergences, American Negro culture is not something independent. . . . It is a distorted development, or a pathological condition, of the general American culture. The instability of the Negro family, . . . the insufficiency and unwholesomeness of Negro recreational activity, . . . the narrowness of interests of the average Negro, . . . superstition, personality difficulties, and other characteristic traits are mainly forms of social pathology which, for the most part, are created by the caste pressures" that arise from exclusion and segregation. Writing in Myrdal's name but drawing heavily on the work of the black sociologist E. Franklin Frazier, Rose claimed that "the average Negro family is more disorganized than the white family." He cited statistics showing that Blacks' illegitimacy rate was about eight times that of native-born whites, and thus the Negro family differed markedly from the "ideal type of the monogamous patriarchal Christian family." Rose also referred to a study that showed that mental illness was three or four times more prevalent among Blacks than among whites, in part because of alcoholism and syphilis.[5] This view of the "pathological" elements of African American culture remained influential. Ralph Ellison would offer a withering critique of Myrdal's portrait of African American culture in an essay published in 1964. But that same year, Daniel Patrick Moynihan's infamous report, entitled "The Negro Family: The Case for National Action," blamed black poverty on the "breakdown" of the Black family, which, he contended, had been headed by women instead of men ever since slavery.[6]

Amidst his personal agony in 1941, Gunnar Myrdal had articulated a "moral dilemma" that held profound meaning for many white Americans struggling with their conscience on the race issue, which had gained a new salience in American society during the war. The psychological tension that Gunnar Myrdal had felt during his personal crisis resonated powerfully with Protestant moral discourse. His efforts to interpret African American families, sexuality, and culture, however, were flawed by his powerful need to avoid these painful subjects.

In his most original remarks on the subject, Gunnar Myrdal compared the status of Negroes and women. He began by arguing that women and children, like African Americans, had been subject to patriarchy throughout American history. The common law had subordinated women and children to "the paternal power," and "when a legal status had to be found for the imported Negro servants in the seventeenth century, the nearest and most natural analogy was the status of women and children." Upon this legal concept of the slave as a subordinated member of the master's household, the South had built an ideology of paternalism, which reached its most elaborate expression in the writings of antebellum pro-slavery theorist George Fitzhugh. Although the cult of southern chivalry claimed that men elevated and protected white women, southern women actually lacked many legal and property rights and had fewer opportunities to obtain an education and conduct a business than women outside the region. The link between the bondage of Blacks and women was best expressed, Myrdal thought, by a statement attributed to Dolly Madison: that the southern wife was "the chief slave of the harem" (1073–1075).

After enumerating various legal restrictions on women in the early nineteenth century, Gunnar Myrdal observed the close connections and ideological similarities between the abolitionist movement and the women's rights movement. He pointed to white leaders such as Angelina and Sarah Grimké, Abby Kelly, Elizabeth Cady Stanton, and Susan B. Anthony, but did not mention the many African American women who were both were feminists and abolitionists. The failure of Congress to include women's suffrage in the Fourteenth and Fifteenth amendments had led to bitter estrangement between the advocates of women's rights and African American men's rights, but Frederick Douglass and W.E.B. Du Bois had continued to support equal rights for all women (1075–1076).

In comparing the changing economic, social, and political status of women and Negroes, Gunnar attempted to reconcile Alva's conception of the position of European women after the Industrial Revolution with Frazier's picture of the Black family. Both theories were influenced by the

Chicago School of Sociology, which focused on adjustment to societal change. "Paternalism was a preindustrial scheme of life," Gunnar wrote, "and was gradually becoming broken in the nineteenth century. Negroes and women, both of whom had been under the yoke of the paternalistic system, were both strongly and fatefully influenced by the Industrial Revolution." Echoing Alva and Frazier, he suggested that "for neither group is the readjustment process yet consummated. Both are still problem groups," as their social condition is incompatible with modern, industrial conditions.

> The women's problem is the center of the whole complex of problems of how to reorganize the institution of the family to fit the new economic and ideological basis, a problem which is not solved in any part of the Western world. . . . The family problem in the Negro group . . . has its special complications, centering in the tension and conflict between the external patriarchal system in which the Negro was confined as a slave and his own family structure.

Both groups are in the process of change, but a "reorganization" of their status involves a change in the attitudes and behavior of men with regard to women and of white Americans in their relations with Blacks.

Comparing ideologies of domination, Gunnar found that "the study of women's intelligence and personality has had broadly the same history as the one we record for Negroes." "The arguments have been about the same: smaller brains, scarcity of geniuses and so on." Negroes and women were each assigned a specific "place" in society. "The myth of the 'contented women,' who did not want to have suffrage or other civil rights and equal opportunities, had the same social function as the myth of the 'contented Negro.'" Turning to racial and gender discrimination, he observed that both groups had been denied access to higher education. Women had been enfranchised only recently, and in most countries still had great difficulty winning election to public office. Most women workers were confined to low-wage "women's jobs," just as most Negroes were stuck in low-paid "Negro jobs," depressing the wage scale for all workers. Gunnar emphasized that "men often dislike the very idea of having women on an equal plane as co-workers and competitors, and usually they find it even more 'unnatural' to work under women," just as whites object to working under a Black supervisor. Returning to the legacy of patriarchy, Gunnar claimed: "In personal relations with both women and Negroes, white men generally prefer a less professional and more human relation, actually a more paternalistic and protective position." Having startled his American readers by comparing the status of white women to that of Black men, Gunnar made another provocative comparison: "As in Germany it is said that every gentile has his pet Jew, so it is said in the South that every white has his 'pet nigger,' or—in the upper strata—several of them."

In his analysis of male paternalism toward women, Gunnar suddenly switched into the first person plural, adding a direct observation: "We sometimes marry our pet woman, carrying out the paternalistic scheme. But even if we do not, we tend to deal kindly with her as a client and a ward, not as a competitor and an equal." In comparing the position of Negroes and women, "we are uncovering a fundamental basis of our culture." "Although it is changing, atavistic elements sometimes unexpectedly break through even in the most emancipated individuals." He reminded his readers that the similarities in the treatment of Blacks and women were not "accidental" because they both originated in a "paternalistic order of society" and that these problems remain, "even though paternalism is gradually declining as an ideal and losing its economic basis." He concluded that "women are still hindered in their competition by the function of procreation; Negroes are laboring under the yoke of the doctrine of unassimilability which has remained although slavery is abolished." Conceding that the barrier against Negroes is "stronger in America today," Gunnar cited Alva Myrdal's *Nation and Family* in support of his claim that the barrier against women "is more eternally inexorable" (1078).

Gunnar Myrdal intended this comparison to be one more "thought experiment" that would startle some white Americans into seeing discrimination against African Americans in a different way. It certainly shocked Frederick Keppel, president of the Carnegie Corporation, who objected that "members of both groups might be offended" by the comparison and persuaded Gunnar to move this section from the body of the text to an appendix. Most readers missed the strong theoretical statement of feminism that Gunnar had intended to give a prominent place in his analysis of the American race issue. Tucked away at the back of the book, "A Parallel to the Negro Problem" attracted little comment from reviewers in the 1940s, but was sometimes cited by feminist scholars who compared the two groups. Although Gunnar Myrdal had great difficulty living his life according to the principles he had advocated concerning equality for women, at least one major feminist theorist of the 1940s seems to have been affected by his work. In 1947 Simone De Beauvoir wrote her American friend Nelson Algren: "I am thinking about a book on women's situation which I started before. I would like to write a book about women as important as [Myrdal's] is about blacks."

Gunnar had confided only to Alva that *An American Dilemma* was "just a fantastic symbolic expression of my own life's problem," but he gave readers a glimpse of his struggle in the final paragraphs of the book. "Social study is concerned with explaining why all these potentially and intentionally good people so often make life a hell for themselves and each other when they live together, whether in a family, a nation, or a world." Summoning a willed optimism, he emphasized his "faith that institutions can be improved and strengthened and that people are good enough to live a happier life." He conceded that "the world catastrophe places tremendous difficulties in our way and may shake our confidence to the depths." In his final sentence, Gunnar Myrdal faced down his personal demons and affirmed his own professional creed, that "we have today in social science a greater trust in the improvability of man and society than we have ever had since the Enlightenment" (1023–1024).

Notes

1 Alva Myrdal, *Nation and Family.* In this section, the page numbers in parentheses refer to her book.
2 This description is strikingly similar to what Betty Friedan later called "the problem without a name" in *The Feminine Mystique.*
3 On Alva's feminism, see Bok, *Alva Myrdal*, 137–142.
4 Festinger, *Theory of Cognitive Dissonance.* Gunnar Myrdal, *American Dilemma.* In this section, the page numbers in parentheses refer to his book.
5 Arnold Rose, The Negro community, chapters 43 and 44 of *An American Dilemma.* These chapters were reviewed and approved by E. Franklin Frazier, author of *The Negro Family in the United States.* Frazier's work, while unsparing in its criticism of the black middle class, was inflected by the disdain that members of the educated black elite often showed for working-class and poor blacks, especially those from the rural South.
6 Ellison, *Shadow and Act.* Moynihan, *The Negro Family.* Echoing Rose's language, Moynihan described the black community as "a tangle of pathology." William Ryan, a psychologist, coined the phrase "blaming the victim" to refer specifically to Moynihan's theory, which disregarded the discrimination against black men in the labor market that forced black women to engage in paid work to support their children.

References

Myrdal, Alva. *Nation and Family: The Swedish Experiment in Democratic Family and Population Policy.* New York: Harper & Brothers, 1941.

Myrdal, Gunnar, with the assistance of Richard Sterner and Arnold Rose. *An American Dilemma: The Negro Problem and Modern Democracy.* New York: Harper & Bros., 1944.

Other Published Sources

Bok, Sissela. *Alva Myrdal: A Daughter's Memoir.* Reading, MA: Addison-Wesley, 1991.

Ellison, Ralph. *Shadow and Act.* New York: Random House, 1964.

Festinger, Leon. *A Theory of Cognitive Dissonance.* Stanford, CA: Stanford University Press, 1957.

Frazier, E. Franklin. *The Negro Family in the United States.* Chicago, IL: University of Chicago Press, 1939.

Friedan, Betty, *The Feminine Mystique.* New York: W.W. Norton, 1963.

Moynihan, Daniel Patrick. *The Negro Family: The Case for National Action.* Washington, DC: U.S. Dept. of Labor, 1964.

Ryan, William. *Blaming the Victim.* New York: Random House, 1971.

Part IV

Alva in Crisis, 1944

16 Together and Separately

When Alva finally travelled to join Gunnar in the United States, she had decided to try to place their marriage on a new basis of equality. The sheer intensity of their engagement in communication and personal reflection might have been persuasive. In the fall of 1941 Alva donned a parachute and flew on a secret British military plane from Sweden to Scotland, knowing that other planes of this type had been shot down by German antiaircraft batteries in occupied Norway. She then spent a month in Britain researching a book on the British home front, which was published the following year in Sweden.[1] Finally, with the help of diplomatic contacts, she flew to Lisbon, where, after another month, she managed to get a coveted ticket on a flight that took her to the Azores, Bermuda, and New York. After ten months of living apart on opposite sides of the Atlantic, Alva and Gunnar were reunited in Princeton in November.

It was under these circumstances, from November 1941 to September 1942, that Gunnar wrote most of *An American Dilemma*. During these ten months, living and working together without the children, Alva and Gunnar thought that they had repaired their frayed relationship. Alva stayed in the marriage for a complex bundle of motives: ensuring the children's welfare; sustaining her multidimensional relationship with a man she still loved; playing indispensable roles as mother figure and counselor for a psychologically vulnerable man as he finished his great book; keeping "the firm" of AGM, social engineers, going; and preserving a broad range of options for herself on the national and international stage.

Political Advocacy

Alva and Gunnar returned to Stockholm in September 1942, settling back into their futuristic house with their three children, who had been under the care of Gunnar's mother. Alva sought to develop a more independent role in public life. She resumed her position as principal of the early child education institute, renewed her connections with Swedish activists, and plunged back into her work with women's organizations. At the same time, seeking to establish herself as a strong, independent voice in the Swedish press, she wrote editorials and opinion pieces on a wide range of international issues, especially American politics and Swedish foreign policy. She actively aided the Norwegian Resistance, and she played a leading role in evacuating thousands of children, many orphaned by war, from Finland to foster homes in Sweden.

In two newspaper articles in the spring of 1943, Alva wrote the fullest discussion of the Nazis' mass murder of European Jews that had been published in Sweden and issued an urgent call to action to save people still at risk. She swept aside the cobwebs of older Swedish discussions of the "Jewish Question" in the first article, focusing instead on anti-Semitism as both a social pathology and a moral issue. In the second piece, which focused on Jewish refugees, she estimated that two million Jews had already been "liquidated" and warned that the remaining four to five million were "in mortal peril." Chastising her fellow citizens for not having accepted more refugees earlier, Alva urged neutral Sweden to undertake diplomatic and humanitarian efforts to rescue as many endangered Jews as possible, which paved the way for Sweden's postwar policy of welcoming refugees.[2]

Gunnar, whose book on race relations was widely hailed in America, had his beloved Alva at his side. The politically ambitious social scientist wanted to put his unique set of talents to work for his country. Sweden was one of the few industrialized nations that had managed to stay out of the war; the economy was poised to grow rapidly, and planning was essential. Gunnar advised the government on fiscal and monetary policy and on relations with the United States, which was emerging as the world's most powerful nation. Reelected to the Riksdag, he sought to continue the social democratic project of building the welfare state and to help reorient Sweden toward a more global perspective. Alva shared his broad international view, was an expert in social welfare and education policy, and had more experience working with organizations at the grassroots level. She was also eager to use her political skills to push the welfare state forward, but she lacked academic credentials and had not served in parliament or at the top level of government. The Social Democratic Party leadership thought that two Myrdals could not hold seats in the Riksdag at the same time, and Alva refrained from running for any elected office. Serving on an important government commission was the main path open to her. Keen on reforming Sweden's hierarchical educational system, she secured a position on the royal commission on education that was appointed after the war.

Alva and Gunnar sought to have a fourth child, but the attempt ended in miscarriage. Their 16-year-old son, Jan, became even more of a problem in their eyes. Their younger daughters, Sissela and Kaj, seemed generally happy and stable. Despite the usual sibling rivalry, they forged a close bond with each other, a pact to protect themselves from the everyone around them. At the dinner table, however, both felt pushed to the periphery as Gunnar and Jan argued and Alva sought to calm them down but not to interfere. Theirs was hardly the "model family" that some admiring Swedes imagined.

The looming problems of the postwar world cried out for social scientists and planners who could look beyond the daily headlines and envision long-range policies for global rebuilding and a durable peace. After years of preparatory study and painful psychological struggle, Gunnar believed that he was indispensable to Sweden, especially when it came to reframing its economic and foreign policy. Alva, too, felt a sense of urgency. She sought not only to meet the humanitarian needs of civilians in a world destroyed, but also to secure the gains that women had made in wartime and to plan for postwar reforms with respect to women and children.

The death of Alva's mother, Lowa Reimer, in the spring of 1943, followed three months later by the death of her father, Albert Reimer, required that she make time in her crowded schedule for self-reflection, which she pursued both through psychotherapy and by writing an autobiographical account of her emotional development during her childhood and teenage years, a dream diary, and a personal journal. Gunnar's total immersion in politics and postwar planning meant that there was no room for the firm of AGM. There would be no more joint research projects. Alva now had to stand alone in public.

A Romantic Rationalist

In December 1943, Alva wrote a brief autobiographical article for the Social Democratic newspaper, *Aftontidningen*, in which she sought to craft a fresh image of herself as a political reformer. During the 1930s, she had been known as an educator who showed people how they might use new social scientific knowledge to lead happier and more rational lives. In this article, subtitled "A Romantic Rationalist," she sought to anchor this image as a modern, scientific problem-solver in the great popular movements through which her father's generation had begun to reshape Swedish society. Alva stressed that she had grown up in a Social Democratic home, nurtured by her father's values of equality, social solidarity, and altruism. She praised the huge wave of rural people who had flooded into the cities and sought to bring order and justice to a society dominated by unscrupulous entrepreneurs, financial speculators, and an irresponsible upper class. Although the social history of the labor movement was yet unwritten, she asserted that her generation had the duty to extend this precious "inheritance." While acknowledging that she and her siblings had been taunted by other children as "socialist kids," she insisted that this experience had produced a "psychic hardening" that is "useful" in times that require extraordinary efforts to rebuild a broken world. She was most concerned about groups that were still fighting for social justice: the unemployed, landless rural residents, women, children, and refugees. Alva challenged Swedes to try to extend "our feelings of equality and brotherhood" to people in other countries and to "other races."[3]

In this self-portrait aimed at working- and middle-class readers, Alva deftly folded the issue of women's equality into a broader, humanitarian advocacy on behalf of subordinated groups, stressing that the global struggle for economic and racial equality requires the inclusion of women and children, as well as alleviating poverty and preventing war. She mentioned her husband only once, obliquely and not by name, positioning herself as the heir of her idealistic but obscure father. More remarkable than what she says is what she does not say: the narrative leaps from her childhood in the "heroic age" of the Social Democrats to the present without mentioning any of her political accomplishments during the 1930s. Alva omitted her early advocacy of affordable housing for working families, daycare centers, parent education, laws protecting married women from being fired from their jobs, birth control, and eugenics, all of which had been institutionalized to some extent by the Social Democratic government. It was as if she had been borne along by the tide of the Social Democratic movement, innocent of any unseemly personal ambition, a voice for the unrealized hopes of tens of thousands of unheralded working men and women. Since her ideas had been enacted into law under the leadership of senior Social Democrats, Alva thought it best not to try to take the credit.

While Alva struck a tone of humility, the newspaper editors burnished her image with photographs: a pensive Alva, fashionably dressed in a business suit with padded shoulders; Alva as a teenager in her confirmation dress; Alva, Gunnar, and the children about to embark for the United States in 1938; and Alva supervising kindergarten teachers. The final photograph of Alva, casually dressed, swinging open the door to her home in Princeton, New Jersey, is captioned: "Alva Myrdal's door is open to the world." In sum, the photo essay depicts her as an elegant, educated woman gracefully balancing work, family, and politics. The article's headlines identify Alva as a "Social Democrat by birth with boundless experience. Academic. Child psychologist. . . . Wife and mother. A person of our time and pathfinder. Courageous woman." Having highlighted her femininity and domestic credentials, the editors added short testimonials from prominent Social Democratic men, one of whom declared: "Just think—what if Alva Myrdal were a man? With her knowledge, she would long ago have been elected to public office."

Two joint portraits of Alva and Gunnar taken by a professional photographer during this time are telling (see Figures 16.1 and 16.2). Creating a sense of intimacy by posing the couple inside their modernist home in Stockholm, the photographer created what the historian Thomas Etzemüller called "the media's symbol of an equal, intellectual marriage." Yet, as he pointed out, these images place Gunnar in the center,

Figure 16.1 Alva and Gunnar at their shared desk, Äpplevik, Stockholm. Photograph by Arne Holmström. Courtesy of Alva and Gunnar Myrdal's Collection, Arbetarrörelsens Arkiv och Bibliotek, Stockholm, Sweden.

looking at the camera, and Alva on the periphery or in a subordinate position, looking at Gunnar. He is actively reading or writing, while she is passive—the conventional bourgeois wife.[4] That image may have made Alva's achievements more acceptable to the public, but it undermined the message that Alva and Gunnar sought to convey: that they exemplified a modern marital partnership. Even more seriously, it obscured the dilemmas that Alva faced as she tried to juggle the multiple, often competing demands made on her by Gunnar and their three children, her professional career, intellectual work, and political advocacy, while emphasizing her poise and equanimity. And it muted her feminist arguments that women's emancipation requires a complete reorganization of society, that there are no purely personal solutions to the problem of gender inequality, and that only the next generation, raised in a freer society, will overcome these difficulties.

Indeed, Alva's public political positioning occluded much of her identity as a feminist. As a young woman, Alva had been influenced by Ellen Key, the most prominent Swedish feminist at the beginning of the twentieth century. Although Key was resolute in her advocacy of political and social equality, she believed that men and women bring different

Figure 16.2 Alva and Gunnar in their library, Äpplevik, Stockholm, Autumn 1942. Photograph by Arne Holmström. Courtesy of Alva and Gunnar Myrdal's Collection, Arbetarrörelsens Arkiv och Bibliotek, Stockholm, Sweden.

temperaments to their relationships with each other and to society. Admitting women to the political sphere, she had argued, would enlarge the possibilities for public discussion and policy making, resulting in a fuller realization of human potential, but men and women would come to the dialogue with different orientations. Alva left the idea of distinct masculine and feminine temperaments rooted in biological differences behind in the late 1920s as she studied psychology, sociology, and anthropology in the United States. As a Social Democratic activist in the 1930s, Alva embraced an optimistic view that men and women could change centuries of socialization as they built new lives in industrial cities. Achieving equality would require a rethinking of marriage, childrearing, education, and women's work as caregivers and breadwinners.

As a social scientist and policy maker, Gunnar strongly supported Alva's proposals for women's equality, advocating many of her ideas in the Riksdag. But while the couple—or, at least, Alva—sought to shape more egalitarian relationships between the sexes and generations, their own family life was a tangle of contradictions. During a period of intense self-scrutiny in 1944, Alva explored the dilemmas she faced.

Notes

All translations from Swedish texts were done by the author, unless otherwise indicated.

1 Alva Myrdal, *Stickprov på Storbritannien.*
2 Alva Myrdal, Antisemitism är en sjukdom; Alva Myrdal, Judar med och utan framtid.
3 Alva Myrdal, En romantisk rationalist.
4 Etzemüller, *Alva and Gunnar Myrdal*, 211–212, and the book's cover photograph.

References

Alva and Gunnar Myrdal's Collection (AGMA). Arbetarrörelsens Arkiv och Bibliotek (Swedish Labour Movement's Archive and Library). Stockholm, Sweden.

Alva Myrdal's published works, 2.1

Myrdal, Alva. Alva Myrdal, En romantisk rationalist (A romantic rationalist). *Aftontidningen*, 7 December 1943.

Alva and Gunnar Myrdal's Published Works

Myrdal, Alva. *Stickprov på Storbritannien* (A spot-check of Great Britain). Stockholm: Bonniers, 1942.

Myrdal, Alva. Antisemitism är en sjukdom (Anti-Semitism is pathological). *Aftontidningen*, 14 March 1943.

Myrdal, Alva. Judar med och utan framtid (Jews with and without a future). *Aftontidningen*, 10 June 1943.

Published Source

Etzemüller, Thomas. *Die romantik der rationalität: Alva & Gunnar Myrdal und "Social Engineering" in Schweden.* Bielefeld: Transskript Verlag, 2010; *Alva and Gunnar Myrdal: Social Engineering in the Modern World*, trans. Alex Skimmer. Lanham, MD, and London: Lexington Books, 2014.

17 The Formation of the Psyche

In the spring of 1944, at the age of 42, Alva Myrdal began composing an autobiographical account of her childhood and adolescence. The following morning she started a dream diary, recording what she could remember of her dreams from the night before. These two acts of self-scrutiny proceeded simultaneously for six weeks, during a tumultuous period of political activities and family strife. Six months later she kept a journal, examining her relationship with Gunnar after almost 20 years of marriage. These unpublished documents, previously unknown to historians, represent the only pause in the midst of an onrushing life that spanned most of the twentieth century. As it turned out, 1944 proved to be the exact midpoint of Alva's extraordinary life. Her career as a social scientist, political reformer, ambassador, cabinet minister, and international disarmament advocate culminated in the Nobel Peace Prize, awarded four years before her death in 1986.

In her autobiography, the psychologist on the verge of middle age probed the roots of her personality in a difficult childhood, straining to recover and analyze half-hidden memories (see Figure 17.1). Writing a year after the death of her mother, she explored the causes of her epic rebellion against her mother's controlling temperament as well as the roots of her strong superego as she struggled to achieve self-control and independence during her teenage years. Nine months after her father's death, she recalled his steady encouragement of her ambitions and traced the process through which her identity was strengthened not only by his love but also by his Social Democratic political ideals. As a feminist, Alva asked why, during her adolescence, she had learned to suppress her childhood fantasies of becoming a great leader and did not compete in her elementary school classes. She remembered early feelings of guilt and unworthiness, how difficult it had been for her to come to terms with her ambition, and how she learned to channel it into a Social Democratic mission of achieving equality for all subordinated groups.

These themes are refigured in Alva's dream diary. Here she abandoned her customary style of careful empirical writing and let the account of her dreams float between past and present, recording stories of imagined events peopled with real and imagined characters. At the end of each

Figure 17.1 Alva at her desk during the 1940s. Photograph by Bo Törngren. Courtesy of Alva and Gunnar Myrdal's Collection, Arbetarrörelsens Arkiv och Bibliotek, Stockholm, Sweden.

narrative, which Freud called the "manifest dream," she wrote a short interpretation in which she strove to elucidate the meaning of the "latent dream." Alva explored how personal ambition might be reconciled with her ideology of service to humanity. She wondered: Is there any time and energy left to nurture three children? Does her activism in in the "masculine" realm of politics require her to suppress what she called the "feminine" side of her personality? Does her involvement in public life deny her valuable opportunities for emotional satisfaction?

In the brief, private journal she kept six months later, Alva examined her feelings about Gunnar and tried to fathom what was going on between them. She also scrutinized her social self—how she thought she appeared to other people and interacted with them. The December journal provides the closest look we have at the emotional costs of playing the conflicting roles demanded of her as the wife of an important politician, mother of three children, educator, social reformer, and writer. The journal brought Alva to a crossroads. She considered various terms on which her marriage might continue, if it continued at all, and she tried to imagine an independent public career for herself. She assessed whether the inevitable conflict of egos with her husband would be tolerable if they pursued separate careers and no longer worked in partnership. She considered the emotional costs of staying in a marriage with a demanding, highly egocentric man who had less and less time for her. Trying to look at herself with critical distance, Alva mapped out alternative strategies of moving forward in or terminating her marriage and considered how she would feel if she carried out each one of them, confronting the stark choices that loomed before her. Honesty had always been the most important virtue in the Myrdals' marriage, but avoiding self-deception posed a daunting challenge. In all three of these personal documents, Alva asked hard questions about herself and assessed where she stood. Each manuscript offers a different window on the self, disclosing distinct fears, vulnerabilities, and strengths.

Patient and Psychiatrist

In her letters to Gunnar in 1941, when she and her husband had been on opposite sides of the Atlantic and he had fallen into a major depression, Alva's deepening feminism had made her more acutely aware of problems in the marriage. She had written with an element of tact and calculation because of his volatile temperament and threats of suicide. At first she had been careful to reveal only as much as she felt he could stand to hear. As their separation during the spring and summer continued, however, Alva had bluntly criticized Gunnar's behavior and insisted on greater equality in the marriage. Yet during their three years at home in Sweden little had changed.

Now Alva wrote for herself. She began the autobiography the same week that she started seeing a psychiatrist, and her therapy formed a point of reference as she interpreted her childhood, dreams, and relationship with Gunnar. Alva would sometimes walk for an hour after these weekly sessions, turning over the conversation in her mind. She intended the autobiography as an exercise in self-understanding and modeled it on life histories and case studies in psychology. In contrast to her recently published political autobiography, the narrative contains no political rhetoric, ideological statements, or attempts to fashion a public image. She sought to make it an honest account of her childhood and youth. Alva not only probed the familial and social influences that had shaped her identity, but also looked critically at the choices she had made. She explored the limits on women's achievement that she had internalized and puzzled at some of the ways in which she had impulsively kicked against those boundaries without knowing why.

Her companion on this journey of self-discovery was neither Gunnar nor any of her close women friends but Dr. Jakob Billström, a psychiatrist she saw weekly from April to June and again in December 1944. Like many psychiatrists at that time, Billström had been trained as a neurologist before he shifted into the new specialization. During the 1920s and 1930s, he presented fundamental concepts of psychiatry to the public and linked them with current social issues. During the Depression, he refuted conservative arguments that the "youth problem" was primarily a moral problem and argued that the main problem was unemployment and the inability of many young adults to support families. Like the Myrdals, he called for a more open discussion of human sexuality. In 1938, Billström and Dr. Axel Höjer spoke out in favor of a motion Gunnar Myrdal made in the Riksdag calling for sweeping reforms in medical education that would devote more resources to public health. Alva was familiar with his work and might have encountered him at public forums, but Billström was not part of the Myrdals' social circle.[1]

Billström's life overlapped with that of Alva's father. Born in 1880, he was a lifelong temperance advocate and supported publicly financed healthcare for the poor. His father died when he was only ten, so his mother, Selma Lundberg Billström, was the formative influence on his life. The daughter of a Lutheran pastor, she was a social activist and was not afraid to take strong public stands on controversial issues. During the 1880s, some middle-class young people became aware of urban poverty and plunged into social reform. For Selma, as for many others, the decline of religious faith triggered an intense desire to reach out to disadvantaged people and a sense of urgency about being part of a democratic community. She and her son lived a Spartan life in Södermalm. Selma took in boarders to help pay for Jakob's education and devoted much of her time to aiding the working-class people who resided nearby. In contrast to many affluent women who made forays into Söder to perform charitable deeds and then went home to more comfortable neighborhoods, Selma lived there and knew many people from everyday encounters. Söder abounded in lessons about social inequality, and she encouraged her son to open his eyes to the world around him.[2]

An outspoken feminist whom some considered a "mannish woman," Selma Lundberg Billström wrote a pamphlet calling attention to the needs of impoverished women who had turned to prostitution and penned a 50th birthday tribute to the radical socialist Hinke Berggren, who had been an early champion of birth control. Her living room was often filled with reformers and radicals of various persuasions, and Jakob, an only child, grew up listening to lively debates. His childhood friends included John Landquist, later a prolific author who introduced Freud to a popular audience in Sweden, and Ruth, the daughter of Kata Dalgren, the best-known socialist-feminist "agitator" in the country. From his mother, young Jakob learned an ethic of solidarity and altruism.[3]

In his gymnasium and university years, Billström participated in a wide range of social movements. On Sunday mornings he attended lectures at the labor movement's People's House. He learned folk dancing and participated in discussions with working-class people through organizations that brought university students together with young socialists, teachers, domestic servants, and office workers. After receiving his undergraduate medical degree in 1907, he did postgraduate work at the University of Berlin, and in 1910 defended a thesis on "traumatic neuroses." Unlike many psychiatrists, he recognized the social as well as individual causes of psychological problems and was committed to the emerging field of social medicine.[4]

Billström and several other young physicians who were concerned about poor people in the capital decided to investigate the living conditions of unemployed men during the cold winter of 1912–1913. Disguising themselves in dirty, ragged clothing, they checked into Stockholm's notorious "bachelor hotels," which reeked of urine and tobacco and had neither adequate insulation nor facilities for washing. The flophouses were rife with infectious diseases, especially tuberculosis. Men were required men to leave the facility between nine in the morning and six in the evening. Often there was no place for them to avoid frostbite except a saloon, exacerbating the problem of alcoholism. Billström and his colleagues aroused public indignation by publishing their findings in *Social Tidskrift* magazine and founded an organization that had these hostels torn down or renovated. A model facility served 340 lodgers, where doctors provided medical care two nights a week. It also organized cultural evenings for homeless and unemployed men. Carl Svedelius, rector of Norra Real gymnasium, arranged performances there by the school's orchestra and boys' choir, to which the teenaged Gunnar Myrdal belonged.[5]

Jakob Billström was vitally interested in educating the public about mental health and lectured widely on medical ethics, nervous disorders, alcoholism, and sexual hygiene. Known for his rich voice and clear articulation, he became the country's first "radio doctor," giving advice in regular broadcasts, some of which were then published as pamphlets. His many books and essays dealt with topics that were of major interest to Alva Myrdal, including psychological viewpoints on child raising, how children learn through play, and parent education. In 1934, when many feared that unemployed, alienated youth would turn to Nazism and Communism, Billström described activities and organizations in which young people from different backgrounds could find common interests and argued that Sweden should promote them to strengthen solidarity and democratic values. Shortly before his sessions with Alva, the psychiatrist had published *Parents and Children*, and at the time of Alva's psychotherapy he was extending his studies of the life course. In addition, he had recently completed a privately printed biography of his mother.[6]

In books and radio talks, Billström lambasted the authoritarian childrearing practices that Alva also detested. When asked how to raise a happy child, he replied: "Leave youngsters in peace and stop giving them advice." Do not forbid too many things, do not dampen children's self-confidence by excessive punishment, and never resort to violence. He emphasized the long-term consequences of parents' use of fear and guilt, which limits children's capacity to make their own decisions and inhibits their emotional development as adolescents and adults.[7]

When World War II broke out, Billström gave radio addresses on how Swedes might prepare psychologically for the possibility that their cities would be bombed. During the difficult, morally ambiguous years when Sweden remained neutral, Billström and Alva both spoke publicly on the importance of Swedes maintaining their morale as a democratic nation and not succumbing to Nazi propaganda. Amidst the Winter War of 1939–1940, Billström volunteer to serve in Finnish field hospitals but was turned down because they needed surgeons, not psychiatrists.[8] A year later, Alva helped to organize the mass evacuation of thousands of Finnish children to foster homes in Sweden. At the time of their therapy sessions, both were involved in aiding the Norwegian people during the German occupation.

Själsbiografi

On April 19, 1944, Alva began composing her *Själsbiografi*.[9] Traditionally the term meant a "spiritual autobiography," but this detailed account of Alva's memories of childhood and adolescence is modeled on the psychological case study. "Biography of the psyche" captures her earnest effort to achieve a critical distance in writing an account of a young girl's emotional development. Her use of clinical terminology and attention to childhood traumas strongly suggest that she thought of Billström as her audience. There is no indication that she gave the manuscript to him or to anyone else to read, but she referred to the doctor in the dream diary she wrote at the same time and in the journal she kept six months later.

In the early pages of her autobiography, Alva recalled the pervasive guilt and self-doubt that inhibited her early emotional and mental development. After grounding the narrative in the painful episode in which she lied about losing her schoolmate's book, she launched a broader inquiry into the sources of these feelings. Focusing on her parents in the wake of their deaths, she drew on her psychological training in an effort to understand them better than she had in her youth. Looking back, she saw her mother's putative ill health as "partly a defense against" her children and husband. In response, Alva had turned to her father for comfort, but now she remembered him as stoical and emotionally withdrawn.

In her study of developmental psychology, Alva had been impressed by Lawrence K. Frank's *The Management of Tensions*, which criticized pediatricians' standard advice to mothers to feed all infants according to a strict schedule. Frank, an American psychologist who had become a friend of Alva's in 1929–1930, emphasized the importance of mothers adapting their care to the differing needs of individual children. Alva suggested that Lowa's failure to breastfeed her adequately was related to a consistent pattern of withholding affection from her children. She pointed to a connection between the physical hunger she experienced as an infant and the emotional hunger for closeness and understanding that engulfed her during her later childhood and adolescence. Her mother's accusations that she was selfish and "greedy" prefigured Lowa's later inability to comprehend the adolescent Alva's ambitions for a distinguished career.

Alva's reconsideration of this story about childhood hunger had been prompted "by the case of my own son," she acknowledged. Although she did not reproach herself for having followed pediatricians' advice, she, too, had fed Jan at strict, regular intervals, and now she regarded this deprivation "as the most important cause in the formation of his impatient and misanthropic character." Alva did not linger on this point and resumed the narrative of her early life: "From here it would be better if I gave a continuous story so that the most traumatic points can be pointed out."

Alva then sketched her development, recording and reconsidering her struggles to understand herself and the people around her. Despite her growing closeness to her father as she learned about politics, she still felt alone. Not only did her mother withdraw from the family, but emotions had to be kept under a tight rein in the household. Her parents had not allowed her to express her feelings when she was angry. In retrospect, Alva saw this as the foundation of her "terribly demanding superego." But the perfectionism she had developed "did not drive me to excel" in school because she feared standing out from her peer group (22).

As a feminist who had authored an important government report on sexuality six years earlier, Alva tried to find humor in the ways she had groped for an understanding of human reproduction when she had been denied any kind of sex education at home and at school. Trying to assess her experience of puberty objectively, Alva wrote that, although she could not talk to anyone about it, the mysterious changes in her body pushed her toward adulthood and helped her to separate her identity from Lowa's. Alva had kept a diary (which she later destroyed) as she experienced these physical and emotional transformations. She did not remember intense sexual longings at this age, acknowledging that "I surely had some sexual fantasies during the time of puberty, but it did not seem to bother me especially." Not until she met her future husband was she "sexually awakened," she concluded.

Right after mentioning her limited comprehension of sexuality, Alva remarked pointedly that during this time "I discovered the seduction of reading." Sublimating her desires into cognitive and imaginative activity, "I gave myself to reading with such gluttonous joy." She remembered her immersion in books as an "orgy in solitude," away from the family's tensions. Her bond with Märta Fredriksson, with whom she shared secrets, teenaged rebellion, and love of ideas, was a crucial source of support.

Her struggle to fashion a unique self was also helped by her correspondence with her former teacher, Per Sundberg.

In her narrative, Alva devoted little time to the religious questions that had tormented her for over a year. She avoided considering why she felt such an intense desire to submit to God because it did not fit the story line she was developing about her growing self-confidence and independence. Now Alva took pride in having been a "freethinker" before her period of religious searching, linked this attitude to her rebellion against her mother, and emphasized her interest in scientific writers and psychology. Employing a concept from Alfred Adler, she saw this period as characterized by "masculinity worship" (44–47).

No stranger to introspection, Alva observed that writing about her teenage years in the autobiography had not upset her as much "this time," suggesting that she had previously found it painful to think about. She had learned to leaven her writing with humor as a way of coping with pain, and paused to ask whether this account of her adolescence relied too much on humor as a way to get past the memories of suffering. She worried that she had not recaptured the "dreadful seriousness" of it all (61).

Toward the end of her autobiography, Alva took up questions of gender. In childhood she knew she was a girl but was aware that it was much better to be a boy. This should not, she explained, be misunderstood as homosexuality or embracing an "Amazon" style. When she dreamed of being a policeman or a general when she grew up, it was always in terms of achieving something. Even beyond childhood, her thoughts had always centered on having a profession and making her own living, not on getting married. She had little of Rut's spontaneous tenderness for children. Looking at aspects of her personality she had kept hidden from everyone, Alva confessed that she had never really liked children that much, except that she had always felt pity for their suffering. Of course, she hastened to add, she has the same "irrational" love for her own children that most mothers have, but others' children only touch her if she sees them being mistreated. Even when it came to her own children, Alva admitted, she had always unhesitatingly chosen her husband over her children when it was "necessary."

Turning to the roots of her feminism, Alva recalled that during her adolescence her "disappointment" with the female sex was transformed into a feminist passion. Then she corrected herself and wrote that it would be more accurate to say that her exclusion from the world of men and dissatisfaction with most women's acquiescence to oppression had led her to an "ambivalence" between contempt for and advocacy on behalf of the female sex. The injustice toward women in the educational system had been a burning issue for her during her teenage years.

The tension between Alva's ambition and the creation of a social self that others would accept was a source of intense inner turmoil for her as a girl. For a long time, she had denied her ambition in order to evade her mother's condemnation of her "selfishness" and to get other girls to like her. During adolescence, she had struggled to transmute that ambition into a vocation of service to humanity; medicine was one of the few narrow portals through which a young woman might squeeze in an effort to reconcile personal ambition with public and popular esteem.

Alva's startling declaration that she had always "unhesitatingly" chosen Gunnar over her children when it was "necessary" was not entirely true, but it is a telling admission. She had resisted Gunnar's plan to leave Jan with Gunnar's parents in 1929, but finally gave in when he convinced her that it would not be good for a 2-year-old to be carted around an English-speaking country and live in hotel rooms for a year. Her guilt over that mistake and concern for her three children's welfare had led her to delay her journey from Stockholm to the United States in the spring of 1941, in spite of Gunnar's abusive bullying. In this context, however, Alva's frank admission about putting husband before the children comes as one of several acknowledgements of the powerful hold that duty had on her.

She regarded the sacrifices she made for her husband, as well as her sense of public obligation, as requirements imposed by a superego forged in a patriarchal society that overrode her children's needs and her own desires. Alva's father had inculcated a strong sense of social responsibility. For Alva, the price of her professional success and of reaching even a modest degree of prominence in the Social Democratic Party had been high. Since childhood she had felt painfully torn between the supposedly "masculine" domain of politics and professional achievement and the supposedly "feminine" world of love and empathy. Over time she had felt increasingly pulled toward politics, especially during the economic crisis of the 1930s and the war when she had been moved to remedy suffering. Alva had a powerful drive for accomplishment in the public arena and knew it should be open to women. Her talent in political negotiations and in writing about public policy refuted conventional stereotypes about women's "natural" limitations, but she worried that the demands of professional and political work had crowded out other parts of her personality. As a whole, the autobiography is not a flattering self-portrait, but an "honest" attempt to understand the tensions that had been so wrenching for her.

In the conclusion of the "biography of the psyche," Alva suggested that something further back in her development must be at the bottom of these conflicting attitudes about the roles of men and women. She remembered her parents' clear signals that boys had a higher status than girls and her mother's criticism that she was not as "soft, sweet, and kind" as a girl should be. The responsibility for her younger siblings that her mother considered the duty of the eldest daughter had been a heavy burden. As a child, Alva envied boys who did not have to be so quiet, clean, and polite, and she keenly felt the injustice of the narrower constraints imposed on girls. Alva traced her interest in feminism to her anger over the "restrictions" that society placed on women.

These societal constraints on women forced her to make difficult choices. Before meeting Gunner, she was afraid of being "only married," and nothing more. She insisted that now she "abandons" herself to love in a "very feminine" manner and enjoys her modern home, but shaping her work life in accordance with conventional gender norms would never be acceptable. The isolation, dependency, and lack of meaningful stimulation of being a housewife would be unbearable. Alva tried to put the best face on her striving to navigate through all these restrictions. She claimed to be "biologically totally happy" with her female role in marriage and "completely prepared" for the male role in work and in the public sphere. Yet she acknowledged that she still felt held back by this "dilemma." "A whole lot of emotional energy, which ought to be channeled into work and sheer living, is instead wasted on reacting against the artificial barriers erected against the female sex."

The *Själsbiografi* ends abruptly here. If she had continued the story past the age of 17, Alva would have had to confront the question of why, if her feminism had been so sharply formed during her adolescence, she had allowed Gunnar to dominate her life so completely during the early years of their relationship and marriage. She might also have wondered why, even at age 42, attending to Gunnar's needs and demands squeezed so much energy out of her own life. The dream diary, which she kept as she was composing the autobiography, offers a few glimpses into these tangled issues.

Notes

All translations of Alva Myrdal's manuscripts were done by the author.

1 Ljungberg, *Jakob Billström*, 12–17; Lagerborg, *Jakob Billström*. See Bröd och befordran locka vår ungdom till feghet, and Reform av läkarutbildningen, both in AGMA. On the "youth problem," see Billström, *Några av ungdomsproblem i subjektiv belysning*.
2 Billström, *En demokratiskt åskådning*, 6–8.
3 Lagerborg, *Jakob Billström*, 7; Luttenberger, *Freud i Sverige*.
4 Billström, *En demokratiskt åskådning*, 7–12; Ljungberg, *Jakob Billström*, 13–14.
5 Halldin, En fattigläkares kamp för hemlösa män i Stockholm; Halldin, Utsattas och hemlösas ohälsa.
6 Ljungberg, *Jakob Billström*, 14.
7 Ljungberg, *Jakob Billström*, 16; Lagerborg, *Jakob Billström*, 92–93.
8 Lagerborg, *Jakob Billström*, 61–62.
9 All page numbers in parentheses in this chapter refer to Alva Myrdal, Själsbiografi, AGMA.

References

Alva and Gunnar Myrdal's Collection (AGMA). Arbetarrörelsens Arkiv och Bibliotek (Swedish Labour Movement's Archive and Library). Stockholm, Sweden.

Alva Myrdal's press cuttings, 5.1

Bröd och befordran locka vår ungdom till feghet: Dr. Billström vill ha till stånd en ungdomsvecka för diskussion av ungdomens problem. *Stockholms-Tidningen*, 16 Nov. 1932.

Billström, Jakob. Reform av läkarutbildningen. *Nya Dagligt Allehanda*, 20 Jan. 1938.

Published Sources

Billström, Jakob. *En demokratiskt åskådning*. Stockholm: Hanssons, 1934.

Billström, Jakob. *Några av ungdomsproblem i subjektiv belysning*. Stockholm, 1936.

Halldin, Jan. En fattigläkares kamp för hemlösa män i Stockholm. *Lakartidningen* 106 (2003): 779–780.

Halldin, Jan. Utsattas och hemlösas ohälsa under de senaste hundra åren. *Socialmedicin Tidning* 1 (2008): 12–16.

Lagerborg, Rolf. *Jakob Billström, 1880–1955: Vivre pour autrui*. Åbo: Finlands boklador, 1957.

Ljungberg, Lennart. *Jakob Billström, 12/12–1880—15/2 1953*. Stockholm: Svensk sällskap för psykiatrins historia, 1985–1988.

Luttenberger, Franz. *Freud i Sverige: Psykoanalysens mottagande i svensk medicin och idédebatt 1900–1924*. Stockholm: Carlsons, 1989.

18 Dream Diary

While Alva struggled to maintain a tone of detachment in her biography of the psyche, she allowed herself a more fluid, immediate, and vivid style in the dream diary that she kept simultaneously. She recorded what she remembered of her dreams in the early morning, while composing her autobiography in the evenings. The diary is comprised of fourteen entries written between April 20 and June 4. Some coincide with the issues from her childhood and youth that she was considering that day, and carefully wrought passages in the autobiography are prefigured as surreal, atemporal fantasies in the dream diary. The narrative floats from one scene to another, cutting back and forth from her daily life to childhood memories refashioned in her imagination. Alva turned to her dreams as a step toward unlocking those parts of the self she had effectively repressed. Yet the analyses at the end of each entry in which she attempted to discern the dream's latent psychological meaning are very brief and add little to their manifest meaning.

Alva had begun thinking about dreams at the age of 16, when she and her best friend Märta had tried to probe the netherworld of their psyches by analyzing each other's dreams. In her first year of correspondence with Gunnar, the lovers had analyzed each other's dreams as part of their effort to draw closer. Her dreams often had a clear reference to some issue in their relationship. In the early 1930s, Alva had completed a master's thesis on "Freud's Theory of Dreams," but it was rejected by Rudolf Anderberg, the positivist experimental psychologist at Uppsala University, on the ground that it lacked scientific rigor. Her interest in Freudian psychology had continued in the 1930s, and in the United States she had many conversations with neo-Freudians who were seeking to reconcile Freud's teachings with a social reform agenda. Freud's theories about women collided with the feminism that informed Alva's thinking. She embraced a strongly environmentalist position on the differences between men and women, differentiating her view from more essentialist beliefs. Yet Freud's theory of personality was still central to her model of psychological development. When Alva referred, in her autobiography, to the formation of her superego during her childhood, she was writing about an internalized judgment that had been implanted in her by her parents, teachers, and other authority figures. As she understood it, this superego was deeply rooted in her unconscious emotional life and was the source both of her striving for excellence and of her feeling of unworthiness. It had also been a driving force in subordinating what was conventionally regarded as the "feminine" side of her personality—expressiveness, interpersonal connectedness, and nurturance—to what was considered the "masculine" side—rationality, individualism, and ambition.

When Alva began therapy in 1941, she did not choose a psychiatrist from Stockholm's circle of Freudian analysts. Jakob Billström was familiar with Freud but resistant to the pessimistic implications of his later work. His views on gender stood in stark contrast to those of many psychiatrists at that time, who were inclined to see women who were active in professions or public life as "compensating" for a sexual problem or their inability to perform the roles of wife and mother that were thought to be biologically based and vital to women's happiness. Billström encouraged Alva to open up and explore those regions of the self that had remained hidden and obscure and to question everything, including the constraints of gender.

Issues of gender socialization and identity formation that are raised obliquely in the early pages of Alva's autobiography are apparent from the beginning of the dream diary. Her first dream narrative recalled the many little domestic tasks she had been required to perform as a girl. Alva's anxious efforts to prevent disasters and pick up lost treasures reflect the development of a powerful sense of duty, as she felt compelled to arrange things to suit other people. Childhood obligations blend with duties to husband and children and to the Social Democratic Party, creating a myriad of imperatives Alva never felt able to fulfill. She was also stunningly candid about the extent to which her professional work had diminished her relationship with her children, who appear in the dreams only sporadically and often disruptively.

Her dream diary, like the autobiography, opens with an attempt to come to terms with the influence of her parents on her life. Since they had recently died, this subject surfaced with new intensity. Many other entries register the conflicts Alva felt between her public service and the emotional needs of her husband and children. Here she often lost sight of herself as she tried to balance and mediate between their incompatible and excessive demands. Finally, the dream diary raises the issues that would reappear in acute form in her private journal six months later.

Her Parents' Legacy

The first entry in Alva's dream diary on April 20 is a montage of images of her family's repeated moves. A donkey is pulling a cart packed with the family's possessions. Alva must pick up precious items that fall off the cart, while Rut holds the reins. The sisters must calm the wayward donkey, tend to the younger children, and care for a sick person lying in a bed on the cart. In the midst of all this, someone decides that everyone's throats, including the donkey's, must be brushed with a soothing medicine. In her dream, Alva recalled, "I tried to speak rationally" to her frightened younger siblings and "said that it was good for all of us . . . even if we don't have a cold." She then hypothesized that "this treatment has a particular inner connection with the fact that I had consulted Dr. Billström. The whole thing is not so bad that I cannot clear it up myself. But it is rational for all people . . . [to have] a mental prophylaxis." In the dream, however, the wagon turns into a bier, a burden that she and Rut are still bearing a year after their mother's death.

Alva's pocket calendar for April 27–30 indicates that the next weekend the four Reimer siblings were meeting to divide their inheritance from their father. In the first of two dreams centered on her parents (April 25), Alva was leaving on a trip when she was struck by the thought that, even if she were killed in a plane crash, she would feel content with the legacy she is leaving as her parents' first-born child. As the scene shifts to Slagsta farm, she realizes that she has forgotten to say goodbye to an adult male figure who seems first to be her father, but then shades into her husband. The next night (April 26), Alva's dream focused on her mother and sister. In a jewelry shop, she admires a bracelet decorated with blue enameled butterflies. Lowa offers to buy it for her since Alva had such a hard time as a child. Her sister Rut lets her choose between two kinds of earrings. Alva wants both but does not dare to say so, as she had been continually scolded about her selfishness during her childhood. Her mother had never attempted to atone for their difficult relationship, although Rut had been generous. Alva concluded that the dream was a wish projection, as she sought to find an internal reconciliation with her mother.

Gunnar

Alva described the second dream she recalled on April 20 as "very curious." She and Gunnar own a valuable scientific discovery, which is enclosed in a partitioned container. She "egotistically" asserts that *she* was the one who had discovered it but concedes that the best thing about it is that it is split in two, which was *his* idea. They agree that the discovery is incomplete. An imaginary female scientist has also participated in this project and is eagerly awaiting the result. "She will probably have a long wait," Gunnar jokes. "It will never be finished, but if it succeeds—and that is what she is hopelessly waiting for—she will end up in a very elevated position." In her analysis, Alva suggested that the female scientist might represent a conception of herself as an independent professional woman who is looking at the Gunnar-Alva relationship from the outside. The partitioned container represents Alva's long years of subordination to Gunnar in a partnership that might bring her a reward in the distant future. The two are tightly bound together, but they are not one, and their project is unfinished. Alva wondered what she might have accomplished on her own if she had developed a separate career. In reflecting on her dream, she worried that enjoyment of their intimacy as a couple seemed to require her to set aside her own ambition. "Therefore, I push it away onto" the female character, she concluded. Alva was aware that, for Freud, the treasure box was a symbol of a woman's sexual organs, but Freud was thinking about men's sexual fantasies about women, not women's own psyches. In her interpretation, the box represents the professional work she has shared with Gunnar. They have a sexual as well as a working relationship, however, while the female scientist has only work. Although Alva is tightly bound to Gunnar in the box, a partition separates them. In the bedroom of their custom-designed home, they had a sliding wall that separated their two beds, giving them a choice between privacy and intimacy. Significantly, the figure Alva identifies with her ambition is a solitary woman who is excluded from the professional and sexual rewards of Alva's partnership with Gunnar. This dream may indicate Alva's subliminal awareness that, whatever she chose, it came at a high price for the other side of her personality.

On April 23, Alva noted that she and Gunnar had intercourse the night before, following two weeks during which they had abstained because they both had manuscripts to finish. In the dream she recalled, she and Gunnar are in a hotel with many corridors. She is moving from one room to another, and they are never together. In her interpretation, Alva speculated that the dream took her back to the first five years of the relationship, when she and Gunnar had been forced to conceal their sexual life from her parents. In this imaginative recreation of those years, Alva spends one pleasurable night with Gunnar in the hotel and then triumphantly announces to others that this took place a few days *before* rather than after their wedding.

On May 6, Alva recorded a dream set in New York City. As Alva goes for a walk with Gunnar, they see a man who appears to be trying to commit suicide. Entirely calm, he is lying flat on the bottom of a riverbed. Another man, dressed in white underwear, goes in too. Then they see a whole group doing the same thing, tucked in under the mud as if it were a blanket. Their calm and relaxed faces are very strange. While Alva did not interpret this scene, we know from their letters to one another that Gunnar had felt the impulse to commit suicide on numerous occasions and that Alva had once considered suicide by jumping into a river. In the dream, the possibility of suicide seems oddly unremarkable. As the scene shifts, Alva and Gunnar realize they are near their own apartment. Their children appear, and they walk home through a neighborhood full of small shops, including funeral parlors.

In the next scene, Alva and her siblings are redoing her father's estate inventory because the tax authorities have found mistakes. Although she is aware that Albert is dead, he sits there with them, a spectral figure meticulously correcting the columns of numbers. This apparition epitomizes the image of Albert on which Alva had modeled her own better self: an honest person conscientiously serving others. The theme of death recurred the following night (May 7), but this time it is Alva who is dead. Lying in a hospital bed, she is definitely deceased but remains interested in the other dead people and those around them. "Can't stop meddling," she observed wryly.

Five days later, Alva was trying to take Dr. Billström's advice to relax and enjoy the aesthetic dimension of life, but her mind was hardly in repose. After an evening when she and Gunnar went to a movie, she jotted down a dream in which she imaginatively remade the film with the two of them as characters (May 13). Although she and Gunnar frequently analyzed movies and discussed how they might have been improved, in her dream Alva reshoots and edits the film. She splits up the group of characters and makes the central secret known only in part to everyone except the central character. As the director, she lets the multiple plots run parallel, so the secret is revealed gradually. As the film is reshot, the story changes again. The resemblance to Alva's ever-shifting relationship with Gunnar and their efforts to re-envision their partnership in times of trouble seems clear.

In one scene, Alva conjures up a lawyer and his secretary. He holds forth hilariously in a modernistic vein about love and life while speaking to his wife, whom he can only reach by phone. Alva noted that this is "our situation approximately." Indeed, during their marital crisis in the summer of 1941 it was precisely their situation. "Life is an accountancy system," the man declares, using a metaphor that Gunnar had employed when he sought to add up his personal moral balance sheet. Sounding like a contractor, the lawyer invokes the building metaphor both of them often used. "Life is a bit like the basic structure of a building where two people are climbing parallel steps but they have nevertheless reached different 'levels of abstraction'" and therefore do not meet.

After several other scenes, the authorities in City Hall insist that the lawyer and his secretary behave in a thinly disguised sexual way that makes them appear ridiculous. The embarrassed typist explains that "this is the office wiggle and you have to do it to avoid hemorrhage of the lungs," which would result if you repressed too much anger in talking politely to a superior. The jerky, mechanical movements, executed by both in unison, emphasize the marionette-like aspect of the whole dream-movie. The typist's explanation echoes the Freudian idea that one must have a "catharsis" or suffer damage from repressed emotions.

On May 23, Alva recorded a dream in which she, her husband, and a girl, all involved in some kind of political work, are walking out of a railroad station. They emerge onto a platform and have to jump down to the street below. Alva hesitates but somehow manages it. They start to walk away, but she remembers she has forgotten something and they all go back. Now she has to leap again. This time she must land on a spot close to the wall, but a baby carriage has been positioned so that she must either land in it or in front of it. Again, she hesitates and considers jumping into it, but decides to follow "the man" and jump over the pram. When she lands, the jump seems very easy. The platform "was only as high as a chest of drawers," she notices, although before jumping she had thought it was two or three stories. The dreamer then finds herself at home in a tiny and very dirty apartment. She hears voices on the stairs and realizes that "the man" has decided to bring "the girl" there. Alva asks her to come in but is ashamed because this place is not fit to be shown to a stranger. At the end of this chimera, Alva speculated that the dream could be linked to her decision not to let herself be nominated in recent election for party office because she felt unprepared, while ignoring the manifest relevance of the dream to Gunnar's sexual infidelities and the risks his behavior posed to herself.

The Demands of Work

Two weeks after beginning the diary, Alva had a dream she considered an expression of the "stress" caused by all the duties that were weighing on her and keeping her from enjoying more emotionally satisfying activities. At the time, her pocket calendar was packed with appointments. May 1 was Labor Day, which kicked off a week of political meetings. Alva's dreams were filled with small household chores. She speculated that these tasks, seemingly about her home life, were linked to the work she had been doing for the Social Democratic Party. Although Alva avoided saying that the chores the party assigned to her were commonly regarded as women's work, she admitted that she would rather be a policy planner than organize social events (May 3).

On May 18, Alva was so busy preparing for the Social Democratic Women's conference that she canceled her appointment with Dr. Billström and went to the family's cottage outside Stockholm to write her talk. The previous night, she had dreamt that she was undergoing some kind of "treatment" that required sunbathing, then jumping into a pool of ice-cold water. She asks her students whether she should follow her psychiatrist's advice to "let go," relax a little, and try to "take life as it comes." The dreamscape dissolves into an apartment in New York as she and her husband are preparing to leave for Sweden, but visitors turn up to say good-bye. She flirts playfully with a Swedish diplomat she knows vaguely. Her husband suddenly turns into a child and vomits on her dress. The other man helps her wipe it off, a little too eagerly. Alva then maneuvers her child/husband away, thinking that "this is a bit strange."

She sits down on the diplomat's lap and they kiss in an explicitly erotic way. They pretend that nothing is happening, then fall on the ground. The man is drunk, and she helps him return to the "Hotel Custido" where he is staying. But he does not want to go in, so they continue walking. She tells him that one should live in the here and now, let things happen, and not think ahead. "But I have a career to think of," he replies. "I don't," says the imagined Alva. After walking along a beautiful lakeside road that ends in a snowy ditch, she feels disappointed. Suddenly she realizes that she has to go and rushes back to the apartment she and her husband are leaving.

After this free-floating narrative of her comical efforts to take Dr. Billström's advice, Alva's superego compelled her to conclude that her disappointment was "only fitting," since this was an obvious attempt at adultery. While Alva did not make the connection, the dream is reminiscent of the one night she had spent with the professor in Stockholm during the terrible summer of 1941. In the dream, however, Alva stops herself from this precipitous act.

Children

On April 22, Alva recorded a dream after a night in which she had not slept much, having stayed up late with a sick child. In her dream, she is away from her family on a speaking tour promoting good parenting. She finds that there are heavy balls attached to her leg by a chain. The incompatibility of her professional work on parenting with taking care of her own children is so obvious that this dream needed no interpretation.

In a dream recorded on April 24, Alva's "9-year-old daughter" had managed to pass the examination to graduate from gymnasium, but when Alva had interrogated her she appeared to know little about punctuation. This posed a dilemma. Should Alva tell her daughter of her ignorance, taking away her joy at having passed the exam? How would she manage with all those gaps in her education? This imagined daughter may have been a composite of Kaj, then 8, and Sissela, then 10. It was Jan, however, who was studying for the all-important exam.

Alva was so frenetically busy during the party congress that she did not record any dreams for four days. When she resumed the diary, her entries centered on motherhood. In two dreams involving her daughters, Alva the psychologist restrained Alva the mother from interfering too much with the children's processes of self-discovery. Reacting against her own mother's hectoring and incessant need for control, Alva had tried to encourage her children to develop spontaneously, strive for autonomy, take pride in their own achievements, and mature at their own pace into reasoning, thoughtful persons.

Three weeks later, Alva's dream leaped to her "zestful middle daughter," who had broken a whole set of furniture in their house. In her dream, Alva had felt less upset at her daughter's action than at herself for not having noticed it for a long time. Later she takes the daughter, wearing a white fur coat, to a "very crowded refuge" where she is jostled and stepped on but enjoys the experience. The 10-year-old dances around and is so happy to be in a place full of people. This mood may not last long, Alva thinks, but she does not want to say anything that might discourage her daughter.

Alva had tried to apply the same modern philosophy of childrearing, in which the parent stands back and lets children experience things on their own, to her son, Jan. In his case the result had not been so happy, and Jan had been a rebellious boy. He was very smart, however, and she assumed that he would succeed academically. On May 28, Alva dreamed that she is standing in line at the Lost Property office in Stockholm when a mother with two children comes in to claim her son's fur coat, which he had left somewhere. The children are wearing a velvet dress and a sailor suit. "The fur coat of the day," sighs the woman working in the office as she hands over the coat. Alva, standing next to her, thinks "the children of today," as if it were strangely normal that children themselves are lost and then handed in to this place. Although Alva had recently helped to resettle Finnish war orphans, her response to the dream was to look inward and blame herself. As she closed that morning's entry, she wondered: "Bad conscience about neglecting my children?"

Two days later, Alva recorded a dream that had helped her "work through" a terrible problem that had kept both her and Gunnar awake until late at night (May 30). Jan had suddenly dropped out of school after failing the entrance exam for gymnasium, moved out of the house, taken a factory job in a town far from Stockholm, turned against his parents, and joined the Communist Party. For several years Alva had tried to mediate the raging oedipal struggle between Jan and Gunnar, but she had not expected anything like this. In the dream, Gunnar rushes home after a newspaper reports that their son has read some of her Social Democratic Party documents and passed on the contents to their Communist rivals. She is torn between double loyalties, but ready to drop her son. Alva commented that the dream's "exaggeration" of what had happened signifies the focus of her anxiety. Adhering to the discipline that she kept up throughout the diary, she limited her analysis to what the dream might reveal about her own emotions; she did not probe the feelings of Jan or others and confined herself to describing them as they appear in her dreams. Forty and fifty years later, Jan and Kaj each published their memories of this bitter confrontation between father and son. In the light of those narratives, Alva's interpretation that her manifest dream had been an "exaggeration" seems to have been sheer denial.[1]

On the morning of June 3, when Alva was scheduled to speak to the Social Democratic youth organization's annual conference in Stockholm, she jotted down a dream that accentuated the many burdens placed on her by her party work. She is in a railway station, loaded down with a suitcase, a briefcase and a large, sooty drainpipe which she clutches against her light-colored coat. It is very heavy and nobody offers to help her, although her husband and some other men are walking next to her carrying nothing. Alva also must pick up a bag at the station, left there for her by Arthur Engberg, the longtime Minister of Education. He had previously given her what seemed like an important letter and awaits her reply. In her account of the dream, Alva remarked that she has been told that Engberg spoke of her in flattering terms. In the letter, he says he wants her to carry on his educational reform work. She felt it was her duty, as nobody else would eliminate the class-bound educational structures that had blocked the aspirations of youth from impoverished families.

After scribbling these notes, Alva moved briskly through a busy day at the youth conference, calmly fulfilling all her responsibilities despite her anxieties about her performance and the blowup with Jan. In parts of the dream she remembered and recorded on June 3–4, Alva shows resilience under pressure and works her way through many precarious situations. But there is a cost: the dreamer is often tired, and her attention shifts abruptly between her husband, her work, and her children. She feels inadequate in everything she does. Always, there are things left undone. In her short bursts of analysis, Alva often denied that others were responsible for the situation, blaming herself for the consequences of other's actions. She also denied the emotional impact on her of the enormous burdens she is bearing and felt compelled to append a cheerful disclaimer that contradicts the content of the dream.

The children occupy a small part of this dreamscape. Alva feels unable to meet all of their needs. When something goes wrong, it must be her fault. In her interpretation, she did not try to excuse herself by mentioning that much of her work outside the home had been for the benefit of children less fortunate than her own. Although Alva insists that she loves her own children, she seems aware that her remarkable ability to think ahead of those around her, to plan, and to organize has come at an emotional cost, the repression of her own other needs and feelings. In the few references to her children in the dream diary, Alva seemed confident that the problems they face are manageable: they will pass their exams, the broken furniture can be mended, and the lost fur coat recovered. Although she felt guilty that she did not have more time with them, she had argued forcefully in her professional writings that children need to become independent, to make their own decisions and learn from their mistakes.

Jan's abrupt departure is figured in the dream diary as a rejection of her, rather than as the culmination of a long-running, deep-seated conflict between Jan and Gunnar. In reality, there was no public scandal at the time of Jan's break with his parents. The dream diary suggests that Alva experienced Jan's actions as an embarrassment to her at precisely the moment when she hoped to reemerge into the political limelight. She had spent weeks preparing her speeches for the Social Democratic Party's congress, women's conference, and youth conference. When she stepped back onto the national political stage, this time by herself and not with Gunnar, Jan's conflict with his father had pulled her off. Sadly, the conflicts between the demands of family and work Alva wrestled with in her inner life were also played out in the interactions between her first-born son and his father, leaving her unable to smooth over the situation. To solve that problem, psychotherapeutic self-examination would not suffice. Six months later, she was plunged into a crisis in her marriage.

Note

All translations of manuscripts written by Alva Myrdal were done by the author. The dates in parentheses refer to her Dream diary.

1 Fölster, *De tre löven*; Myrdal, *Barndom*.

References

Alva and Gunnar Myrdal's Collection (AGMA). Arbetarrörelsens Arkiv och Bibliotek (Swedish Labour Movement's Archive and Library). Stockholm, Sweden.

Alva Myrdal's personal documents, 1.1

Alva Myrdal. Drömdagbok (Dream diary). April–June 1944.

Published Sources

Fölster, Kaj. *De tre löven: En Myrdalisk efterskrift*. Stockholm: Bonniers, 1992.

Myrdal, Jan. *Barndom*. Stockholm: Norstedts, 1982. *Childhood*, trans. Christine Swanson. Chicago, IL: Lake View Press, 1991.

19 Politician's Wife or Independent Woman?

In her autobiography and dream diary, Alva kept the focus squarely on herself in an effort to take responsibility for her own actions and understand her own emotions. Gunnar appeared in the dream diary as the senior partner of AGM, a child vomiting on Alva's dress, a lawyer talking to his wife on the phone before he doing an erotic but therapeutic dance with his secretary, a prominent figure in the Social Democratic Party leadership, a man who brings a girl upstairs while Alva cooks in a shabby apartment, and, perhaps, a raging donkey. Oddly, there are no obvious scenes from the marital crisis they had endured three years before and nothing about the intensity of Gunnar's continual oscillations between grandiose visions of himself as a world-historical figure and self-lacerating depression.

Six months after she completed the dream diary, Alva started another notebook in which she observed her interactions with Gunnar and used them a springboard for more general assessments of her feelings about the marriage. Parts of this journal take the form of a dialogue with herself about what to do. Her rhetorical questions to herself are reminiscent of her Diary of Him and Her in 1926, yet with an important difference. The 1926 diary was intended as a joint project, but Gunnar had contributed just once, and her observations became more honest and more frantic as she realized she was undergoing an emotional crisis that Gunnar did not understand. Her December 1944 journal was strictly her own, and in it she brought the difficulties of the marriage into clear focus.

The journal opens on December 2, after Alva and Gunnar had attended a party together. She found herself stuck in a role she had outgrown long before: the attractive, witty wife of an ambitious member of the Riksdag. Reflexively, she compared her persona with the self-presentations of the other politicians' wives. The masks she and other women put on at gatherings of women's organizations, the Social Democratic Party, and reform-minded intellectuals were not "the woman as she really is" Alva had wanted to discover. In these settings, she realized, she was strictly a satellite of Gunnar—and not the only one orbiting around him. "The truth is Gunnar does not like me when he sees me with other people," Alva sighed. He was not jealous of her appeal to others, but he resented the limits that her presence imposed on him. Her husband felt that she was getting in the way of his flirtations with other women. "And when it is time to go home, he is simply in a foul mood. 'I can't get rid of you that easily,' he said tonight when I wanted [taxicab] money to go home and liberate him."

Then Alva shifted into the voice of the psychologist: "Let us try to analyze." Alcohol was behind some of Gunnar's behavior, along with "tiredness, bad temper—projected onto whoever is nearest." But that was not the full explanation. The problem is that "Gunnar dislikes me in the same measure as he is interested in someone else" or "can only see me at all in comparison with someone else."

Returning to the voice of the diarist, she wondered whether she could turn herself into the kind of woman Gunnar found more attractive. If she did,

> Would I be myself, would I be me? Would I not be that which I often feared being, a vacuum that gives in and yields and pretends to live. Should I do this to win him? And should I dedicate even more of my life to . . . pretending to be something that I am not? God—I don't know. Not that I want to lose—but I can't help shrinking away from what I notice he values.

Alva had invested so much energy and emotion in cultivating a self that was both independent and in love with Gunnar that to settle for an empty shell of a marriage or to retreat into a dependent role would be to lose her self, as well as the equal relationship with her husband she prized. She had believed that after 1941 she had negotiated a better balance between her independent career and their joint social scientific work, as well as a more honest emotional relationship with her husband. But now she felt that she was being cut adrift emotionally and pushed out of a substantive role in politics. She was accustomed to being seen by an important segment of the Swedish public as a full partner in "the Myrdal couple," a marriage that symbolized all that was modern, reform-minded, and egalitarian. That the reality of the marriage was quite different hurt her deeply, but did not invalidate the ideal of partnership as an alternative to patriarchal domination. Perhaps other couples would succeed where she and Gunnar had failed. Thus, either divorcing Gunnar or retreating into a conventional wifely role would be to "lose" the "gamble" their marriage represented. Men and women in the bourgeois parties would exult publicly in their breakup, and there would be whispering and backbiting among Social Democrats. "I told you so," their enemies would exclaim, pointing to the Myrdals as proof that feminism and partnership marriage do not work. It might even have consequences for the public policies Alva had championed.

"What shall we do?" Alva asked. We could "pretend there is nothing wrong," but then the problem would continue. She found that approach "undignified" and reiterated her long-held view that "such repression can result in catastrophe one day." Alternatively, Alva could "just retreat." Would she be satisfied if in her husband's eyes she represented "the boring part of his life," if she became "the one who is identified with 'those irritating kids' and the tiresome house?" That would not be fair to her, and she felt that "surely this cannot be what he truly wishes in his innermost self."

A third possibility would be for Alva to "play the same game." Could she be "just as good" at it," "showing more interest" in other men? Could she "become as successful as the hungry women—and men—always are?" Turning the problem around, she speculated that Gunnar is not "that desirable to others" when he is in a political or business role, although "to me he is, in some mysterious, comradely loyal way." "But when he is on the hunt for something," she observed, he attracts other women. For Alva, however, "switching over to this style would require me to give up the style I now have. And I just cannot be bothered as long as I am supposed to be a happily married wife." The post-divorce options, as she saw them, were engaging in sexual affairs without emotional commitment or marrying another man. She could not imagine herself as a divorced woman with a career and three children entering into emotionally satisfying relationships with a succession of lovers. In a burst of candor, she confessed that "I am certainly not ashamed to admit that I would be a great deal unhappier if forced to enter the marriage market."

She then presented herself with a fourth alternative: a legal separation. "Is it more practical that he should try to live the kind of life that he now apparently so unhappily has to give up?" "If he really believes he is missing out," she concluded with a touch of irony, "we must of course not make any effort to keep anything going." Alva tried to consider the plusses and minuses of the marriage in a strictly objective analysis. Affirming a principle that did not fully express her own feelings, she asserted that "this marriage does not need to be maintained for the sake of the children." Alva hypothesized that Gunnar might think he would come out ahead if freed of the necessity of supporting her financially. Since he is "aging," he is naturally "worried that time is passing and he is no longer able to experiment with more women." "Perhaps it would be more fulfilling not to have to drag me along, to go alone to parties, to graze among the available mistresses." Maybe he would think a separation better for the sake of "sexuality" or for "the lonely self." For Alva, scientific accuracy required a cool detachment from her own emotions. "I want to see this from his point of view, but always without sentimentality, without getting upset." In contrast to her mother, she would not be a whiner. In her view, the stronger person always wins despite the emotional cost.

"And me?" she asked. "That is still a question of secondary importance. Not because it is less important, but because I cannot force myself into anything that might not be meant for me." "If we belong together, we ought to be happier than this." To herself she was able to joke that "I do not want the job of a kill-joy, even if the pay is good." The whole idea that Gunnar should reproach her for denying him a little fun is deeply ironic, she observed wryly.

> This was never what we intended, my beloved and I. But we started off in the forest. It may not be so easy to continue in the drawing rooms. As it turns out, the maladjustments have been loaded on me. If Gunnar is not enjoying [himself] in a ballroom, the fault is mine. And I am so crushed inside that I myself don't even like to remind him that it was not I who took the dance out of our youth. *Then*, I had to put up with all that semi-scorn from Rut and school friends, etc. because I let myself be dominated by such a solemn, high-minded man that all dancing had to come to an end. *Now* there is the same reproach, only from another direction. Would it not be a little disappointing, though, if our lives should end this way when we intended so much more? If I [only] knew.

That was a question with no possible answer.

Alva could not embrace any of the alternatives: playing the loyal and dumb wife while her husband fooled around; demanding fidelity and trying to stop his amorous extramarital activities; agreeing to an open marriage, which would require her to change her own needs for emotional satisfaction in a fundamental way; or to embark on a divorce or separation. "The only thing I can see," she concluded, "is that we should not continue with these half measures."

> I am not going to be the one who just drags him down into the hell of kids, like a ball and chain [away from his] tempting social life, something to be kissed a couple of times a week in an effort to discharge his duty. But what?

There was always work. Alva constantly wrote articles and attended meetings; her energy level remained extraordinary. In a second entry written six days later (Dec. 18), she tried to analyze what she was doing in politics. Although her marriage posed insoluble problems, it was also not easy to throw herself into the feminist movement. That day she had argued with a more senior member of the Social Democratic women's organization. They shared the goal of achieving greater representation for women on party committees; their conflict had more to do with personalities, leadership styles, and tactics. The woman had proposed a measure that "gave her all the power—against the wishes of the majority." But Alva was the only one willing to speak up. She felt "nauseated" by the whole business and resolved to stay away from organizations where conflicts were likely. For Alva, her position as principal of the college she had founded for training preschool teachers was most rewarding. "Gunnar is entirely right when he says that it is better for me physically and in terms of subjective satisfaction and objective prestige the less I involve myself" in organizations. She vowed to "complete what I have started in other areas, for example [the Social Democratic youth association], refugees, translations, etc." and above all to "maintain my independence." Emotionally numb from the protracted conflict with her husband, Alva struck a note of resignation as she tried to sum up her "life's balance sheet": "I can enjoy being at home, I can complete my duties, I can maintain my freedom in order to choose something later." This was a rather modest set of goals for an accomplished author, scholar, activist and emerging politician. She had been striving for more and would aim higher in the future. But at the end of 1944, she felt exhausted by her problems with Gunnar and by the angry departure of their son.

When Alva looked back at the journal eight years later, on August 30, 1952, she added a note observing that she and Gunnar had been out of balance "almost all the time, in spite of other things being so good." Placing the journal in the context of a longer period, she suggested that things had gone wrong in the 1920s due to her lack of self-confidence. "Following the passivity with which I seem to have reacted in the 20s and the flowering of external activities in the 30s, the 40s was a period of impatiently waiting." "One may wonder," she mused, "how much would have been different if the earlier attempts to be more active, based on self-confidence, had developed along normal lines."

So Alva saw her life at age 42 in her autobiography, dream diary, and private journal. The three manuscripts reveal a chain of self-discoveries leading to an uncertain future. In the autobiography, she found the roots of her "terribly demanding superego" in her protracted conflict with her mother and explored how, after separating her identity from her mother, this superego still prodded her to ever-greater achievements in the "masculine" world of career and politics while crowding out emotions that she connected to the "feminine" side of her personality. This realization brought her face-to-face with the paradox that, while she was fighting battles on behalf of women and children, she was annoyed by what she saw as the superficiality of many contemporary women and was not sure that she really liked other people's children, except insofar as they were in need of her help.

In her private journal, we see that, having built her early career as a junior member of the firm, the only way Alva could attain political influence on her own was by building a base in women's organizations, serving as advisor to the Social Democratic youth organization, and shaping her public image as an expert on families, women, and education—the sole sectors of public policy in which an ambitious woman had any hope of achieving political influence. Alva had painstakingly cultivated a public persona as a confident, capable, and, above all, rational woman, but the dream diary discloses the legacy of the self-doubt, guilt, and inadequacy whose roots she had traced in the autobiography.

The dream diary offers kaleidoscopic glimpses of the many roles she had been required to play in her relationship with Gunnar: lover, mother figure, and counselor in private, and loyal subordinate in public. We see her re-enacting the pattern she learned in childhood, putting others' needs ahead of her own while quietly pursuing her own goals. Her record of dreams sheds light on her matter-of-fact statement in the autobiography that she had always placed duty to her husband ahead of duty of her children. Alva's superego had been forged in a patriarchal society and, in response to the crises of the Depression and the war, she felt forced to take the expedient course of subordinating herself to husband, party, and state in the hope of achieving a more equal society. She had resolutely stepped into those public arenas in which women were able to participate, but found it necessary to content herself with supporting Gunnar in enclaves from which women were largely excluded. In contrast to wives who had sacrificed all for their husband's career, Alva observed and learned about these citadels of male power and privilege, especially the Riksdag and international organizations, carefully laying the groundwork for the day when she would finally enter them.

Did she still need Gunnar, and, if so, on what terms? This was the question she considered in December 1944. The choices were not as clear-cut as she tried to make them seem. For the next five years, Alva continued to live with her husband during his service as Minister of Commerce in the Swedish cabinet and director of the United Nations Economic Commission for Europe (ECE), while she opened up new opportunities for poor children and combatted gender inequity as a member of Sweden's Education Commission. Alva continued to broaden her international contacts, focusing on postwar reconstruction in Europe and development aid to newly independent nations in Africa and Asia. In 1950, she left home to serve as an official of the United Nations in New York and then at UNESCO in Paris, becoming an administrator with global influence on issues of women, families, children, education, and poverty. In 1955 she was appointed Sweden's ambassador to India. She was elected to the Swedish Riksdag in 1961, quickly promoted to the cabinet, and then became Sweden's international negotiator on international nuclear disarmament.

Alva and Gunnar had a long-distance marriage for eight years during the 1950s, until he completed his work at ECE and moved into the Swedish ambassador's quarters in New Delhi, where he headed a large-scale study of poverty in South Asia. They lived together in Stockholm for the last 25 years of their lives. Some kind of partnership survived: Gunnar continued his research on the economics of development, while Alva grew into one of Sweden's best-known political leaders. As the only prominent Social Democratic feminist from the 1930s who was still active in politics, her moment finally came in the 1960s and 1970s. The marriage endured, at least as a partnership of two political intellectuals and reformers, but much of the emotional core that bound them together had been irretrievably lost along the way.

Note

All translations from Alva Myrdal's private journal were done by the author.

References

Alva and Gunnar Myrdal's Collection (AGMA). Arbetarrörelsens Arkiv och Bibliotek (Swedish Labour Movement's Archive and Library). Stockholm, Sweden.

Alva Myrdal's personal documents, 1.1

Alva Myrdal. Journal *intime* (Private journal). December 1944.

Index

Note: Page numbers followed by 'n' refer to notes.

For Product Safety Concerns and Information please contact our EU representative GPSR@taylorandfrancis.com
Taylor & Francis Verlag GmbH, Kaufingerstraße 24, 80331 München, Germany

www.ingramcontent.com/pod-product-compliance
Ingram Content Group UK Ltd.
Pitfield, Milton Keynes, MK11 3LW, UK
UKHW022348190926
475702UK00015B/2177
* 9 7 8 0 3 6 7 4 9 7 0 8 8 *